The Certainty
of the
Third Angel's
Message

Louis F. Were

The Certainty of the Third Angel's Message

© 1999 by *LMN Publishing International, Inc.*
ISBN: 0-9665788-2-7

Published by:

Laymen Ministries

LMN Publishing International, Inc.
HC 4, Box 94C
St. Maries, ID 83861

Alan Collins is the designer of the original sculpture, "Three Angels of Revelation 14," a photograph of which appeared on the cover of the previous printing of this book. The cover of the current printing is based on this photograph, adapted and designed by Terri Prouty.

INTRODUCTION

The widespread confusion in contemporary Christianity regarding the understanding of biblical prophecies about the future of Israel and the final battle of "Armageddon" is largely due to a lack of clearly defined *principles* of prophetic interpretation. Such principles or rules are indispensable as a safeguard against exegetical anarchy and the speculations of an unwarranted literalism or spiritualization. The certainty of true religious convictions is not based on isolated Scripture passages but rather on the central teaching of the totality of Holy Scripture.

Students of Bible prophecy will be delighted to find renewed access to this masterwork of prophetic interpretation from a Seventh-day Adventist perspective by the late Australian evangelist, Louis F. Were.

The subject of *unfulfilled* prophecy in the Bible is of increasing importance and relevance to our generation which stands in the urgent need of being prepared for the final conflict between good and evil, between God's revealed will and the traditions of men. The author has sought to guard himself against speculations by focusing on those principles of interpretation which are inherent in the Holy Scriptures themselves. Basing himself on the assumption of faith that there exists a basic continuity between the Old and New Testaments, between Israel and the Church, Louis Were has tried to articulate the principles of this spiritual unity in a Christ-centered hermeneutic.

The author honors both the *conditional* aspects of prophecy and the *unconditional* divine assurance of its fulfillment in Messiah Jesus and His faithful people. In this Christological principle of fulfillment, Louis Were is in fundamental agreement with the position of the great Reformers of the sixteenth century. Only, Were confronts us with his consistent application of those time-honored principles to the apocalyptic portions of Holy Scripture, including the vision of the millennium. This book provides a fundamental answer to the hermeneutic of *literalism* in prophetic interpretation as set forth by Dispensationalism, popularized by such writers as Hal Lindsey, Salem Kirban, and by their motion pictures.

3

In our time of superficiality and scepticism this challenging study of Evangelist Were is a great help in understanding more clearly the truth which God has given in the New Testament for the Church of Christ in the last days.

Especially the meaning of the three angels' messages of Revelation 14 — the divine credentials of the remnant church — becomes more transparent than ever before.

May this study book find its way to all those students of biblical prophecy who long for greater clarity and deeper assurance regarding our individual responsibility in the final conflict between God and Satan.

Hans K. LaRondelle, Th.D.
Professor of Theology
Theological Seminary
Andrews University
Berrien Springs, Michigan
October 3, 1979

FOREWORD.

"We have not followed cunningly devised fables" (2 Pet. 1: 16)—the Third Angel's Message as taught by the Spirit of Prophecy is, indeed, the truth of God. This is not a dogmatic assertion based upon the blind acceptance or acquiescence of statements made by men, but is a belief definitely established upon inspired principles of interpretation revealed in the Scriptures and the Spirit of Prophecy. God desires that His people *know* the truth for themselves. He says: "Have not I written to thee excellent things in counsels and knowledge, that I might make thee *know* the certainty of the words of truth?" Prov. 22: 20, 21. In the introduction to his Gospel, the Apostle Luke states the reason for writing his book: "That thou mightest *know* the certainty of those things, wherein thou hast been instructed." Luke 1: 4. One is impressed with the frequent use of the word "know" by the New Testament writers. For instance, John uses the word over thirty times in his First Epistle. It is the privilege of every believer to know his personal relationship to God as well as to know what is the truth concerning Christian doctrines and prophecies. Whatever privileges have been for believers in the past, the time is coming when it will be imperative that God's children *know* positively for themselves what is the truth for the last days. God's servant has written:

"The people of God are directed to the Scriptures as their safeguard against the influence of false teachers and the delusive power of spirits of darkness. Satan employs every device to prevent men from obtaining a knowledge of the Bible; for its plain utterances reveal his deceptions . . . he is now putting forth his utmost efforts for a final struggle against Christ and His followers. The last great delusion is soon to open before us . . . In order to endure the trial before them, they [Commandment keepers] must understand the will of God as revealed in His Word. . . . *None but those who have fortified the mind with the truths of the Bible will stand through the last great conflict.*" G.C. 593. "Only those who have been diligent students of the Scriptures, and who have received the love of the truth, will be shielded from the powerful delusion that takes the world captive." G.C. 625.

Through a study of the Scriptures and the Spirit of Prophecy, the writer, having in a measure sensed the greatness of the struggle which lies before the people of God, desires to strengthen the foundations of the faith of God's people. My efforts have been to point out by Biblical laws of interpretation why the message of God which has been entrusted to our care is truly established upon the Word of God. Many of God's people do not know how wonderfully strong are the walls of Zion, nor how impervious to the assaults of the enemy are the deep, broad, and irrefragible foundations of "the faith of Jesus." The writer is burdened with a desire that all of the members of spiritual Israel know for themselves the laws governing the interpretation of Scripture so that their faith will not depend upon another's word, but upon their own intelligent understanding of the Word of God.

As we study the Bible laws of interpretation *proving the certainty of the Third Angel's Message* we are also led, *by those same principles,* to see that the teaching of a military-Palestinian "Armageddon" is entirely out of alignment with the principles forming the basis of the Third Angel's Message. One of Satan's devices in the interpretation of prophecy is to create misunderstanding concerning the importance of the issues involved, or to belittle the subject. Would that all could say with Paul: "We are not ignorant of his devices." 2 Cor. 2: 11. God's servant has written: "There is nothing that the great deceiver fears so much as that we shall become acquainted with his devices." G.C. 516.

If verses 12-16, of Rev. 16, merely predicted national events to occur after probation has closed and our eternal destinies have been decided, and if they could be isolated in their interpretation from other portions of the Scripture, then the subject of Armageddon could be dismissed with a shrug of the shoulders or some impatient mood which thrusts it aside as unimportant. However, a logical study of the underlying *principles* shows that the understanding of "Armageddon" is of far greater consequence than many have hitherto thought—what is involved is the principle of interpretation applied in our understanding of the Third Angel's Message as taught by the Spirit of Prophecy.

Nearly twenty years ago the writer realized that, in order to positively know the Message for themselves, and to provide an adequate answer to false theories based upon erroneous interpretations of last-day prophecies, believers in the Third Angel's Message would need to have a definite and a clear cut understanding of the fixed PRINCIPLES of the Biblical laws of interpretation which are the foundations of the Third Angel's Message. These definite laws of interpretation form the immovable basis for the great Message which God has commanded us to give to the world.

6

They are the proof positive that our denominational interpretation of the Third Angel's Message is correct.

As the days of peril thicken around the remnant church its members must "be ready always to give an answer to every man that asketh [them] a *reason* of the hope that is in them" (1 Pet. 3: 15).

"The members of the church will individually be tested and proved. They will be placed in circumstances where they will be forced to bear witness for the truth. Many will be called to speak before councils and courts of justice, perhaps separately and alone. The experience which would have helped them in this emergency they have neglected to obtain, and their souls are burdened with remorse for wasted opportunities and neglected privileges." 5T. 463.

"You will be brought before councils, and every position of truth which you hold will be severely criticised." 5T. 717.

"Our ministers will have to defend the truth against base apostates, as well as to measure Scripture evidence with those who advocate specious errors." 5T. 528.

"I have been shown that *many* who profess to have a knowledge of present truth, know not what they believe. They do not understand the evidences of their faith. They have no just appreciation of the work for the present time. When the time of trial shall come, there are men now preaching to others, who will find, upon examining the positions they hold, that there are many things for which they can give no satisfactory reason. Until thus tested, they knew not their great ignorance . . . And there are many in the church who . . . will be surprised to see how confused are their ideas of what they accepted as truth." 5T. 707.

"Not all our ministers who are giving the Third Angel's Message *really understand* what constitutes that message." 5T. 715.

"I have been shown that but a *small number of people* in our churches know for themselves what constitutes the Third Angel's Message."

"The days are fast approaching when there will be great perplexity and confusion. Satan, clothed in angel robes, will deceive, if possible, the very elect." 5T. 80. "Fearful tests and trials await the people of God." 9T. 17. "The conflict that is right upon us will be the most terrible ever witnessed." 6T. 407.

7

These, and other statements from the pen of the servant of the Lord, point out the necessity for all believers in the Message—preachers and church members—to thoroughly understand the essential principles of the Message.

The following pages set forth some of the principles of prophetic interpretation which are necessary to a proper grasp of present truth. May the dear Lord guide and keep our hearts and minds as we study His Holy Word in preparation to endure the coming time of trial, and finally stand before His eternal throne clad in the perfect robe of the righteousness of our Lord and Saviour Jesus Christ.

LOUIS F. WERE.

Melbourne,

    October 25, 1945.

CONTENTS.

Chapter   CONTENTS (Continued).   Page

KEY TO ABBREVIATIONS.

SP. .... The Spirit of Prophecy.

IT. .... Testimonies, Vol. 1.

GW. .... Gospel Workers.

GC. .... The Great Controversy.*

EW. .... The Early Writings

TM. .... Testimonies to Ministers.

AA. .... The Acts of the Apostles.

MH. .... The Ministry of Healing.

DA. .... The Desire of Ages.*

PP. .... Patriarchs and Prophets.

PK. .... Prophets and Kings.

Early Edition

11

"Progress does not consist in increasing truth, but in liberating it from its veils."—
Tolstoy.

CHAPTER I.

HOW TO UNDERSTAND THE BIBLE.

"Multum in parvo," or much in little, may be discerned, written with the divine imprint across each verse of Scripture, for nothing is unimportant in all of God's works and words. The Bible is not a heterogeneous assemblage of verses on history and isolated doctrines, it is a book of principles dealing with eternal realities so necessary for the child of God to understand in these last days.

We learn the arts or the sciences by commencing with the rudimentary things, going on from the simple to the profound, from the known to the unknown. After much patient study one gradually learns to absorb facts as the mind adjusts itself to them. Should it be thought that the Bible which teaches the grandest of all sciences—the science of salvation—may be more easily understood, and does not require the same faithful study and meditation necessary to master other subjects?

To know the Bible we should read it often until we become familiar with its contents. Some read the Bible without thoroughly grasping the import of what they read. In 2 Pet. 3: 16 we are told that in some portions of the Scriptures there are "some things hard to be understood, which they that are unlearned and unstable wrest, as they do also the other Scriptures, unto their own destruction." However, the way of salvation is made simple and plain. The Bible makes it clear that all have sinned and come short of the glory of God, and that salvation may be obtained only through the substitutionary death of Christ. These essential facts are clearly stated again and again in different ways, and most understand these teachings of Scripture better than the prophecies. It is in the prophetic portions of Holy Writ that difficulties are encountered. These should be read in the fear of God—for by wrong interpretations some have been blinded to the Third Angel's Message. The prophecies of the Bible contain marvellous light for the lover of God who delves deeply into the Scriptures, but they are not to be understood by casual readers. The importance of prophecy is stressed in 2 Pet. 1: 19, "We have a *more sure* word of prophecy whereunto ye do well that ye take heed."

Upon the rudiments of salvation many people agree; it is in the interpretation of the prophecies that disagreements are prolific. This should not discourage the study of the predictions of Scripture, but stir us to seek God's guidance to ascertain their true meanings. "For prophecy came not in old time by the will of man: but holy men of God spake as they were moved by the Holy Ghost. 2 Pet. 1: 21. As the writers of the prophecies were "moved by the Holy Ghost" in making their predictions, it is very evident that in order to understand them we, too, must be "moved by the Holy Ghost."

When Jesus promised the Holy Spirit He called that Spirit "the Spirit of truth." John 14: 17; 15: 26. "Howbeit when He, the Spirit of truth, is come." John 16: 13. Jesus informs us that the work of the Spirit in guiding us into "all truth" is to show us "things to come." The prophetic element enters into the wonderful ministry of the Spirit of God. And if we would be guided into "all truth" we need to follow the leadings of the Spirit, for only as we follow His guidance are we assured of being shown the things which are "to come."

In order to receive the Holy Spirit's guidance in our study of the prophetic portions of the Scriptures we must first be obedient to God. Notice Acts 5: 32: "The Holy Ghost Whom God hath given to them that obey Him." Many err by seeking to know the prophecies without first yielding to the call of God. Observe the following verses:—

"The secret of the Lord is with them that fear Him." Ps. 25: 14. "I will instruct thee and teach thee in the way which thou shalt go: I will guide thee with Mine eye." Ps. 32: 8. "Thou shalt guide me with Thy counsel, and afterward receive me to glory." Ps. 73: 24. "And all thy children shall be taught of the Lord." Isa. 54: 13. "For his God doth instruct him to discretion and doth teach him." Isa. 28: 26. These, and many other Scriptures, state that God will teach those who seek to know His will and who endeavour to obey His voice. If we desire to obtain light on the prophecies in order to know and to do God's will better, then we shall be taught of God. But if we study these holy utterances only to satisfy our curiosity regarding the future so that events are like passing mileposts of material interest along the highway of life, and if we do not live a life of obedience to God, we will never grasp the deeper, spiritual depths which are reserved for those who fear the Lord. Jesus declared: "If any man will do His will, he shall know of the doctrine." John 7: 17. Thus the Master gives the essential for the

14

acquisition of the knowledge of true doctrine—namely, the consummate passion to know God's will at whatever the cost, and to do whatever is revealed.

It should be regarded as certain that interpretations of prophecies which do not set forth in clearer light the gospel of Christ are not God-inspired. Interpretations of prophecies which do not find their centre in Jesus as the Saviour, or as the Destroyer of evil, are wrong applications of Scripture.

The Jewish religionists were masters in the outside knowledge of the Bible, yet, with all their reading of the Old Testament, they did not understand the prophecies. In Acts 13: 27 Paul declared, "For all they that dwell at Jerusalem, and their rulers, because they knew Him not, nor yet the voices of the prophets which are read every Sabbath day, they have fulfilled them in condemning Him." Because they knew not Jesus they misread the prophecies of the Old Testament.

"The Jewish leaders had studied the teachings of the prophets concerning the kingdom of the Messiah; but they had done this, not with a sincere desire to know the truth, but with the purpose of finding evidence to sustain their ambitious hopes." D.A. 212.

In the old sanctuary, and later in the temple of the Jews, only those dedicated to the holy office of the priesthood were permitted to view the wonderful glories to be seen within the sacred edifice. And only those whose lives are dedicated to God are permitted to see the inner beauties of the temple of Scripture. Said Jesus to the Jewish leaders: "Search the Scriptures; for in them ye think ye have eternal life: and they are they which testify of Me." John 5: 39, 46.

The New Testament shows how Jesus brought fulfilment to the Old Testament predictions. The first words we read in Matthew's Gospel direct our minds back to the prophecies which were given to David and Abraham. While Solomon was the son who sat upon David's throne in the days immediately following the prediction, the longer and the real fulfilment is to be fulfilled by "a greater than Solomon." Matt. 12: 42. The peacefulness and the wisdom of the earlier part of Solomon's reign when people came from afar to learn of him, find their larger application in Christ. David was to have a son who would sit upon his throne. 2 Sam. 7: 12, 13, 16; Luke 1: 32, 33. Abraham was promised a son who would be the channel of blessing. Isaac was the immediate fulfilment; but Isaac prefigured the greater fulfilment in

15

Jesus Who, through His church, blesses the world. Gal. 3: 16, 29; 4: 28. The Old Testament prophecies which set forth the coming of the sons of Abraham and David are concentrated in the first verse of Matthew. Thus, from its commencement, the New Testament takes the things of the Old Testament and applies them in connection with Christ and His work of redemption. Christ and His salvation is the central theme of the Bible, and to make plain the way of salvation was the sole purpose for which the Scriptures were written. As the sun is reflected in each of the millions of dew-drops so Jesus, the Light of the world, shines forth in every verse of the Bible.

"In every page, whether history, or precept, or prophecy, the Old Testament Scriptures are irradiated with the glory of the Son of God. So far as it was of divine institution, the entire system of Judaism was a compacted prophecy of the gospel. To Christ give all the prophets witness.'" (Acts 10: 43.) D.A. 211.

Failing to read the prophecies in the light of Christ's work of salvation caused the Jews to misunderstand the prophecies they knew so well. Unless our interpretations of the prophecies reveal Christ we, too, will fail to grasp their true meaning.

"SPIRITUAL THINGS ARE SPIRITUALLY DISCERNED."

By inspiration Paul wrote that men unenlightened by God can never understand the Scriptures. He said: "But the natural man *receiveth not* the things of God: for they are foolishness unto him: *neither can he know them, because* they are *spiritually* discerned." I Cor. 2: 14.

One may be able to read the words of the Bible in the original languages, but this is not sufficient to enable the most educated mind not yielded to Christ to understand the full illumination of Scripture, which comes through the gracious ministry of the Holy Spirit. Before Paul accepted Christ, with all his knowledge of the Bible, he really did not understand it. He persecuted the followers of Jesus in ignorance. See I Tim. 1: 13.

God has declared: "I will destroy the wisdom of the wise, and will bring to nothing the understanding of the prudent. Where is the wise? Where is the scribe? Where is the disputer of this world? Hath not God made foolish the wisdom of this world? For ye see your calling, brethren, how that not many wise men after the flesh, not many mighty, not many noble, are called: but God hath chosen the foolish things of the world to confound the wise; and God hath chosen the weak things of the world to confound the things which are mighty; and base things of the world, and things which are despised, hath God chosen, yea, and things which are not, to bring to nought things that are: that no flesh should glory in His presence." 1 Cor. 1: 19-29. A brain which has been dedicated to the acquisition of knowledge pertaining to this present life can never understand that which belongs to another realm. Paul stresses the fact that without the continued operation of the Holy Spirit upon the human mind the things of the kingdom of God will never be understood. "But as it is written, Eye hath not seen, nor ear heard, neither have entered into the heart of man, the things which God hath prepared for them that love Him." 1 Cor. 2: 9. Then Paul proceeds to show that these "things which God hath prepared for them that love Him" are revealed to the believer: "But God *hath revealed* them unto us by His Spirit: for the Spirit searcheth all things, yea, the deep things of God." The illuminations of the Spirit are granted to those who are obedient to God, thus enabling them to see "the deep things of God." The keenest unspiritual mind touches the surface, but cannot penetrate into "the *deep* things of God."

"The things of God knoweth no man, but the Spirit of God. Now we have received, not the spirit of the world, but the Spirit which is of God; that we might know the things that are freely given to us of God. Which things also we speak, not in words which man's wisdom teacheth, but which the Holy Ghost teacheth; comparing spiritual things with spiritual." 1 Cor. 2: 11-14. As it is necessary to be born again in order to enter the kingdom of God, so the deeper knowledge of the things of His kingdom comes only to those whose lives are wholly dedicated to Him. God's servant has well said: "The soul that turns to God for its help, its support, its power, by daily, earnest prayer, will have noble aspirations, *clear perceptions of truth* and duty." "Thoughts from the Mount of Blessings." P. 127.

This fact is expressed in the wonderful promise which Jesus gave on the eve of His departure from this world back to His Father's throne in glory. He said: "He that hath My commandments, and keepeth them, he it is that loveth Me: and he shall be loved of My Father, and I will love him and *will manifest Myself to him.*" John 14: 21. Blessed, indeed, is the communion of the obedient soul with Christ. He has promised: "I will come in to him, and will sup with him, and he with Me." Rev. 3: 20.

Only those who are careful to obey all the commandments of God are assured of knowing the inner secrets of the kingdom of God. As the hymn writer states it: "None but Zion's children know." God and His Son will manifest themselves by the revelations of the Holy Spirit to those who love God enough to obey His voice.

It is by prayer and the study of the Bible that we obtain power to resist evil; to go contrary to our natural inclinations. As we bend our energies to submit our wills to God's commands our characters grow in strength, and spiritual discernment increases as character develops. Those who refuse to feed the carnal desires and who lay hold on to the power of Christ to transform the life, will know more of the things of the spiritual realm explained in the Bible than those who endeavour to serve both God and the world. Jesus declared: "If thine eye be single thy whole body shall be full of light." Matt. 6: 22. As we cultivate the natural desires, the things of Satan's kingdom—pride, selfishness and worldliness—we learn to understand more about the things of time and sense; but as we cultivate resistance to the things of the world which rejected God as its Lord and crucified Christ, the mind grows more and more spiritually inclined, and understands more and more the meaning of the divine things contained in the Scriptures.

It is not a mere coincidence that the two men who had the deepest and clearest light of all the New Testament writers were those who had personal, intimate communion with Christ. To Paul, who had "the abundance of the revelations" (2 Cor. 12: 7), Christ appeared personally on the road to Damascus. Acts 9: 4-6. Paul spent three years (Gal. 1: 15-18) in communion with Christ studying the meaning of the Old Testament predictions, the words of which he knew so well, but the real meaning of which he did not grasp until he saw their fulfilment in Jesus.

At the Lord's Supper, held in the upper room the evening before Christ's crucifixion, we have a picture of the close association of John and Jesus. John is not only described as the disciple "whom Jesus loved" (John 13: 23, 27) but also as the one "leaning on Jesus' bosom." Peter knew that a close bond—a spiritual tie—linked Jesus and John. "Simon Peter therefore beckoned to him, that he should ask who it should be of whom He spake. He then lying on Jesus' breast saith unto Him, "Lord, who is it?" John 13: 25. When John asked Jesus the question the answer was given. Jesus selected John to reveal the most wonderful, the most spiritual book of the New Testament—the Book of Revelation. "The secret of the Lord is with them that fear Him." Those who love the Lord the most and who are ever seeking to grow more like Him, even if they lack academic degrees, will have a clearer knowledge of the prophecies than the better educated who do not love and fear the Lord. This does not mean that God will not reveal clear light to those with scholastic attainments. Ignorance is never to be coveted; nor is it to be a cloak for superstitution or laziness; neither is learning to be substituted for the unction of the Holy Spirit, through Whom, alone, can be understood the spiritual things of God.

To appreciate the arts and the sciences one must be trained. And to understand spiritual things one must be trained spiritually. As Christ declared to Nicodemus: "Except a man be born of the water and of the Spirit, he *cannot* enter the kingdom of God. That which is born of the flesh is flesh; and that which is born of the Spirit is spirit. Marvel not that I said, Ye must be born again." John 3: 5-7.

It is a true saying that "the humble saint can see further upon his knees than the philosopher can see upon his tip-toes." Of course, if the saint is also a philosopher he will see further than the saint who is not a philosopher. Our constant effort must be to combine education with prayer and a life of obedience to God's will.

Daniel's stirling spiritual qualities made him a man greatly beloved of God. The angel who gave him the visions addressed him as, "Daniel, a man greatly beloved." Dan. 10: 11, 19; 9: 23. This thrice-repeated designation shows the reason why he was selected by God to reveal the wonderful prophecies found in his book. John the beloved, and Daniel the beloved, were the ones selected by Heaven as mediums through whom were given the amazing predictions which are found in their books.

One commentator (Benson) has well observed concerning the Book of Revelation:—"The Revelation was not written without tears, neither without tears will it be understood." This spirit of humility and devotion to God is necessary in our experience if we would understand the inner, spiritual truths of all the Bible.

Jesus promised: "When He, the Spirit of truth, is come, He will guide you into all truth." We cannot approach unto the holy ground of Biblical knowledge without first removing the shoes of our sins and worldliness. We must be in the right spiritual condition to understand spiritual things. "The Bible should never be studied without prayer. The Holy Spirit alone can cause us to feel the importance of those things easily understood, or prevent us from wresting truths difficult of comprehension." GC. 599.

The Lord's servant has written:—"The perception and appreciation of truth, He [Jesus] said, depends *less upon the mind than upon the heart*. Truth must be received into the *soul;* it claims the homage of the will. If truth could be submitted to the reason alone, *pride* would be no *hindrance* in the way of its reception. But it is to be received through the work of grace in the heart; and *its reception depends upon the renunciation of every sin that the Spirit of God reveals*. Man's advantages for obtaining a knowledge of the truth, however great these may be, will prove of no benefit to him *unless the heart is open to receive the truth*, and there is a conscientious surrender of every habit and practice that is opposed to its principles. To those who thus yield themselves to God, having an honest desire to know and to do His will, the truth is revealed as the power of God for their salvation."—Desire of Ages, p. 455.

"Only those who love and fear God can understand the mysteries of the kingdom of heaven." P.K. 516.

"The fear of the Lord is the beginning of wisdom: a good understanding have all they that do His Commandments." Ps. 111: 10.

Concerning the understanding of last-day prophecies, the prophecy and the promise is given: "None of the wicked shall understand; but the wise shall understand." Dan. 12: 10.

CHAPTER II.

THE IMPORTANCE OF PRINCIPLES REVEALED IN NATURE AND REVELATION.

Everything in nature is governed by laws or principles. Chemists, scientists working in all branches of natural research, horticulturists, botanists, etc., spend time and energy discovering the laws with which God has endowed nature: the principles by which the Creator sustains His vast and complicated creation. Success comes as they discover and use the laws of God in the natural world: failure comes through a disregard of these laws.

God appointed the sun, moon, stars, planets, comets, etc., to move according to definite laws. These heavenly bodies act as mighty hands in the heavenly chronometer, moving with faultless precision, across the vaulted dome, following the path planned by their Almighty Creator and Sustainer. Law and order are fixed in the mighty expanse of the stellar regions, and on earth—except in the rebellious hearts of men. We know the times for the rising and setting of the sun, moon, and stars; the tides are governed by certain principles; the seasons come and go; and the whole course of nature is governed by definite laws. Horticulturists know that the growth of leaves and branches on plants and trees is governed by definite mathematical laws. The gardener knows when to plant his seeds, and when they should grow to maturity. By the shooting of the buds, flowers, and leaves of the trees, we know that summer is at hand. From this simple fact Jesus made His remark that we can know with the same certainty the time for the harvest of the world. See Matt. 24: 32, 33. The ornithologist knows the various times it will take for different species of eggs to hatch; but all are governed by the septenary law which governs so much of insect, bird, and animal life.

The law of resonance, or vibration, to which the ears and eyes are adapted by the Creator, governs all the lovely and wonderful things men see and hear, as well as the rays invisible and inaudible to man.

As never before, men now see that everything in nature is controlled by certain laws or principles. Seventh-day Adventists maintain that the law of God uttered from the rugged heights of Mt. Sinai is as unalterable as the other laws by which God controls His illimitable universe; and that man's happiness and usefulness depend upon his strict obedience to the spirit, as well as to the letter, of that law. Everything the Creator—"Palmoni, the wonderful Numberer" (see Dan. 8: 13, margin)—has made is subject to definite laws. As the Bible has been inspired by God (2 Tim. 3: 16; 2 Pet. 1: 21; etc.), is it not reasonable to believe that the Scriptures are based upon definite laws which we must study and follow if we would obtain a true understanding of the Word of God?

How are the laws of nature discovered? In his patient research the scientist constantly tabulates isolated facts until many such facts prove that a certain law operates throughout nature. Until the law is positively established, theories are advanced to try to explain why the facts exist. Theories are not facts—they are the attempts to explain how or why certain facts are as they are. When enough proof has been gathered to demonstrate that the theory is true, then that theory becomes a law. Similarly, he who patiently and prayerfully searches the Scriptures, learns from his "study" that there are laws which govern in *"rightly dividing* the word of truth." 2 Tim. 2: 15.

Especially in the study of the prophecies, one needs to apply all the laws of interpretation. The failure to learn and to apply these laws is responsible for a great amount of theological confusion and false teaching regarding last-day events.

The Bible is scientifically constructed; there are certain principles upon which it was written, and those who interpret it without regard to these principles do injustice to its Divine Author. Only when these principles are recognised and applied will a beautiful harmony be found to exist in all its parts. The Holy Spirit reveals the true meaning of prophetic imagery after much prayer and patient Spirit-led research, which leads to the knowledge of the laws of interpretation. "The secret of the Lord is with them that fear Him." Ps. 25: 14.

CHAPTER III.

BIBLE PRINCIPLES ARISE OUT OF THE NATURE AND CHARACTER OF THE GODHEAD.

As Creator, God is Supreme, and to Him should be rendered trustful obedience. The great controversy between Christ and Satan is *a clash of principles*. Before the inception of sin, God's creatures were governed by the *principle* that God was supreme, and that His will, being perfect and holy, should be obeyed without hesitation or question. So long as that principle was maintained peace, harmony, and joy prevailed throughout God's limitless kingdom. The thoughts of the sinless children of God were God-centred, not introspective and "self"-centred. The bliss of heaven was marred by Lucifer's *principles* of pride and "self"-exaltation, which led to revolt against God's supreme authority.

Repeatedly, Jesus stated that the purpose of His coming to earth was to reveal the character of His Father, and to teach the principle of implicit trust and obedience to the will of the infinite God—"our heavenly Father." John 4: 34; 5: 30; 6: 3; Matt. 26: 39-44; Phil. 2: 8; Heb. 5: 8.

Actuated by the *principle* of humble obedience to the will of God, the church has faced hostile forces following the principles of Satan's kingdom. In describing the final acts in the great drama of the conflict between the forces of good and evil, God's servant declares: "The Sabbath is to be the issue in the great final conflict in which all the world will act a part. Men have honoured *Satan's principles* above the *principles that rule in the heavens.* They have accepted the spurious Sabbath, which Satan has exalted as the *sign of his authority.* . . . . It is our work to lead people to understand this." 6T. 352. Thus we are instructed to deal with the Sabbath from the viewpoint of the *principles* involved. It is not a matter merely of a day, but of the principle of perfect trust and obedience to the will of a loving, all-wise, and Almighty God— "a faithful Creator." 1 Peter 4: 19.

The Third Angel's Message is based upon definite *principles governing the interpretation of the Scriptures.* In his opposition to

God, Satan has devised a system of interpretation which, if followed, will blind people to the Third Angel's Message.

That the Sabbath is still binding is evident from the *principle* that God has made all vital matters pertaining to His work on earth a subject of prophecy. "Surely the Lord God will do *nothing*, but He *revealeth* His secret unto His servants the *prophets.*" Amos 3: 7. All texts in the Bible must be interpreted to agree with this fundamental principle. God's nature causes Him to clearly reveal His will. God did not predict that He would change His Sabbath day; therefore, the fourth Commandment is still obligatory on all mankind.

The perpetuity of the Law of God is established upon the principle that God's law is the expression of His character. As God's character is unchangeable, so is His law.

The teaching of an eternally burning hell in which sin would be perpetuated throughout eternity is contrary to the nature of God. God "canst not look on iniquity" (Hab. 1: 13), and, therefore, would not make provision to behold sin throughout eternity. All texts dealing with the punishment of the wicked must be interpreted to agree with this principle. Other doctrines, also, may be sustained by well-defined Bible principles which have their origin in the character of God.

Because of God's holiness sinners cannot live in His kingdom. "The wages of sin is death." God's character also prompted the "unspeakable gift" (2 Cor. 9: 15) of His Son. In order to give us eternal life Jesus was obliged to die. In the plan of redemption life comes from death. See John 12: 24, 25. To receive new life from Christ the believer, too, must die—die to the "old man," the old nature. Rom. 6: 11-13, etc. The more we die to sin and self, the more strength we develop in the new life. As in nature new life springs from the dead, so we obtain new life spiritually now, and literally at the resurrection. Therefore, from God's holiness arises the principle of life from death caused by sin. This oft-repeated Bible principle must guide in the interpretation of prophecy. There cannot be a millennium of peace and blessedness on earth to follow as the harvest from a world steeped in sin and iniquity. The doctrine of a desolate—"dead"—earth and the cleansing of the earth by the fires of the last days alone harmonizes with the principle of new life—a new world—emerging from death.

God, by nature, is a great Giver—but nothing is wasted, nothing uselessly destroyed. Throughout His kingdom there is a conservation of energy—even when things are apparently wasted. Dead leaves may fall from the trees, but they become life in the soil for next year's growth. Fruit that is not picked and eaten by man either becomes the birthplace and food supply for new plants, or rots and nourishes the soil. The substance that locks up energy may be destroyed, but the energy released serves some other purpose. Even the wicked who are destroyed in the fires of the last days are turned back to ground from whence they came. Mal. 4: 1, 3. All nature agrees with Revelation that man's struggles after righteousness are not for nought. The God Who brings new growth, new life from decay, will certainly bring forth immortal life out of a life pleasing to Him. If He did not, it would be wasted effort. God permits nothing to waste. This world, itself, though marred by sin, will rise from the cleansing fires to be the saints' abode and the place of the Lord's throne.

In nature we also see evidence that God has more than one object in view. The flowers provide the bees with honey, but the bees in seeking for the honey carry the pollen for reproducing the flowers. The flowers not only attract the bees and the insects, and thus reproduce themselves, but they gladden the heart of man with their beauty. In the spiritual realm, also, we see this principle. By destroying the wicked, God preserves the peace and happiness of His children. In sending Jesus to save the people of this world, God demonstrated to all the worlds on high that He is a God of goodness and righteousness and deserving of all their confidence and love. Thus He met Satan's false accusations against His character. God plans that man shall be instrumental in saving his fellowman because in helping another he helps himself.

God wastes nothing in nature, and He has more than one purpose in all that He does. Similarly, we see the principle that nothing is wasted in the Scriptures, and that God has more than one purpose in the experiences of ancient Israel: all that pertained to literal Israel is now useful to the church—even the conditional prophecies (such as Ezek. 38-48, etc.) which were not fulfilled in the experiences of literal Israel because of their failure to meet the conditions necessary for their fulfilment.

Jesus commands His followers: "Gather up the fragments that remain, that nothing be lost." John 6: 12. The "fragments" filled twelve baskets. By heeding Bible principles of interpretation we are able to fill our "baskets" with what many regard as mere "fragments" of little value. "Man shall not live by bread alone,

25

but by *every* word that proceedeth out of the mouth of God." Matt. 4: 4.

In the prophecies (such as Joel 3; Zech. 14; Ezek. 38, 39; Rev. 16: 12-16; 19: 11-21) outlining "the final conflict," God does not waste valuable space in His Word referring to specific nations, for these prophecies relate to the church and her spiritual enemies. "The final conflict" concerns only the two opposing forces of good and evil.

The Godhead is a Trinity, and therefore the Scriptures constantly employ the number three—not only in the many instances where such use is plainly stated, but also intricately woven into the very warp and woof of the words and structure of Holy Writ.

In the Apocalypse (where the principles of interpretation for the whole of the Scriptures are found), Jehovah is mentioned *three* times in relation to the *three* divisions of time: "the Lord which *is*, and which *was*, and which is *to come*." Rev. 1: 4, 8; 4: 8. The name Jehovah signifies God's eternal existence: "The I AM" of the past, "The I AM" of the present, "The I AM" of the future. "Jesus Christ, the same *yesterday*, and *to-day*, and *forever*." Heb. 13: 8. Not only is time divided into *three*—past, present and future —but space is also divided into *three* planes—above, our plane of existence, and below. As in time and space it is the *central*, or *second* division and plane in which we live, so the *second* Person of the Godhead, Jesus Christ, incarnate Deity, *visibly* contacted our time and mortal plane. "The Word was made flesh, and dwelt among us (and we *beheld* His glory as of the only begotten of the Father)." John 1: 14. "That which was from the beginning . . . which we have *seen* with our eyes . . . and our hands have handled, of the Word of Life." 1 John 1: 1-3.

In the plan of redemption, Jesus is the *visible* manifestation of the Deity to man, and because of this the New Testament reveals the principle that the *literal* interpretations of Scripture are applicable when and where His *literal* Presence is manifested: (1) in the days of literal Israel, (2) in heaven now, (3) in the eternal kingdom on earth. Wherever Jesus is, *there* will be found the *literal*, the real, the tangible.

In dealing with national Israel, God spoke audibly to His people, and the evidences of His Presence were *literally* seen by them. When on earth, Jesus was *literally* seen, but with His death the period in which God revealed Himself through *literal* things—

temple, priests, sacrifices, etc.—ended (Matt. 27: 50, 51, etc.), and "the dispensation of the Holy Spirit" (T.M. 511) was ushered in. During this "dispensation of the Holy Spirit," the things of the kingdom of *grace* are based upon the *spiritual* and the invisible. Jesus declares: ". . . Even the Spirit of truth, Whom the world cannot receive, *because it seeth Him not.*" John 14: 17.

Jesus *visibly* appeared to man, and ministers among *literal* things: the Holy Spirit *invisibly* represents Christ to man, and glorifies Christ (John 16: 14) by *spiritually* interpreting literal things. While Jesus is ministering in "the *true* tabernacle, which the Lord pitched" (Heb. 8: 2)—the *literal* temple in heaven—the Holy Spirit is ministering in the *spiritual* temple—the church—on earth. Ephes. 2: 21. 22; 2 Cor. 6: 16, etc. While Jesus is ministering among the seven candlesticks (Rev. 1: 12, 13) in the heavenly temple, the Holy Spirit is ministering among the seven *spiritual* candlesticks in the *spiritual* temple. "The seven candlesticks which thou sawest *are the seven churches.*" Rev. 1: 20. The principle of the *literal* wherever Jesus is, and the *spiritual* now, while the Holy Spirit represents Jesus, gives rise to the principle of the triple application of the Scriptures, whereby the things relating to Israel must be interpreted to be: (1) *literal* before the cross; (2) *spiritual* on earth after the cross and the subsequent rejection of the Jewish nation; (3) *literal* after the second advent. This *triple* application establishes the certainty of the Third Angel's Message. For further consideration of the triple application, see later chapters.

From the principle that the *literal* things are always *grouped* around Jesus, and the *spiritual* things are *grouped* around the Holy Spirit while He represents Christ, arises the principle that other things in the Scriptures are also grouped together. In the days of literal Israel things were grouped on a *literal*, national basis: in the times of *spiritual* Israel things are *spiritually* grouped together. Jerusalem, which was God's centre, and Babylon, Satan's centre, and *all that were grouped with them,* are brought into the New Testament and applied in a *spiritual, world-wide sense.*

As stated in my "Christ Conquers," pp. 76, 77: "When a person, place, or battle mentioned in the Old Testament is applied in the New Testament in a spiritual, or antitypical world-wide sense, the *whole* of the picture presented in the Old Testament narrative becomes an *imagery* in the antitypical application—even though all the associated features are not separately applied. Thus, once we see *Babylon,* the literal city which was built upon the literal river Euphrates, applied spiritually, or antitypically, as it is in the Apocalype, then we know that the river Euphrates, in Rev. 16: 12, also must be applied spiritually, or antitypically—which is, of course, world-wide. Things in the *antitypical* application must *stand together* in the *same relation* as they did in the *literal* setting. . . . The same principle operates in relation to Elijah and Jezebel. Both of these Old Testament characters are typical. In the Apocalypse there is no *specific* antitypical application of Elijah to the last message of God now about to sound with its loud cry. . . . But, the very fact that Rev. 2: 20 applies Jezebel, *Elijah's opponent,* in an *antitypical* sense, is quite sufficient for us to see that *all* of the factors involved in the Old Testament presentation of the conflict between Elijah and the sun-worshiping forces in his day, are to be antitypically applied in the last days in connection with the world-wide spiritual conflict. Having drawn our attention to the fact that *Jezebel* is to be understood in an antitypical sense, the Lord expects us to see that the *whole* of the Old Testament picture is to be *applied in exactly the same way.* . . .

"Nowhere in Scripture are we instructed that Ahab (the king and husband who introduced sun-worship into Israel to please Jezebel his wife) is typical of the State that will enforce Sunday keeping, to please the antitypical Jezebel, the apostate church; but such is the obvious application because of the fact that Jezebel, in Rev. 2: 20, is applied by the Lord in an antitypical manner. An antitypical application of *one* of the features of the Old Testament narratives is an indication from God—*the principle revealed*—that *all that is associated with it* should also be understood in a world-wide, antitypical sense."

The book of Revelation is a divine example of this principle of things being grouped together, for *all* the places, proper names and designations are employed *symbolically.* By this group-principle we know that, as Babylon in Rev. 16 is interpreted spiritually, so the *Euphrates* and *Armageddon,* which are grouped with her, must also be interpreted in a *spiritual, world-wide sense.*

Prophetic interpretations must harmonize with clearly-stated principles which are based on the nature and work of God.

CHAPTER IV

HOW GOD TEACHES HIS PEOPLE TO SEE THE INVISIBLE.

"By faith he [Moses] forsook Egypt . . . for he endured, as *seeing* Him Who is *invisible.*" Heb. 11: 27. He who constantly practices the spiritual vision grows in character and purpose. The Christian looks beyond the things of time and sense and *sees an invisible world.* "Now *faith* is the *substance* of things hoped for, the *evidence* of things not seen." Heb. 11: 1. Of the Old Testament saints we read: "These all died in faith, not having received the promises, but having *seen them* afar off [i.e., by *spiritual* vision], and were persuaded of them, and embraced them, and confessed that they were strangers and pilgrims on the earth . . . they desire a better country, that is, an *heavenly.*" Heb. 11: 13-16. Abraham "looked for a city which hath ˀfoundations, whose builder and maker is God." Heb. 11: 10.

The Christian's gaze is upon unseen things. Paul declares: "While we *look not* at the things which are seen, but at the things which are *not seen:* for the things which are *seen* are temporal; but the things which are *not seen* are eternal." 2 Cor. 4: 18. God says: "*Look unto Me,* and be ye saved, all the ends of the earth." Isa. 45: 22. "Thou wilt keep him in perfect peace, whose mind [margin, *thought,* or *imagination*] is stayed upon Thee." Isa. 26: 3.

Imagination is a natural endowment, and by it God desires man to *picture* divine things. 1 Chron. 29: 18; 28: 9; 2 Cor. 10: 5, etc. "Perfect peace" is assured him "whose imagination is stayed upon" God. Satan causes men to pervert this gift of imagination. Gen. 6: 5, margin; 8: 21; Deut. 29: 19; 31: 21; Ps. 2: 1; Zech. 7: 10; Acts 4: 25; Rom. 1: 21; 2 Cor. 10: 5, etc.

"No man hath *seen God* at any time." John 1: 18. "Ye have neither heard His voice at any time, nor *seen His shape.*" John 5: 37. "And no man hath ascended up to heaven." John 3: 13. How, then, can we look to God Whom we have not seen, or picture heaven, having not been there? As by *earthly things* God teaches us concerning heavenly things, so Jesus, in His human life, revealed the *likeness* of His Father. Jesus declared: "He that hath *seen Me* hath *seen the Father."* John 14: 9.

Our vision of God and of heaven comes as we study the Scriptures, for in them we have *word pictures* of heavenly things. "Eye [i.e., the *natural* eye] hath not seen . . . the things which God hath prepared for them that love Him. *But* God *hath revealed them unto us* by His Spirit: for the Spirit searcheth all things, yea, the deep things of God . . . Which things also we speak . . . comparing *spiritual* things with *spiritual* . . . they are *spiritually* discerned." 1 Cor. 2: 9-14. Spiritual vision develops as we continue to study the Word of God and pray for heavenly enlightenment. Living in the atmosphere of the inspired writers, one learns to see things as they saw them.

The infinite Teacher "used similitudes" (Hos. 12: 10) by which to instruct His people. By comparing Jas. 3: 9 with Gen. 1: 26, 27, we see that a "similitude" is an "image" or "likeness." In His Word, God employed "similitudes"—likenesses, or imagery— because He created the mind capable of conjuring up *pictures.* Educationalists rightly stress the value of "visual education." The blessings of eyesight are very great; but the blessings of mind-sight are greater. It is possible to casually see an object without observing it with the mind.

The ear has been marvellously created to receive vibrations of sound, which reach the brain via the auditory nerves, and the brain translates those vibrations into pictures. Whether learning through the eyes or the ears, we arouse the mind to take pictures of that which we seek to memorize. The mind is a photographic plate, and is constantly taking pictures. Clear thinking is an alert mind taking clear pictures, which are stored up in the memory. Logic is the manipulator which adjusts the focus of the camera. When seeking to recall something to memory, we concentrate on making the brain throw on to the screen the pictures we have stored in our minds. We forget easily when we fail to expose the mind-plate long enough to enable the picture to be indelibly stamped upon the mind. Meditation is a Christian duty. 1 Tim. 4: 15.

Because God has endowed the mind with the ability to make pictures—to visualize what we read or hear—He has so inspired the writing of His Holy Word that it forms a long gallery of *word pictures*—"likenesses," "similitudes," "imagery." Two ideals are attained in the Scriptures—clarity and brevity. *By · word-*

pictures God has made the truths of His Word *clear,* and *by them* He has been able to present *"much in little."* By the law of association, the mind can visualize all which is *connected with a symbol.* In the sanctuary and its services we see clear and definite *illustrations* of the various features connected with the plan of redemption. An innocent, unblemished lamb slain because of an individual's sin presents an impressive picture of Christ's substitutionary death. The word-picture of the Israelites sheltering behind the blood-sprinkled door lintels while the death angel passes by, graphically portrays the effectiveness of the blood of Jesus to save us from God's wrath against sin. By the pictures presented in the sacred narratives of the *physical* exploits of Samson, we see clearly illustrations of the power of the Holy Spirit in our lives, overcoming the difficulties and dangers from our *spiritual foes.* "The people that do know their God shall be *strong,* and *do exploits."* Dan. 11: 32. "Be strong in the Lord, and in the *power of His might."* Ephes. 6: 10. David's victorious conflict with Goliath provides us with a clear picture of what it means to live the victorious life in the power of Christ. Satan, our Goliath, is far too strong for us to slay, but with Paul we can say: "I can do all things through Christ which strengtheneth me." Phil. 4: 13. We obtain "the victory through our Lord Jesus Christ." 1 Cor. 15: 57.

The *historical incidents* recorded in the Old Testament provide us with *word pictures* by which God teaches us *spiritual truths.* In them we are to see things world-wide in scope: *corresponding likenesses in the spiritual realm,* which are *"spiritually* discerned." 1 Cor. 2: 14.

The New Testament reveals the principle of *"spiritually"* discerning *"spiritual things"* in the historical narratives of the Old Testament. In this way "God *hath revealed them* unto us"—the things which He *"hath prepared* for them that *love Him."* The *natural* eye does not see these *"spiritual things,"* and often interprets literally that which should be *"spiritually* discerned." See 1 Cor. 2: 6-16.

During His earthly ministry Christ proclaimed heavenly truths by means of parables: *word-pictures* of earthly things with heavenly meanings. "The unknown was *illustrated* by the known; divine truths by *earthly things* with which the people were most familiar. The Scripture says, 'All these things spake Jesus unto the multitudes in parables' . . . *Natural things* were the *medium for the spiritual; the things of nature* . . . were connected with the truths

31

of the written word. Leading thus from the *natural to the spiritual kingdom,* Christ's parables are links in the chain of truth that unites man with God. . . .

"Parable-teaching was popular, and commanded the respect and attention, not only of the Jews, but of the people of other nations. *No more effective method* of instruction could He have employed." "Christ's Object Lesson," pp. 17-21.

Natural or *literal* objects illustrated divine truths: "Natural *things* were the *medium* for the *spiritual*." Christ's word-pictures lead us "from the *natural* to the *spiritual* kingdom." As shown in later chapters, all the natural, or literal history of literal Israel was recorded to present *pictures* leading "from the *natural* to the *spiritual* kingdom." In this way God teaches His children to see the invisible, and, by seeing the things of the *spiritual* realm, to grow strong in character and purpose.

God calls the Laodicean church to develop *spiritual sight:* "I counsel thee to . . . anoint thine eyes with eyesalve, that thou mayest *see.*" Rev. 3: 18. Only by much prayerful study of the Word of God is it possible for this heavenly injunction to be obeyed. The development of *spiritual* vision depends upon the co-operation of human effort with Divine power. See Matt. 13: 13-17, etc.

CHAPTER V.

THE LAW OF THE LITERAL AND THE SPIRITUAL: THE PRINCIPLE OF "ACTED PARABLES."

The Bible contains both the literal and the spiritual. People holding divergent views recognize this fact. They differ, mainly, concerning the *time* and *place* of the literal or spiritual application. The true understanding of last-day prophecies depends on *"rightly dividing* the word of truth" (2 Tim. 2: 15). The literal is the commencement of, or the foundation for, the spiritual. God leads our minds from the material world to the spiritual: from the seen and the known to the unseen and the things unknown to us through our physical senses. "That was *not first* which is *spiritual, but* that which is *natural; and afterward* that which is *spiritual."* 1 Cor. 15: 46.

As the things belonging to the material world and those belonging to the spiritual realm were both created by God, the seen harmonizes with, and illustrates, the things of the spiritual realm. When on earth Jesus pointed to nature in teaching spiritual truths. In many of her books, such as "Christ's Object Lessons," God's servant has demonstrated to us that this was the Master's method of instructing His children. From the material things limited to certain places He taught spiritual truths which are of world-wide application.

BY "ACTED PARABLES" GOD INSTRUCTS IN SPIRITUAL THINGS.

"A wise purpose underlay *every act* of Christ's life on earth." D.A., p. 206. The *physical* work He accomplished in Palestine was done to illustrate the *spiritual* work which He would do in all the world.

"The work of Christ in cleansing the leper from his terrible disease is an *illustration* of His work in cleansing the soul from sin." D.A., p. 266. "In the healing of the paralytic at Capernaum, Christ again taught the same truth. It was to manifest His power to forgive sins that the miracle was performed. And the healing of the paralytic *also illustrates* other precious *truths."* D.A., p. 267.

Concerning the experience of the disciples in the storm on the Sea of Galilee, the servant of the Lord has written:

"In their efforts to save themselves, they forgot Jesus; and it was only when, in the despair of self-dependence, they turned to Him, that He could give them help. How often the *disciples' experience is ours!* When the tempests of temptation gather, and the fierce lightnings flash, and the waves sweep over us, we battle with the storm alone, forgetting that there is One Who can help us. . . . Then we remember Jesus, and if we can call upon Him to save us, we shall not cry in vain. . . . Whether on the land or on the sea if we have the Saviour in our hearts, there is no need of fear. Living faith in the Redeemer will smooth the sea of life, and will deliver us from danger in the way that He knows best. There is *another spiritual* lesson in this miracle of the stilling of the tempest. . . ." D.A., p. 336.

The miracles and experiences of Jesus in His Palestinian ministry were recorded as *illustrations of world-wide spiritual truths,* having their counterpart in the world-wide spiritual kingdom in the spiritual land of Israel. Employing the literal to illustrate the spiritual is one of the principles upon which the Bible was written —a principle clearly taught in the New Testament and in the Spirit of Prophecy. "Thus the Lord . . . [in the days of Jeremiah] taught the people by means of a series of *acted parables.*" P.K. 423.

"The cursing of the fig-tree was *an acted parable.* That barren tree, flaunting its pretentious foliage in the very face of Christ was a *symbol* of the Jewish nation. The Saviour desired to make plain to His disciples the cause and the certainty of Israel's doom. For this purpose He invested the tree with moral qualities, and *made it the expositor of divine truth.*" D.A., p. 582. "*Every act* of His life, *every word* spoken, *every miracle* wrought, was to make known to fallen *humanity* the infinite love of God." P.K. 696.

After proclaiming a spiritual truth Jesus performed a physical miracle to *illustrate His spiritual meaning,* or, after performing a miracle, He then taught some spiritual truth *illustrated* by the miracle. Christ had performed His miracle of changing the water into wine before He informed Nicodemus concerning a change of heart. Christ's first cleansing of the temple also preceded His statement to Nicodemus. See John 2 and 3. The miracle of the new birth *changes* the heart and *cleanses the heart-temple.* The morning after Jesus stilled the storm on Galilee and spoke peace to the troubled hearts of His disciples, they encountered two madmen.

"The disciples . . . fled in terror . . . He Who had stilled the tempest . . . did not flee before these demons . . . Jesus raised that hand which had beckoned the waves to rest and the men could come no nearer." D.A., p. 337. The demons possessing the two men were the cause of their misery; and evil spirits were the cause of the troubles of the disciples, and are still the cause of the misery and the storms of all mankind. "The encounter with the demoniacs of Gergesa had a *lesson* for the disciples. *It showed* the depths of degradation to which Satan is seeking to drag the *whole human race*, and the mission of Christ to set men free from his power." D.A. 341.

After feeding the multitudes with the literal bread, Jesus gave a deeply spiritual sermon concerning "the Bread which came down from heaven," declaring, "I am that bread of life." John 6. In this sermon, Jesus applied the giving of manna to the children of Israel in the wilderness as the giving of Himself—the living Bread—to His children in their wilderness journey to the promised land. As the children of Israel partook of the manna daily so, also, must we partake of the spiritual bread each day.

In both the Old and the New Testaments operates the principle that the *literal* things which were enacted in Palestine were "acted parables"—*illustrations* or *types* of *world-wide, spiritual* things pertaining to Christ's kingdom of grace. As Jesus is the Author of the whole of the Word of God, we know that His method of teaching in the Old Testament is the same as in the New. As generally recognized, all the gospel was shown by the types—acted parables—of the sanctuary services. Ps. 77: 13. *"All"* the recorded experiences of literal Israel "were our examples," or *"our figures,"* as stated in the margin of 1 Cor. 10: 6. "Now *all* these things happened unto them for ensamples [margin, "types"]: and they are written for our admonition, upon whom the ends of the world are come." 1 Cor. 10: 11. In this instance, the Apostle Paul does not point out the types of the sanctuary services, but *"all"* the experiences of the children of Israel.

"For *whatsoever* things were written aforetime were written for our learning." Rom. 15: 4. "In *every* page, whether history, or precept, or prophecy [including Ezek. 38-48, etc.], the Old Testament Scriptures are irradiated with the glory of the Son of God. So far as it was of divine institution, the *entire system of Judaism* was a compacted *prophecy* of the gospel. To Christ 'give all the prophets witness.' Acts 10: 43. From the promise given to Adam, down through the patriarchal line and legal economy, heaven's glorious light made plain the footsteps of the Redeemer. . . . In *every* sacrifice, Christ's death was shown. In *every* cloud of incense His righteousness ascended. By *every* jubilee trumpet His name was sounded. In the awful mystery of the holy of holies His glory dwelt." D.A. 212.

After His resurrection, Jesus taught His disciples the *spiritual* nature of His kingdom: He had endeavoured to teach them these things before His death, but then they were too filled with the erroneous teachings of the Pharisees concerning the establishment of a *literal* kingdom. After Pentecost the disciples clearly understood the Old Testament. The New Testament writers reveal the principle for interpreting the Old Testament: to see in the *literal, types* of the *spiritual* and *world-wide*.

35

THE LORD REVEALS THE PRINCIPLE OF INTERPRETING THE SCRIPTURES.

OLD TESTAMENT HISTORY.	THE NEW TESTAMENT SPIRITUAL APPLICATION.
"The *first* Adam"—father of a sinful, mortal race.	1 Cor. 15: 45-49. Jesus, "the *last* Adam," the Father of a sinless, immortal race.
Eve—Adam's wife.	Ephes. 5: 31, 32; Gen. 2: 23, 24. The church—the bride of "the last Adam."
Saved by the ark from the flood of God's wrath, and landing on to a new world.	1 Pet. 3: 19-21. Salvation from God's wrath and, some day, stepping on to a new world. "The *like figure* whereunto even baptism doth also now save us." Baptism, in its fuller meaning, points forward to the new life in the new world.
Melchisedec, the king-priest of Salem, the "king of righteousness," "the king of peace."	Heb. 7: 2-6. Typified Jesus, the "King of Righteousness," the "King of Peace," Who reigns in "the heavenly Jerusalem." Christians are also "kings and priests." Rev. 1: 6, etc.
Abraham, the father of the tribes of Israel.	Rom. 4: 11-18. "The father of all them that believe." Rom. 9: 7, 8; Gal. 3: 7-9, etc.
Isaac, the promised seed.	Matt. 1: 1; Gal. 3: 16; 4: 28. Type of Jesus, the promised Seed; also type of those who are Christ's.
Isaac, the miraculously born of a freewoman, was free.	Gal. 4: 28. "Now we, brethren, as Isaac was, are the children of promise." The Christian, being born again of the Holy Spirit, is free and is a child of "the heavenly Jerusalem," which is built of God.
Ishmael, born of natural birth by a bondwoman, was in bondage, and persecuted Isaac, the freeborn. The bondwoman and her son were cast out of Abraham's camp.	Gal. 4: 22-31. Paul applies as *"an allegory."* Ishmael, the persecutor of the promised seed, typifies those who oppose the children of God. As "dogs" that bite and devour, they will be "without the city," "the *camp* of the saints." Rev. 20: 9; 22: 15.

Old Testament History.	The New Testament Spiritual Application
Jacob, the supplanter, whose nature was changed during the long *literal* night of wrestling with God. His name was then changed to "Israel."	John 1: 47-50; Rom. 2: 28, 29; Rev. 7: 4-8, etc. Type of all whose characters are changed through wrestling with God during the *spiritual* night till the dawn of eternity.
Israelites.	Rom. 2: 28, 29; 9: 7, 8; Gal. 3: 29; Rev. 7: 4-8; 21: 12-14, etc. Christians.
Circumcision.	Col. 2: 11-13. Dedication of new life to God.
The ladder which Jacob saw in vision reaching from heaven to earth.	John 1: 51. Typified Jesus, Whose sacrificial death has thrown a ladder from heaven to earth.
Joseph, the rejected brother, sold as a slave, later the saviour of the world, having abundant food for all who came to him. Raised to the throne.	Acts 7: 9-13. Typified Jesus—Who was rejected, being sold for the price of a slave—the Saviour and Provider of spiritual food for all who come to Him. Raised to His Father's throne.
Moses, deliverer, lawgiver, etc.	Heb. 3: 2-6; Acts 3: 22; 7: 37-40. Typified Jesus, the Deliverer, Lawgiver, etc.
Egypt, "the house of bondage."	Rev. 11: 8, etc. The type of Satan's bondage.
The deliverance from Egypt.	Luke 4: 18. The deliverance from bondage.
Israel going through the Red Sea, being led by the cloud and fire; partaking of the bread from heaven, and the water from the smitten rock.	1 Cor. 10: 1-11. Typified the Christian as he walks to the heavenly Canaan. Baptism, like Israel having passed through the sea, separates from the old life of bondage, and commences a new life in Christ's service.
Israel's pilgrimage to the land of promise.	1 Pet. 2: 11. Typifies the Christian's pilgrimage across the wilderness of sin to the land of promise.
The manna.	John 6: 31-63. Jesus definitely applied the manna as a type of Himself, "the true bread from heaven."
The tabernacle in the wilderness— plain on the outside, but beautiful and full of glory within .	John 1: 14. Typified Christ's incarnation—His Deity veiled by humanity. See D.A. 23, 24.
Aaron, the High Priest.	Heb. 5: 4, 5, etc. Typified Christ as High Priest.

Old Testament History.	The New Testament Spiritual Application.
The people of Israel bitten by serpents in their wilderness journey.	Rev. 12: 9; 20: 2. Typified God's spiritual Israel suffering from Satan's vicious attacks on their journey to heaven.
By looking to the uplifted serpent they found healing from the serpent's stings.	John 3: 14; 8: 28; 12: 32. By looking to Jesus we, too, find healing from the wounds caused by Satan.
The unbelief of the Israelites in their walk to the land of promise, and their failure to reach Canaan.	Heb. 3: 8-19. Applied by Paul to Christians who do not exercise faith, and who will not reach the heavenly Canaan.
Israel's promised rest in the promised land after their sojourn across "the wilderness of sin" (Ex. 16: 1).	Heb. 4. Paul applies to the saints' eternal rest after their sojourn across the wilderness of sin. The Sabbath rest at the end of a week of toil is a type of the eternal rest at the end of life's labours.
National Israel.	1 Pet. 2: 9; Matt. 21: 43. The church a "nation."
National Israel, a kingdom of priests.	1 Pet. 2: 9; Rev. 1: 6, etc. Christians are "priests."
National Israel had national enemies.	Rev. 11: 1, 2; 20: 8. These same enemies are employed as antitypical—*spiritual*—enemies of the church.
The Old Testament temple.	1 Cor. 3: 9-16; 2 Cor. 6: 16; Ephes. 2: 20-22. Typified the spiritual temple—the church.
The priests of the Old Testament.	Heb. 8: 1-6. Typified (1) Christ in His heavenly ministry; (2) All of His believers ministering the spiritual things of His spiritual kingdom on earth. 1 Pet. 2: 9.
The destruction and rebuilding of the temple.	Acts 15: 12-19. Applied by James as a type of the re-building of Christ's spiritual temple — the church.
Treading down of Jerusalem by Gentile, or heathen nations.	Rev. 11: 1, 2. Applied by Jesus, through John, to the treading down of spiritual Jerusalem—the church —by spiritual Israel's spiritual enemies. The "Gentile" or "Heathen" nations of the Old Testament who attacked Israel (mentioned in such prophecies as Joel 3; Ezek. 38, 39; Zech. 14, etc.) are applied by Christ as the spiritual enemies of spiritual Israel.

Old Testament History.	The New Testament Spiritual Application.
The measuring of the temple and city of Jerusalem.	Rev. 11: 1, 2. Applied by Jesus, through John, to the spiritual measuring of the church.
Solomon reigning in his kingdom of peace and splendour, and people coming from afar to hear his wisdom.	Matt. 6: 29; 12: 42. Pointed to One Who is "greater than Solomon."
David, King of Israel.	Luke 1: 32, 33; John 1: 49. Typified Jesus "the King of Israel."
Zion.	Joel 2: 32 compare with Rom. 10: 13; Isa. 28: 16 with 1 Pet. 2: 6-8; Isa. 59: 20 with Rom. 11: 26, etc. "Zion," in the New Testament interpretation, refers to the church.
The camp of Israel, and, later, Jerusalem, with God's Presence in Israel's midst.	Heb. 12: 22, 23; 1 Pet. 2: 4-9, etc. Typified the church, and also the New Jerusalem. See Rev. 20: 9; 21: 2, 3, 12-14.
The precious stones on the breastplate of the High Priest.	Rev. 21: 19, 20. "The breast-plate, the most sacred of the priestly vestments. . . . It was in the form of a square. . . . The border was formed of a variety of precious stones, the *same that form the twelve foundations of the city of God.*" P.P. 350.
The feasts and services mentioned in Lev. 23, etc.—	
The Passover, leaven.	1 Cor. 5: 7, 8. "Christ, our passover." "The leaven of malice and wickedness."
The first fruits.	1 Cor. 15: 20, 23. "Christ, the first fruits." James 1: 18. "That we should be a kind of first fruits of His creatures." Rev. 14: 4. "Being the first fruits unto God and to the Lamb."
Pentecost.	Acts 2: 1. "And when the day of Pentecost was fully come."
Blowing of trumpets.	Rev. 14: 6, 7,; Joel 2: 1, etc. The Judgment-hour Message.
Day of Atonement.	Rev. 14: 6, 7; Dan. 8: 14, etc. The Investigative Judgment in the heavenly sanctuary.

Old Testament History.	The New Testament Spiritual Application.
End of Day of Atonement—cutting off of those who did not afflict their souls: who did not avail themselves of the ministry of the High Priest.	Rev. 22: 11, 12; 14: 9-11; 15: 5-8, etc. Close of probation. Rev. 16; 19: 11-21. Destruction of those who did not avail themselves of the ministry of Jesus, the High Priest, in the heavenly temple.
Lev. 16. Scapegoat sent to "a land not inhabited," where he eventually perished.	Rev. 20: 1-10. Satan, the scapegoat, confined to this depopulated earth during the 1,000 years. Satan perishes on this earth.
Lev. 25. Jubilee—everything was restored to the rightful owners.	Acts 3: 21. "The restitution of all things."
The land of Canaan promised Abraham.	Rom. 4: 13. Typified the world.
The mountains of Israel.	Ezek. 34: 13-16, 23-26, 28-31; Ezek. 38; 39; 40: 2; D.A. 52, 479; A.A. 9, 10. Typified the spiritual, world - wide highlands where spiritual Israel feed in spiritual pastures. Ephes. 1: 3; Isa. 58: 14; Rev. 14: 1.
Israel's enemies perish on the mountains of Israel. Ezek. 38, 39.	Rev. 16: 16. "Har" means "Mount." Rev. 19: 17, 18, 21 compare with Ezek. 39: 4, 17-19. The prophetic picture describes the world-wide slaughter, on "the mountains of Israel," of the enemies of spiritual Israel.
The tabernacle was pitched in the midst of the children of Israel. Num. 1: 51-53; 2: 1-34.	John 1: 14; Rev. 1: 13, 20, etc. Jesus in the midst of His people.
"Israel, a people [literally] near unto Him." Ps. 148: 14.	Heb. 10: 22. Spiritual Israel is spiritually near to Him.
They literally approached His visible Presence within the Sanctuary.	Heb. 4: 16; Luke 15: 13-20. The movements of people away from, or to God, mentioned in the New Testament (after the rejection of the literal centre—the temple), are spiritual applications of the literal movements of ancient Israel. Rev. 18: 4, etc.
The Gentiles inhabited lands far off from the literal centre—the temple.	Acts 22: 21; 13: 47, etc. "But now in Christ Jesus ye [Gentiles] who sometimes were far off are made nigh by the blood of Christ . . . and preached peace to you which were afar off, and to them that were nigh." Ephes. 2: 13-18; Acts 2: 39, etc.

Old Testament History.	The New Testament Spiritual Application.
Gen. 10: 10; 11: 1-9, margins, "Babylon," "confusion," rebellion.	Rev. 14: 8; 16: 19; 17: 5; 18: 2, 10. Spiritual Babylon—rebellion, confusion.
Jer. 51: 13; PK. 523. Literal Babylon built on the literal Euphrates. The Annotated Para. Bible comments on Jer. 5: 13: "The Euphrates and its numerous canals, which passed through and near the city."	Rev. 17: 1, 5, 15. Spiritual Babylon built on the spiritual Euphrates.
Jer. 50: 38; 51: 36; Isa. 44: 27. The waters of the river Euphrates were "dried up."	Rev. 16: 12. The waters of the spiritual Euphrates to be "dried up."
Cyrus, the deliverer of Israel, and the destroyer of Babylon.	Type of Jesus, the Deliverer of spiritual Israel, and the Destroyer of Babylon. For further details, see later chapter.
Jer. 50: 8; 51: 6, 46; Isa. 48: 20. Israel called out of literal Babylon "to restore and to build Jerusalem" (Dan. 9: 25); rebuild the literal temple the Babylonians had destroyed, and "repair" (Neh. 3) the walls of Jerusalem.	Rev. 18: 4. Spiritual Israel called out of spiritual Babylon to "restore all things" (Matt. 17: 11; Rev. 14: 6-14, etc.): to rebuild the spiritual temple (Rev. 11: 1, 2; GC. 266) and repair the spiritual walls of the church (Isa. 58: 12-14, etc.), which spiritual Babylon had attacked and spoiled. P.K. 677, 678.
Isa. 21: 9; Jer. 51: 8. Babylon's literal fall.	Rev. 14: 8; 18: 2. Spiritual Babylon's spiritual fall.
See "What is Armageddon?" pp. 34-36, for further citations of Old Testament references to the things of literal Babylon which are spiritually applied in the Book of Revelation.	
1 Kings 16: 30-33. Jezebel, aided by Ahab at the head of the State, fostered sun-worship among literal Israel.	Rev. 2: 20. The apostate church, aided by the State, fosters Sunday observance among spiritual Israel.
Elijah calls Israel back to the true worship of God.	Mal. 4: 5, 6; Rev. 14: 6-14. Typified God's last-day Message calling professing Christians back to the true worship of God.
See my "Christ Conquers," pp. 76-85, for further consideration of the New Testament, spiritual application of the experiences of Elijah—typifying the experiences of the remnant church.	

Old Testament History.	The New Testament Spiritual Application.
Literal Babylon's "flood"—the Euphrates. Josh. 24: 2, 3, 14, 15; Isa. 8: 7, 8; 28: 2, etc.	Rev. 12: 15, 16; 16: 12; 17: 1, 15. Employed to symbolize the people of Babylon who *persecute* the church.
Judg. 4: 3. The Canaanites who "mightily oppressed the children of Israel" were destroyed: "there was not a man left" (v. 16)—"by the waters of Megiddo." Judg. 5: 19.	Rev. 16: 16 etc. Typify those who will "mightily oppress" spiritual Israel; all Israel's enemies will be destroyed in the antitypical Megiddo "slaughter."
Dan. 3: 1, etc. Nebuchadnezzar's literal image erected on the plains of literal Babylon. Decree—all to *literally* bow to image or suffer in the *literal* fiery furnace.	Rev. 13: 15; 14: 9, 11, etc. *Spiritual* image to be erected in *spiritual* Babylon. Decree—all *spiritually* bow or suffer *spiritual*, fiery furnace.
Jesus preserved, and delivered from death, the three faithful Hebrews.	Rev. 17: 14; 15: 2-4. Jesus brings His people through their fiery ordeal (Rev. 3: 10). "Jesus would be honoured by translating without their seeing death, the faithful waiting ones." EW., pp. 283, 284.

These examples, and many others, show that the New Testament writers based their interpretations and their prophecies upon the principle that the Old Testament literal, national things pertaining to Israel and her enemies have their *spiritual, world-wide* application in connection with the church in this "dispensation of the Holy Spirit." Not only Israel's sanctuary and its typical services foreshadowed greater things to come, but the liberation from Egypt, the victory at the Red Sea, the desert experiences, the wars, the entrance into the promised land—all recorded in the Old Testament *concerning Israel*—were written as "types," "figures" (1 Cor. 10: 6, 11, margins), or "acted parables" illustrating the experiences of the church and her enemies.

CHAPTER VI.

EXAMPLES FROM THE SPIRIT OF PROPHECY OF THE SPIRITUAL INTERPRETATION OF SCRIPTURES.

"In *every* page, whether *history*, or *precept*, or *prophecy*, the Old Testament Scriptures are irradiated with the *glory of the Son of God*." D.A. 211.

Abraham offering his son on Mt. Moriah is applied as a *type* of God permitting His Son to die on Calvary. See D.A. 468, 469.

"The ladder *represents* Jesus . . . All this was revealed to Jacob in his dream." P.P. 184.

Christ's incarnation "had been *shadowed* forth in *types* and *symbols*. . . . The *symbol* chosen for the *representation* of the Deity was a *lowly shrub*, that seemingly had no attraction. This enshrined the Infinite. The all-merciful God shrouded His glory in a most humble *type*." D.A. 23.

"The Passover was to be both commemorative and *typical*, not only pointing back to the deliverance from Egypt, but forward to the *greater deliverance* which Christ was to accomplish in freeing His people from *the bondage of sin*." P.P. 277.

"The deliverance of Israel from Egypt was *an object lesson of redemption*, which the Passover was intended to keep in memory. The slain lamb, the unleavened bread, the sheaf of first fruits, *represented* the Saviour." D.A. 77.

The incense offered in the sanctuary "*represents* the merits and intercession of Christ." P.P. 353.

"In every part it [the ritual service] was a *symbol* of Him; and it had been full of vitality and *spiritual beauty*." D.A. 29. "The Saviour *typified* in the rites and ceremonies of the Jewish law is the very same that is revealed in the gospel." P.P. 373.

"By his rash act, Moses took away the force of the *lesson* that God purposed to teach. The rock, being a *symbol* of Christ, had been once smitten, as Christ was to be once offered. The second time, it was needful only to speak to the rock, as we have only to ask for blessings in the name of Jesus. By the second smiting of the rock the *significance* of this beautiful *figure* of Christ was destroyed." P.P. 418.

"Its [the temple] services were *typical* of the sacrifice of the Son of God. The priesthood was established to *represent* the . . . work of Christ. The *entire* plan of sacrificial worship was a *foreshadowing* of the Saviour's death. Since the *whole* ritual economy *was symbolical* of Christ, it had no value apart from Him." D.A. 165.

"The Jews lost the *spiritual* life from their ceremonies, and clung to the dead forms." D.A. 29.

"Thus the Lord . . . taught the people by means of a series of *acted parables*." PK. 423. ". . . the ceremonial sacrifices ordained by God as a *type* of the coming Redeemer, Satan discerned in these a *symbol* of communion between earth and heaven." P.K. 685. "In *patriarchal* times . . . and . . . with the *entire ritual* of the *sanctuary* services throughout Israel's history. In the ministration of the *tabernacle*, and of the *temple* that afterward took its place, the people were taught *each day*, by means of *types* and *shadows*." PK. 684.

"The lamb *representing* Christ had been brought to be slain. Clothed in his *significant* and beautiful dress, the priest stood with lifted knife as did Abraham when he was about to slay his son. . . . *Type* has met *antitype* in the death of God's Son." D.A. 756, 757.

"Christ arose from the dead as the first fruits of those that slept. He was the *antitype* of the wave-sheaf. . . . For more than a thousand years this *symbolic* ceremony had been performed. . . . So Christ the first fruits *represented* the great *spiritual* harvest to be gathered for the kingdom of God. His resurrection is the *type* and pledge of the resurrection of all the righteous dead." D.A. 785, 786.

"He was the *spiritual* light that in *symbol* and *type* and prophecy had shone upon Israel. . . . As the sunbeams penetrate to the remotest corners of the earth, so does the light of the Sun of Righteousness shine upon every soul." D.A. 464.

"John the Baptist was the *type* of the second advent messenger." D.A. 103; 8T. 9, 332. "As a *symbol* of cleansing from sin, he baptized them in the waters of the Jordan." D.A. 104.

The above extracts from the Spirit of Prophecy show that the Bible contains rich spiritual truths expressed in types, symbols, and acted parables. The following example shows that the Spirit of Prophecy also draws attention to *spiritual* lessons found in Old Testament *narratives:*

"Many are the *spiritual* lessons to be gathered from the story of the healing of the waters. The new cruse, the salt, the spring—*all are highly symbolic.* In casting salt into the bitter spring, Elisha taught the same *spiritual* lesson imparted centuries later by the Saviour to His disciples when He declared, 'Ye are the salt of the earth.' The salt mingling with the polluted spring purified its waters, and brought life and blessing where before had been blighting and death." P.K. 231. "The polluted stream *represents* the soul that is separate from God." PK. 233.

Similarly, *spiritual lessons* may be drawn from every part of Holy Writ.

The New Testament principle of seeing something "greater" in Old Testament narratives and prophecies, even though fulfilled in Palestine, is also the principle followed in the Spirit of Prophecy. For instance, the triumphal entry of the Messiah into Jerusalem, fulfilling Zechariah's prophecy (Zech. 9: 9; Matt. 21: 4, 5; John 12: 15, 16), is applied as *"a dim foreshadowing* of His coming in the clouds of heaven with power and glory, amid the triumph and rejoicing of the saints." D.A., p. 580.

Literal rains which fell in *Palestine* are employed as *types* of *spiritual* rain falling in *all the world.* God's servant says:—

"Under the *figure* of the early and the latter rain, that falls in Eastern lands at seed-time and harvest, the Hebrew prophets foretold the bestowal of *spiritual* grace in extraordinary measure upon God's church." A.A. 54, 55; TM. 506, 507; 8T. 21, etc.

The principle of applying, in a *spiritual, world-wide sense,* Old Testament history, geography, etc., is maintained throughout the Spirit of Prophecy and the New Testament. The Book of Revelation was constructed on this principle. Writing of the Revelation, God's servant declares:

"This book demands close, prayerful study, lest it be interpreted according to the *ideas of men* and false construction be given to the sacred word of God, which in its *symbols* and *figures* means so much to us." E.G. White, Letter 16, 1900.

The importance of the *"symbols* and *figures"* of the Revelation is again emphasized by the Lord's servant:—

"In *figures* and *symbols,* subjects of vast importance were presented to John . . . that the *people of God* . . . might have an intelligent understanding of the perils and *conflicts* before *them.* . . . In the Revelation are portrayed the deep things of God. . . . In the Revelation all the books of the Bible meet and end. . . . The names of the seven churches are *symbolic* of the church in different periods of the Christian era. The number seven *indicates* completeness, and is *symbolic* . . . the *symbols* used . . .Christ is *spoken of as* walking in the midst of the golden candlesticks. Thus is *symbolized* His relation to the churches." A.A. 583-586.

Throughout the Spirit of Prophecy we see applied the use of type and antitype in connection with the Third Angel's Message:

"Arguments drawn from the Old Testament *types* also pointed to the autumn as the time when the event *represented* by the 'cleansing of the sanctuary' must take place. This was made very clear as attention was given to the manner in which the *types* relating to the first advent of Christ had been fulfilled. The slaying of the passover lamb was a *shadow* of the death of Christ. . . . The sheaf of first fruits . . . was *typical* of the resurrection of Christ. . . . These *types* were fulfilled. . . . And as the *antitype* of the wave-sheaf, our Lord was raised from the dead . . . the first fruits of them that slept,' a *sample* of all the resurrected just. . . . In like manner, the *types* which relate to the second advent must be fulfilled at the time pointed out in the symbolic service." GC. 399.

Types abound in the Old Testament, and the *principle* of *antitypes* operates *throughout the New.* The *types*—historical incidents, "acted parables," etc.—were *literal* foreshadowings of *spiritual* things to come. The New Testament shows that the disciples' faith was based upon the fact that Christ fulfilled "the *types* and *prophecies* of the Old Testament." D.A. 796. The Third Angel's Message is also based upon "the *types* and *prophecies* of the Old Testament." We can prove that we have the truth of the Third Angel's Message *only as we employ the New Testament principle* of applying in a *spiritual, world-wide* sense the *literal* types of the Old Testament.

Many futurists employ a system of types and antitypes but, because they believe that the things of *Israel* still belong to the *literal* Jews, they misapply the *antitypes,* in connection with *literal* Israel *in Palestine.* But, since Christ was enthroned in the heavenly temple and the Holy Spirit became His representative on earth, the types do *not have any literal, Palestinian* meaning: they are *spiritual* and *world-wide* in their *antitypical* application.

45

CHAPTER VII.

OLD TESTAMENT TERMINOLOGY EMPLOYED SPIRITUALLY IN THE NEW TESTAMENT: THE CHURCH IS NOW THE "NATION" OF ISRAEL.

"The Kingdom of God shall be taken from you [*literal* Israel] and given to a *nation* [*spiritual* Israel] bringing forth the fruits thereof." Matt. 21: 43. "Ye [the church] are . . . an holy *nation.*" 1 Pet. 2: 9.

The following references show that the terminology employed in the Old Testament relating to *national* Israel enters unchanged into the New Testament but, while the *designations* are unchanged, and the *same phraseology* used, they are lifted from their *national* setting *in Palestine* into the realm of the Messiah's *spiritual, world-wide* kingdom.

IN THE OLD TESTAMENT.	IN THE NEW TESTAMENT.
National Israel.	*Spiritual Israel.*
Literal kingdom; visible King, city, temple, sacrifices, altars, etc.	Spiritual kingdom. Luke 17: 20, 21, margin; 1 Pet. 2: 5, 9; 1 Cor. 10: 3, 3; Col. 1: 13; AA. 30, 28, 39; GC. 347, 348; DA. 506; Heb. 4: 16; Heb. 8: 1; Zech. 6: 13, etc .
Holy nation. Ex. 19: 5, 6.	Holy nation. 1 Pet. 2: 9; Zeph. 2: 1; Matt. 21: 43.
Kingdom of priests. Ex. 19: 5, 6.	Kingdom of priests. 1 Pet. 2: 5, 9; Rev. 1: 6; Rev. 4: 4; 5: 10.
A peculiar treasure. Ex. 19: 5, 6.	A peculiar treasure. 1 Pet. 2: 9.
God's people. Hos. 1: 9-10; Rom. 9: 6-8.	God's people. 1 Pet. 2: 9.
A holy people. Deut. 7: 6.	A holy people. 1 Pet. 1: 15, 16.
A people of inheritance. Deut. 4: 20.	A people of inheritance. Eph. 1: 18.
Israel's Shepherd Jer. 31: 10.	Israel's Shepherd. John 10: 11.
Israel's salvation. Isa. 45: 17.	Israel's Salvation. Heb. 5: 9; 9: 15.
God's tabernacle among Israel. Lev. 26: 11.	God's tabernacle among Israel. John 1: 14.
God walked among them. Lev. 26: 12.	God walks among His people. 2 Cor. 6: 16-18.

In the Old Testament.	In the New Testament.
Christ married to His people. Isa. 54: 5; Jer. 3: 14; Hos. 2: 19; Jer. 6: 2; 31: 32.	Christ married to the church. Ephes. 5: 23-33; 2 Cor. 11: 2; Jas. 4: 4; Rom. 7: 1-4; Rev. 12 (Christ's bride); MH. 356.
Christ reigned in Jerusalem. 1 Chron. 29: 3; Zech. 8: 3; Ps. 132: 13; 43: 2; Matt. 5: 35; Zech. 2: 5, 10, 11; Joel 3: 21, 27; Isa. 2: 2; Micah 4: 2.	Christ reigns in the church. Ephes. 2: 20-22; 1 Cor. 3: 16; 2 Cor. 6: 16; John 14: 16-23. Acts of Apostles, pp. 11, 12, 600.
Literal gathering to Jerusalem for their festivities, and after their captivities.	Spiritual gathering to Jerusalem—the church. Isa. 11: 11, 12; PK. 375, 376; E.W. 74, 75; 6T. 133; 7T. 172; 9T. 51; Isa. 60: 3, 4, 6, 7, 9; PK. 375; AA. 595; Rev. 18: 4.
Literal Zion. Ps. 50: 2; 2: 6.	Spiritual Zion—the church. Joel 2: 32; Rom. 10: 13; Isa. 28: 16; 1 Pet. 2: 6-8; Isa. 59: 20; Rom. 11: 26; Ps. 2: 6.
Enemies *literally* gather against Israel. Isa. 8: 7, 8; 36: 1, 2, 37; 54: 15, 17; Ezek. 38, 39; Zech. 12: 3, 9; 14: 1, 2, 13, 14; Joel 3.	Enemies *spiritually* gather or "unite" against the church. Isa. 54: 15, 17; Rev. 14: 20; 16: 13-16; Rev. 17: 14; 19: 19; Joel 3; Zech. 14; Ezek. 38, 39, etc.
The *literal* points of the compass referred to in connection with Israel—their temple services, their triumphs, and the destruction of their enemies—centred literally in the Presence of God in the Tabernacle or Temple.	The points of the compass are *spiritually applied* when in connection with spiritual Israel—they centre in the Holy Spirit's Presence in the spiritual temple—the church.
Ex. 25: 8, 22; Num. 2: 2, 10, 18, 25; 1 Kings 8: 13, 16-18, 21, 29, 30, 33, 35 38, 42, 44, 48; 9: 3; Ezek. 39: 7; 43: 7; Dan. 6: 10; Ps. 5: 7; Isa. 60: 3-9; 1 Chron. 29: 3; Ps. 132: 13; 43: 2; Zech. 8: 3; 2: 5, 10, 11; 12: 3, 9; Joel 3: 2, 9-14, 17, 21; Jer. 3: 17; Isa. 54: 15, 17, etc.	Matt. 18: 20; Rev. 1: 12, 13, 20; John 14: 16-23; Heb. 12: 18-24; Ezek. 39: 7; 38: 5, 6, 12; Joel 3: 2. 9-14 17, 21; Isa. 54: 15, 17; 6T. 23; Zech. 14: 2, 12; GC. 657; EW. 289, 290; 1 Cor. 3: 16, 17; 6: 19; 2 Cor. 6: 16; Ephes. 2: 21; Rev. 14: 20; 16: 14; 17: 13, 14; 19: 19; etc.

Many other references could be given showing that the New Testament writers use the phraseology pertaining to *national* Israel when writing of *spiritual,* world-wide Israel. This important principle must be remembered when interpreting last-day prophecies.

When the enemies of Israel gathered to destroy her, they gathered to fight God, Who reigned within the temple in Israel's midst. Since God's rejection of national Israel, the church—spiritual Israel—stands in her place, and the Old Testament prophetic forecasts of enemies attacking Israel now apply to the church. The combined forces of the enemies of Israel, pictured in Ezekiel 38, 39 as gathering from the four quarters to attack her, are led by Satan against God, Who is "in the *midst* of My people *Israel*," the church. See Ezek. 39: 7; 43: 7, etc. The promise of Israel's deliverance, declared in Ezekiel's prophecy, refers to the church in "the final conflict." The church has inherited all the promises and blessings assured to Israel. Note the following extracts from esteemed Bible commentators:—

"Those who put their trust in Jesus constitute *the true Israelites, the new, the Messianic Israel,* who have been obedient to God and to his Messiah. . . . Hence the believers in Jesus are *the true people of God,* the possessors of *all the privileges which had once belonged to Israel after the flesh.*" "The People of God," by H. F. Hamilton, D.D., Vol. 1, Preface, p. 7

Vol. II, p. 28, chapter "The New Israel":—

"*All* that belonged to the Israel of the old *now belonged to the new; what was true to the pre-Messianic Israel was true to the post-Messianic Israel.*"

"*We* are the community of the Messiah, and therefore *the true Israelites.* In this one sentence is summed up the whole philosophy of the foundation of the church. . . . But the new Israel not only inherited *all the exclusive privileges of the old,* it also had received yet greater blessings through the Messiah." Ibid., p. 31.

In "The Revelation of St. John," p. 27, Prof. W. Milligan, D.D., has written of the church: "She had an interest in Zion and Jerusalem; she saw in Babylon the type of her enemies; *she felt herself to be the Israel of God.*"

T. W. Christie, B.A., in his book, "The Book of Revelation," p. 329, says: "*All* those names, 'Abraham,' 'children of promise,' with their *attendant country, promises, and blessings, belonged* not to Israel after the flesh, *but to the Israel of God.*"

Note the following from Ellicott's Commentary, Notes on Revelation: "*The Christian Church absorbs the Jewish, inherits her privileges,* and adopts, with wider and nobler meaning, *her phraseology.*" P. 96.

"*The historical basis of the Apocalypse is the past history of the chosen people;* God's dealings with men always follow the same lines. The Apocalypse shows us the principle working in higher levels and in a wider arena. *The Israel of God, the church of Christ, takes the place of the national Israel.*" (p. 125.)

Matthew Henry's Commentary, in notes on Joel 3, says: "*The saints are the true Israel of God,* they are His people, the church is His Jerusalem."

And so have written many of the old, spiritual commentators.

In his "Bible Handbook," pp. 203, 285-292, Dr. Angus says:—

" . . . Fairbairn (Typology of Scripture), maintaining that the *whole of the previous economy is affirmed in the New Testament to be typical.* . . .

"As the future was thus represented in visions, and under a *typical* dispensation, it can excite no surprise that the *whole* is often described in *figurative,* and *allegorical* or *symbolical* terms. . . . Besides, as everything earthly supplies *images* for describing things *spiritual,* the law is therefore appropriate as it is necessary. The unity and vastness of God's plans are *illustrated by it all.* "Under the gospel, for example, Messiah is to be a king, and hence the prophets represent Him as possessed of all the characteristics of the most distinguished princes of the Jewish theocracy, and more than once apply to Him the title of

David. . . . Hos. 3: 5; Jer. 30: 9; Acts 13: 34. . . . In the same way, they speak of *His kingdom, either of grace or glory,* as the highest perfection of the Jewish economy. *It is called Jerusalem, or Zion.* Isa. 62: 1, 6, 7; 60: 15-20; Gal. 4: 26-28; Heb. 12: 22. See also Isa. 60: 6, 7; 66: 23. . . .

"In the same way, the enemies of the kingdom of the Messiah are not *only called by the name given to the enemies of the ancient theocracy,* viz., *the nations of the Gentiles,* but they *often bear the name of some one people,* who, at the time, were peculiarly inimical or powerful. In Isa. 25, they are called by the name of *Moab;* in Isa. 63 and Amos 9: 12, by the name of *Edom;* and in Ezek. 38, by the name of *Gog.* . . . Nor need this peculiarity of prophetic language excite surprise. It is *found pervading the whole ancient dispensation.* . . ."

After giving further examples, the learned Dr. says:—

"All these expressions, however, are in *the New Testament applied to the church.* . . . Nearly all the *characteristic names of Israel are applied to the body of believers.* In the first case, the blessings and relations, so far as the people were concerned, are *earthly and temporal;* in the second, *spiritual and eternal.* . . . *The apostles reason throughout their writings on the same principle.* We who believe, and are united to Christ, are children of Abraham, and heirs of His promises (Gal. 3: 29; Rom. 4: 11, 16); the *Israel of God* (Gal. 6: 16); as distinguished from the Israel according to the flesh (1 Cor. 11: 18); the true circumcision (Phil. 3: 3), who therefore appropriate ancient promises (Gen. 22: 16, 17, applied to all believers; Heb. 6: 13, 20; Deut. 31: 6; Josh. 1: 5; quoted Heb. 13: 4-5; Hos. 1: 10; 2: 23, quoted Rom. 9: 24-36). "After the exode comes the institution of the ritual law, its sacrifices, priesthood, mercy seat, tabernacle and temple and worship. *All* these, it need hardly be remarked, are represented in the prophets as being restored in the latter days, and *in the Gospels each expression is applied to our Lord or to His church.* He is priest, and propitiatory. tabernacle (John 1: 14) and temple (John 2: 19); as also, since His ascension. is His church (1 Cor. 3: 16). Her members offer spiritual offerings. They form a royal priesthood, a holy nation. . . .

"Haggai and Zechariah foretell the rebuilding of a temple, and under that figure speak of the church. . . . In a word, not only the prophets, but *all* the inspired writers *describe the church in terms borrowed from successive stages in the history of the ancient economy.* . . .

"From the *typical* character of ancient dispensations arises another peculiarity of prophecy. It not only *speaks their language,* but it *has often a double application.* It applies to one object by anticipation and partially. and to another completely; the *earlier* object being the *representative of the later.* . . .

"As the *history of the Jews foreshadows the history of the church,* so does prophecy the experience of both. . . . Prophecies on the restoration from Babylon (Jer. 31; Isa. 52), on the setting up of the Tabernacle of David (Amos 9), and on His kingdom (2 Sam. 7), had all to a certain extent, an immediate fulfilment, and are yet *applied in the New Testament to the gospel dispensation.* To that dispensation in itself. or in its results, this *double application must be confined.* . . .

"It follows from *this double sense that, as in the first fulfilment there is a limit to the blessing foretold, so, in the second, there is a fulness of meaning which it seems impossible to exhaust.* To David, for example, the promise was partly conditional. partly absolute. As conditional, it cannot be applied to Christ, and as absolute, it cannot be applied in its fullest literal meaning to David. 2 Sam. 7: 13-15. The condition both David and God repeat (1 Kings 2: 4; 9:4), and the promise that David's seed should occupy the throne *for ever,* had, of course. in a literal sense, but a limited fulfilment. For ever may mean till the end of the kingdom, or till the end of the polity. . . . There was, therefore, a *literal* fulfilment of the promise, but clearly less glorious than when applied to the Messiah."

Notice the following extracts from the authoritative work, "The Progress of Doctrine in the New Testament," by T. D. Bernard, M.A., pp. 128-129, 131, 114, 115, 218, 221, 222:—

"The other principle which is contended for and secured is that the *Gospel is the heir of the Law;* that it *inherits* what the Law had prepared. The Law, on its *national* and ceremonial side, had created a vast and closely woven system of ideas. These were wrought out and exhibited by it in forms according to the flesh—an elect nation, a miraculous history, a special covenant, a worldly sanctuary, a perpetual service, an anointed priesthood, a ceremonial sanctity, a scheme of sacrifice and atonement, a purchased possession, a holy city, a throne of David, a destiny of dominion. Were these ideas to be lost, and the *language which expressed* them to be dropped when the Gospel came? No! *It was the heir of the Law.* The Law had prepared these riches, and now bequeathed them to a successor able to unlock and to diffuse them. The Gospel claimed them all, and developed *in them a value unknown before.* It asserted *itself* as the proper and *predestined continuation of* the covenant made of God with the fathers, *the real and only fulfilment of all which was typified and prophesied,* presenting the same ideas which had been before embodied in the *narrow* but *distinct limits of carnal forms,* in their *spiritual, universal, and eternal character. The body of types* according to *the flesh died with Christ,* and with Christ it arose again a *body of antitypes according to the Spirit.* Those who were after the flesh could not recognise its identity; those who were after the Spirit felt and proclaimed it.

". . . The principle that the *same things* which were done under the *old covenant* in the *region of the flesh* are done under the *new covenant* in the *region of the spirit* opens out into the doctrine of the mediatorial work of Christ in the true tabernacle . . . the sanctification of *believers as a kingdom of priests and a holy nation,* and their destined inheritance in a *promised land* and a holy city of their God. The expansion of these doctrines *fills* and forms all the Epistles. . . .

"*All is founded upon the old Jewish expectation of a kingdom of God;* but it is now explained how *that expectation is fulfilled* in the person of Jesus. The complete exposition of the Gospel was the result of a *combination of the facts and the words of the old dispensation* with the facts and the words of the new, a combination effected in the minds of the Apostles under the teaching of the Holy Ghost, who thus brought to light the meaning and the scope of His own *earlier inspirations, preserved in the Law and the Prophets* . . . 'Which the Holy Ghost teacheth, comparing spiritual things with spiritual' (v. 13) . . . the interpretation of these words is best derived from the fact everywhere apparent in the Apostles' writings, namely, *his habit* of working out *all* the more recondite and (if I may use the word) scientific parts of the evangelical doctrine *by the aid of the Old Testament, the types, images, and sentences* of which were, we know, in His sight '*spiritual*' . . . The appropriation of the *Old Testament words* to *express the New Testament doctrines* is a part of this elucidation."

That the church is now the nation of Israel is maintained throughout the New Testament and the Spirit of Prophecy: this principle is the basis of the Third Angel's Message.

CHAPTER VIII.

THE SPIRIT OF PROPHECY EMPLOYS THE NEW TESTAMENT PRINCIPLE THAT THE CHURCH IS NOW "THE ISRAEL OF GOD": THE PROPHETIC NATURE OF ISRAEL'S HISTORY.

The Spirit of Prophecy, throughout, employs Biblical principles of interpretation. In this we find proof of the divine leadership of the messenger of God. The following extracts show the importance in the Spirit of Prophecy of the principle that the remnant church is the Israel of God and that the experiences of ancient Israel were *typical* of the experiences of present-day, spiritual Israel:—

"The history of the wilderness life of Israel was *chronicled for the benefit of the Israel of God to the close of time.* . . . God would have His people in these days review with a humble heart and teachable spirit the trials through which ancient Israel passed, that they may be instructed in their *preparation for the heavenly Canaan.*" P.P., p. 293.

"The *history of ancient Israel* is a striking *illustration* of the past experience of the Adventist body." G.C. 457.

"The apostle Paul plainly states that the *experience of the Israelites* in their travels has been *recorded for the benefit of those living in this age of the world,* those upon whom the ends of the world are come." 3T., p. 358. See also 1T., p. 283 .

"Satan's snares are laid for us as verily as they were laid for the children of Israel just prior to their entrance into the land of Canaan. *We are repeating the history of that people.*" T. No. 31, p. 156. See also S.T., Nov. 3, 1890.

"With the *history of the children of Israel before us,* let us take heed, and not be found committing the same sins, following in the same way of unbelief." Rev. & Her., 1893, No. 16.

"The *experience of Israel,* referred to in the above words [1 Cor. 10] by the apostle, and as recorded in the 105th and 106th psalms, contained lessons of warning that the *people of God in these last days especially need to study.*" S.T., quoted in "Healthful Living," p. 284.

"*We* are numbered with *Israel. All* instructions *given to the Israelites of* old concerning the education and training of their children, *all the promises* of blessing through obedience, are for *us.*" Min. of Healing, p. 405.

"The trials of the *children of Israel,* and their attitude just before the first coming of Christ, have been presented before me *again and again* to *illustrate the position of the people of God in their experience before the second coming of Christ.*" Rev. and Her., 1890, No. 7.

"This song was not only *historical* but *prophetic.* While it recounted the wonderful dealings of God *with His people in the past,* it *also foreshadowed* the great events of *the future, the final victory of the faithful* when Christ shall come the second time in power and glory." P.P., p. 467.

"As the angel of God presented these facts in the *travels* and *experience* of the *children of Israel,* I was deeply impressed with the especial regard of God

51

for His people. . . . *I was also shown* that those who are trying to obey God and purify their souls through obedience to the truth. are God's chosen people. *His modern Israel.*" 2T., 108, 109.

"*The Israel of God to-day . . . the true church of Christ.*" P.K. 74. ". . . *spiritual Israel—His church* on earth." P.K. 370-372. See also P.K. 22, 188, 189, 298-300, 375, 376, 398, 392, 703, 704, 713, 714, 720; P.P. 447; E.W. 33, 42, 43, 60, 125, 285, 286; 5T. 454-456, etc.

The principle that Israel's history is *prophetic* of the experiences of the church is continually employed in the Spirit of Prophecy. Under the heading, "The Church the Light of the World," in 5T. 454-467, the Lord's servant urges the church to carry the gospel to the world. She says: "God has called His church in this day, *as He called ancient Israel,* to stand as a light in the earth."

Concerning ancient Israel we read: "Thus the work which God had given His people to do in *prosperity* . . . was done by them in captivity, *under great trial and embarrassment.*" God's servant enquires: "Shall we let the history of Israel be repeated in *our experience?*" (p. 456). The answer is given on page 463: "The work which the church has failed to do in a time of *peace and prosperity,* she will have to do in a terrible crisis, under most discouraging, forbidding circumstances . . . under the fiercest opposition from enemies of the faith." Literal Israel failed to do her appointed work in times of "prosperity"; *spiritual Israel* has failed to do her work "in a time of peace and prosperity." *Literal Israel's* work was "done . . . under great trial and embarrassment"; *spiritual Israel's* work will be done "under discouraging, forbidding circumstances." Thus the *history* of *national* Israel is employed by God's servant as a *prediction* concerning the *church.*

Though the work will be completed amid discouraging circumstances, "the Lord will give us *favour* before the world until our work is done." 6T., p. 21. We read God's thrice-repeated promise to ancient Israel: "I will give this people *favour* in the sight of the Egyptians." Ex. 3: 21; 11: 3; 12: 36.

"A little time of peace," mentioned by the Spirit of Prophecy (1T. 267, 268), is a last-day application of that which occurred in ancient Israel's experience before the completion of the work of repairing Jerusalem after the Babylonian captivity. See Ezra 9: 8.

"God's church on earth was as verily in *captivity* during this long period [of Papal supremacy] of relentless persecution, *as* were the *children of Israel* held captive in *Babylon* during the period of their exile. But, thank God, His church is no longer in bondage. *To* spiritual Israel have been *restored the privileges accorded the people of God at the time of their deliverance from Babylon* . . . and to *spiritual* Israel is given the message, 'Come out of her, My people.' . . . As the captive exiles heeded the message, 'Flee out of the midst of Babylon' (Jer. 51: 6), and were restored to the land of promise, so those who fear God to-day are heeding the message to withdraw from *spiritual Babylon.*" P.K. 714, 715.

"The opposition and discouragement that the builders in Nehemiah's day met from open enemies and pretended friends, is *typical* of the experience that those to-day will have who work for God." P.K. 644. Among other *anti-typical* applications concerning Nehemiah's work, God's servant says: "As the time of the end draws near, Satan's temptations will be brought to bear with greater power upon God's workers. He will employ human agents to mock and revile those who *'build the wall.'*" P.K. 659.

"The work of restoration and reform carried on by the returned exiles under the leadership of Zerubbabel, Ezra, and Nehemiah, presents a *picture* of a work of *spiritual restoration* that is to be wrought in the closing days of earth's history. . . . Varied were the experiences that came to them as they rebuilt the *temple* and the *wall of Jerusalem.* . . . The spiritual restoration of which the work carried forward in Nehemiah's day was a *symbol,* is outlined in the words of Isaiah [Isa. 61: 4; 58: 12 are then quoted]. The prophet here describes a people who, in a time of general departure from truth and righteousness, are seeking to *restore* the principles that are the foundation of the kingdom of God. They are *repairers* of a *breach* that has been made in God's law—the *wall* that He has placed around His chosen ones for their protection. . . . In words of unmistakable meaning, the prophet points out the specific work of this *remnant* people who *build the wall* [the words of Isa. 58: 13, 14 are then quoted]. In the time of the end every divine institution is to be *restored.* The breach made in the law at the time the Sabbath was changed by man is to be *repaired.* . . . Constrained by the love of Christ, they are to co-operate with Him in building up the *waste places.* They are to be *repairers* of the *breach,* the *restorers* of paths to dwell in." P.K. 677, 678.

Thus the Spirit of Prophecy makes a *spiritual* application of the call out of *literal* Babylon, the *literal* repairing of the breaches in the wall of Jerusalem, and the *rebuilding* and *restoring* of the temple and city of Jerusalem. Those *literal* experiences of *literal* Israel are applied as "a *symbol*" or "a *picture* of a work of *spiritual* restoration that is to be wrought in the closing days of earth's history."

A study of Neh. 2: 1, 6; 5: 14-16; 6: 15; 13: 6 reveals that within a short space of twelve years Nehemiah had completed *all* his work. The "repairing" (see Neh. 3) of the walls of Jerusalem was done in 52 days. See Neh. 6: 15. This quick work will be repeated in the experience of spiritual Israel. "The final movements will be rapid ones." 9T. 11. "The bright light going among the living creatures with the swiftness of lightning represents the speed with which this work will finally go forward to completion." 5T. 754. See also Rom. 9: 28.

The *sealing* brought to view in Neh. 9: 38; 10: 1, 29 was done in a short space of time. The Spirit of Prophecy says: "The *sealing* time is very short, and will soon be over." E.W. 58.

In the chapter, "The Coming Crisis," in 5T. 449-454, God's servant tells us that "God means testing truth shall be brought to the front, and become a subject of examination and discussion, even if it is through the contempt placed upon it. The minds of the people must be agitated. Every controversy, every reproach, every slander, will be God's means of provoking inquiry, and awakening minds that otherwise would slumber. *Thus it has been in the past history of God's people."* P. 453. Examples are then cited from the experiences of Israelites.

When writing of the coming world-wide threat to destroy the remnant people of God, the servant of the Lord bases her statements upon the Old Testament record of Jacob being threatened with death by his brother Esau. Gen. 32: 6-11; GC. 616, 618-621. Jacob's deliverance *typifies* the deliverance which will come to God's people. See Jer. 30: 7 and GC. 635-652. When writing of the coming death decree, which will be passed upon spiritual Israel in the last days, God's servant directs us back to the Old Testament to the death decree passed upon the *literal* Jews in the days of Mordecai and Queen Esther: *"The decree* which is to go forth against the people of God will be *very similar to that issued* by Ahasuerus *against the Jews* in the time of Esther. . . .

"On this battle-field comes the last great conflict of the controversy between truth and error. And we are not left in doubt as to the issue. *Now, as in the days of Mordecai,* the Lord will vindicate His truth and His people." 5T. 450, 451; P.K. 605, 606.

"Elijah was a *type* of the saints who will be living on the earth at the time of the second advent of Christ, and who will be 'changed, in a moment, in the twinkling of an eye, at the last trump,' without tasting of death. It was as a *representative* of those who shall be thus translated that Elijah . . . was permitted to stand with Moses by the side of the Saviour on the mount of transfiguration. In these glorified ones, the disciples saw *in miniature a representation of* the kingdom of the redeemed . . . they saw Moses, *representing* those who will be raised from the dead at the time of the second advent; and there stood Elijah, *representing* those who at the close of earth's history will be changed from mortal to immortal, and be translated to heaven without seeing death." PK. 227.

Writing of the care God will have over His people in the last days, God's servant says: "That God Who cared for *Elijah* will not pass by one of His self-sacrificing children." GC. 629.

Many other statements in the Spirit of Prophecy concerning the closing up of the work of God on earth, the time of trouble, the persecution and deliverance of the church and the destruction of her enemies can be traced to the experiences of *literal Israel* recorded in the Old Testament. Thus the Spirit of Prophecy is in harmony with the principle followed throughout the New Testament that the history of ancient Israel is typical of the experiences of the church. This principle proves the divine origin and certainty of the Spirit of Prophecy, and also proves that the Third Angel's Message we are proclaiming to the world is of God. "We have not followed cunningly devised fables." 2 Pet. 1: 16. We *"know* the certainty of those things, wherein [we have] been instructed." Luke 1: 1-3.

CHAPTER IX.

THE BOOK OF REVELATION: CHRIST'S MESSAGE TO SPIRITUAL ISRAEL.

"Christ [is] the Revelator." G.C. 342. The book of Revelation was written for the church of Jesus Christ. See Rev. 1: 11; 22: 16; 2: 7, 11, 17, 29; 3: 6, 13, 22, etc. "In figures and symbols, subjects of vast importance were presented to John . . . that *the people of God* . . . might have an intelligent understanding of the perils and *conflicts* before *them.*" A.A. 583-586. "To John were opened scenes of deep and thrilling interest in the *experience of the church.* He saw the position, dangers, conflicts, and final deliverance of the *people of God.* Subjects of vast importance were revealed to him, *especially for the last church,* that those who turn from error to truth might be instructed concerning the perils and *conflicts* before *them.*" G.C. 341, 342.

As already shown, Old Testament terminology is employed *spiritually* in the New Testament in describing the church—spiritual Israel. This principle is especially manifest in the Revelation. All that comes into the Revelation is mentioned as either belonging to Israel, or to her foes. The latter are mentioned *only because they are the enemies of God and His people.* Bcause of their opposition as a counterfeiting system, Israel's enemies are described in *similar language* to that pertaining to Israel.

GOD AND ISRAEL.	SATAN AND BABYLON.
Rev. 1: 4, 5. The Trinity—Father, Son, and Holy Spirit.	Rev. 12; 13; 16: 13, 19. False trinity —dragon, beast, false prophet.
Rev. 1: 1; 6: 2. God commissions His Son, and gives Him authority and power.	Rev. 13: 2. The dragon gave the beast his "power, and his seat, and great authority."
Rev. 5: 6. Christ is likened to a Lamb with seven horns—all power in heaven and on earth.	Rev. 13: 11. False prophet has two horns like a lamb, but speaks later as a dragon—*political* power controlled by *church.*
Rev. 22: 16. Jesus, means Saviour.	Rev. 9: 11. Apollyon or Destroyer. Rev. 12: 7-9; 20: 2. Satan or Adversary.

Rev. 1: 18; 3: 7. Keys of death and of hades.	Rev. 9: 1. Key of bottomless pit.
Rev. 3: 21. Christ's "throne."	Rev. 2: 13; 16: 10. "Throne" of Satan.
Ps. 113: 5; Isa. 40: 18. "Who is like unto the Lord."	Rev. 13: 4. "Who is like unto the beast?"
Rev. 5: 6. "A Lamb as it had been slain."	Rev. 13: 3. One of the heads of the beast "as though it had been slain." See margin.
Rev. 2: 8. Christ died and lived again.	Rev. 13: 14. Beast received stroke of death "and lived." R.V.
Rev. 1: 4. God: "He which is, and which was, and which is to come."	Rev. 17: 8. Beast "was, and is not," and is about to come out of the bottomless pit.
Rev. 11: 17. R.V. drops last term of the above description.	Rev. 17: 11. Last term of above description is dropped.
Rev. 6: 16. The wrath of the Lamb —comes down with great wrath.	Rev. 12: 12. The wrath of the dragon—comes down with "great wrath."
Rev. 7: 2. God's seal.	Rev. 13: 17. Beast's mark.
Rev. 7: 3. Seal in forehead.	Rev. 13: 16; 20: 4. Mark in forehead or the hand.
Rev. 14: 1. Contains the name of God.	Rev. 13: 17. Contains the name of the beast.
Rev. 7: 4. The tribes of Israel.	Rev. 1: 7. The tribes of the earth.
Rev. 16: 12. The kings of the east.	Rev. 16: 14. The kings of the earth and of the whole world.
Rev. 19: 11-14. The armies of heaven.	Rev. 19: 19. The armies of earth.
Rev. 21: 24-26. Nations saved.	Rev. 16: 19; 20: 8. Nations destroyed.
Rev. 12: 7; 16: 14, 16; 19: 11. The "war" or "battle" against Satan and his followers.	Rev. 12: 17; 17: 14; 20: 8. The "war" or "battle" against Christ and His people.
Rev. 7: 1-4; 14: 6-17. Christ's messengers come "down" from heaven "above." See John 3: 3, 7, margins; v. 31, etc.	Rev. 11: 7; 13: 1, 11. Satan's messengers come "up" from the earth "beneath." See John 8: 23, etc.
Rev. 19: 9. The marriage supper of the Lamb: the triumph and joy of Israel.	Rev. 19: 17-20. The supper of the birds: the defeat and death of Israel's enemies.
Rev. 21: 10. The Lamb's wife.	Rev. 17: 1, 5, 18. The harlot of Babylon.
Rev. 21: 14. Apostles of the Lamb.	Rev. 2: 2. False apostles.
Rev. 11: 2; 14: 20. The holy city, Jerusalem—God's church.	Rev. 14: 8; 16: 19; 18: 2, etc. The unholy city, Babylon — Satan's church.

Because of the imagery pertaining to Israel so abundantly used in the book of Revelation, futurists say that it is a book largely pertaining to the literal Jew in Palestine. Failure to understand the New Testament principle that Old Testament terminology is now employed in a spiritual, world-wide sense in connection with the church is responsible for much theological confusion. "Israel" is the key-word which unlocks prophetic problems—especially those in the book of Revelation. Only as they relate to the church can the prophecies be fully understood. Many commentators rightly emphasize that "the symbolism of the Revelation is *wholly* and *exclusively Jewish"*: only spiritual Israelites can understand the prophecies of the Apocalypse. It is estimated that at least 550 quotations from the Old Testament are found in the book of Revelation. The following extract from "The Revelation of St. John," by Prof W. Milligan, D.D., pp. 27-30, illustrates what others have pointed out concerning the exclusively Jewish nature of the Revelation:

"The Christian church, even among the Gentiles, had been grafted upon the stem of David. She had an interest in Zion and Jerusalem; she saw in Babylon the type of her enemies; she felt herself to be the *true Israel of God.* She was well acquainted with the *tabernacle and the temple,* with their *pillars* and *incense,* with their different *altars,* with the *high priest's robes,* with the seven-branched *golden candlesticks,* with the *ark* of the *testimony,* with the *hidden manna, and* with the parchment *rolls written* both within and on the back. These symbols were therefore closely adapted to her condition ,and must have gone home to her with peculiar power.

"But the symbolism of the *Revelation* is *wholly and exclusively Jewish.* Even 'the crown of life' in Chap. 2: 10 is not the wreath of the victor in Grecian games, but the Hebrew crown of royalty and joy—the crown of 'King Solomon, wherewith his mother crowned him in the day of his espousals, and in the gladness of his heart.' Song of Sol. 3: 11. The 'white stone,' with the new name written in it, of chapter 2: 17, is not suggested by the white pebble which cast in heathen courts of justice into the ballot box, expressed the judge's acquittal of the prisoner at the bar, but in all probability by the glistering plate borne by the high priest upon his forehead. And all good commentators are agreed that the palms of chapter 7: 9 are not the palms of heathen victors either in battle or the games, but the palms of the Feast of Tabernacles when, in the most joyful of all her national festivals, Israel celebrated that life of independence on which she entered when she marched from Rameses to Succoth, and exchanged her dwellings in the hot brickfields of Egypt for the free air of the wilderness, and the 'booths' which she erected in the open country. *The symbols of the Apocalypse are to be judged of with the feelings of a Jew,* and not with those of our own country or age."

After presenting other "Israel" features in the Revelation, Prof. Milligan continues:—

"If from the trumpets we turn to the bowls the following particulars claim our notice:—

1. The very mention of bowls at once connects us, not with the world, but with the *church* The vessels so designated were not vials, but bowls or basins, broad and shallow, rather than narrow and deep. They were the gifts presented by the *princes of the twelve tribes of Israel*

for the service of the *Tabernacle,* Num. 7, and they were used for offering on the golden altar of the sanctuary, the incense which had been kindled by coals from the altar in the court. They were instruments of religious service, and were peculiarly fitted, according to the law of recompense in kind, pervading the whole Apocalypse to contain those judgments of the Almighty, which were designed . . . for the faithless church. . . . [The plagues, primarily, fall upon *spiritual* Babylon —the *apostate* church.]

2. A similar remark applies to the fact that, as mentioned in chapter 15: 6, the angels which bear the seven last plagues, come forth from the *'temple'* or innermost shrine of the *tabernacle* of the testimony in heaven, dressed as *priests* in pure white linen, and with golden girdles." pp. 54, 55.

"The Book is absolutely steeped *in the memories,* the *incidents,* the *thoughts,* and the *language* of the *church's past.* To such an extent is this the case that it may be *doubted whether it contains a single figure not drawn from the Old Testament, or a single complete sentence not more or less built up of materials from the same source.* Nothing can convey a full and adequate impression upon the point, except the careful study of the book itself in this particular aspect of its contents." p. 72.

And then he enumerates examples of the many persons, places, incidents, etc., associated with ancient Israel and mentioned in the Revelation. Prof. Milligan then continues:—

"The great earthquake of chapter 6 is taken from Haggai; the sun becoming black as sackcloth of hair, and the moon becoming blood of the same chapter, from Joel; the stars of heaven falling, the fig tree casting her untimely figs, the heavens departing as a scroll, in the same chapter, from Isaiah; the locusts of chapter 9 from Joel; the gathering of the vine of the earth in chapter 14 from Joel; and the treading of the winepress in the same chapter, from Isaiah; the wings of the eagle upon which the woman is borne for protection to the wilderness are those of Deuteronomy and Isaiah, and the whole description of the New Jerusalem in chapter 21, is moulded upon Ezekiel.

"If we look at several of the larger visions, we shall have the same lesson brought home to us—that of the throne in heaven in chapter 4, having its prototype in Isaiah and Ezekiel; that of the opening of the seals in chapter 6, in Zechariah; that of the beast from the sea in chapter 13, in Daniel; that of the olive trees in chapter 11, in Zechariah; that of the measuring of the temple in chapter 21, in Ezekiel and Zechariah; that of the little book in chapter 10, in Ezekiel.

"Or, once more, if we take any single vision and examine its detail, we shall find that its various portions are often gathered out of different prophets, or different parts of the same prophet. Thus, in the very first vision of the book, that of the glorified Redeemer, in chapter 1: 12-20, the golden candlesticks are taken from Exodus and Zechariah; the garment down to the foot, from Exodus and Daniel; the golden girdle, from Isaiah and Daniel; the hairs like white wool, from the same two prophets; the feet like unto burnished brass, from Ezekiel; the two-edged sword, from Isaiah; and the Psalms; the countenance as the sun shineth in his strength, from Exodus; the falling of the Seer as dead at the feet of the person who appears to him, from Exodus, Isaiah, Ezekiel, and Daniel; the laying of the right hand of Jesus upon the Seer, from Daniel.

"It is impossible to enlarge without going over *every chapter, verse,* and *clause* of the book, which is *a perfect mosaic of passages from the Old Testament,* at one time quoted verbally, at another referred to in distinct allusion, now taken from one scene in *Jewish history,* and now again from *two or three together.* . . . The sacred books of his people had been more than familiar to him. They had penetrated his whole being. . . . In the whole extent of sacred or religious literature there is to be found nowhere else such *a perfect fusion of the revelation given to Israel* with the mind of one who would either express *Israel's ideas,* or give utterance, by means of the *symbols* supplied by *Israel's history,* to the purest and most elevated thoughts of the Christian faith.   pp. 75, 76.

"If from persons, we turn to *places* the same rule is observable. Jerusalem and Mount Zion and Babylon and the Euphrates and Sodom and Egypt, *all familiar to us in the history of Israel,* play their part in order to denote the holiness and happiness of the saints, or the coming in of judgment, or the transgressors from whom the righteous must separate themselves. The battle of Har-Magedon has undoubted reference to one or the other, if not both, of the two great slaughters connected in the Old Testament with the plain of Megiddo—Judges 5: 19; Ps. 83: 9; 2 Kings 23: 29. . . .

"While nothing can explain the last attack *upon the saints* as a gathering of Gog and Magog from the four corners of the earth, but the fact that these names had already been consecrated to a similar purpose in the prophecies of Ezekiel (chaps. 38, 39)." Ibid. 72, 73

"A Commentary of the Bible, by Bishops and other Clergy of the Anglican Church," says concerning Rev. 20: 8:—

"The terms 'Camp' and 'City' are *images borrowed* from the condition of *Israel in the wilderness,* and in the *Promised Land.* Ex. 14: 19; Ps. 107: 36."

The "Hebrew" emphasis runs throughout the Apocalypse. Even to many Greek words John gives a "strong *Hebrew* colouring." Notice the following extract taken from the pen of Prof. W. Milligan, D.D.:—

"The writer *does,* then, *intentionally Hebraise.* . . . Nothing can be more decided that his statement (Ewald's) that the imitation of Hebrew idiom in the Apocalypse goes so far as to lead to many a change in Greek construction *with the view of imitating the constructions of the Hebrew tongue."* Milligan's "The Revelation of St. John," p. 260.

Referring to Rev. 9: 11, the Professor states:—

"When we turn to the root of the Greek name Apollyon . . . we discover that it expresses the same meaning as the *Hebrew."*

Uriah Smith, in his "Daniel and the Revelation," p. 479, in commenting upon Rev. 9: 11, says: "His name. In Hebrew, 'Abaddon,' the destroyer; in Greek, 'Apollyon,' one that exterminates, or destroys. Having two different names in two languages, it is evident that the *character,* rather than the name of the power, is intended to be represented . . . as expressed in both languages he is a destroyer."

In describing the destruction of the enemies of the church, John is careful to emphasise the symbolic "place called in the *Hebrew* tongue Armageddon." Rev. 16: 16. As the *character* of the power and not its *literal* name is expressed in the Hebrew name of Rev. 9: 11, so it is because of the *character* or the *meaning* "in the *Hebrew* tongue" of the word Armageddon that it is mentioned in Rev. 16: 16. The meaning of Armageddon is given by Christopher Wordsworth: "Armageddon or Harmageddon is formed of *two Hebrew words,* the one, har, signifying a mountain, the other a cutting to pieces; and thus it means the *mountain of excision or slaughter."* For further consideration of the meaning of the Hebrew word Armageddon, see chapter on "The Significance of the Meaning of Names Mentioned in Connection with the Great Battle of Armageddon."

Ellicott's Commentary states:—

" 'The Greek is moulded by the Hebrew tendencies of the writer.' . . . Thus the *strong Hebrew* colouring is precisely what we should expect from one . . . *constantly talking over Messianic hopes and prophecies."* pp. 5, 6.

"The prevalence of *Hebraic* influences noticeable in the Apocalypse might well fit in with the later date." p. 11.

"The interpreter is too readily caught by *external resemblances,* and *pays too little heed to inner spiritual and ethical principles.* . . . Of these principles the chief seem to be the following: (1) the *root passages in the Old Testament prophecies must be considered."* p. 12, 15.

In "The New Testament in Greek, General Epistles and Revelation," Bishop C. Wordsworth states:—

"The diction of the Book of Revelation is more Hebraistic than that of any other portion of the New Testament. It adopts *Hebrew* idioms and *Hebrew* words. It studiously disregards the laws of *Gentile* Syntax, and even courts anomalies and solecisms; it *christianizes Hebrew* words and sentiments, and clothes them in an evangelical dress, and consecrates them to Christ. Thus, for instance, it never uses the Greek form Hierosoluma, but always employs the *Hebrew* Hierusalem; and by this name it never designates the literal Sion, but the *Christian church."*

By many illustrations Bishop Wordsworth shows the Hebrew setting, sentiment, etc., prevailing throughout the Revelation. He further says:—

"In a similar spirit of genuine catholicity, expanding the mind, and *spiritualizing the language of the Jewish nation,* and investing them with the light of the Gospel, the Apocalypse *designates the Universal Church* of Christ under the terms of a *Hebrew* nomenclature by the names of the Twelve Tribes of Israel.' Thus it extends the view of the Hebrew people, and enlarges the walls of Sion and the borders of Palestine till they embrace within their ample range the family of mankind. . . . The Apocalypse also elevates the heart and voice of the *Hebrew nation,* even to the court of the church glorified. Here the *Hebrew* language sounds in the solemn service of the heavenly ritual, in which the angelic choir sing praises to God, Amen, Hallelujah. . . . It deals in a similar way with *Hebrew* prophecy. It is characteristic of *Hebrew* prophecy to repeat the same predictions at different times. The Apocalypse proceeds on a similar plan."

How true are the words of A. W. Anderson in "The World's Finale," pp. 69-72:—

"The 'four corners of the earth, and the four winds of the earth, are evidently phrases which are meant to convey the *idea of the world-wide extent* of the *conditions which the Relevator is describing.* The seal of the living God. and the white robes, and the *twelve* tribes are also *symbols,* for no one would suppose that a *literal* seal was to be actually stamped upon the foreheads of God's servants; nor that the saints *literally* washed their robes in the blood of Christ nor that the sealing work was confined to the twelve *literal* tribes of Israel, of whom all means of identification have been lost for many centuries. . . . *Much of the real meaning of such passages of Scripture as Rev. 7 is lost when an attempt is made to deal with them literally. Beautiful truths* are revealed in these *symbolic passages,* once we can *define the symbolism* which is used . . . Ezekiel, in describing a vision of judgment which was given to him, tells us of a man with a writer's inkhorn going through *the midst of Jerusalem* setting a mark upon the foreheads of the men that sighed for all the abominations that were done therein."

Thus commentators and expositors point out that only in the light of Israel—only as a revelation to *spiritual Israel*—can the prophecies of the Apocalypse be understood.

THE THIRD ANGEL'S MESSAGE AND ARMAGEDDON UNDERSTOOD BY SPIRITUAL ISRAELITES.

Only spiritual Israelites can fully accept the Third Angel's Message. It can be understood only in the light of the literal types of ancient Israel's sanctuary services. The complete understanding of "Armageddon," also, is known only by spiritual Israelites. It can be understood only in the light of the typical battles fought between Israel and her foes. In the Old Testament, Megiddo is mentioned as the place of Israel's conflict with Satan-led forces, who were destroyed there (Judges 5: 19-21)—"and there was not a man left." Judg. 4: 16. Because of its historical connection with Israel's victory and the place of the destruction of her enemies, as well as for the significance of its meaning, Megiddo is *symbolically* referred to in Rev. 16: 16. Jesus, the Revelator, refers to "a place called in the *Hebrew* tongue Armageddon." The emphasis is not upon the place, but upon the meaning of the name in the *Hebrew* tongue— "the mountain of slaughter," referring to the slaughter of the *enemies of Israel*. The beast and the false prophet are mentioned in the Revelation only because they are Israel's enemies.

The dragon, also, is mentioned only because it symbolizes "the kings, and rulers ,and governors" (T.M. 39) who enforce the keeping of Sunday, the counterfeit of the Sabbath, which is the "sign" between God and Israel. Ex. 31: 13-18.

"The prophets of Israel" must prepare "the house of Israel to stand in the *battle in the day of the Lord.*" Ezek. 13: 2, 5. Through His Sabbath message, God calls spiritual Israel to prepare for the coming storm. See Rev. 7: 1-4. The angels are holding back the winds of universal strife and trouble until the sealing "of all the tribes of the *children of Israel.*" Verses 5-8 name the twelve tribes of Israel who are sealed and thus assured God's protection (see E.W. 43) during the world-wide carnage which will follow when the angels let go "the four winds of the earth." "Armageddon" is to be considered only as it is related to Israel and her enemies. As Israel is protected in all the world, so the Armageddon slaughter from which they are sheltered is also worldwide.

In the midst of His description concerning Armageddon, Jesus addresses the members of spiritual Israel: "Behold, I come as a thief. Blessed is he that watcheth, and keepeth his garments, lest he walked naked, and they see his shame." Rev. 16: 15. Commenting on Rev. 16: 15, "The New Testament Pocket Commentary" says: "May allude to the *Jewish* watchman. The 'man of the mountain,' as he was called, used to go around the temple, and if he found any of the watchmen asleep, would set fire to their clothes. If they were compelled to appear in them the next day, it would cause them much shame." That Christ should refer to a symbolical "place called in the *Hebrew* tongue Armageddon" and, in the midst of a description of the events connected with that slaughter, address spiritual *Israel*, referring to a *Jewish* custom, is congruous *only* when Armageddon is understood as the slaughter of *the enemies of Israel*.

ISRAEL AND THE NATIONS.

Old Testament terminology is employed spiritually in the New Testament. Because ancient Israel was a nation, the church is said to be a nation. Because ancient Israel's enemies were nations, the enemies of the church are referrd to by national terms. Because Israel's enemies gathered against her and assaulted Jerusalem, the enemies of the church are also described as gathering against the Israel of God—the spiritual Jerusalem. Because the ancient people of God came out of the land of their captivity and gathered to their own land, spiritual Israel is said to "come out" of the land of spiritual captivity (Rev. 18: 4) and *"gather"* to their own spiritual land. See Isa. 11: 11, 12: E.W., pp. 74-76.

In our interpretation of the Old Testament we must be guided by New Testament teachings. "The way of man is not in himself: it is not in man that walketh to direct his steps." Jer. 10: 23; Prov. 3: 5; etc. The Scriptures must be their own expositor. T.M. 476, 106. Were this counsel heeded, passages such as Joel 3; Ezek. 38, 39; Zech. 14; Rev. 16: 12-16, etc., which depict a gathering of nations against Israel. would not be interpreted to refer to the *literal* Jews in Palestine, but to a gathering, or uniting of spiritual forces against *spiritual Israel*.

According to Dr. Strong, the Hebrew word for nation means: "A *foreign* nation; hence a . . . Gentile, heathen, nation, people." According to the same authority, the Greek word for nation means: "A race . . . a *foreign* (non-Jewish) one (usually by impl. pagan): Gentile, heathen, nation, people." In Scripture the word is usually employed in contrast to the nation of Israel. When mentioned in relation to the closing conflict, "nations," "gentiles," "heathen" must be interpreted as *enemies of spiritual Israel.* A comparison of Isa. 9: 1-3 with Matt. 4: 14-16 shows that the words "nations" and "gentiles" are used for "peoples." In Ephes. 2: 11, 12 we have the inspired interpretation of the word "gentiles"—those who are not Israelites. In Rev. 11: 2 the Papal persecutors of the church are said to be "gentiles." A person who is not a member of spiritual Israel is an "heathen man." Matt. 18: 17. That the term "gentile," or "heathen" is used in Scripture to designate those out of Christ, or the enemies of God's people, is completely sustained by the writings of the servant of the Lord. For examples, see E.W., pp. 282-284, and G.C. 618, 635, where "heathen" is the word employed when referring to the *enemies of the church.* See "What is Armageddon?" pp. 7-10.

Joel 3; Ezek. 38, 39, etc., depict the gathering, or uniting of the "nations," "heathen," or "gentiles" against spiritual Israel, and their destruction outside spiritual Jerusalem. The final conflict will be waged *"without the city."* Rev. 14: 20. "The fugitives whom the Eternal calls shall be *inside Jerusalem."* Moffatt's Trans. Joel 2: 32.

The fact that the church is definitely called a "nation" (1 Pet. 2: 9; Matt. 21: 43) shows that the word is employed in the New Testament without reference to armies or military strength. As already shown, the word "nation" is used for "people." Depicting the gathering of the "heathen," "gentiles," "nations" against Israel, Joel 3 describes them as "multitudes" gathered into the valley of judgment. Jesus speaks of the nations as being made up of sheep and goats—the people of God, and the unsaved. See Matt. 25: 31-33. The leaves of the tree of life are "for the healing of the *nations."* Rev. 22: 2. "The glory and honour of the *nations"* will be brought into the *"New Jerusalem."* Rev. 21: 26. "And the *nations* of them *which are saved* shall walk in the light of it." Rev. 21: 24. In these three references it is evident that the word "nations" refers to people redeemed from "every nation, and kindred, and tongue, and people" (Rev. 14: 6) who, through the new birth, constitute *spiritual* Israel.

CHAPTER X.

THE JEWS, DESIRING A LITERAL KINGDOM, REJECT THE KING OF A SPIRITUAL KINGDOM.

The servant of the Lord informs us that the Jews were led to reject Christ because of their mis-interpretation of the prophecies concerning Israel. In "The Desire of Ages," p. 30, she says:—

"While the Jews desired the advent of the Messiah, they had no true conception of His mission. They did not seek the redemption from sin, but *deliverance from the Romans.* They looked for the Messiah to come as a conqueror, to break the oppressor's power, and *exalt Israel to universal dominion.* Thus the way was prepared for them to reject the Saviour. . . . Hatred of the Romans, and national and spiritual pride, led the Jews still to adhere rigorously to their forms of worship. . . . The people in their darkness and oppression, and the rulers, thirsting for power, longed for the coming of One Who would vanquish their enemies and *restore the kingdom to Israel.* They had studied the prophecies, but without *spiritual* insight. *Thus* they overlooked those Scriptures that point to the humiliation of Christ's advent, and *misapplied* those that speak of His second coming. *Pride obscured* their vision. They *interpreted prophecy* in accordance with their selfish desires."

By applying *literally* the prophecies concerning Israel, the Jews mis-interpreted them. Again we read:—

"The Jews had *misinterpreted* God's promise of *eternal favour to Israel* [Jer. 31: 33, 34 is then quoted]. 'Thus saith the Lord. . . . If those ordinances [sun, moon, and stars] depart from Me, saith the Lord, then the seed of Israel also shall cease from being a *nation* before Me forever.' Jer. 31: 35-37. The Jews regarded their *natural* descent from Abraham as giving them a claim to this promise. But they overlooked the conditions which God had specified." D.A. 106.

In the promise the word "nation" is employed. The Jews interpreted the prophecy to mean a *literal* nation, but the New Testament shows that the promise refers to the *spiritual* nation— the church. Similarly, all the Old Testament prophecies which *seem* to refer to *literal* Israel in the *literal land* of Israel must now be interpreted according to the light shining from the New Testament, where the things of Israel are applied *spiritually* in connection with the church.

So deceived were the Jewish leaders regarding the *literal* fulfilment of the prophecies concerning Israel that, even when Rome, in A.D. 70, was battering down the city of Jerusalem, the priests continued to offer *literal* sacrifices in the *literal temple,* believing that somehow *national* Israel would continue to be under the favour of God. How strong are the delusions based upon a belief in the *literal* fulfilment of prophecies concerning *Israel!* Not only was national Israel deceived, but the most popular prophetic teachings in professed Christendom to-day are those which apply *literally* the things of Israel. The powerful hold of that false system of interpretation is illustrated in the experience of the disciples. Jesus, the world's Master Teacher, constantly endeavoured to turn His disciples from the interpretations of the Scriptures taught by the religious leaders of His day. It was their failure to accept the Lord's interpretations which found them unprepared for the crucifixion of Christ. As stated by the Lord's servant:—

"Before His crucifixion, *the Saviour explained to His disciples* that He was about to be put to death, and to rise again from the tomb; and angels were present to impress His words on minds and hearts. *But the disciples were looking for temporal deliverance* from the Roman yoke. . . . The words which they needed to remember were banished from their minds, and when the time of trial came, it found them unprepared. The death of Jesus as fully destroyed their hopes *as if He had not forewarned them.* So in the prophecies the *future* is opened before us *as plainly as it was opened to the disciples* by the words of Christ. . . . But multitudes have no more understanding of these important truths than if they had never been revealed." GC. 594.

Even on the day of the resurrection the disciples did not know the true interpretation of the prophecies concerning Israel. Before Jesus revealed Himself to the two disciples of Emmaus, He explained the prophecies, for "it was necessary for them to understand the witness borne to Him by the *types* and *prophecies* of the *Old Testament.* Upon these their faith must be established. Christ performed no miracle to convince them, but it was *His first work to explain the Scriptures.* They had looked upon His death as the destruction of all their hopes. Now He showed from the prophets that this was the very strongest evidence for their faith. . . . The miracles of Christ are a strong proof of His divinity; but a *stronger proof* that He is the world's Redeemer is found in comparing *the prohecies of the Old Testament* with the *history of the New.*" D.A. 796-799.

As the spiritual condition of a church declines, more attention is paid to the literal—including a literal application of prophecies which should be interpreted *spiritually* in connection with the church. *Literal* things which have been instituted because of their *spiritual* significance lose their *spiritual* meaning, and the service of the church degenerates into formalism: the letter is emphasised as the spirit wanes. Thus it was in the experiences of literal Israel, and it has been repeated in the experience of the Christian church. "The Jews lost the *spiritual* life from their ceremonies, and clung to the dead forms." D.A. 29.

As an example of the Jews' loss of spiritual vision notice the following extract:—

"To Moses God had said concerning His commandments, 'Thou shalt bind them for a sign upon thine hand, and they shall be as frontlets between thine eyes.' Deut. 6: 8. These words have *a deep meaning*. As the word of God is meditated upon and practised, the whole man will be ennobled. In righteous and merciful dealing, the hands will reveal, as a signet, the principles of God's law. . . . The eyes, directed toward a noble purpose, will be clear and true. . . . But by the Jews of Christ's day all this was undiscerned. The command given to Moses was construed into a direction that the precepts of Scripture should be worn upon the person. They were accordingly written upon strips of parchment, and bound in a conspicuous manner about the head or the wrists." D.A. 612.

The *literal* application of that which God designed should be *spiritually* applied is Satan's plan of substituting a counterfeit for the genuine.

Isaiah had prophesied: "And the *glory* of the Lord shall be revealed, and *all flesh shall see it* together: for the mouth of the Lord hath spoken it." Isa. 40: 5. But before the *visible* glory of God would be manifested at the second advent, the *spiritual* glory of God would be revealed in the character and life of the Lord Jesus. See P.K. 689, etc. Through seeking after *literal* things the Jews failed to see the *spiritual:* they failed to discern that the prophet spoke of the revelation of *spiritual* glory before the *literal* glory of God should be revealed. The Jews' need of *spiritual* vision was also illustrated by their blindness to the meaning of the prophecy in Hag. 2: 7-9. Commenting upon this prophecy, God's servant says:—

"This temple [Solomon's] was the most magnificent building which the world ever saw. Yet the Lord had declared. . . . 'The *glory* of this latter house shall be *greater than of the former*. . . . I will *fill* this house with *glory.'* . . . But the second temple had not equalled the first in magnificence; nor was it hallowed by those visible tokens of the divine presence which pertained to the first temple There was no manifestation of supernatural power to mark its dedication. . . . For centuries the Jews had vainly endeavoured to show wherein the promise of God given by Haggai had been fulfilled; yet *pride and unbelief blinded their minds* to the *true meaning* of the prophet's words. The second temple was not honoured with the cloud of Jehovah's *glory*, but with the living presence of One in Whom dwelt the fulness of the Godhead bodily. . . . In the presence of Christ, and *in this only*, did the second temple *exceed the first in glory.*" G.C. 23, 24; P.K. 597.

"*Spiritual* things are *spiritually discerned.*" That which God designed should be *spiritually* applied, Satan will cause to be *literally* applied: in this way he blinds the eyes of millions to the truth of God. Some day, in the eternal kingdom, "the glory of the Lord shall be revealed, and all flesh shall see it together." P.K. 733. But, until then, in this "dispensation of the Holy Spirit," the things of Israel are to be *spiritually* applied.

66

THE MESSIAH'S SPIRITUAL KINGDOM.

The Old Testament contains many predictions concerning the Messiah's kingdom.

"At the time . . . when our Lord appeared, there was a *general expectation among the Jews of the coming of the Messiah*, and His reign was called 'the world to come,' 'the heavenly Jerusalem,' 'the kingdom of heaven,' or 'of God.' To enter the kingdom was to become His disciple. The Jews had very erroneous conceptions of its nature; and it was necessary that our Lord should correct them. This He does in the teachings of Himself, and of His disciples. *The nature of the kingdom of God must be learned, therefore, from the New Testament." "Angus's Bible Handbook," p. 203.*

When the Messiah came "unto His own," "His own received Him not." John 1: 11. The Jews rejected Christ because His kingdom was not what they expected or wanted:—

"Some of the Pharisees had come to Jesus demanding 'when the kingdom of God should come.' More than three years had passed since John the Baptist gave the message, that like a trumpet call had sounded through the land, 'The kingdom of heaven is at hand.' And as yet these Pharisees saw no indication of the establishment of the kingdom. Many of those who rejected John, and at every step had opposed Jesus, were insinuating that His mission had failed. Jesus answered, *'The kingdom of God cometh not with outward show; neither shall they say, Lo here! Lo there! for, behold, the kingdom of God is within you.' The kingdom of God begins in the heart.* Look not here or there for manifestations of earthly power to mark its coming. . . . *Because* it is *not* attended by *worldly pomp, you are in danger of failing to discern the glory of My mission."* D.A. 506.

The Jews looked forward to the time when, with the advent of the Messiah, all the predictions regarding the exaltation of Israel in His *literal* kingdom would have their grand fulfilment. The two-fold nature of the Messiah's kingdom their unspiritual natures could not grasp.

Not wishing to see this two-fold nature prophesied by the seers of Israel, they failed to heed the truth that the *first* phase of the kingdom had to do with humiliation and the battle against evil within. Christ had to *suffer* before He entered into *glory.* Luke 24: 25-26, 46; 1 Pet. 1: 11. Similarly, the Israel associated with Him would likewise first suffer before they reigned in glory with Him. 2 Tim. 2: 12; 1 Pet. 4: 13.

The proud human heart would like to share in the glory, but not in the humiliation and the suffering, which are essential for entrance into the kingdom. Acts 14: 22. The first phase of the Messiah's kingdom is the kingdom of grace, during which, time and opportunity are afforded for a heart preparation for the glory to follow.

"The kingdom of God" and its cognate phrases are found 47 times in Matthew; 13 times in Mark; 31 times in Luke; and 5 times in John. "Life" is a synonym for "the kingdom of God" (Mark 9: 45, 47; Matt. 18: 9), and "everlasting life" occurs about 40 times in John's gospel. In the kingdom of grace Jesus gives *spiritual* life. In the kingdom of glory He gives eternal life.

Christ not only reigns upon "the throne of grace" in heaven, but also, by His Spirit, reigns in every heart on earth subject to Him. Col. 1: 13; 1 John 3: 14; 5: 11-13; Col. 1: 26, 27; 3: 4; John 3: 3, 7; Phil. 3: 20; Heb. 12: 23, margin; Ephes. 2: 6, etc. This was the kingdom which was "at hand." See Matt. 3: 2; 4: 17, etc. This was the burden of Paul's sermons. See Acts 20: 25; 28: 23, 31.

"And *'the kingdom of God'* which they had declared to be at hand, was *established by the death of Christ.* This kingdom was *not,* as they had been taught to believe, *an earthly empire.* Nor was it that future, immortal dominion, which shall be set up when 'the kingdom and dominion, and the greatness of the kingdom under the whole heaven, shall be given to the people of the saints of the Most High;' that everlasting kingdom, in which 'all dominions shall serve and obey Him. . . .

"The throne of Grace represents the kingdom of grace; for the existence of a throne implies the existence of a kingdom. In many of His parables, Christ uses the expression 'the kingdom of heaven,' to designate the work of divine grace upon the hearts of men. . . .

"The kingdom of grace was instituted immediately after the fall of man. . . . It then existed in the purpose, and by the promise of God; and through faith, men could become its subjects. Yet it was not actually *established* until the *death of Christ.*" GC., p. 347, 348.

The work of the Messiah was not only to establish an eternal kingdom of glory, but also to prepare characters for it. But the Messiah's kingdom is just as truly established in the *spiritual* kingdom as it will be in the eternal world. Christ reigns from "the throne of grace" (Heb. 4: 16)—a real throne in heaven. Heb. 8: 1; Zech. 6: 13. He is the "King eternal, immortal, *invisible"* (1 Tim. 1: 17)—invisible to earth now, but visible in heaven. After His ascension, Christ was enthroned as the King-priest (Zech. 6: 13), typified by Melchisedec. Gen. 14: 18; Ps. 110: 1-4; Heb. 6: 10; 7: 1, 2, etc.

"Christ's ascension to heaven was the signal that His followers were to receive the promised blessing. . . . When Christ passed within the heavenly gates, He was *enthroned* amidst the adoration of the angels. As soon as this ceremony was completed, the Holy Spirit descended upon the disciples in rich currents, and Christ was indeed glorified. . . . The Pentecostal outpouring was heaven's communication that the *Redeemer's* inauguration was accomplished. According to His promise He had sent the Holy Spirit from heaven to His followers, as a token that He had, *as priest and king,* received all authority in heaven and on earth, and was the *Anointed One* over His people." A.A., pp. 38-39.

When believers associate with Jesus, the King-priest, in the work of soul-saving and destroying sin, and thus help spread His spiritual kingdom they, too, become kings and priests. See Rev. 1: 6; 5:10; 20: 6; 1 Pet. 2: 5, 9. Since Christ's enthronement as King-priest, the Holy Spirit represents the "invisible" King of Israel. Predictions concerning the Messiah's kingdom are being fulfilled *spiritually* during this "dispensation of the Holy Spirit."

AT PENTECOST THE DISCIPLES WERE GIVEN DISCERNMENT CONCERNING THE SPIRITUAL KINGDOM.

"Just before leaving His disciples, Christ once more plainly stated the *nature* of His kingdom. He recalled to their remembrance things He had previously told them regarding it. He declared that it was *not His purpose* to establish in this world *a temporal kingdom."* AA., p. 30.

"Because of their selfishness and earthliness, even the disciples of Jesus could not comprehend the *spiritual glory,* which He sought to reveal unto them. *It was not until after Christ's ascension* to His Father, and the outpouring of the Holy Spirit upon the believers, *that the disciples fully appreciated the Saviour's character and mission."* D.A., p. 506.

Not until the spiritual kingdom of grace was established, not until the outpouring of the Holy Spirit did the disciples understand the *spiritual* interpretation of Old Testament predictions regarding the kingdom.

After Pentecost, while teaching a *literal,* physical salvation of the *future,* they also taught that *spiritual* salvation was a *present blessing.* See 1 Pet. 1: 5; 1 Thes. 5: 8; Rom. 13: 11; Heb. 9: 28; Isa. 25: 9; 35: 4; 62: 11; Rom. 8: 23; Acts 3: 21 and 2 Cor. 6: 2; Heb. 3: 13; Acts 13: 26; 28: 28; Titus 2: 11; 2 Tim. 2: 10. The *spiritual* salvation of the kingdom of grace will be *followed* by a *literal, physical salvation* in the kingdom of glory.

"Undoubtedly our natural bias is in favour of the so-called 'literal' interpretation of the prophecies in question; for to the natural man the things that are seen are the *real* things; and to that view we are disposed to cling tenaciously, notwithstanding the plain teaching of the New Testament, that the seen things are fleeting shadows of things unseen, the latter being the spiritual and eternal realities with which the promises of future blessing have mainly to do. . . . Evidently then our difficulty in understanding prophecies of the class referred to above is due to our lack of faith and our spiritual dullness." *"The Hope of Israel,"* p. 15, 17, by P. Mauro.

"The Desire of Ages," p. 506, states that the disciples could not, at first, see "the *spiritual* glory" of Christ's work fulfilling the Old Testament predictions "because of their *selfishness* and *earthliness."* The Jews *"knew Him not, nor yet the voices of the prophets* which are read every Sabbath day, *they have fulfilled them* in condemning Him." Acts 13: 27. Their *wrong interpretation* of the Messianic prophecies led them to fulfil the very predictions they so frequently read. They failed to grasp the *spiritual* nature of the

Messiah's kingdom *because they looked for a literal fulfilment of the kingdom prophecies,* and this led them to crucify Him. The Scriptures make it plain that the prophecies concerning the reign of David's promised Son were to be fulfilled by His death and resurrection. See Acts 2: 29, 32; 13: 22-24, 32-34; Rom. 1: 4; 2 Tim. 2: 8. By crucifying the Son of God the Jews brought about the fulfilment of the predictions which they relegated to the future.

Paul preached the kingdom of God and of Christ as a *then reality, into which every believer of the gospel was, and is, instantly translated.* Col. 1: 12, 13; 1 Cor. 15: 11; Acts 20: 24, 25; 1 Cor. 4: 20; Acts 17: 6, 7; 19: 8; 28: 31. By the *new birth* we *enter into the kingdom* of God. John 3: 3, 5; Rom. 14: 17; God *has* "raised unto *Israel a Saviour,* Jesus," Acts 13: 22, 23; Luke 2: 10, 11, 30-32, 68-70; Matt. 1: 21; Acts 5: 30-31. By the work of the Holy Spirit in Messiah's spiritual kingdom of grace, Christ is *now* saving, redeeming Israel, out of "all people." Luke 2: 30-32, etc. *That salvation is "in Zion"* (Joel 2: 32; Rom. 11: 26; 9: 33; 1 Pet. 2: 4-7), *the church, where Jesus reigns.*

The spiritual kingdom of Israel is world-wide, Rom. 4: 13. The expressions "the land of Israel," "His land," "their land," mentioned in the prophecies, now refer to wherever spiritual Israel —His church—is found. The Shepherd and the flock of Israel, and "the mountains of Israel" are mentioned in Ezek. 34: 13, 14. Commenting on Ezek. 34: 23, 16, 25, 28, "The Desire of Ages," p. 477, states: *"Christ applied these prophecies to Himself."* On p. 479 we read: "As an earthly shepherd knows his sheep, so does the divine Shepherd know His flock, that are *scattered throughout the world."* Ezek. 34: 31 is then quoted. Quoting Ezek. 34: 26, 29, 31 in "Acts of the Apostles," pp. 9, 10, we read: "Many and wonderful are the promises recorded in Scripture *regarding the church."*

The Holy Spirit clearly teaches that the sheep of "the house of Israel," on "the mountains of Israel," in "their own land," are the church "scattered *throughout the world."* Thus we have Divine guidance in the interpretation of such prophecies as Ezek. 38, 39; 40-48; Joel 3; Zech. 14; Rev. 16: 12-16, etc. They can be understood only when spiritually applied in connection with the *church:* spiritual Israel is pictured as being attacked by her enemies, who are destroyed by the intervention of God. As the kingdom of Israel is spiritual and world-wide, prophecies relating to this kingdom must have a spiritual, world-wide application.

A SPIRITUAL KINGDOM AND ITS SPIRITUAL SYMBOLS.

Baptism was instituted as an outward sign of inward grace. It *symbolizes* a death of the old life—a crucifixion with Jesus—a burial "with Him," and a resurrection "with Him." It also points forward to the blessed expectation of passing from this world of death at the second advent to the new life with Him in the new world. Without its *spiritual* significance the rite of baptism is worthless.

The emblems of our Lord's broken body and His shed blood—the bread and the wine used in the Lord's Supper—are *spiritual* symbols. By taking *literally* Christ's statement: "This is My body . . . this is My blood," Roman Catholics have been led into the error of transubstantiation. Protestants repudiate the idolatry of the Mass by interpreting Christ's statement *symbolically,* and not *literally.* Error is often the *literal* interpretation of that which God intended to be applied *spiritually.*

Writing of the *spiritual* significance of the service of feet-washing, which Christ instituted in connection with the Lord's Supper, God's servant says:—

> "These words *mean more* than *bodily* cleanliness. Christ is still speaking of the *higher cleansing* as *illustrated* by the lower. . . . So Peter and his brethren had been washed in the great fountain opened for *sin and uncleanness* . . . they still needed His *cleansing grace.* . . . Their *hearts* must be *cleansed.* Pride and self-seeking create dissension and hatred, but *all this Jesus washed away in washing their feet.* A change of feeling was brought about. Looking upon them, Jesus could say, 'Ye are *clean.'* Now there was union of heart, love for one another. . . . Like Peter and his brethren, we too have been *washed in the blood of Christ,* yet often through contact with evil the heart's purity is soiled. We must come to Christ for *His cleansing grace."* D.A., p. 646.

The Lord teaches His people the *spiritual* nature of His kingdom of grace. The symbols and prophecies relating to *spiritual* Israel must be *"spiritually discerned."*

CHAPTER XI.

THE SABBATH—THE "SIGN" BETWEEN GOD AND SPIRITUAL ISRAEL—IS A SPIRITUAL INSTITUTION.

The Third Angel's Message is a call from the Lord Jesus Christ to His people to show their loyalty to Him by obedience to all His Commandments. The Sabbath is the "sign" of this obedience. The Scriptures teach that when the seventh-day Sabbath is faithfully observed it is proof that the heart is spiritually united to Christ. "Wherefore the children of Israel shall keep the Sabbath, to observe the Sabbath throughout their generations, for a perpetual covenant. It is a *sign* between Me and the children of *Israel* for ever: for in six days the Lord made heaven and earth, and on the seventh day He *rested,* and was *refreshed.*" Ex. 31: 13-17; Ezek. 20: 12, 20; Rev. 7: 1-4, etc. In the Scriptures the Sabbath is inseparable from the sanctuary. Lev. 19: 30; 26: 2; Rev. 1: 10, etc. The books of the Bible particularly explaining the sanctuary and its services, invariably mention the Sabbath. In this connection study Heb. 4 and 10: 25; Rev. 1: 10 and its contexts, etc.

When God's last-day Message brought light concerning the ministry of Jesus in the "true tabernacle which the Lord pitched," it also brought light concerning the importance of the Sabbath in the plan of God. The Third Angel's Message is based upon the spiritual interpretations of the *typical* services of *ancient Israel.* The Lord and His Sabbath were the central features of the Old Testament; they are also the central features in the New Testament. In the Book of Revelation, a solemn warning is sounded against "the mark of the beast" (Rev. 13: 17, etc.), which is Satan's *counterfeit* of "the *seal* of God." Rev. 7: 2-4. Both are *spiritual* signs or marks: one the sign of loyalty to God, the other the sign of disloyalty to God. In picturing the scenes of "the final conflict," John applies terms familiar in the history of ancient Israel to describe *spiritual* Israel; and her enemies are designated by terms only understood because of their *opposition to Israel*—hence "the *mark* of the beast" is mentioned only because it is the spiritual counterfeit of the *"sign"* (the Sabbath) between God and His people.

Israel's literal deliverance from 'the land of Egypt, out of the house of bondage" (Ex. 20: 2, etc.), *was typical* of the *spiritual* deliverance from Satan's kingdom of bondage. Sabbath-keeping was a sign of gratitude for the deliverance God had wrought. Deut. 5: 12-16. *Spiritual* Israel observes the Sabbath as a "sign" of deliverance and sanctification. Ex. 31: 13.

The Sabbath was not intended to be confined to Palestine, but being a spiritual institution, it is for all time, and for all people. See Mark 2: 27, 28; Isa. 66: 22, 23. By its very nature it must be as *universal*, and as *enduring* as the *unseen things*, which are eternal. 2 Cor. 4: 18. Time is both intangible and universal. The seventh day, continually recurring in our material existence, lifts our minds beyond *the things of sense*, to the *invisible* Creator of all. This *invisible* memorial of the Creator's power and goodness appeals to our *spirituality*. It is presented as the crucial test of obedience to the *spiritual*. By observing the Sabbath, we subordinate the demands of the material world to those of the invisible and spiritual.

Grasping after *material* things will not satisfy the craving for the spiritual which God, the infinite Spirit, has placed within us. While there is a fever for *material* things, there will be unrest of heart and mind. The Israelites established their hopes upon *material* things, and could not enter into God's "rest." In Hebrews 3 and 4 Paul shows the relationship between Sabbath observance, present *spiritual* rest, and *eternal* rest. Journeying to the promised land, the Israelites looked forward to a *physical* rest from the toils of the pilgrimage and the trials of the desert. Many were materially minded, and lived for the *things of sense* and, consequently, did not enjoy *rest of spirit*, while looking forward to the *rest of body* to come. After all their anxious expectancy, most of the pilgrims, because of unbelief or disobedience, did not enter the promised land.

Through faith and obedience we obtain present rest of heart and mind, while looking forward to eternal rest. This "rest" is illustrated by Sabbath-keeping: physical toil is laid aside, and the heart and mind commune with God, being lifted beyond earthly things to contemplate the invisible, and the eternal. The Sabbath is the trysting time of the spirit of man with his Creator. The Sabbath rest is the consummation of that spiritual rest enjoyed throughout the week.

The Israelites' pilgrimage across the desert is employed in the New Testament to picture the saints' pilgrimage across life's desert to the promised land. 1 Pet. 2: 10, 11. The Sabbath rest, which is the weekly entering into "that rest" of God by both body and spirit, foreshadows the eternal rest awaiting the tired pilgrims at the end of the journey. What the Sabbath is to the week, so eternity is to a life's journey. The certainty of eternal rest is assured by the rest of spirit which comes through faith and a life of obedience. "Rest" begins the moment we believe. Matt. 11: 28, 29. As *spiritual* rest must precede the *physical* rest of Sabbath-keeping, so must there be *spiritual* rest on earth before the eternal rest of body, soul and spirit in the future kingdom.

CHAPTER XII.

THE ERRORS OF ROMAN CATHOLICISM ARE BASED UPON THE *LITERAL* APPLICATION OF THE THINGS OF NATIONAL ISRAEL.

How does the Roman Catholic Church justify its ornate ritual, etc.? The following extracts from "The Question Box" explain the Catholic view:—

"Why do you Catholics make so much of a show in your churches during divine worship? Why do you have so many silly and meaningless ceremonies? . . . So Catholics, believing with the certainty of faith that Jesus Christ is really present upon the altar, so that our *churches* are indeed *temples* of the living God, wish to give outward expression to their love of Him. Therefore, silver, gold, flowers, incense, lighted candles, processions, architecture, sculpture, painting, music—all strive to pay their homage. If it were silly or superstitious, how then do you account for God's sanction of the minutest detail of *the Mosaic* ritual? Ex. 26: 27, 28; Num. Lev."

Roman Catholics fail to see that the *literal* Mosaic ritual terminated at the cross: the Old Testament ritual now meets its literal antitype in the heavenly sanctuary. From p. 187 we quote:—

"Why are so many thousands of dollars put into the building of churches? . . . *The Jews* of the Old Law did not spare gold or precious stones in the *Temple of Solomon, which was merely a figure of the Catholic Church* on whose *altars* Jesus Christ was to be *really* present—the Emmanuel—*God with us.*"

The New Testament teaches that Christ's temple on earth is now *spiritual* and world-wide. See 1 Cor. 3: 9, 16, 17; 2 Cor. 6: 16; Ephes. 2: 21, 22; Rev. 11: 1, 2, etc. Christ (the Emmanel—"God with us") is *spiritually* in His church—temple. The *literal* temple is in heaven. Heb. 8: 2; Rev. 11: 19, etc.

On page 188 of the "Question Box" an endeavour is made to justify the use of incense:—

"Why do you burn fragrant spices during your service? . . . The burning of incense before the altar was part of the *prescribed ceremonial of the Old Law.* Ex. 30: 7; cf. 25: 6; 30: 23; Lev. 26: 13; Num. 16: 46."

The appeal to the literal service of the Old Testament to justify the present use of incense condemns, not justifies. The offering of literal incense on earth terminated at the cross: incense is now offered in the heavenly sanctuary. Rev. 5: 8; 8: 3.

In the Old Testament, literal incense offered on a literal altar symbolized prayer. Ps. 141: 2. Prayer is now offered on a spiritual altar. Mal. 1: 11; Heb. 13:15; 1 Cor. 9: 13; "Gospel Workers," p. 255. We also have spiritual altars upon which spiritual sacrifices are offered. 1 Pet. 2: 5; Rom. 12: 1; Heb. 13: 15, 16. Since the Old Testament typical services ceased at the cross (Matt. 27: 50, 51), the *literal* and the *spiritual* do *not* have *simultaneous* application *upon earth,* and will not do so in "this dispensation of the Holy Spirit."

Page 189 seeks to justify holy water—literal water—by the same principle of applying literally the things of literal Israel:—

"Why do Catholics sprinkle themselves on entering a church? What warranty in the Bible for the use of holy water? . . . How explain the *use of holy water in the Old Law?*—Viz., 'Aaron and his sons shall wash their hands and feet in it [a brazen laver], when they are going into the tabernacle.' Ex. 30: 19; Num. 5: 17; 8: 7; cf. Ex. 19: 10-14; Lev. 8: 6."

Water is the symbol of the Holy Spirit. See Isa. 44: 3; Zech. 9: 1; John 7: 37, 39, etc. Therefore, the cleansing in the *spiritual* temple—"to drive forth the evil one"—is done by *spiritual* water, not literal.

On page 190 of the same book we read: "Why do Catholic priests wear such peculiar clothes during services? The vestments worn by the priests at Mass mark him a man apart from the world, *as in the Old Law.* Ex. 28: 4."

In Rev. 1: 12-20 Jesus Christ is pictured in heaven wearing the vestments of the priesthood; but on earth, *spiritual* robes (Isa. 61: 10; Rev. 3: 4, 5; 6: 11, etc.) and the *spiritual* priesthood belong to the church.

"Keenan's Catechism," p. 193, says:—

"Was the manna of the desert a figure of the Christian sacrament of the Eucharist? Yes, Christ Himself declares it. But if the Protestant bread and wine be the Christian Pasch, then the figure is greater than the reality, and Christianity is degraded even below the level of the Judaic rite. The manna was miraculous bread. The manna was a heavenly food, given only to the people of God; the Protestant sacrament is the common food of all men. . . .
"But when we look at the Catholic Pasch, and believe in the illustrious sacrifice and sacrament in which the body and blood of Jesus are offered and received, we are extricated from such difficulties; our understanding becomes unclouded; we perceive at once the noble and significant *figure of the Old,* and the infinitely superior reality of the New Law."

The above reasoning is contrary to the Biblical law of interpretation, which teaches that the literal things of the Old Testament are spiritually applied in the New. The manna, a *literal* substance, could not typify the *Mass, another literal* substance, notwithstanding their claim that the bread becomes Christ. Christ is the *living* reality of the manna; the Bible is the *spiritual* manna. Matt. 4: 4, etc. The *literal* is in heaven; the *spiritual* is on earth.

On page 202 of the same catechism, we read:—

"Do Catholics act properly in carrying the Adorable Sacrament with religious pomp and solemnity in processions? If *the Israelites carried the ark of the alliance with great solemnity (Joshua 6),* Catholics have much more reason to carry in triumph the holy sacrament, of which the *ark was only a mere figure.*"

Instead of being the "shadow of *heavenly* things," as we are explicitly informed by God's Word, the ark is erroneously taken to be a figure of the sacrament—an earthly thing.

Pages 209-210 show the Catholic belief that their priesthood is the continuance of the Melchisedek priesthood. A *literal* Old Testament priesthood is thus erroneously interpreted to foreshadow another *literal* earthly priesthood. The *literal* priesthood is in heaven, and the *spiritual* priesthood is on earth. See 1 Pet. 2: 5.

Pages 210-212 maintain that as the priest of the Mosaic economy was ordained "that he may offer up gifts and sacrifices for sins," so the priest of the Catholic Church offers the sacrifice of the Mass as "a true, propitiatory sacrifice or sin-offering." But the Scriptures state that Christ is our Priest, and He is constantly offering the merits of His own blood, as a propitiation for our sins. Heb. 9: 11-12; Rom. 3: 24-25, etc.

Page 111 of "Keenan's Catechism" teaches that the Pope is "the *visible* head of the church." In an editorial in the *Tablet* (Roman Catholic) of June 13th, 1914, Italy is mentioned as that nation:—

"Whose capital is also the centre of Christendom, and against the spoliation of which as the seat of his necessary temporal dominion, *Christendom's head, in the person of our High Priest,* still makes his dignified protest."

Thus Roman Catholics regard the Pope as "our High Priest." Paul states that "our High Priest" is in heaven sitting on "the throne of grace." Heb. 8: 1; 4: 14-16. On earth there is no "*visible* head of the church." The Holy Spirit is the *invisible, spiritual* head of the church. John 14: 16-17; 16: 7.

Cardinal Manning wrote:—

"God has instituted His kingdom upon earth, and fixed the head and centre of it *in Rome, as of old in Jerusalem.*"

The teaching that God has established a kingdom upon earth, with Rome as the new, *literal* centre, is really the basic error of the Papacy. From that *literal* kingdom idea, with a *visible* city, and a *visible* head, have come all the other Papal errors—even the putting to death of those who disagreed with the Pope may be justified by the destruction of the enemies of the Jews, as recorded in the Old Testament. The theocracy was a government of God, through a *visible* head. And God's enemies were slain by the Israelites when He ordered them to go to battle. *If* the *literal* still operated, the Papal idea would have much to support it. But the church is the *spiritual* Jerusalem, and uses the *spiritual* sword of the Spirit—God's Word. Heb. 4: 12; Ephes. 6: 17.

Instead of adorning churches, clothing, etc., with *literal* crosses, Christ asks each believer to take up his *spiritual* cross and follow Him. Matt. 10: 38; 16: 24, etc. In the Scriptures, the *literal* things are associated with Jesus, and the *spiritual* application is always associated with the ministry of the Holy Spirit. Jesus bore a *literal* cross; we bear a *spiritual* cross. The thief on the cross was *literally* crucified "with" Jesus, but we are to be *spiritually* crucified "with Him." Rom. 6: 6-8, etc. We must have a *spiritual* death, burial and resurrection "with Him," and must *spiritually* reign "with Him" before we can have a *literal* resurrection, and literally reign "with Him" in the eternal kingdom. The New Testament Epistles contain many spiritual applications concerning death and resurrection.

By a process of sanctification—of fighting against unholy desires and keeping the will subjected to God's authority—the believer goes through a *spiritual,* purifying process. 1 Pet. 1: 22, etc. Satan, who *literalizes every spiritual truth,* places a *literal* purgatory after death, as the purifier of the soul to fit one for habitation with God.

The east was employed in the Old Testament as a *symbol* of the place of the rising of "the Sun of Righteousness" to give light and blessing to God's people (see P.K. 688, 719; D.A. 261, etc.). By literalizing the east, Satan led the people into the idolatries of sun-worship, and by it also brought *Sun-day keeping into the Christian church.* By *literalizing* the number eight, which is employed in Scripture as a *symbol* of Christ's resurrection, Satan, by specious reasoning, deceived people into making Sunday, the first day of the week, a kind of "eighth day," to be observed in honour of the Lord's resurrection. See my "Christ Conquers or Why Christ Rose on Sunday, the First Day of the Week," pp. 12, 14, 38, 42-44, 123-129.

The *literal* east, the *literal* number eight with reference to Sunday, a *literal* king (the Pope), a *literal* throne, *literal* bread, *literal* "holy" water, *literal* altars, *literal* priests, *literal* robes, *literal* candles, *literal* incense, *literal* earthly sanctuaries, *literal* images instead of *mental* images. *literal* interpretations of the prophecies pertaining to Israel and the anti-christ, and the *literal*, Palestinian "Armageddon," are all *literal* counterfeits of those things which are *spiritually* applied in the New Testament in connection with *spiritual* Israel. The Papacy is Satan's counterfeit of the ministry and kingdom of the Lord Jesus. Fostered by the Papacy is that system of interpretation which *literalizes,* in connection with Palestine and the *literal* Jews, those prophecies outlining the details of the final conflict involving *spiritual* Israel and the Sabbath.

In "this dispensation of the Holy Spirit," the *literal* interpretation of the things of *Israel* is contrary to the Scriptures. The *principle* of interpreting *spiritually* that which is mentioned in the Old Testament concerning Israel and her enemies is expressed by Paul:—

"No, you have *not* come near to *something material.* . . . No! you have come to Mt. Zion, and to the city of the living God, the heavenly Jerusalem." Weymouth's Translation, Heb. 12: 18-22.

In this "dispensation of the Holy Spirit" (T.M. 511) the things of the kingdom of Christ are *spiritual.* Jesus, the King, is "*invisible*" (1 Tim. 1: 17; 6: 16), and His Representative, the Holy Spirit, is also unseen to human eyes, and because the world "*seeth Him not*" (John 14: 17) it rejects the *spiritual* things of the *spiritual* kingdom: even the Third Angel's Message.

CHAPTER XIII.

SATAN DECEIVES TO-DAY AS HE DECEIVED THE JEWS.

History repeats itself. As Satan blinded the eyes of the Jews to the true understanding of the prophecies (see P.K. 686, 687) "in order to prepare the way for the rejection of Christ at His [first] coming," so, to-day, the evil one causes people to reject the Third Angel's Message by misinterpreting the same prophecies in the same way as the Jews.

In "The Desire of Ages," p. 509, we read:—

"But to-day in the religious world there are multitudes who, as they believe, are working for the establishment of the kingdom of Christ *as an earthly* and *temporal* dominion. They desire to make our Lord the *ruler of the kingdom of this world*. . . . They expect Him to rule through legal enactments, enforced by human authority. . . . *The establishment of such a kingdom is what the Jews desired in the days of Christ.* They would have received Jesus, had He been willing to establish a *temporal* dominion, to enforce what they regarded as the laws of God, and to make them expositors of His will, and the agents of His authority. But He said, 'My kingdom is not of this world.' *He would not accept the earthly throne.*"

The Jews looked for "an earthly and temporal dominion." The people of to-day, also, look for "an earthly and temporal dominion." The Jews claimed the *literal* fulfilment of the prophecies concerning Israel, refusing to see that they forfeited their right to them because of their failure to meet the conditions. Because of their false interpretations of the prophecies concerning the kingdom promised to Israel, the Jews rejected Christ and His *spiritual* kingdom. Similarly, to-day, many professing Christians fall into the same error of interpreting the prophecies concerning Israel in a *literal* Palestinian sense, failing to see that the Jews, by their rejection and crucifixion of Christ, forfeited all right to them. As the *literal, Palestinian-centred system of interpretation was the means of the Jews' rejection of Christ* and His spiritual kingdom, so, to-day, *the literal, Palestinian-centred system of interpretation causes people to reject Christ's last-day Message* concerning the spiritual kingdom of Israel.

THE DIFFERENCE BETWEEN FUTURISM AND THE THIRD ANGEL'S MESSAGE.

Whereas the Papacy-fostered system of interpretation known as Futurism applies *literally*, in a Palestinian sense, the things pertaining to Israel, the Third Angel's Message follows the system of interpretation outlined in the New Testament and Spirit of Prophecy and applies the things of Israel in a *spiritual*, world-wide sense.

The New Testament teaching is clear and decisive that, since the rejection of the *Jewish nation*, city and temple, the church—spiritual Israel—is now God's "Jerusalem" or "temple." See Rev. 11: 1, 2; Ephes. 2: 21, 22, etc. "The man of sin" who was to sit "in the *temple of* God, showing himself that he is God" (2 Thess. 2: 3, 4) is the Papacy within the *spiritual* temple—the professedly Christian church. Futurists—whether Papal or supposedly-Protestant—apply this prophecy in connection with a *literal* temple yet to be built in *literal* Jerusalem by an enemy of the *literal* Jews. The Roman Catholic teaching is stated in the following extract from the "Controversial Catechism," p. 115, by the Rev. Stephen Keenan:—

"Is it clear from Scripture that Rome will be the seat of Antichrist? Ans.: No; it is much more evident that *Jerusalem will be his seat*. In the Gospel of St. Matthew (24: 1-15) Christ speaks first of the *temple* of Jerusalem, and immediately after connects this with the abomination of desolation to be seen standing in the holy place; evidently pointing out that *temple* as the holy place, *where the beast should be enthroned*; and this is clearly confirmed by the Apocalypse (11: 8), where, speaking of the wars to be carried on by the Antichrist, and of those that were to be slain by him, St. John says: 'And their dead bodies shall lie in the streets of the great city, which spiritually is called Sodom and Egypt, where also our Lord was crucified.' Now, the Lord was crucified in *Jerusalem*, not in Rome, therefore *Jerusalem*, not Rome, *will be the seat of Antichrist*. See also on this subject: Apoc. 11, 12, 13, 17."

Thus, by interpreting *literally* the things which at one time pertained to *national* Israel, Roman Catholics and many Protestants are blinded to the truths of the Third Angel's Message, which has for its basis the teaching that the things which were *literal* and *Palestinian* in the days of *national* Israel now have their *spiritual, world-wide* application in connection with *spiritual* Israel —the church.

Advocating the erroneous Futuristic system of interpretation, the comments in Schofield's Bible declare:—

"Israel *as a nation* . . . is *yet to have its greatest exaltation as the earthly* people of God. . . . According to the prophets, Israel, regathered from all nations, restored to her own land. and converted, is *yet* to have her greatest earthly exaltation and glory." *Notes on Rom. 11.* "Jerusalem is yet to be the religious centre of the earth." "In the days when *Jerusalem* has been made the *centre* of earth's worship, *the Jew will then be the missionary, and to the very nations now called Christians. Notes on Zech. 8.*"

Futurists ignore the plain declarations of Scripture that "wrath is come upon them [the *literal* nation of Israel] to the *uttermost*" (1 Thess. 2: 16); that as a nation they have been so broken that they *"cannot* be made whole again" (Jer. 19: 11); and that Christ had explicitly declared to them: "The kingdom of God shall be *taken from you*, and *given to a nation* [the church, 1 Pet. 2: 9] bringing forth the fruits thereof." Matt. 21: 43. Had the Jews been faithful, they would have *literally* fulfilled the prophecies which Futurists say the Jewish nation will yet fulfil. Writing of "what *might have been* the condition of Jerusalem" had the Jews "heeded the light which heaven had sent" them, God's servant states:—

"*Had Israel* as a nation preserved her allegiance to heaven, Jerusalem would have stood forever the elect of God." G.C., p. 19.

"If the leaders in Israel had received Christ, He *would have* honoured them as *His messengers to carry the Gospel* to the world. To them was given the opportunity of becoming the heralds of the kingdom of the grace of God . . . Jesus . . . turned to another class to proclaim His message." D.A., p. 231. See also pp. 576, 577.

The Jews, clinging tenaciously to the belief that the prophecies concerning Israel must be *literally* fulfilled through the Jewish *nation*, were so blinded that they did not recognise the fulfilment of those prophecies in the experiences of the Messiah and *spiritual* Israel. The Apostles declared: "But those things, which God before had shewed by the mouth of *all His prophets*, that Christ should suffer, *He hath fulfilled*." Acts 3: 18. "Yea, and *all the prophets* from Samuel and those that follow after, *as many as have spoken, have likewise foretold of these days*." Acts 3: 24. See also Acts 13: 27, 29, 33, etc. Similarly, to-day, modern theologians are so blinded by the belief of a *literal* Palestinian fulfilment of the prophecies pertaining to Israel, that they do not recognise the *spiritual* fulfilment now taking place. The temple described in Ezek. 40-48 has its fulfilment in the Christian church—the spiritual temple which the Messiah is *now* building, and in which He *now* reigns in power. Zech. 6: 12, 15; A.A. 595-600. The river of living spiritual water is *now* emerging from the church to bless a needy world. Ezek. 47: 1-12; Joel 3: 18; Zech. 14: 8; A.A., p. 13; John 7: 37-39. The spiritual latter rain is *now* falling. A.A. 54, 55. The spiritual gathering of Israel and Judah is *now* taking place. Isa. 11: 11, 12. The walls of spiritual Jerusalem are *now* being built. Isa. 60: 1-11. In the Person of His Holy Spirit, Jesus is *now* reigning in spiritual Jerusalem. Micah 4: 7; Joel 3: 17, 21; Isa. 24: 23; Ezek. 48: 35, etc. Satan is now endeavouring to assemble his hosts against spiritual Israel. Ezek. 38, 39; Joel 3; Zech. 14.

Had the Jews been faithful, such prophecies as Ezek. 38, 39; Zech. 14; Joel 3, depicting the gathering of many nations *against Israel*, followed by their destruction and *Israel's triumph*, would have been fulfilled in their *literal*, Palestinian sense. Now, however, they meet their *spiritual* fulfilment in connection with *spiritual* Israel. Writing of the last days, God's servant says: "If he could blot them from the earth, his triumph would be complete. *As he* influenced the *heathen* nations [referred to in Ezek. 38, 39; Joel 3; Zech. 14] to destroy Israel, *so in the near future he will stir up the wicked powers of earth to destroy the people of God."* P.K. 587, 588. As we have shown elsewhere, the Spirit of Prophecy applies the gathering of the nations against Israel and Jerusalem, depicted in Zech. 14, in connection with the attempt of the people of *spiritual* Babylon to destroy *spiritual* Israel. Ezek. 38, 39; Joel 3, etc., are parallel prophecies giving additional features of the *same spiritual struggle*, and must be interpreted in the same way as Zech. 14. By interpreting these prophecies in a *literal*, Jewish, Palestinian sense, Futurists fail to recognize the Third Angel's Message. The Revelator points to our day (Rev. 12: 12, 17) as the time of special Satanic hatred against the remnant of Israel. Those prophecies depicting the final gathering of the forces of evil against Jerusalem and Israel, and Israel's triumph over her enemies through the wonderful intervention of God, are precious messages of encouragement for the remnant church.

CHAPTER XIV.

THE PRINCIPLE OF THE WORLD-WIDE SYMBOLIZED BY THE LOCAL.

"History repeats itself"—this oft-quoted statement contains truth deserving of our study. King Solomon uttered the same thought when he declared: "That which hath been is now; and that which is to be hath already been." Eccles. 3: 15.

However, we are desirous of dealing with explicit facts and not with vague generalities, and so turn our attention to the Scriptures for definite instruction regarding the correct application to be made from the events of Biblical history.

Sin is a world-wide disease. Men may differ in nationality, may live in different countries, but one thing is common to all—"all have sinned and come short of the glory of God." Rom. 3: 23. Because of this inescapable fact it has been possible for God to illustrate His attitude towards all sin and righteousness by His dealings with His chosen nation and their enemies who opposed the working out of God's purpose in Israel. Observe the following statement from God's servant:—

"The work of God in the earth presents, from age to age, *a striking similarity in every great reformation* or religious movement. *The principles of God's dealing with men are ever the same.* The important movements of the present have their *parallel in those of the past,* and the *experience of the church in former ages has lessons of great value for our own time.*" GC. 343.

From the local events which occurred in Palestine we are instructed in the New Testament to discern world-wide happenings in the "church" period. This is the application made by the inspired writers of the New Testament—they took hold of the *local* things of *ancient* Israel and employed them as *prophecies* or as *typical principles* applicable to the *world-wide church.* The history of the struggle between the forces of right and wrong repeats itself in the church—spiritual Israel—as it did in national Israel. The principles involved are the same—God has not changed, and Satan still hates God and all who endeavour to obey the law of God—the only difference being that, in the days of the Palestinian Israel, God had a *national* people who had *national* enemies. *Then* things operated on a *national basis centred in Palestine* and, hence, in the very nature of that economy, were largely *literal.* Since God's rejection of the Jewish nation as His chosen people, and His callihg of the church—spiritual Israel—to be His elect, the literal things of the *national* regime have been sublimated into the *spiritual* things of *spiritual* Israel.

The New Testament application of the Old Testament economy (sanctuary services, types, prophecies, etc.) does not refer to literal things in Palestine but to the spiritual in all the world— the application is *based* on the *literal, national* things of the old *Palestinian regime,* but they are lifted on to a spiritual, *world-wide plane.* Thus history repeats itself—"that which is to be hath already been; and God requireth that which is past." The past becomes the present—*the past is a prophecy of the future*—no longer restricted to the literal things of the Jewish nation or its country, but applying to the world-wide realms of the church; no longer limited to the visible kings and priests of the literal throne of David and the visible things of the literal sanctuary or temple, but applicable to the things of the invisible Lord—the spiritual kingdom and the heavenly sanctuary services on behalf of spiritual Israel in all the world.

In national Israel certain laws and principles of God's dealings with sin were represented by *national* types, but the application of these laws and principles in the *spiritual* realm is world-wide.

By observing this principle we can see why the different letters of instruction sent to different people and churches are included in the Bible and in the Testimonies of God's servant. Letters of instruction to the Romans, Galatians, Colossians, Thessalonians, Hebrews, Philippians, Ephesians, Corinthians, etc., or to individuals such as Philemon, Titus, Timothy were included in the Canon of Scripture because the counsel, principles, and the truths contained therein are suitable for the members of Christ's church in *all parts of the world.* The inspired writers were not parochial in their prophetic descriptions of the last days; they looked beyond the narrow confines of their national boundaries to the world field, *though they gave vivid pictures of world events steeped in the atmosphere, customs and diction of their native land.*

The Bible was not written for the benefit of one nation more than another—it is the world's Book. "God so loved the *world* that He gave His only begotten Son, that *whosoever* believeth in

Him should not perish, but have everlasting life." John 3: 16. John pointed to Jesus and declared: "Behold the Lamb of God, which taketh away the sin of the *world*." John 1: 29. "He is the propitiation of our sins: and not for ours only, but also for the sins of the *whole world*." 1 John 2: 2. The whole Bible is centred in Jesus and His church, and all that is written is related to the plan of redemption. "God is no respecter of persons." Acts 10: 34. The New Testament makes it clear that, when God finally rejected the Jewish nation as His chosen people, He had no further use for any earthly, literal nation, land, city, temple, priest or sacrifice. The church is now the Israel of God—a spiritual, world-wide Israel —and the national things which belonged to the literal nation in the promised land are now applied by the Scriptures and the Spirit of Prophecy to the church in a spiritual, world-wide sense.

The visions of the prophets, *though couched in a local setting,* broaden in their New Testament application to portray *world-wide events*. They have a two-fold application—a *local* during the days of *national* Israel, and a *world-wide* during the dispensation of the church—*spiritual Israel*. The land which God promised to Abraham and his seed (Gen. 12: 1, 7; 13: 15-17; 15: 7, 18; 17: 8) was a *type of the world*. Rom. 4: 13. Many prophetic students fail to see this principle of interpretation because they are blinded by doctrines based upon the future literal, *Palestinian* fulfilments in reference to the *literal* Jewish people.

That misconception of prophetic interpretation prevents them from seeing the Third Angel's Message—thus the importance of adhering to the divinely-given laws of interpretation is fully demonstrated. In another chapter we have shown that the millennium is the dividing line between the dispensation when the things of Israel have their spiritual application, and the kingdom of glory when Israel will enter into her everlasting land. Those things which Israel will then enjoy as eternal realities are presented as *spiritual* possessions *now* in this "church" dispensation. Thus the promise of Palestine (see texts given above) will find its larger fulfilment in the world to come and also has a spiritual application now in this "dispensation of the Spirit." The promised land—Palestine—was a *miniature world* in which God illustrated His kingdom and His way of dealing with sin. "Thy way, O God, is in the sanctuary." Ps. 77: 13. The sanctuary, also, was a miniature representation of something far greater—it was only a "shadow of heavenly things.' Heb. 8: 5, etc. In the same way Jerusalem, the throne of David, the land, the people, and history and prophecy relating to Israel, were all "shadows of heavenly things." By this principle we can thus see world-wide events depicted in the records giving the history of literal Israel. The experiences of Israel—including the unfulfilled conditional prophecies—were recorded as "types," "figures"—local events typifying world-wide occurrences in the experiences of the church. See Rom. 15: 4; 1 Cor. 10: 6, 11, margins.

CHAPTER XV.

THE PRINCIPLE OF THE WORLD-WIDE SYMBOLIZED BY THE LOCAL—DEMONSTRATED IN THE REVELATION.

The visions of the prophets, though couched in a local setting, broaden out in their New Testament application to portray *world-wide* events. They have a two-fold application: a local during the days of National Israel, and a world-wide during the dispensation of the Church—Spiritual Israel.

To show that this principle is employed throughout the Book of Revelation, attention is directed to the following verses:—

Rev. 1: 6 —"Hath made us kings and priests unto God." "Melchizedek, king of Salem . . . was the *priest* of the most high God." Gen. 14: 18. Thus this ancient *king-priest* of Salem was a type of Christ the world-wide *King-Priest* (see Ps. 110: 1, 4; Heb. 7: 1-24; 8: 1, etc.). Believers share with the Lord the privileges of ministry and service and are also designated as king-priests. See also Rev. 5: 10; 20: 4-6; 1 Pet. 2: 9. Here, in the commencement of Revelation, we see the principle of that which was local and literal being employed in a spiritual, world-wide sense in connection with the Saviour and His church. As the Revelation in its opening verses adopts this principle it should be expected that it would be maintained— as one of the unalterable laws of God—throughout the book. Wherein expositors do not abide by this principle in their study of this book they err in their interpretations—as Futurists do by applying again in a local, literal sense, as in the days of national Israel, the things of Israel mentioned in the Revelation. In this category is the erroneous belief of a literal conflict of nations to be fought in Megiddo (Rev. 16: 16), taken from the reference (Judges 4 and 5) to the ancient conflict of Israel with the kings of Canaan "by the waters of Megiddo." Judg. 5: 19. The following examples will also show the principle of the true interpretation of the Scriptures, namely, that the literal, *local* things of the Old Testament are brought into the imagery employed by the Revelator in depicting *world-wide* things in connection with our Lord and His church—and their enemies.

Rev. 1: 7—"All kindreds of the earth shall wail because of Him."
In this verse John takes us back to Zech. 12: 11-14, to which
the translators have turned our attention by placing it in the
margin. In Zech. 12: 11-14 we read: "In that day there shall
be a great mourning in Jerusalem, as the mourning of *Hadadrimmon* in the *valley of Megiddon*. And the land (i.e.,
Palestine) shall mourn, every family apart, the family of the
house of David . . . the family of Nathan . . . the family of
the house of Levi . . . the family of Shimei . . . all the families
that remain, every family." The Hebrew for "family"—
—mishpachah—according to Dr. Strong, means "kindred, tribe."
Zech. 12: 11-14, speaking of the mourning in Jerusalem as "the
mourning of Hadadrimmon in the valley of Megiddon," says:
"The land shall *mourn, every* family . . . *all* the families"—
or kindreds, or tribes. When quoting this passage of Zechariah
in predicting the world-wide scenes associated with His second
coming, Jesus said: "Then shall all the *tribes* of the earth
mourn." Matt. 24: 30. John's application of the same verses
in Zechariah is: "All *kindreds* [or "tribes," as in Matt. 24: 30]
of the earth shall wail because of Him." It is to these same
"tribes"—"every kindred"—that the message of Rev. 14: 6 is
being heralded. These are not Palestinian "families," "tribes,"
or "kindreds"—the Message is world-wide. Zech. 12:10
points to a Palestinian event—the crucifixion of Christ
(compare Zech. 12: 10 with John 19: 37). It was the custom
of the prophets to look at some Palestinian fulfilment and, at
the same time, to look beyond to the great world-wide scenes
of Armageddon. Some readers of the prophecies fail to take
into account the ancient, local setting and, consequently, misapply the Palestinian aspect in a literal sense when considering the final scenes associated with Armageddon. John shows
how the factors which at one time had a local significance are
now to be applied in a world-wide sense—and that is how he
brings into his pictures of the world-wide Armageddon all the
Old Testament persons, events, and places, including
Megiddo.

Rev. 1: 7 quotes from Zech. 12: 11-14, and gives it a world-wide
application at the coming of Christ. Zech. 12: 10-14 prophesied the mourning to take place in "the land" of Palestine
when Christ was crucified—the despairing grief of the disciples
when Jesus, their only hope, was dead. Matt. 24: 30; Rev.
1: 7, apply that dark and terrible grief as belonging to the

wicked in all the world at the last day. Their grief will be in the realisation that, by a life of sin, they have crucified "the son of God afresh, and put Him to an open shame" (Heb. 6: 6)—that they have been at "war" with their Saviour, Who then will be their Judge and destroyer. The mourning of the wicked in that day is declared by Zech. 12: 10 to be "as the mourning of Hadadrimmon in the *valley of Megiddon."* Hadadrimmon was "a place in Palestine"—Dr. Strong. This place was "in the valley of Megiddon." It is self-evident that "the valley of Megiddon" has the same world-wide application as have the other factors quoted from the same passage by Jesus in Matt. 24: 30, and by John in Rev. 1: 7, in their description of the world-wide events to transpire at the time of the second advent. "Necho, king of Egypt, came up to fight against Charchemish by Euphrates; and Josiah went out against him," despite the "words of Necho from the mouth of God, and came to fight in the valley of Megiddon." As an *ally of Babylon,* Josiah fought and was slain at Megiddo—against the express desire of God. The mourning and lamentation for Josiah at Megiddo mentioned in 2 Chron. 35: 24, 25, form the basis of Zech. 12: 10-14, which, in turn, is that upon which Jesus in Matt. 24: 30, and John in Rev. 1: 7, base their statements regarding the mourning of all the wicked *in all the world—* —the antitypical Megiddo ("Armageddon")—at the end of the world. In Rev. 16: 12-16 the Euphrates and Megiddo are also associated together as they are in 2 Chron. 35: 20-22; 2 Kings 23: 29, 30. Their mention in Revelation in connection with the mourning of all kindreds and tribes at the second advent is, of course, in a world-wide sense—nothing less can possibly measure up to the principle of interpretation—that local things of the Old Testament are employed in a worldwide sense—clearly demonstrated throughout the Revelation.

Rev. 1: 20—In this verse the seven candlesticks of the old sanctuary are used to represent the seven periods of the *world-wide church* in the gospel dispensation. The seven cities "in Asia" (Rev. 1: 11) in which were located the seven symbolic churches represent *world-wide* activity during seven periods of this era.

Rev. 2: 14—A description of apostasy in the Christian church is based upon the experience of Balaam.

Rev. 2: 20—The Papal apostasy, bringing the customs and practices of ancient sun-worshippers into the world-wide Christian church, finds its local analogy in Jezebel's introduction into

Israel in the land of Palestine of the same sun-worshipping customs and practices.

Rev. 3: 4, 5—"White raiment" is promised the faithful from all the world. The priests of the literal sanctuary services wore "fine linen" called the "holy garments" (Lev. 6: 10; 16: 4, 32; Ezek. 44: 17, 18).

Rev. 6: 1-8—The four horses of the Apocalypse symbolize the work of the professed church of Christ in spreading the gospel story to the world. In these symbols we can read the struggle the true church had, and still has, with spiritual Babylon. The basis of this vision is found in Zech. 1: 8-12; 6: 1-8, where Zechariah had a vision of coloured horses. Israel had been taken into Babylon, and had not been delivered from the bondage or hindrances of the latter. God encouraged His people to look to Him to lead them on to final and complete victory from Babylon. Those things which pertained to *literal Israel and literal Babylon* are employed in the Revelation in connection with the *world-wide* struggle between *spiritual Israel* and *spiritual* Babylon.

Rev. 6: 14—"The heavens shall be rolled together as a scroll; and all their host shall fall down . . . as a falling fig from the fig tree." Isa. 34: 4. This prophecy in its *local setting* was *part* of the prediction of Isa. 34 regarding the *destruction of the Idumeans,* but, in its secondary application, the falling of the stars represents a sign to the *world* of the coming doom, followed by the opening heavens revealing the descending *Son of God coming to destroy all the wicked of the entire globe*—the world-wide Idumeans, the enemies of spiritual Israel.

Rev. 6: 15—Depicting the terror of the wicked at the second advent, the Revelator quotes from Isa. 2: 10-22. After the glorious promise, given in Isa. 2: 1-5, of what God would do for them if they would "be willing and obedient" (ch. 1: 19), the prophet proceeds to describe the wrath of God which would fall on *impenitent Judah.* The prophecy of the threatened judgments of the Lord, given through Isaiah to the rebellious house of Judah, is taken by John to describe "the judgments that are to fall upon *an impenitent world at the time of the second advent of Christ.*" See P.K. 389.

Rev. 6: 16—The threat of divine judgment upon *the northern kingdom* included the statement "And they shall say to the mountains, Cover us; and to the hills, Fall on us." Hosea 10: 8.

The Revelator takes these words of threatened *judgment upon wicked Samaria,* and refers them *to the wicked of all the world at the second advent.*

Rev. 6: 17—The great day of wrath to come upon *the wicked Babylonians,* as pictured in Isa. 13: 1-22, depicts the great day of wrath *upon all the wicked at the coming of Christ.* The severe judgment *against Judah* in Zeph. 1: 14, etc., portray the wrath of God upon *the entire world at the Saviour's return.* See margin, Rev. 6: 17.

Rev. 7: 1-4—The sealing of the tribes of Israel refers back to the times of literal Israel. After their acceptance of the call to come out of Babylon (see Isa. 48: 20; Jer. 50: 8; 51: 6) the God-fearing among literal Israel determined to "make a sure covenant, and write it; and our princes, Levites, and priests, *seal unto it"*—or, as the margin says, "are at the *sealing,* or *sealed."* In Neh. 10: 1-29 we have "the names of them that *sealed* the covenant" as the synopsis at the heading of the chapter states. Thus the *local* event in Palestine is applied by the Revelator in a *world-wide* sense. Those who heed the call to come out of Babylon (Rev. 18: 4) prepare for the scourging seven last plagues which will be poured out upon all the unsealed—and especially upon those with the counterfeit sign, seal or mark—the mark of the beast. The Revelator describes the coming of *world-wide events,* but bases his prophecies of the future upon the *local* events of the past.

Rev. 7: 1-8—The *marking* of the foreheads of people *in Jerusalem,* described in Ezekiel 9, is a representation of a world-wide sealing message in connection with a work of Sabbath reform; and the *angels* going through *Jerusalem* bringing destruction upon the disobedient Jews is a picture of the *destroying angels bringing destruction to all the unprepared of the world at the seecond advent.*

Rev. 7: 9—*The promise to Abraham* of an *innumerable posterity* (Gen. 15. 5) finds its larger fulfilment in the total number of *the redeemed—*"a *great multitude,* which no man could number." The God-given name "Abraham" means "Father of a *great multitude."* See Gen. 17: 5.

Rev. 7: 14—Joshua's change of raiment in Zech. 3: 3-5 becomes the lot of all the saved.

Rev. 7: 17—David's Shepherd becomes the Shepherd to all the redeemed. Ps. 23: 1.

Rev. 7: 17—"The Lord God will wipe away tears from off all faces"—which Isa. 25: 6-8 states would be done *"in this mountain"*—points forward to the time when the *whole world* will be free from tears.

Rev. 11: 1—The measuring of the temple of Ezekiel's vision (40-48) becomes the measuring of *the world-wide church.* 1 Cor. 3: 9-16; 1 Cor. 6: 19; Eph. 2: 20-22; 1 Pet. 2: 4-5; A.A. 595, 413; PK. 36; 9T. 180; TM. 17.

Rev. 11: 2—The city of *Jerusalem* becomes the world-wide church. GC. 266.

Rev. 11: 3-12—The two olive trees seen by Joshua in Zech. 4: 2-14 symbolize the *Bible* which now goes to *all the world.*

Rev. 12: 9—*The serpent of the garden of Eden* is stated to be "The devil and *Satan,* which *deceiveth the whole world."*

Rev. 12: 17—*The woman's seed of Gen. 3: 15* is the *world-wide church* of Jesus Christ—the remnant of her seed, particularly, which is a *world-wide organization.*

Rev. 13: 3, 4, 8, 12, 15—The Revelator's picture of the struggle between spiritual Israel and the spiritual Babylonians over the Sabbath of God or the mark of the beast is based upon the experiences of the three faithful Hebrews. As stated in my "Christ Conquers," p. 115: "The three faithful Hebrews who refused to bow to the image of Babylon, represent the people of the Third Angel's Message who will refuse to bow to the spiritual image of the beast in spiritual Babylon. In literal Babylon the people had to literally bow before a literal image; in spiritual Babylon people will spiritually bow before a spiritual image. What was literal then, is spiritual to-day. There cannot be the slightest doubt that John had the experience of Shadrach, Meshach, and Abed-nego before him, when he wrote of the final scenes regarding the beast and his image. . . . The people in Babylon were to 'worship the golden image' that Nebuchadnezzar had set up. This fact is stated six times—Dan. 3: 5, 7, 10, 12, 14, 18. In the Book of Revelation the fact of *worshipping* the *beast* and his *image* is mentioned six times—Rev. 13: 15; 14: 9, 11; 16: 2; 19: 20; 20: 4. . . . In the experiences of these men we are to see the prophecy of the struggle between Israel and Babylon over the *image* of the beast."

Rev. 13: 13—Sometimes God allowed false teachers to do their deceptive wonders to test Israel's love for Him. Deut. 13: 1, etc. In the last days God will permit "the false prophet" to work miracles to test spiritual Israel's loyalty.

Rev. 13: 16, 17—When Israel obeyed God's commands they were marked in their foreheads and in their hands. Deut. 6: 8; 11: 18; Ex. 13: 9, 16. Spiritual Israel, by obeying the Sabbath Commandment which contains *God's seal, sign, or mark* (Ex. 31: 1-18; Ezek. 20: 12, 20), show their loyalty to all of God's Commandments. Those who reject God's last-day Message and continue to observe Sunday (instituted by the instigation of Satan to turn people from obedience to God) will receive "the *mark* of the *beast*."

Rev. 14: 1—"A Lamb stood on Mount Sion and with Him an hundred and forty-four thousand." Lambs typifying Jesus were slain on Mount Sion where the temple was built. The 144,000 is made up of the twelve tribes of Israel, and there are 12,000 to each tribe. See Rev. 7: 1-4. Jerusalem, the temple, and the sacrificial services performed in the midst of the twelve tribes of Israel, are mentioned in the Revelation in connection with spiritual Israel in all the *world*.

Rev. 14: 4—"Being the *first fruits* unto God and to the Lamb." "Israel . . . the *first fruits* of His increase." Jer. 2: 3; James 1: 18. Concerning the reaping of their harvests in the promised land God commanded Israel: "When . . . ye reap the harvest thereof, then ye shall bring a sheaf of the *first fruits* of your harvest unto the priest." Lev. 23: 9-14. Paul applies the symbolism of the waving of the first fruits before God to "Christ the first fruits; afterward they that are Christ's at His coming." 1 Cor. 15: 23. That which pertained to the first fruits and harvests in *Palestine* is applied by the Revelator in a *world-wide* sense, in connection with spiritual Israel.

Rev. 14: 5—The description, in Zeph. 3: 13, of "the remnant of Israel" who would not "speak lies" nor have a "deceitful tongue" is applied by John to the *world-wide* remnant of the last days.

Rev. 14: 6, 7—The *local* day of Atonement (or Judgment day) in the economy of literal Israel was the type of the Investigative Judgment. Spiritual Israel is to proclaim to the *world* the Judgment-hour Message, which can be understood only in the light of the *local* services of ancient Israel. The Third Angel's Message is God's Message *because* it is based upon the *local* things of *literal Israel*.

Rev. 14: 8—The literal *fall of the city of Babylon* depicts the moral fall of spiritual world-wide Babylon. Isa. 21: 9; Jer. 51: 8.

Rev. 14: 8—"That great city" which "made all nations drink of the wine of the wrath of her fornication" refers, in a *world-wide sense,* to what was said of the ancient city of Babylon. Jer. 51: 7.

Rev. 14: 11—The burning of the *land of Idumea,* in Isa. 34: 5, 9-10, typifies the burning of *the wicked in all the world.*

Rev. 14: 15—The *reaping of the harvest in the valley of Jehoshaphat,* near Jerusalem (Joel 3: 13), is employed by John to picture the reaping of the *world's harvest at the second advent.*

Rev. 14: 18—The reaping of *the grapes in the valley of Jehoshaphat,* just outside the walls of Jerusalem (Joel 3: 13), is *the reaping of a world-wide harvest of the wicked,* ready for the wine-press of God's wrath.

Rev. 14: 20—John describes the winepress of God's wrath, which Christ treads at His second advent (Rev. 19: 15), as being trodden *outside the city of Jerusalem,* and thus he carries out the *picture* given in Joel 3 of the valley of Jehoshaphat where the harvest of grapes is obtained. The city of Jerusalem becomes the church in all the world and, consequently, the *harvest of grapes in Jehoshaphat's valley becomes a world-wide slaughter at the end of the world.*

Rev. 14: 20—One thousand and six hundred furlongs are equivalent to 200 miles, which is the circuit of the Holy Oblation where, in his symbolic vision of the church, Ezekiel pictures a mighty temple and city on the "very high mountain" *"in the land of Israel."* See my "What is Armageddon?" p. 16. John applies this vision concerning the city, temple and Holy Oblation in "the land of Israel" in a *world-wide* sense.

Rev. 15: 3-4—The song of Moses and the voice of triumph of the Israelites—over their persecutors who sought to physically enslave or to destroy them—at the Red Sea becomes the song of the remnant from the *whole world* over their persecutors who will seek to spiritually enslave or destroy them.

Rev. 15: 5—"The temple of the tabernacle of the testimony in heaven." The Book of Revelation centres around Jerusalem, the temple, the High Priest (Rev. 1: 12, 13), the 24 assistant priests (Rev. 4: 4-10; 5: 8-10, compare Ezek. 8: 16, etc.), and the various articles of furniture—the seven candlesticks (Rev. 1 to 3), the prayer altar (Rev. 5: 8; 8: 3-5), the ark of the testimony (or the golden chest wherein God's testimony—the Ten Commandments—was deposited), etc. All the visions and prophecies of the Revelation are inseparable from, and cannot be thoroughly understood without, a knowledge of the Old Testament temple and services at Jerusalem or the tabernacle in the midst of the camp of Israel in the wilderness.

Rev. 15: 8—When "the glory of the Lord filled the tabernacle, Moses was not able to enter into the tent of the congregation." Ex. 40: 34. We also read concerning the temple at Jerusalem: "When the priests were come out of the holy place the cloud filled the house of the Lord, so that the priests could not stand to minister because of the cloud: for the glory of the Lord had filled the house of the Lord." 1 Kings 8: 10, 11. Hence the Revelator's prophecy that when Jesus ceases His ministry in the heavenly temple, the temple will be "filled with smoke from the glory of God" and there will be no ministry of mercy during the outpouring of the seven last plagues. When Israel disobeyed God and provoked His wrath He plagued them. Aaron, the High Priest, then "stood between the dead and the living; and the plague was stayed." Num. 16: 44-50. The Revelator directs us to the time when, Christ's mediatorial work having been completed, He no longer stands between God's wrath and the living. Once again we see that the *local* things of literal Israel are applied by the Revelator in a *world-wide* capacity.

Rev. 16—The plagues of Egypt were God's judgments upon the *persecutors* of *national* Israel just before Israel's deliverance. The seven last plagues will be God's judgments upon the *persecutors* of *spiritual, world-wide Israel,* just preceding spiritual Israel's deliverance. Some of the seven last plagues will be similar to some of the plagues of Egypt. That which was *local* in Egypt will be *world-wide* in the last days.

Rev. 16: 12—The literal city of Babylon was built on the literal river Euphrates. Jer. 51: 13; P.K. 523. As a part of the strategy in the overthrow of literal Babylon, Cyrus turned the waters of the Euphrates from their accustomed bed. This drying of the waters of the Euphrates was predicted, and Cyrus was definitely named as the one who should do it. See Isa. 44: 27, 28; 45: 1. "As the king (Cyrus) saw the words foretelling . . . the manner in which Babylon should be taken; as he read the message addressed to him by the Ruler of the universe, 'I have girded thee . . . that they may know from the rising of the sun.'" PK. 557. The words of Jer. 50: 38, "A drought is upon her *waters; and they shall be dried up"* are quoted in Rev. 16: 12. See also Jer. 51: 36. The record of the overthrow of *literal* Babylon is thus used to depict the overthrow of the *world-wide, spiritual* Babylon. The Euphrates is Babylon's river and has no reference to any local nation or nations. The terminal of the prophecies which are *based upon Old Testament allusions is world-wide.*

Rev. 16: 12—The Medes and the Persians came "from the rising of the sun" (Isa. 41: 2, 25; Isa. 46: 11; 45: 6) to overthrow literal Babylon. The reference in Rev. 16: 12 to the kings of the east refers back to the *literal armies* which overthrew *literal Babylon*—the Revelator's use of the Old Testament narrative can mean nothing less than the coming of *spiritual* forces— —the *armies of heaven,* depicted in Rev. 19: 11-21, which will descend the eastern heavens to bring destruction to the world-wide, spiritual Babylon. For further consideration of this theme see my "What is Armageddon?" pp. 34-36.

Rev. 16: 13—The false teachers and *unclean spirits* (see Zech. 13: 2), who troubled the *land of Palestine* in the days of literal Israel are here referred to in connection with the *world-wide* apostasy of formal Christianity when "the kings and governors" (represented by the *"Dragon"*—see T.M. 39, 62) enforce the Sunday laws dictated by the *beast* and *the False Prophet.*

Rev. 16: 16—The first recorded conflict of literal Israel opposed by the sun-worshipping Canaanites who were *"all"* destroyed "by the waters of *Megiddo"* (Judges 5: 19-21; 4: 16) becomes part of the background to picture the *world-wide spiritual* conflict where the sun-day worshippers who have been attacking spiritual Israel are destroyed.

Rev. 16: 19—The cup of wrath given to the *enemies of Jerusalem,* mentioned in Isa. 51: 17, 22; Jer. 25: 12-29, becomes the cup for the three sections of spiritual Babylon, which include the *whole of rebellious mankind.*

"The *great* city," Babylon of the Old Testament (Dan. 4: 30), is *the world of confusion* in the New Testament—Rev. 16: 19; 17: 5; 18: 10, 21.

Rev. 16: 21—The plague of hail upon Egypt (Ex. 9: 23-25) is a world-wide plague at the end.

Rev. 17: 1—*The city Babylon* "that dwellest upon many waters," of Jer. 51: 13, becomes a *world-wide organization*—"The waters which thou sawest. *where the whore sitteth,* are peoples, and multitudes, and nations, and peoples." Rev. 17: 15. *A literal city on the river Euphrates becomes the apostate system of religion controlling the world.*

Rev. 17: 2—*The wine of the city of Babylon* (Jer. 51: 7) which made the nations of antiquity mad is the wine or *teachings of the spiritual, world-wide Babylon.* This false teaching causes the nations to think and act wrongly.

Rev. 17: 4—The golden cup in the hand of the city of Babylon (Jer. 51: 7) becomes the golden cup in the hand of the *world-wide Babylon.*

Rev. 18: 1—*The glory of the Lord which filled the temple Ezekiel saw* in vision—a temple which, in a measure, would have been built, had the Jews been faithful (Ezek. 43: 2)—becomes the *spiritual glory of the loud cry of the Third Angel's Message.* This glory will lighten the whole earth. Also the *literal* glory of the second coming of Christ is pre-figured. Ezek. 43: 2. EW. 15, 286. GC. 640.

Rev. 18: 2—The doom pronounced upon the city of Babylon (Isa. 13: 19; 21: 9; Jer. 51: 8) becomes the doom pronounced upon the *world-wide Babylon.*

Rev. 18: 2—*When the ancient city of Babylon* was overthrown, *it became the habitation for wild creatures* (Isa. 13: 21; 21: 9; 34: 14; Jer. 50: 39; 51: 37). With this historic event as a background, the Revelator pictures *Babylon as the dwelling of devils.* Again, a world-wide meaning is given to local things. (See EW. 274, 277.)

Rev. 18: 2—*The ruins of Babylon* (and *Edom,* too) became the *habitation of unclean birds* (Isa. 13: 21; 14: 23; 34: 11); this description *is taken to represent the unclean state of members of the spiritual, world-wide Babylon.* Unclean birds in a certain locality represent people in all the world who are spiritually unclean. See EW. 274, 277.

Rev. 18: 3—The nations which traded with Babylon prospered (Isa. 47: 15), and those who have gone the way of the world-wide, spiritual Babylon have enjoyed worldly advantages.

Rev. 18: 4—As the *people of God were called out of Babylon* before its doom (Isa. 48: 20; Jer. 50: 8; 51: 6, 45) so *the remnant in all the world will be called out* before the outpouring of the plagues. However, it is well for us to note that the Jews removed their *bodies* from the *literal* locality of Babylon. To-day, in *all the world*, the church withdraws *spiritually* from a *spiritual* Babylon.

Rev. 18: 5—The judgment of literal Babylon "reacheth unto Heaven, and is lifted up even to the skies" (Jer. 51: 9); this is likewise said of the *world-wide*, spiritual Babylon.

Rev. 18: 6—Babylon of old was to be treated as she had treated Jerusalem (Jer. 50: 15, 29; 51: 24, 49); the *world-wide*, spiritual Babylon is to be treated as she had made God's people suffer.

Rev. 18: 7—Ancient Babylon said, "I shall be a lady forever." "I shall not sit as a widow, neither shall I know the loss of children" (Isa. 47: 7-8); the *world-wide Babylon* is to say the same things.

Rev. 18: 8—The city of Babylon was to have these "things come to thee in a moment in one day" (Isa. 47: 9); the *world-wide Babylon* is to have "her plagues come in one day, death, mourning, and famine."

Rev. 18: 8—Fire was to play a part in the destruction of the proud city (Isa. 47: 14; Jer. 32, 58; 50: 32); *spiritual Babylon* "Shall be utterly burned with fire."

Rev. 18: 8—Babylon was judged by Israel's "strong Redeemer" (Jer. 50: 34); "strong is the Lord God Who judgeth her"— *world-wide Babylon*.

Rev. 18: 9—There was a cry "among the nations" "at the noise of the taking of Babylon" (Jer. 50: 46); the nations of the world "shall bewail her, and lament for her"— the *world-wide, spiritual* Babylon.

Rev. 18: 20—There was rejoicing over the downfall of literal Babylon (Jer. 51: 48; Isa. 44: 23); there is to be rejoicing at the overthrow of the *universal Babylon*.

Rev. 18: 21—Jeremiah's servant, Seraiah, threw a stone into the *literal* river Euphrates to illustrate that Babylon would sink, and not rise again (Jer. 51: 63-64); the *world-wide Babylon* is to be thrown down and never rise again.

Compare Jer. 51: 36 with Jer. 50: 38. "Sea" is used in Jer. 51: 36 for the waters of the Euphrates in Jer. 50: 38. See also Isa. 44: 27, where "deep" is also used to describe the Euphrates. See also Josh. 24: 2, 14, 15, where the Euphrates is called "the flood." See also Rev. 12: 15, 16, etc.

Rev. 18: 24—"As Babylon hath caused the slain of Israel to fall, so at Babylon shall fall the slain of all the earth"—margin "country" (Jer. 51: 49); of the spiritual Babylon we read, "And in her was found the blood of prophets, and of saints, and of *all that were slain upon the earth.*"

Rev. 19: 13—In Isa. 63: 1-6 the Saviour is represented as coming *"from Edom,* with dyed garments *from Bozrah.* . . . Wherefore are thou red in thine apparel, and thy garments like him that treadeth in the winefat? I have trodden alone . . . . for I will tread them in mine anger, and trample them in My fury; their blood shall be sprinkled upon My garments, and I will stain all My raiment." *The Revelator quotes from that passage relating to Edom and Bozrah in describing the universal slaughter at the second advent.*

Rev. 19: 15—This verse links Isa. 63: 1-6 with Joel 3: 13 (and Rev. 14: 19-20), where the harvest of grapes is reaped in the valley of Jehoshaphat. *The valley of Jehoshaphat is to be no more a literal valley than Edom, or Bozrah.* The play is upon the meaning of the words—Edom for "red," and "Bozrah," "a vintage;" the valley of Jehoshaphat, "the valley of God's Judgment." The same principle of the significance of the meaning of names is employed in the other names in the Apocalypse. See the names of the seven cities "in Asia" (Rev. 1: 11), and read Uriah Smith's "Thoughts on the Revelation" dealing with the first three chapters of Revelation. A significance is attached to the use and meaning of names such as Jerusalem "the city of peace," and Babylon, meaning "confusion." Babylon, founded by Nimrod, whose name means "rebellious," is employed in the Revelation as the designation of a world in rebellion against God's law—a rebellion which ends in the *world-wide* slaughter of "Armageddon." The number 13 is employed in Scripture as the number for rebellion, and the 13th time Megiddo occurs in Scripture is in Rev. 16: 16. "Armageddon," meaning "the mountain of destruction," brings destruction to the Babylonian *world* of *rebellion* against the rulership of God.

For further examples of the meanings of names, see the chapters dealing with "The law of the Significance of Bible Names."

Rev. 19: 17—The call of the birds to come to "the land of Israel" to feast on the bodies of Gog and his army, mentioned in Ezek. 38, 39, is interpreted in Rev. 19: 17 as the call to all the fowls of the *world* to come to feast upon the bodies of *all the wicked* who will be destroyed in *all parts of the world.* Jer. 25: 30-33.

Rev. 19: 18—The description of the feast of the fowls on the bodies of Gog and his army (Ezek. 39: 18, 20) "upon the mountains of Israel" (Ezek. 39: 4) is employed in the Revelation as a picture of the feast of the fowls upon "the flesh of *all* men, both free and bond, both small and great."

Rev. 20: 7-9—Gog and Magog of Ezek. 38, 39 are applied to the world-wide forces led on by Satan against Christ and His church—they do not apply to Russia as taught by the Futurists. Only as we interpret Gog and his army in the light given by God in Rev. 20: 7-9 can we understand the words concerning Gog in Ezek. 38: 17: "Thus saith the Lord God; Art thou *he of whom I have spoken in old time by my servants the prophets of Israel,* which prophesied in those days *many years* that I would bring thee against them?" Surely no one would maintain that God *often* inspired His prophets, *over a long period of time,* to prophesy about Russia! But God has shown through His servants the prophets down through the centuries that Satan is constantly plotting against God's people and is ever stirring up the multitudes of the world to oppose the work of Christ on the earth.

To further prove that the use of Old Testament places, persons and events are brought into the Revelation by Jesus (Who is its Author, see Rev. 22: 16) in a world-wide sense in connection with His church and her enemies, we will observe this same law brought to view in the pronouncement of doom given by the prophets of literal Israel against ancient cities, and referred to by the Revelator in picturing the final downfall of spiritual Babylon:—

LITERAL, LOCAL IN THE OLD TESTAMENT.	SPIRITUAL, WORLD-WIDE IN THE REVELATION.
Bozrah—Isa. 34: 6, 7. 9, 10; 63: 1-6.	Compare with Rev. 14: 10, 11, 18-20; 19: 3. These verses are taken from the texts in Isaiah where the destruction of the Edomites, or Idumeans, is described. Bozrah was one of their capital cities.
Ezek. 16—*Jerusalem* the harlot, the whore. Study the emphasis on these words. Disloyal to God—looked to other nations for support—her lovers. Her lovers leave her "naked and bare." See vs. 36-44. In Isa. 1: 21 we read of Jerusalem:	Rev. 17—*Babylon* the harlot, the whore. Compare with Ezek. 16. Disloyal to God—supported by beast and ten horns—her lovers. Her lovers turn and hate the whore and "make her desolate and bare." V. 16.

"How is the faithful city become an *harlot!*" See also Jer. 2: 20, 21, etc. "I was an husband unto them, saith the Lord." Jer. 31: 32. "For thy Maker is thine Husband." Isa. 54: 5; 61: 4, 5; Rev. 21: 2, 9, etc.

"Shall burn thine houses with fire."— V. 41.

Lev. 21: 9—"And the daughter of any priest, if she profane herself by playing the whore, she profaneth her father: *she shall be burned with fire.*"

Rev. 17: 16—"And burn her with fire."

Rev. 17: 16—"*Burn her with fire.* 1 Pet. 2: 5, 9, Christians are priests; 2 Cor. 11: 2; Rom. 7: 1-4; Jas. 4: 4—friendship with the world— spiritual adultery."

Nah. 3: 4—*Ninevah* the harlot. "The mistress of witchcrafts, that *selleth nations* through her whoredoms, and families *through her witchcrafts.*"

Rev. 18: 23—*Babylon* the harlot. "For by thy *sorceries* were *all nations deceived.*"

Ezek. 26: 13—*Tyre* ("the city of confusion," Isa. 23: 1; 24: 10). "I will cause the *voice of thy songs to cease;* and the *sound of thy harps shall be no more heard.*" See Isa. 14: 11, where the same is predicted of Babylon. Isa. 24: 8. "The mirth of tabrets *ceaseth,* the noise of them that rejoice *endeth,* the joy of the *harp ceaseth.*"

Rev. 18: 22—"And the voice of *harpers,* and musicians, and of pipers, and trumpeters, *shall be heard no more at all* in thee."

Ezek. 28: 2-6, 17—Tyre glorified herself.

Ezek. 26: 16, 17; 27: 35—*Kings* distressed at the downfall of Tyre.

Ezek. 27: 27-36—*Merchants* lament the destruction of Tyre. Among these were the *merchants of Tarshish* who came in the ships of Tarshish (v. 12, 25). Other traders were—Persia, Tubal, Meshesh, the house of Togarmah, Dedan, Sheba—*the same as those mentioned in Ezek. 38.* They are *grouped as one unit*—both in Ezek. and Rev.

Rev. 18: 7—"How much she has glorified herself."

Rev. 18: 9, 10—*Kings* lament the downfall of Babylon.

Rev. 18: 11-21—*Merchants* lament the destruction of Babylon. As merchants of Tarshish are included as *enemies of Israel*—friends of Babylon—*they cannot be friends of Israel in Ezekiel 38.* It is the merchants of Tarshish who are particularly selected to lament the most bitterly. See Isa. 23: 1, 6, 14; Ezek. 27: 25-32; Rev. 18: 17-18.

Ezek. 27: 13—*Tyre* traded in *men.*

Rev. 18: 13—*Babylon* trades in the "*Souls of men.*"

Old Testament.	Revelation.
Ezek. 27: 29-32—The *shipmasters* lament the destruction of Tyre. Mariners, *pilots*, etc., "stand upon the land" and "cry bitterly."	Rev. 18: 17—*Shipmasters* lament the destruction of Babylon. "All the company in ships" (Variorum Bible: "Helmsman, or *pilot*") "stood afar off" "and cried."
Ezek. 27: 30, 32—"What city is like Tyrus?"	Rev. 18: 18—"*What city* is like unto this great city!"
Ezek. 27: 30—"And shall cast *dust* upon their heads."	Rev. 18: 19—"And they cast *dust* on their heads."
Ezek. 27: 31—"And they shall *weep* for thee with bitterness of heart and bitter *wailing*."	Rev. 18: 19—"And cried, *weeping* and *wailing*."
Ezek. 27: 5-24—*Tyre* traded with merchants for gold, silver, precious stones, purple, fine linen, etc.	Rev. 18: 12—*Babylon* trades in the same jewels, etc.
Ezek. 27: 13-22—*Tyre* traded in spices, wine, oil, wheat, sheep, etc.	Rev. 18: 13—*Babylon* trades in the same commodities.

Because of the sinfulness of the inhabitants, five ancient cities received God's judgments. These cities are brought into the Revelator's picture of the judgments of God upon *spiritual* Babylon. The last three enumerated below are said to be *harlot* cities:—

1. Bozrah. Rev. 14: 18-20; 19: 3, compare with Isa. 34: 6; 63: 1-6.
2. Babylon. Rev. 14: 8; 16: 19; 18: 2, 4, 10, 21.
3. Tyre. Isa. 23: 17. See texts given previously.
4. Ninevah. Nah. 3: 4, compare with Rev. 18: 23.
5. Jerusalem. (A harlot city when the professed people of God turned from God.) Rev. 17: 16, compare with Ezek. 16: 37-44, and verses 15, 20-59; Isa. 1: 21; Jer. 2: 20, 21, etc.

The fact that *three* ancient cities described as *harlot* cities—the harlot Jerusalem (Ezek. 16: 15, 20-59; Isa. 1: 21), the harlot Ninevah (Nah. 3: 4), and Tyre the harlot (Isa. 23: 17)—are brought into the Revelation in describing "The great whore . . .

BABYLON THE GREAT, THE *MOTHER OF HARLOTS*"

(Rev. 17: 1, 5)—though those *three harlot* cities were actually removed from and independent of Babylon—shows that spiritual Babylon includes all who reject the Third Angel's Message. See my "Christ Conquers," pp. 60-62, for fuller details explaining who are included in "Babylon" of the Apocalypse.

The employment of the five ancient literal cities in the Revelator's picture of the final doom of *spiritual* Babylon shows clearly the principle governing the interpretation of the book of Revelation, namely, that literal, local places mentioned in the Old Testament are employed in the Revelation in a spiritual, *world-wide* sense.

By this wide selection of *representative cities* the Holy Spirit, Who inspired the writers of the Bible, shows that all those who are worldly, and disloyal to God—even in Jerusalem, the church—are included under the term "Babylon," and will share in her doom. *Apostate* Israel in the Old Testament is a type of modern *apostate* Israel—apostate Protestantism. The analogy between national Israel as a whole (nominally professing to obey God, and yet not obeying all God's commandments) and Christendom (which also professes to obey God, and yet does not obey all of God's Commandments) is clear and decided, and Old Testament predictions of calamities to overtake *national* Israel in its apostasy set forth the judgments of God upon professing Christians who do not obey *all* His word. The principle that Old Testament local places and events are applied in the Revelation in a world-wide sense, and thus Jerusalem, in its harlot experience of unfaithfulness to God, is brought into the prophet's description of the downfall of spiritual Babylon, shows the Scriptural basis for the statement made by the servant of the Lord that Zephaniah's "prophecies of impending judgment upon *Judah* apply with *equal force* to the judgments that are to fall upon an *impenitent world* at the time of the second advent of Christ." P.K. 389. Thus we see that a knowledge of the Biblical laws of interpretation shows the Divine reliability of the Spirit of Prophecy, as well as proving that our Message is, indeed, the Third Angel's Message. The Spirit of Prophecy applies the *local* judgments to fall upon Judah as also foreshadowing "the judgments that are to fall upon an impenitent *world.*" The second, or double, application of Palestinian, or local, disasters, etc., is always world-wide. As shown elsewhere, the basis of Futurism is to make the second application of Old Testament Jewish and Palestinian things *again* Jewish and Palestinian. This is Satan's counterfeit of the true, world-wide application, which is *the foundation of our Message.*

104

From our survey of the contents of the Revelation given above (and other facts showing the same principle could have been presented) we can readily see that Old Testament places, etc., are mentioned in the Revelation according to the law governing their use, namely, that the *local* things of the Old Testament are employed in the Apocalypse in a *world-wide* sense. By this clear-cut, God-given principle we are able to *prove* that our Message is the Message of the living God. The literal, local things pertaining to *national* Israel are the basis of the *spiritual, world-wide* things of *spiritual Israel*—the church.

The *world-wide*, Judgment-hour Message, brought to view in Rev. 14: 6, 7, is based upon the *local* services in the tabernacle or temple of the Jews. The cleansing of the sanctuary was the last in the yearly round of the typical services in the economy of literal Israel. Lev. 16 and 23: 26-32 give details of significant ceremonies on that solemn day. Throughout the year the forgiven sins were recorded in the sanctuary. The final disposition took place at the end of the year's services, when, in type, they were removed from the sanctuary and placed on the head of the evil one, Satan—typified by the scapegoat. The sins recorded in the sanctuary were committed, firstly, by Satan, the author and instigator of all sin and, secondly, by the people led by the evil one into sin. The repentant people who availed themselves of the forgiveness extended by God through the shed blood of their Substitute were forgiven for *their* part in the sins recorded in the sanctuary, but Satan, the instigator, has no Saviour for *his* part in those sins, and must perish with them.

The last service of the year was known as the cleansing of the sanctuary, the day of atonement, or the day of judgment. Thus, in the typical services of literal Israel, God pre-figured the investigative judgment—the closing phase of Christ's heavenly ministry on behalf of *spiritual* Israel. Daniel's prophecy of the cleansing of the sanctuary (Dan. 8: 14, etc.) points to the final work of Christ in the heavenly temple, which will be accomplished just immediately prior to His second advent.

On the typical day of judgment the High Priest, having completed His ministry within the sanctuary, came out to bless the waiting people of Israel and to send the sin-laden scapegoat out into the wilderness, where it subsequently perished. In these final acts in the typical service of the day of atonement we see depicted the second coming of Christ and the events that follow. When our

Lord completes His heavenly ministry **He** will come from His place of mediation to bless His waiting people and to give them eternal life. He comes to charge Satan as being the author of all sin and to make him wander (for the 1,000 years of Rev. 20) on the desolate world he has ruined. As the scapegoat in the typical service was sent "unto a land *not inhabited*" (Lev. 16: 22) so Satan will be confined to this depopulated world. See also Jer. 4: 23-27: Zeph. 1: 2, 3, etc. Thus we see that the heavenly ministry of our Lord, His second advent, the bestowal of eternal life upon His people, the desolation and depopulating of the world and the binding of Satan in the bottomless pit—this earth in its empty and void condition—for the 1,000 years, the judgment at the end of the millennium, and the final destruction of Satan and his followers, and the eternal happiness of sin-freed Israel, were all typified in the services of the day of atonement. As these are the themes which are enlarged upon in the Revelation, we see that *the understanding of the Revelation depends upon a knowledge of the typical services in the economy of literal Israel.*

We cannot prove that our Message is God's Message except by employing the principle that the literal, *local* things of *literal* Israel are employed in the Revelation concerning the *world-wide* things of *spiritual Israel.* The understanding of this principle is vital to the proper grasp of the Third Angel's Message. By not heeding this principle Futurism applies the Hebrew things of the Revelation to literal Israel in Palestine. We must choose between the two systems of interpretation. The belief that there will be a *literal*, military conflict of all nations at "a place called in the *Hebrew* tongue Armageddon" (Rev. 16: 16) is part of the Futuristic system. There cannot be the slightest doubt that the first typical battle, involving *national* Israel and her sun-worshipping enemies who were destroyed "by the waters of *Megiddo*" (Judges 5: 19-21), forms part of the background of the Lord's prophecy in Rev. 16: 16 which points us to the destruction of the *enemies of spiritual Israel.* Having proved that our Message is God's Message by the principle that the *literal* things of *national* Israel mentioned in the Old Testament have a world-wide spiritual application in relation to spiritual Israel, shall we then discard that principle and accept the Futuristic principle of interpretation that "a place called in the *Hebrew* tongue Armageddon" has a *literal* meaning in relation to the *literal* Jews in the *literal* land of Israel? Thus we see that the acceptance of the belief of a Palestinian "Armageddon," logically, is a *blow at the principle upon which the Message of God is estab-*

lished. The very foundations of the great world-wide Judgment-hour Message are at stake in the *principle* involved.

In the 550 Old Testament quotations or allusions found in the Apocalypse the Divine law of interpretation—that the local things of the Old Testament are employed in the Revelation in a world-wide sense—is abundantly demonstrated. If the reference to Megiddo (in the word Armageddon) is *again,* in Rev. 16: 16, applied in a *literal* and *local* manner *as in the Old Testament,* that would be the *only* instance in the prophecies of the Revelation of the *literal* use of a place. Such an application is so obviously a violation of the law of interpretation revealed throughout the Apocalypse that it bears the mark of the evil one whose hands also have sought to interfere with and change the law of the Ten Commandments. Like the moral law, the laws governing the interpretation of the prophecies of the Apocalypse are unchangeable.

The instances presented above fully illustrate the fact that when Old Testament prophets were describing some calamity, etc., of a local character pertaining to Old Testament times, they were looking beyond the restricted area mentioned in the actual wording of the prediction (suited to the people of the time) *to world events at the close of the world's history.* The New Testament writers, and particularly John in the Revelation, by inspiration, have so applied the Old Testament predictions. The *imagery* employed to portray *world events* is taken from the Old Testament prophecies concerning *local* events. Old Testament predictions, when employed by the New Testament writers, are not used again by them with reference to local events. There is never a second *local* application. The belief in a literal conflict of nations in Palestine for Armageddon, based upon Rev. 16: 12-16, *violates every law of prophetic interpretation which the Holy Spirit has given us by which to know the truth.*

In my brochure on "Futurism and the Antichrist of Scripture," written nearly twenty years ago, I pointed out that the futuristic system of interpretation (which directs us to Palestine as the place for the fulfilment of the prophecies concerning the work of the antichrist and for the fulfilment of the other prophecies which the Third Angel's Message interprets in relation to all the world) is inspired by "a spirit of opposition to the unchanging nature of God's law, for the two things always go hand in hand." Or, stated in other words, Futurism is Satan's device in his warfare against the law of God, to turn people away from the true understanding of the prophecies which explain the attempt by the Papal antichrist to change God's law, and from a true interpretation of the prophecies depicting the final scenes in the great controversy between Christ and Satan over the Sabbath versus Sunday-keeping issues. By turning people's minds over to Palestine for the fulfilment of the prophecies which, rightly understood, present the final scenes in the conflict between truth and error, Satan successfully blinds their eyes to the truth taught by those predictions. Futurism teaches that the law of God was changed when Jesus died on the cross, and that the Sabbath was nailed to the cross; it also teaches the Palestinian fulfilment of the prophecies of the final struggle.

The Futuristic, or Palestinian-centred, system of prophetic interpretation, which applies to the *literal* Jews in Palestine the things pertaining to *Israel*—her perils and her deliverance from her enemies by the intervention of the Son of God—is Satan's prophetic scheme by which he attacks the law of God and blinds the eyes of millions to a true understanding of the things pertainings to *spiritual* Israel and to a knowledge of the "war" being waged between Christ and Satan over the law of God. To facilitate his deception that the Moral Law of God was changed at the cross, Satan introduced the Palestinian-centred system of prophetic interpretation.

The deceptions of the changed law at the cross, and the changed law of interpretation seen in the Futuristic system are integral parts of the one deception—they stand or fall together. And every sermon or book upholding the Palestinian "Armageddon" assists the work of God's enemy in his attack on the law of God. It would be incongruous for upholders of the perpetuity of the Law of God to present the Futuristic belief of a Palestinian "Armageddon" when, by so doing, they further the design of the evil one. Every sermon or article maintaining the view of a military, Palestinian Armageddon delays the coming of the Lord, confuses truth and error, and prevents God's people from learning the right interpretation of the prohecies giving the pictures of "the final conflict."

In His Holy Word God has shown us that the principle governing the understanding of the Revelation is that *local* things are brought in from the Old Testament and applied in the Revelation in a *world-wide* sense in connection with *spiritual* Israel, the church. To rightly proclaim God's Message upholding the perpetuity of His law we need also to abide by this God-given law of interpretation.

CHAPTER XVI.

THE LAWS OF REPETITION AND ENLARGEMENT.

The Bible contains much repetition, for, by the principle of enlargement through repetition, the divine Teacher increases our knowledge. "For God speaketh once, yea *twice*, yet man perceiveth it not." Job 33: 14. "And for that the dream was *doubled* unto Pharoah *twice*; it is *because the thing is established by God.*" Gen. 41: 32. God also repeated the prophetic dream to Nebuchadnezzar. See Dan. 2: 1. "God hath spoken once; *twice* have I heard this." Ps. 62: 11.

To give emphasis, certain words or phrases are repeated, as: "Comfort ye, comfort ye, My people." Isa. 40: 1; "Awake, awake," Isa. 51: 9, 17; 52: 1; "Depart ye, depart ye, go ye out from thence . . . go ye out of the midst of her." Isa. 52: 11; "Woe to Ariel, to Ariel." Isa. 29: 1; "O Jerusalem, Jerusalem." Matt. 23: 37; "Jesus cried with a loud voice, saying, Eli, Eli . . . that is to say, My God, My God." Matt. 27: 46. Seven persons were addressed by God with a double name, such as "Abraham, Abraham." Gen. 22: 11; "Samuel, Samuel." 1 Sam. 3: 10; "Saul, Saul," Acts 9: 4. In John's Gospel Jesus used the double form of "Verily, Verily" twenty-five times.

We also find repetition in the Hebrew manner of expressing the superlative degree: "Thou wilt keep Him in perfect peace," margin; Heb., "Peace, peace," see Isa. 26: 3, margin, Isa. 57: 19; "I will make thee most desolate"—margin, "Desolation and desolation." Ezek. 35: 3. "They were not of a double heart," margin, "without a heart and a heart." 1 Chron. 12: 33, etc.

Concerning the standard time measurements to be employed in interpreting symbolic prophecies we are told: "I have appointed thee each day for a year," margin, Heb., "A day for a year, a day for a year." Ezek. 4: 6.

Regarding the study of the Scriptures we are informed that: "Precept must be upon precept; line upon line, line upon line; here a little, and there a little." Isa. 28: 9-13.

By reading the Gospels we notice that Jesus repeated certain expressions. To each temptation in the wilderness Jesus replied, "It is written." Matt. 4: 4-10. As the earthly ministry of the Master proceeded, He saw the need of keeping before His disciples the fact of His coming death. *"From that time forth began* Jesus to shew unto His disciples, how He must suffer many things of the elders and chief priests and scribes, and be killed, and be raised again the third day." Matt. 16: 21. "From that time forth *began Jesus"* to tell the disciples of His coming death, and He repeated this instruction at different occasions. In His second advent sermon He again stressed the warning which He had given at other times, for we read, "Behold, *I have told you before."* Matt. 24: 25. In His illustrations showing the necessity of perseverance in prayer Jesus admonishes us to "ask," "seek," "knock," "for everyone that asketh . . . seeketh . . . knocketh." In our English translation the first letters of these three words form an acrostic as follows:

*A*sk   for everyone that *A*sketh.
*S*eek   *S*eeketh.
*K*nock   *K*nocketh, etc.

In stating the necessity of continuing in prayer, the Master repeated these words, by which we see that importunate prayer means to *ask, ask,* and keep on *asking.* To further illustrate His teaching, He gave two parables which bear such striking similarities that they appear to be repetition. See Luke 11: 5-8 and Luke 18: 1-8. A comparison of these two parables shows that they *do* contain repetition, not of detail, but of *principle;* namely, the necessity of *perseverance in prayer.* Luke 11: 5-8 teaches us to be importunate in our *asking on behalf of others;* Luke 18: 1-8 teaches us to be importunate in our *asking for ourselves.*

THE SCRIPTURES ARE WRITTEN UPON THE PRINCIPLE OF ENLARGEMENT BY REPETITION.

Jesus has warned against the use of *"vain* repetitions." Matt. 6: 7. Instances of vain repetitions by the heathen are given in 1 Kings 18: 26; Acts 19: 34. But the Divine Teacher employed *useful* repetitions. God selected the Hebrew nation to proclaim His truth, and they expressed themselves by repetition—the *repetition* being an *enlargement* of that which preceded it. Illustrations of this will be seen in such texts as Isa. 1: 10, 16; 28: 23; 41: 8; 44: 1-3, etc. In these, and the many other instances in the Scriptures, we notice that the repetition is not "vain," for it is used to explain and enlarge upon what has been already said.

The Rev. W. F. Wilkinson, M.A., in his "Personal Names in the Bible," p. 17, says:—"According to the genius of Hebrew poetry, when words or phrases of substantially the same import occur in two parallel or antithetical clauses, the variation of the second from the first consists of its being *explanatory*, or *expansive*, or augumentative of the notion which the first contains."

Bruce Barton, in "The Book Nobody Knows," p. 41, says:—

"Hebrew poetry does not consist of rhyme or meter, but in balance of thought, a Parallelism. One line says a thing, and the next repeats it with slight and skilful variations."

"In the way of righteousness is *life;* and in the pathway thereof there is *no death.*" Prov. 12: 28.

The Bible is not only full of *enlarging repetitions* in individual verses, but it is full of *explanatory* repetitions in parables, sermons, prophecies, history, etc.

Bible themes are written upon the crescendo plan. The earlier books lay the foundations for later developments. The details accumulate until, like an artist dipping his brush in different colours, a complete picture is produced. To change the metaphor, the seeds of truth planted in Genesis grow to large plants in later books. "The path of the just is as the shining light, that *shineth more and more* unto the perfect day." Prov. 4: 18. The Bible is written on this growing-brighter plan. Christ's miracles were performed on the accumulative method. He raised three people from the state of death—a child, a youth, and a fully grown man. And progressive conditions are also observed in the details of the Scriptural narratives—the girl was in bed, having just died; the young man had been dead some time and was on the way to the cemetery; while the fully grown man was decomposed in his grave.

The second chapter of Genesis enlarges on the important phases of the story of creation given in the first chapter. Some are confused over what they term the "two creations" brought to view in these two chapters. Some say that in chapter 1 of Genesis a "pre-Adamic" creation is referred to, whereas Gen. 2 presents the creation of Adam. This error occurs as false teachings originate, namely, by not heeding the Divine laws of interpretation —in this instance, the law of repetition and enlargement.

The erroneous teachings of evolution are based partly on the fact that in living things upon the earth there is a gradation of species from the lower to the higher forms of life. From this similarity of design and structure materialists suppose that the higher species have evolved from the lower. A failure to understand the Creator's laws of repetition and enlargement leads to this error. In the Genesis record of creation week we see how God commenced with the lowest forms of life and worked through to man—the highest. Certainly there is a gradation of species—the higher forms of life do appear as improvements on the lower forms of life—but the first object of His creation is just as perfect as the last thing He has created. In His creative and redemptive work, God commences from the lower and goes to the higher. He leads us from the material things to the spiritual; from our earthly abode to our heavenly. "The path of the just is as the shining light that shineth *more and more* unto the perfect day." Prov. 4: 18. God's method expressed in creation and revelation is that of working on the "more and more" plan—keeping the best wine until the last. John 2: 10. In the Scriptures, we see the Gospel of John—the Gospel which especially reveals Christ's divinity—and the Revelation—the most intricate and embracing of the prophetic books—kept till the last. The description of the glorious new world—the best of all God's creation—is reserved until the end of the Bible. Rev. 21 and 22.

The 7th day Sabbath came at the end of six days of labour. Gen. 2: 1, 2; Ex. 20: 8-11. The 7th year Sabbath came at the end of six years of work. Lev. 25: 2-7. "And thou shalt number *seven sabbaths of years* unto thee, *seven times seven years;* and the space of seven sabbaths of years shall be unto thee *forty and nine years.* Then shalt thou cause the trumpet of the jubilee to sound . . . and ye shall hallow the *fiftieth* year." Lev. 25: 8-13. The 1,000 years of earth's desolation—the earth's sabbath—comes at the end of 6,000 years of labour. In brief, we see that at the close of six days of labour came the *weekly* Sabbath: after six years of labour came the *yearly* sabbath: at the end of "seven times seven years" came the year of *Jubilee.* At the close of 6,000 years comes the *millennium.* These illustrate God's system of enlargement—a system discerned throughout Scripture.

The prophecies which follow Daniel 2 are but the enlargements of this foundational prophecy: the prophecy of Daniel 7 covers the same course of history as that covered in chapter 2; this is again repeated in the prophecies of Dan. 8 and 9, and again in chapters 10 to 12. But with each repetition additional truths are brought to view. In the book of Revelation, also, we see the same principle.

The Revelation is the consummation of all preceding books. "In the Revelation all the books of the Bible meet and end." A.A. 583-586. It contains 550 references to Old Testament passages. The Revelator repeats the past in prophesying the future—the past is repeated, but is enlarged upon. The New Testament contains 1,500 quotations of sentences and phrases from the Old Testament. The New Testament writers go over the history of the past, building on it in relation to the present and the future.

The deliverance of the children of Israel at the Red Sea is a type of the deliverance of the church at the end of human history. Rev. 15: 1-3. The record of every succeeding deliverance of God's people adds details concerning the final deliverance of His people at the time of the outpouring of the 6th plague, when He completely overthrows the enemies of spiritual Israel at "Armageddon."

HOW TO TEST A MESSAGE.

Messages emanating from God are built upon the past. "Surely the Lord God will do nothing but He revealeth His secret unto His servants the prophets." Amos 3: 7. This prophetic test we are admonished to heed. 2 Pet. 1: 19-21. A movement arising to-day must look to the *past* for its support: prophets in the past must have foretold its rise. The Exodus from Egypt of the children of Israel was based upon a prophecy given earlier. See Gen. 15: 13-16, and compare with Ex. 2: 23, 24: 3: 6-8, 15; Ex. 12: 40, 41. God reminded Moses of this prophecy when placing on him the responsibilities of leadership. Moses also reminded the Israelites of this prophecy given by God to Abraham. The return of the Jews from their Babylonian captivity was based upon definite predictions given sometime before. See Jer. 25: 11, 12; 30: 3, etc. "Now in the first year of Cyrus, king of Persia, *that the word of the Lord spoken by the mouth of Jeremiah might be accomplished,* the Lord stirred up the spirit of Cyrus, that he made proclamation. . . . Thus saith Cyrus . . . [God] hath charged me to build Him an house in Jerusalem. . . . Who is there of all His people? The Lord His God be with him, let him go up." 2 Chron. 36: 22, 23.

Daniel, in his perplexity regarding the future, turned to the prophecy of the past. Dan. 9: 1, 2.

When John was challenged as to his authority to preach, he directed his enquirers to the prophecy of Isaiah (40: 3-5) which predicted the work he was doing. The first verse of Matthew shows one of the main reasons for the writing of the book of Matthew and the New Testament; namely, to show the fulfilment of the Old Testament prophecies. Matt. 1: 1 refers us back to the prophecies that Abraham's seed should be the heir of the world (Rom. 4: 13), and that David's son should sit on his throne (Luke 1: 32, 33). Through Jesus the fulfilment of the Old Testament prophecies is made certain. See 2 Cor. 1: 20; Acts 13: 27-37. The Book of Matthew contains 99 *direct references* to the Old Testament Scriptures. Nine times he employed the formula, "That it might be fulfilled" (see Matt. 1: 22, 23; 2: 15, 17, 23, etc.), and at other times he referred to the fulfilment of the Old Testament prophecies, saying, "For thus it is written by the prophet" (Matt. 2: 5); "Then was fulfilled that which was spoken by the prophet" (Matt. 27: 9); "But all this was done, that the Scriptures of the prophets might be fulfilled" (Matt. 26: 56); "For it is written" (Matt. 26: 31, etc.). Thus Matthew illustrates the burden of the writers of the New Testament to show that Jesus' birth, life, ministry, death, resurrection, and the development of His Church and her work, all fulfil the prophecies of the Old Testament.

At the commencement of His ministry, Jesus appealed to the prophecy which outlined His work. Isa. 61: 1; Luke 4: 17-21; Dan. 9: 25, 26; Mark 1: 14, 15. When John sought confirmation from Jesus that He was the true Messiah, Jesus said: "Go shew John *again* those things which ye do hear and see." Matt. 11: 2-4. Jesus *"again"* pointed to the things He was saying and doing— things which the prophecies had declared that He would do.

When Jesus met the two disciples on the way to Emmaus, He said: "O fools, and slow of heart to believe *all that the prophets have spoken* . . . and beginning at *Moses and all the prophets,* He expounded unto them in all the Scriptures *the things concerning Himself."* Luke 24: 19-27. Before revealing Himself, Jesus proved to them that He was the Messiah by showing how He fulfilled the Old Testament Scriptures. See D.A. 796-799. Later, when He met with the other disciples, Jesus again directed their minds to the prophecies concerning Himself: "These are the words which I spake unto you, while I was yet with you, that *all things must be fulfilled,* which were written in the law of Moses, and in the prophets, and in the Psalms, concerning Me." Luke 24: 44. What made Peter's sermon so powerful? The outpouring of the Holy Spirit, and the declaration of the fulfilment of prophecy! Peter showed how the outpouring of the Spirit fulfilled the prophecy of Joel 2: 28, 29. He also pointed to other Old Testament prophecies fulfilled by the death, resurrection and ascension of Christ. See Acts 2: 25 (Ps. 16: 8), 31 (Ps. 16: 10), 34 (Ps. 110: 1).

Later, in the development of the church, Peter, and then Paul, declared that God had visited the Gentiles "to take out of them a people for His name" (Acts 15: 14). James, the President of this church council, said that this was the fulfilment of the prophecy found in Amos 9: 11, 12. See Acts 15: 12-17.

Peter (2 Pet. 3: 13) directs us to the prophecy found in Isa. 65: 17. John's description of the New Jerusalem is based upon prophecies found in Isaiah and Ezekiel. The last book in the Old Testament (Mal. 4: 4) refers to the writings of Moses. All the New Testament writers refer back to the Old Testament for their authority: and the Old Testament writers refer to, confirm, and build upon the writings of the prophets which preceded them.

Dr. S. H. Brooks affirms that Genesis is quoted nineteen times in nine New Testament books; Exodus, twenty-four times in twelve New Testament books; Leviticus, twelve times in nine books; Numbers is quoted or alluded to in nine books; Deuteronomy, twenty-six times in thirteen books; the Psalms, fifty-nine times in twelve books; Isaiah, fifty times in eleven books; Proverbs, six times in six books; and Zechariah, six times in four books. To these must be added 376 allusions to the Old Testament in the New. The epistle to the Hebrews and Jewish portions of the epistle to the Romans are entirely dependent on the Old Testament. Concerning the book of Revelation, Professor W. Milligan says: ". . . it may be doubted whether it contains a *single figure not drawn from the Old Testament*, or a *single sentence not more or less built up of materials brought from the same source* . . . [it] is a *perfect mosaic of passages from the Old Testament*." "The Revelation of St. John," p. 72.

The Old Testament is the foundation for the New. The New Testament elevates and magnifies the teachings and prophecies of the Old.

"The New is in the Old contained;
The Old is by the New explained.
The New is latent in the Old;
The Old is patent in the New.
The New is in the Old concealed;
The Old is by the New revealed.
The New is in the Old enfolded;
The Old is in the New unfolded."

Strange doctrines may find apparent support from isolated passages or texts interpreted without reference to their contexts. But the test of true doctrine is its agreement with the rest of the Scripture. A spirit of unity prevails throughout the Word of God. "The spirits of the prophets are subject to the prophets." 1 Cor. 14: 32.

By prophesying, many centuries in advance, future messages or movements in His work of salvation, God safeguards His children from deception. The miracle of prophecy not only guides His people, but is a powerful convicting force in the proclamation of their message, as there could not possibly be any collusion between the prophets of long ago and people proclaiming a message in later centuries. As the movement is seen to be in perfect harmony with the prediction, to the honest in heart the conviction is irresistible that both the prediction and the fulfilment are God ordained.

A God-inspired movement does not destroy the foundations of the past—it does not destroy, but *fulfils*. Matt. 5: 17-19. The teaching of Sunday sacredness destroys the past: destroys not only the Sabbath, but also teaches the abolition of the law on the cross. The Third Angel's Message is based upon the united testimony of the prophets: it fulfils all the specifications of the prophetic Word: past revelations form its foundations. It does not destroy, but fulfils.

CHAPTER XVII.

THE THIRD ANGEL'S MESSAGE IS BASED UPON THE PRINCIPLE THAT "DOUBLE" APPLICATIONS, WHEN APPLIED TO "ISRAEL," ARE SPIRITUAL AS WELL AS WORLD-WIDE.

The principle of "double" applications of prophecy is recognised by Bible students. Writing on matters of prophetic interpretation, Prof. George McCready Price states:—

"Some scholars have spoken of an *apotelesmatic* accomplishment of the prophecy, by which is meant that a partial or preliminary fulfilment may take place in one age, then long afterward *a much more complete* fulfilment. For instance, Christ's prophecy in the 'little apocalypse' of Matt. 24 seems to apply initially to the destruction of Jerusalem under Titus, while its *full* and *final accomplishment* will be seen in the destruction of the *nations of the world at the second coming.* In fact, many prophecies in the Old Testament seem to have been partly accomplished in events which took place near the times of the prophets, but will be completely fulfilled on *a vaster scale* and with more minute accuracy in *the events associated with the end of the age.*

"This is because the prophecies deal with the general principles of God's management of world events, so that whenever similar conditions prevail, we might speak of the prophecy as applying. Thus we might speak of a sort of *double* fulfilment according to the laws of analogy; for whenever a similar set of conditions occurs, the prophecy would seem to apply. . . .

"Thus, if we wish to speak of a *double* application of the prophecy, we must bear in mind that it is the final or the *apotelesmatic* meaning, *which is the true meaning after all,* when the prophecy is fulfilled on the *largest scale* and with the most complete and detailed accuracy." (Italics mine.) "The Ministry," September, 1939.

Dr. W. G. Wirth also refers to the "double" application, in which the local setting, or the first use of the prophecy, forms the basis for the "double," or larger fulfilment. He says:—

"There is nothing strange in this apparently *mixed time* method of Christ's prophecy, in which in one place He deals with that which is *immediate* in time and close at hand, as was the destruction of Jerusalem; and then, abruptly and at once, *projects* Himself into the future, to His second advent; or *merges* these two events together in *double* application of principles and fulfilment. A study of the Old Testament reveals this to be the method of Isaiah, Jeremiah, Ezekiel, and many other of the prophets, aided by the flexible time character of the Hebrew verb. From the consideration of the *immediate time* situation, suddenly, abruptly, they will project themselves into the *future, suggested by the present background.* Again, they will merge the *present or immediate condition* into that which will be in *the future,* in *double* application of principle and fulfilment. A careful study of the context and historical setting will make manifest which of the three methods the prophet is using in a particular case. It must be ever remembered that God does not look upon time in the limited sense that we do, in definite past, present, and future relations. He sees the *whole time* relation of world history and human events as one; and where *facts and principles at one time meet their application in another time*, He directs the inspired writer to treat of both in the same recording." (Italics mine.) American "Signs of the Times," December 8, 1931.

In his "Bible Handbook," pp. 285-292, Dr. Angus states:—

"From the *typical* character of ancient dispensations arises another peculiarity of prophecy. It not only *speaks their language*, but it has often a *double application*. It applies to one object by anticipation and partially, and to another completely; the earlier object being the *representative* of the later. . . .

"As the history of the Jews *foreshadows* the history of the *church*, so does prophecy the experience of both. . . . Prophecies on the restoration from Babylon (Jer. 31; Isa. 52), on the setting up of the Tabernacle of David (Amos 9), and on His kingdom (2 Sam. 7), had all, to a certain extent, an immediate fulfilment, and are yet applied in the New Testament to the gospel dispensation. To that dispensation in itself, or in its results, this *double* application must be confined.

"It follows from this *double* sense that, as in the *first* fulfilment, there is a limit to the blessing foretold, so, in the *second*, there is a fulness of meaning which it seems impossible to exhaust."

In the prophecy of the downfall of Jerusalem, Christ also predicted the downfall of *all* the cities at the end of the world. The "double" application of this prophecy does not refer merely to the fall of Jerusalem. The "double" application is never *another local* fulfilment: the prophets always saw in local events the foreshadowing of *world-wide* events at the end of time.

The *God-rejected* Jewish nation typifies the God-rejected world. The servant of God writes:—

"Christ saw in *Jerusalem* a *symbol of the world* hardened in unbelief and rebellion, and hastening on to meet the retributive judgments of God. . . . Jesus, looking down to the last generation, saw *the world* involved in a deception similar to that which caused the destruction of Jerusalem." G.C. 22. "The prophecy which He uttered was *twofold* [having a "double" application] in its meaning: while foreshadowing the destruction of Jerusalem, it prefigured *also* the terrors of the last days." G.C. 26. "The Saviour's prophecy concerning the visitation of *judgments* upon *Jerusalem* is to have *another* [a "double"] fulfilment, of which that terrible desolation was a faint shadow. In the fate of the chosen city we may behold *the doom of a world* that has rejected God's mercy and trampled upon His law." G.C. 37. "Christ, upon the Mount of Olives, rehearsed the fearful judgments that were to precede His second coming. . . . While these prophecies received a *partial* fulfilment at the destruction of Jerusalem, they have *a more direct application to the last days.*" 5T. 753. See also T.M., 232; Education, p. 129.

Thus the Lord has given abundant light concerning the *principle* of the "double" application of prophecy. Judgments prophesied to fall upon Jerusalem, Judah, Israel, etc., *because of their disobedience and impenitance*, foreshadow God's judgments to fall upon the *impenitent* world in the last days.

"His [Zephaniah's] prophecies of impending judgment upon *Judah* apply with equal force to the judgments that are to fall upon *an impenitent world* at the time of the second advent of Christ." P.K. 389.

If we are guided by the divinely-given principle that the second application of prophecies concerning local things always refers to things of a world-wide character we will not err by applying those prophecies *again* in a local setting.

Futurism, which has been so zealously fostered by the **Papacy**, teaches that the Jewish-Palestinian things in the prophecies are to be interpreted again to-day as they were when the Jews were God's chosen nation: that the "double" application refers *again* in the same *limited, national, Palestinian* sense as in the first fulfilment. As we have shown elsewhere, Futurism disregards the laws of God—the laws of interpretation, and the immutability of the moral law. Thus Satan opposes God's last-day message.

The Biblical principle, so clearly enunciated in the Spirit of Prophecy, is that the "double" fulfilment will be (to use the words of Prof. Price) "on a *vaster scale* . . . in the events associated with *the end of the age.*"

WHEN APPLIED IN CONNECTION WITH SPIRITUAL ISRAEL, "DOUBLE" APPLICATIONS ARE SPIRITUAL AS WELL AS WORLD-WIDE.

In Old Testament times the judgments of God fell upon various nations because of their sins. These same judgments, in the last days, will fall upon all the nations of the world because they are committing the same sins. The "double," or second application of the Old Testament narratives of judgments upon nations, without any specific "church" aspect, is world-wide and applies to *literal* judgments upon the wicked. An example of this principle is seen when comparing the seven last plagues with the plagues which fell upon Egypt. Elsewhere we have pointed out their similarities, stressing that those of the seven last plagues which are similar to the ones which fell upon ancient Egypt are described in *literal* language, whereas the 6th plague, referring us back to the judgments of God upon *Babylon,* is couched in *symbolic* language. In Rev. 11: 8, when picturing France under its atheistic revolutionaries, the Revelator refers to "the great city which spiritually is called Sodom and *Egypt.*" In his "Thoughts on the Revelation," p. 501, Uriah Smith says: "Mark! this beast, or kingdom . . . is an atheistical power, is 'spiritually Egypt.' (See Ex. 5: 2: 'And Pharoah said, Who is the Lord, that I should obey His voice to let Israel go? I know not the Lord, neither will I let Israel go.') Here is atheism." Thus the Revelator based his description of the national spirit of France during the Revolution upon the Old Testament narrative of the words and attitude of Pharoah. The Revelator does not refer to Egypt from a "church" angle, but from a "non-church" angle. In striking contrast, the Revelator brings "Babylon" into his imagery as Satan's false system of worship—the *counterfeit* of the worship of the God of Israel.   His imagery is based upon the Old Testament, where Babylon is constantly mentioned as the seat of Satan's kingdom, the rival to Jerusalem, the Lord's city.   Hence we can see why the Revelator, in describing the judgments which will be similar to those which fell upon *Egypt*, employs *literal* language, while in describing the judgments of the 6th plague, he uses *spiritual symbolism* because the description is based upon the overthrow of ancient *Babylon*.

Old Testament narratives of judgments upon nations, merely as nations, have, in the last days, a "double" or *world-wide* application.   But Old Testament narratives of nations *attacking Israel* are employed in the Revelation in connection with the *church and her enemies:* when applied in connection with the *church* the "double" application is *spiritual* in addition to being *world-wide*. The plagues similar to those which fell upon Egypt will fall upon the nations who (by enforcing Sunday laws), like Pharoah, will not recognise God's authority.   The 6th plague is poured out upon those who seek to destroy God's people.

In 1 Cor. 15: 46, the Apostle Paul enunciates the principle governing the right use of the *literal* and the *spiritual:* "Howbeit that was *not first* which is *spiritual,* but that which is *natural;* and *afterward* that which is *spiritual.*"   That is, the *first* use is to be understood in its "natural" sense: "and *afterward* that which is *spiritual.*"   The *"double"* use, or second application, is the *"spiritual.*"

In Vol. 5, pp. 451, 464, God's servant makes a "double," *"spiritual"* application of the prophecy of the surrounding of Jerusalem by the Roman armies.

The Lord inspired His servant to demonstrate the principle of "double" applications: the "double" application is, firstly, *world-wide,* and secondly, where Jerusalem and Israel and her enemies are mentioned, is applied in a *spiritual* sense in connection with the great controversy between Christ and Satan.   This principle is clearly taught in the book of Revelation.   In Luke 21: 24 we read the Master's prophecy: *"Jerusalem shall be trodden down of the Gentiles."*   The Roman nation came, and Jerusalem was, and ever since, has been trodden down by "the Gentiles."   That was the "first" fulfilment of the Lord's prophecy; the "double," "spiritual" application is presented by the Lord, in Rev. 11: 2: "But the court which is without the temple leave out, and measure it not; for it is *given unto the Gentiles:* and the *holy city shall they* [the Gentiles, as stated in Luke 21: 24] *tread under foot forty* and *two months."*

The Papacy—the *spiritual* Romans—by persecuting "the church of Christ" trod underfoot the *spiritual* "holy city" as, similarly, the *literal* Romans brought destruction to *literal* Jerusalem in A.D. 70. This interpretation is given in G.C. 266: "Said the angel of the Lord: *'The holy city (the true church)* shall they tread under foot forty and two months. . . .

"The periods mentioned—'forty and two months,' and 'a thousand two hundred and threescore days'—are the same, alike representing the time in which the *church of Christ* was to suffer *oppression from Rome. . . .The persecution of the church."*

Thus the Lord has clearly shown the principle underlying "double" applications: the first fulfilment is the "natural"; the "double" application is *world-wide* when applied to nations as *nations,* and *spiritual* and *world-wide* when referring to the *church and her enemies.* Prophecies of the perils of Jerusalem, Judah, Israel, etc., and of their deliverances when the people of God were penitent and obedient, have a "double" application in a *spiritual* sense in relation to the *world-wide church* in the last days.

The gathering of the nations to fight against Jerusalem, prophesied in Zech. 14: 1-3, 12-14, had a *local,* partial fulfilment in A.D. 70 when the Roman armies (made up of many nationalities) were permitted to destroy the Jews' city because of the iniquities of the rejected nation. God promised Israel: "Jerusalem shall be safely inhabited. And this shall be the *plague* wherewith the Lord will smite all the people that have *fought against Jerusalem."* Verses 11, 12. The *literal* Roman armies were not plagued in "their *tongue"* (v. 12), but the Revelator, quoting from this passage when describing the people of *spiritual* Rome being smitten with the 5th plague, says: "and they gnawed their *tongues* for pain." Rev. 16: 10. In G.C. 657; E.W. 289, God's servant quotes Zech. 14: 12, 13 when describing the fate of "those who have professed to be *spiritual* guardians of the people" (G.C. 656), but have "fought against Jerusalem"—the true church. Thus the Spirit of Prophecy presents a "double," *"spiritual"* application of this prophecy in connection with the final conflict over the Sabbath. The futuristic conception of a *literal* gathering of nations against the *literal* Jews in Jerusalem is Satan's counterfeit. But to apply such prophecies to a gathering, or uniting of spiritual forces against God's spiritual Jerusalem, "the true church" (see Rev. 11: 1, 2; G.C. 266), is in complete harmony with the Third Angel's Message. Thus we see that the great slaughter of Armageddon (likened to the treading of *red* wine from grapes in the winepress of God's wrath), which is said to take place *"without the city"* (Rev. 14: 20), will occur without the spiritual Jerusalem, "the true church." The triple application of the prophecies concerning Jerusalem being surrounded and attacked by enemies will be dealt with in later chapters.

The necessity for believers in the Third Angel's Message to have a thorough grasp of the true principle of "double" applications becomes apparent when we consider the prophecy of the 2,300 days of Dan. 8: 14. The importance of this prophecy is stated in an editorial on the sanctuary, which appeared in the "Review and Herald," January 6, 1944. We quote the first paragraph:—

"No other prophecy in the Bible is so important to Seventh-day Adventists as the twenty-three hundred days of Dan. 8: 14. Our very being as a separate people is *dependent on the accuracy of its interpretation.* Undermine our teaching on the cleansing of the sanctuary, and you *undermine the cornerstone of our message.* It is this that makes us distinctive." P. 4. (Emphasis is mine.)

The 2,300 days commenced (457 B.C.) with the decree for the return of the Jews from Babylon "to restore and to build Jerusalem" (see Dan. 9: 25; Ezra 7, etc.)—to "repair" (see Neh. 3; Isa. 58: 12, 13) the damage done by the Babylonians. By the principle of the "double," *"spiritual"* application of the experiences of ancient Israel (which forms the basis of the Third Angel's Message) we know that the ending of the 2,300 days (1844) brings us to the time *spiritual* Israel comes out (Rev. 18: 4) of *spiritual* Babylon to "restore all things" (Matt. 17: 11; Mal. 4: 5)—the true temple service (Rev. 11: 1, 2)—and to "repair" the breach. Isa. 58: 12, 13. Thus Seventh-day Adventists, in a *spiritual* sense, are fulfilling the "double" application of the experiences of *literal Israel* coming out of Babylon, etc. Not knowing the principle of the "double," *"spiritual"* application, and being blind to the *spiritual* fulfilment now taking place, many look to the future to see a "double," *literal* application in relation to the *Jews in Palestine.* The fulfilment of the 70th week, mentioned in the prophecy of Dan. 8 and 9, Futurists apply to the Jews in Palestine. See notes in Schofield's Bible, etc. Historicists, also, teach a "double," *literal* application of the return of the Jews from Babylon "to restore and to build Jerusalem." Dr. Gratton Guinness taught that the 2,300 days ended in 1844, and from that date would commence a "Restoration Era" in which the Jews would be restored to Palestine. He taught that, as the Jews were restored to Palestine at the *commencement* of the 2,300 years, there must be a "double," *literal* repetition of this after 1844, at the *ending* of the 2,300 years. He says:—

"Where does this long period run out? and to what events does its termination lead? . . . The expression. 'unto 2,300 years then shall the sanctuary be cleansed,' seems to mean, then shall the cleansing process begin, not then shall it come to an end. *Jewish restoration* is going on gradually and by stages . . . as the *former Persian restoration did 2,300 years ago.* . . . That the sanctuary will be cleansed, or Syria freed from Moslem domination, at the close of this cycle of twenty-three centuries, there seems little room for doubt . . . *the rapid restoration* of a considerable number of the Jewish people to the land of their forefathers. . . . This cycle of the twenty-three centuries *from the Persian restoration* era leads no further than the *deliverance of the Holy Land from Gentile rule!*" "Light for the Last Days," pp. 224-234.

Though a stalwart Protestant and strongly opposed to Futurism, Dr. Guinness employed the false principle of the "double," *literal* application of the things of ancient Israel, which is the basis of Papal and Futuristic errors. Historicists, such as Dr. Guinness, valiantly contended that the prophecies concerning antichrist have met their fulfilment in connection with the persecution of the church by the Papacy in Europe. The Futurists, with equal vigour, have maintained that the same prophecies refer to a future antichrist whose deadly work would be done in *Palestine* against the *Jews.* It is remarkable that these two opposing systems of interpretations should agree regarding the *future of Palestine and the Jews,* and that such agreement should come through different interpretations of the prophecy of Dan. 8 and 9. The reason for this agreement lies in the use of the erroneous principle of the "double," *literal, Palestinian* application of the things of ancient Israel. But, according to the New Testament principle, this prophecy of Dan. 8 and 9 pertains to spiritual, world-wide Israel. God's people called out of spiritual Babylon to the spiritual land of Israel, and to the spiritual work of rebuilding and repairing the temple of God.

In contrast to Futurists teaching a future *Palestinian* antichrist, Historicists, by interpreting *spiritually* in connection with the church such prophecies as the "war with the saints" (Rev. 13: 7; Dan. 7: 25) and the "man of sin" sitting "in the *temple* of God" (2 Thess. 2: 3, 4), have taught the truth regarding the Papacy being the antichrist. Were Historicists to continue to interpret *spiritually* in relation to the church the prophecies concerning Israel, they would see the truth of the Third Angel's Message. But, forsaking the principle of the "double," *"spiritual"* application of the things of literal Israel which has led them to correctly interpret the prophecies concerning the antichrist and his "war" with *spiritual* Israel, they change over from that principle and adopt the Futuristic principle of applying to the literal Jews and Palestine last-day prophecies concerning Israel.

The prophecies of Daniel, from chapter 7 to 12, are of great importance for the last days (see P.K. 547). From Dan. 2: 4 to 7: 28, the book of Daniel is written in Aramaic, the ancient language of Syria, and substantially identical with Chaldaic, the language of ancient Babylonia. The language returns to *Hebrew* from chapter 8 to 12. Elsewhere, we have pointed out that because "Armageddon" is said to be "a place called in the *Hebrew tongue*," it is of vital interest to *spiritual* Israel as the *symbolical* place of the slaughter of *her* enemies. Similarly, the prophecies of Daniel, commencing with the prophecy of the 2,300 days (which commences with the return of the Jews from Babylon to the land of Israel), are written "in the *Hebrew* tongue" because of their special importance to *spiritual* Israel.

Without the light of the Third Angel's Message, Historicists agree with Futurists in believing that, in the prophecies of Daniel, the return to the Hebrew tongue, which commences with the prophecy of the 2,300 days, indicates the special importance of these prophecies to the *literal* Jews in Palestine. In his "Light for the Last Days," p. 214, Dr. G. Guinness says:—

"It is a remarkable fact that the Book of *Daniel* is written in two different languages. It opens in Hebrew; but from chapter 2: 4 to the end of chapter 7 is Aramaic in the original, the *remainder of the book reverting to the Hebrew*. Thus the prophecies of the 'times of the Gentiles' are given in the Gentile Aramaic, and the *employment of Hebrew in the remaining predictions seems to indicate that the events foretold in them are viewed from a more Jewish standpoint*, and that the revelation has a more direct reference to *the Jewish people and the Holy Land*. On examination such is found to be the case. . . . They [the 'times of the Gentiles'] start with the *literal*, and end with the *spiritual* Babylon [if only he had also referred to *spiritual* Israel and *spiritual* Jerusalem, as given in the book of Revelation! How near the truth he was, and yet how far away!]. . . . But with the three last prophecies of Daniel the case is somewhat different. The second—the celebrated prophecy of the seventy weeks in chapter 9—foretells the events of history from a decidedly *Jewish point of view*."

In this, Dr. Guinness, representing the Historicists, agrees with Dr. Schofield, representing the Futurists. See Dr. Schofield's notes on Dan. 2: 4:—

"The language *returns to Hebrew* in the predictive *portions which have to do with the future of Israel*."

Satan endeavours to blind people to the light of God's last-day message by *literalizing* in relation to *the Jews in Palestine* the prophecies and things concerning Israel. The New Testament teaches that *all* things pertaining to Israel—*including references to the Hebrew language*—pertain to the church or her enemies. When referring to the *symbolic* place of the slaughter of the enemies of *spiritual* Israel, the Revelation terms it "a place called in the *Hebrew* tongue Armageddon." Rev. 16: 16.

The Third Angel's Message is based upon the New Testament and Spirit of Prophecy principle of the "double," *"spiritual," world-wide* application of the things of Israel.

CHAPTER XVIII.

THE LAW OF THE WORLD-WIDE SYMBOLIZED BY THE LOCAL, DEMONSTRATED IN THE MASTER'S SECOND ADVENT SERMON: A GUIDE IN UNDERSTANDING DANIEL AND REVELATION.

In His second advent sermon, Jesus (as all the prophets of God have done) employed the principle of the world-wide symbolized by the local. He employed the description of an event near at hand when foretelling of a greater event to transpire at the end of time. He pointed His hearers to a Palestinian tragedy, when depicting a far greater tragedy—the world-wide woes and destruction of the last days. In local events He saw symbolized last-day, world-wide events. The signs preceding the downfall of Jerusalem, and the scenes of that awful catastrophe are to be repeated on such an enlarged scale that the whole world will be involved. The pen of inspiration, guiding our minds to the true principles governing the interpretation of the Scriptures, says:—

"Christ saw in *Jerusalem* a *symbol of the world* hardened in unbelief and *rebellion,* and hastening on to meet the *retributive judgments of God.*" G.C. 22.

"The Saviour's prophecy concerning the *visitation of judgments* upon *Jerusalem* is *to have another fulfilment,* of which that terrible desolation was *but a faint shadow.* In the fate of the chosen city we may behold *the doom of a world that* has rejected God's mercy and trampled upon His law." G.C. 37.

It is significant that the book, "The Great Controversy," which presents the events leading to the final overthrow of the Babylonian world, should commence with a portrayal of the overthrow of Jerusalem. The tragedies which befell the Jewish nation and city prefigure, in a limited way, the overwhelming destruction awaiting the *world* and its cities at the end of time.

The comparison between the destruction of Jerusalem and the end of the world may be briefly set out as follows:—

THE DESTRUCTION OF JERUSALEM.	THE DESTRUCTION OF THE WORLD.
GC. 35, 36, 21. Completely destroyed.	GC. 22, 37. The *world* to be destroyed. "Christ saw in Jerusalem a *symbol* of the *world.*" "The *doom* of a *world.*"

The Destruction of Jerusalem.	The Destruction of the World.
GC. 26. "Judgments . . . retributive vengeance."	GC. 26. *"Prefigured* also the terrors of the last great day."
GC. 23. Message given—and rejected.	GC. 37. Message given—and rejected.
Luke 19: 41-44; Matt. 23: 38; CC. 21. Probation closed.	Rev. 22: 11, 12, etc.; GC. 38, 491. Probation closes.
Matt. 24: 15; Luke 21: 20: 5T. 451, 464; GC. 26, 37, 38. *Last sign*— Roman armies outside city walls.	5T. 451, 464. *Last sign*—spiritual Romans outside walls of spiritual Israel; Sunday laws, the sign of Satan's wrath to come in its fulness; sign also of fulness of God's wrath.
GC. 26, 38. Escape when see sign, Matt. 24: 16.	5T. 464. Escape when sign seen, GC. 38.
GC. 31. Christians fled to mountains.	5T. 465 (top page). Flee to mountains.
GC. 30. *"Not one Christian perished in the destruction of Jerusalem."*	Dan. 12: 1; GC. 37. *As in the time of Jerusalem's destruction,* God's people will be delivered. *"Every one* that shall be found written among the living in *Jerusalem"* (i.e., the church), see Isa. 4: 3.
GC. 26. "Retributive *vengeance* . . . for their rejection and *crucifixion of the Messiah."*	GC. 627. "God's *judgments* will be visited upon those who are *seeking* to oppress and *destroy His people."*
GC. 27. Destroy Christ to save nation and city.	GC. 590, 614, 615. "It will be urged that the few who stand in opposition to an institution of the church and a law of the State ought not to be tolerated; that it is better for them to suffer than for whole nations to be thrown into confusion. . . . *The same argument* 1800 years ago *was brought against Christ.* . . . 'It is expedient for us,' said the wily Caiaphas,' that one man should die for the people, and that the whole nation perish not.' This argument will appear conclusive; and a decree will finally be issued . . . giving the people liberty . . . to put them to death."
GC. 27. Thus they would escape the threatened calamity—but this brought about their final doom.	GC. 587, 590, 591. Sunday laws expected to prevent God's wrath, but bring the world's final doom. 1 Thess. 5: 3. Peace and safety cry when Sunday laws are passed; but this does not prevent the coming calamities—"sudden destruction . . . they shall not escape."

The Destruction of Jerusalem.

GC. 28, 29, 36. God's protection withdrawn—Satan controls *nation*.

GC. 28, 29. "Satan aroused the fiercest and most debased passions . . . blind rage . . . Satanic in cruelty . . . family, nation, suspicion, envy, hatred, strife, rebellion, murder. . . . Parents slew their children, and children their parents. . . . The leaders . . . opposing factions . . . torture their wretched victims . . . slaughtered without mercy. Unhappy Jerusalem! rent by internal dissensions, the blood of her children slain by one another's hands crimsoning her streets, while alien armies beat down her fortifications and slew her men of war." See also GC. 31-37.

Dan. 9: 26. "Destroy the city and sanctuary; and the end shall be with a flood, and *unto the end* of the war desolations are determined." Some interpret this last phrase: *"unto the end* wars and desolations are determined."

Luke 21: 20-24. "Days of *vengeance,"* "distress in the land, and *wrath* upon this people."

Luke 21: 20-24. God's wrath upon the rebellious Jewish nation.

Matt. 24: 15-20. Pagan Rome surrounded and destroyed Jerusalem.

The Destruction of the World.

GC. 37, 286, 589, 614. God's protection withdrawn—Satan controls the *world*.

GC. 37. "But a scene *yet darker* is presented in the revelations of *the future.* . . . What are these, in contrast with the *terrors of that day* when the restraining Spirit of God shall be wholly withdrawn."

GC. 614. "The *whole world* will be involved in ruin *more terrible* than that which came upon *Jerusalem of old."*

GC. 622. "The most vivid presentation cannot reach the magnitude of the ordeal."

For further details see my "What is Armageddon?" pp. 35, 36, and "Christ Conquers," pp. 93-95.

"Soon *grievous times* will arise among the nations—*trouble that will not cease till Jesus comes.* The judgments of God are in the land. The wars and rumours of wars, the destruction by fire and flood, say clearly that the time of trouble, *which is to increase until the end,* is very near at hand." R. & H., November 24, 1904.

"For it is the day of the *Lord's vengeance,* and the year of recompences for the controversy of *Zion."* Isa. 34: 8; 62: 2; 63: 4; Rev. 16. Days of vengeance. Rev. 14: 9-11; Luke 21: 25. *"Distress* of nations." Rev. 15: 1. "The *wrath* of God." Rev. 11: 18.

Luke 21: 25-28. God's wrath upon the rebellious Babylonian world. Rev. 16. In His sermon, Christ passes from the scenes of the destruction of the Jewish nation, temple, and city in Palestine, to the world-wide scenes to be enacted at the time of the end.

Matt. 24: 21, 22. Papal Rome surrounded spiritual Jerusalem and killed millions of saints in the dark ages.

JESUS DEMONSTRATES THE USE OF THE "DOUBLE," "SPIRITUAL" APPLICATION.

Without a break in His sermon, Jesus passed from *literal* to *spiritual* Rome; from *literal* Rome's destruction of the literal Jewish nation, city and temple (Matt. 24: 15-20), to *spiritual* Rome's destruction of spiritual Israel—the spiritual city and temple of God. Matt. 24: 21, 22. This "double," "*spiritual*" application of literal Rome's "war" on Israel is definitely presented in the Revelation. Compare Rev. 11: 1, 2 with Luke 21: 24. See also Rev. 13: 7, etc. The "double," "*spiritual*" application of the literal Roman armies surrounding Jerusalem is also made in 5T. 451, 464. The statements in the Spirit of Prophecy always harmonize with Bible principles of interpretation. All God's prophets agree. See 1 Cor. 14: 32, etc. All prophecies commencing with the literal Jewish nation, temple and city have their ending in relation to spiritual Israel and the whole world.

IN HIS SECOND ADVENT SERMON AND THE REVELATION, JESUS EMPLOYS THE PRINCIPLE OF THE "DOUBLE," "SPIRITUAL" APPLICATION.

Jesus is the Author of the Revelation. See Rev. 22: 16; G.C. 342.

Commentators draw attention to the fact that the Apocalypse is really an enlargement of Jesus' second advent sermon, which is sometimes termed the "little apocalypse." As one author has stated: "The *Apocalypse* is nothing else than a *transfigured form of the prophecy on the Mount of Olives.*" Prof. Milligan, D.D., in his "The Revelation of St. John," p. 42, says:—

"*The Apocalypse is moulded by that great discourse of our Lord upon 'the last things'* which has been preserved for us in the first three Gospels. Matt. 24: Mark 13; Luke 21. (It is remarkable that we find no account of this discourse in the Gospel of St. John.) The parallelism between the two is to a certain extent acknowledged by all enquirers, and is indeed in many respects *so obvious* that it can *hardly escape the notice of even the ordinary reader.* Let any one compare, for example, the account of the opening of the sixth seal in Rev. 6: 12-17 with the description of the end in Matt. 24: 29, 30, and he will see that the *one is almost a transcript of the other.* Or let the three series of apocalyptic visions—the seals, the trumpets, and the bowls be compared with the other parts of the discourse, and it will be found that, speaking generally, they are *filled with the same thoughts*—with wars, pestilences, famines, earthquakes, signs in sun and moon and stars, false teachers doing wonders and trying to deceive the very elect, the elect preserved, angels sent forth to gather them with the great sound of a trumpet, the victorious progress of the Gospel, the Son of Man coming in the clouds of heaven, the final deliverance of the good, and the just judgment of the wicked. These things *reveal in a way not to be mistaken a very intimate relation between the last prophecy of Christ and the Revelation of St. John.* When we look still further into the matter, the correspondence is much more marked."

Prof. Milligan then examines the book of Revelation and the Master's second advent sermon. Their correspondences are so striking that it is evident that John was inspired to omit from his Gospel the second advent sermon so that the close of the sacred Canon of Scripture would be the complete enlargement of the Saviour's prophecy.

In His second advent sermon Jesus passed from literal Israel to spiritual Israel; from the literal temple and city to the spiritual temple and city; and from literal to spiritual Rome. Similarly, in the Revelation, He fully demonstrates the principle of employing the experiences of ancient Israel, her city and temple, and her enemies, when outlining the experiences of the church and her enemies. Futurists, not understanding the principle of passing *from the literal to the spiritual*, apply Matt. 24: 21, 22, and the things of Israel mentioned in the Revelation, to the Jews in Palestine in the last days.

Concerning the Revelation, Prof. W. Milligan, D.D., says:—

"The *imagery* of the *Old Testament* certainly lived in the mind of the Seer with not less vivacity than in the minds of its original authors."

Jesus inspired John to reach into the past to obtain his imagery when prophesying concerning the future experiences of the church. All the prophets have done this—which is one of the proofs of their inspiration. They used the past in prophesying the future: they based their predictions upon the earlier records of the sacred historians and prophets of ancient Israel. They all so quote each other, and are so interwoven that they either stand or fall together, and must be interpreted as a whole, with adherence to the principle that local matters become world-wide—particularly in the last days.

In His second advent sermon and in the Revelation, Jesus took things which happened in Palestine as foundational imagery backgrounds for His predictions concerning the future experiences of spiritual Israel in all the world. He did not work in reverse—from all the world *to* Palestine (as in the Futuristic teaching of a Palestinian "Armageddon") but *from* a Palestinian *background* He turned to the *whole world*. Elsewhere in this book, attention has been drawn to the crescendo plan of Scripture: the principle by which the past, as it becomes the future, is enlarged. Thus Jesus, when forecasting the world-wide destruction of the enemies of the church, inspired John to write of the great battle of God at a "place called in the Hebrew tongue Armageddon"—referring back to Megiddo, described in the Old Testament as a place of Israel's conflict with her foes. Only by the principle of the transition from the literal to the spiritual do we see perfect harmony existing between the second advent sermon, the Revelation and all the prophets—including the Spirit of Prophecy.

THE PRINCIPLE OF THE "DOUBLE," "SPIRITUAL" APPLICATION EMPLOYED IN THE SECOND ADVENT SERMON GUIDES IN THE UNDERSTANDING OF THE PROPHECIES OF DANIEL.

When outlining the work of literal and spiritual Rome, Jesus directed us to that which was "spoken by Daniel the prophet." Matt. 24: 15. Thus we are guided in our understanding of the prophecies of Daniel by the principle of the transition from the literal to the spiritual; from the local to the world-wide; from literal to spiritual Israel; from literal to spiritual Rome.

In His second advent sermon, Jesus used several expressions which are keywords of the book of Daniel. He said: "When ye therefore shall see the *abomination* of *desolation,* spoken of by Daniel the prophet, stand in the holy place (whoso readeth, let him understand)." Matt. 24: 15. In Dan. 9: 26, 27 we read of the coming of the Romans who would "destroy the city and the sanctuary; and the end thereof shall be with a flood, and unto the end of the war *desolations* are determined . . . and for the overspreading of *abominations* he shall make it *desolate,* even unto the consummation, and that determined shall be poured upon the desolator." See margin. The "abominations" are mentioned *three* times in Daniel (Dan. 9: 27; 11: 31; 12: 11): thrice mentioned because the power thus designated counterfeits the *Third* Angel's Message. "Abominations" is the word employed in Scripture when referring to idolatrous worship. Commenting on Matt. 24: 15, God's servant says:—

"When the *idolatrous standards* of the *Romans* should be set up in the holy ground, which extended some furlongs outside the city walls, then the followers of Christ were to find safety in flight." GC. 26.

The Greek word for "abomination" ("bdelugma") occurs six (Babylon's number) times in the New Testament. Matt. 24: 15; Mark 13: 14; Luke 16: 15; Rev. 17: 4, 5; 21: 27. In describing the spiritual Roman power, the Revelator designates her "the mother of harlots and *abominations* of the earth." Rev. 17: 5. Thus, in Rev. 17: 4, 5 and also in Matt. 24: 15, Jesus applies, in a "double," *"spiritual"* sense, Daniel's prophecy concerning "the *abomination* of desolation." Both *literal* and *spiritual* Rome are designated by the same word: Pagan Rome was an idolatrous power, and Papal Rome, also, is an idolatrous power.

131

To His disciples Jesus declared: "When ye therefore shall see the *abomination* of desolation . . . *stand in the holy place* . . . then let them which be in Judea flee into the mountains." Matt. 24: 15, 16. As the sign for the flight of the disciples was that *literal* Rome was standing where she should not have stood, so, by the principle of the "double," *"spiritual"* application, the sign for the flight of God's people in the last days will be when *spiritual* Rome also stands "in the holy place"—presumptuously stands in the place of God by enforcing the keeping of Sunday in defiance of the command of God.

This "double," "spiritual" application is given in the Spirit of Prophecy:—

"As the approach of the Roman armies was a sign to the disciples of the impending destruction of Jerusalem, so may this apostasy [the enforcement of the Papal Sunday] be a sign to us that the limit of God's forbearance is reached." 5T. 451. "As the siege of Jerusalem by the Roman armies was the signal for flight to the Judean Christians, so the assumption of power on the part of our nation, in the decree enforcing the papal Sabbath, will be a warning to us. It will then be time to leave the large cities, preparatory to leaving the smaller ones for retired homes in secluded places among the mountains." 5T. 464.

The safety of the church in the final conflict is illustrated by the successful flight of all Christians from Jerusalem just before its overthrow. The Spirit of Prophecy declares that the awful horrors of that siege present a limited picture of the frightful, world-wide scenes of carnage of the last days. The disciples, watching for the Master's sign (vs. 15-20), heeded His counsel, and were protected in the regions of Pella. Writing of the time of the disciples' flight to the mountains, Pastor W. A. Spicer states: "Graetz, the Jewish historian, works out carefully the schedule of the days, showing that Cestius must have withdrawn from the city on Wednesday, October 7. It was 'not in the winter, neither on the Sabbath day.' " Again, it will be noted that that which occurred in Palestine—the disciples' flight to the mountains—will have a world-wide application in the last days.

No doubt, the Lord will again overrule so that the flight to the mountains in the last days, likewise, will be "not in the winter, neither on the Sabbath day."

The word "desolation," accompanying the word "abomination" in Christ's sermon, referring to the work of pagan and papal Rome, is mentioned seven times in Daniel 8: 13; 9: 17, 18, 26, 27; 11: 31; 12: 11. ("The desolate" of 9: 27, and "the desolations" of 9: 2 are from different words.) When Jesus referred to the book of Daniel, saying: "Whoso readeth let him *understand*" (Matt. 24: 15), He used one of its keywords. In the important prophecy of the 2,300 days (Dan. 8 and 9) the words "understand," "understanding," "understood," from the Hebrew "Biyn," "Biynah," are mentioned seven times. (In Dan. 9: 13, 25 the Hebrew "Sakal" is used.) Throughout the book of Daniel the thought of "understand," in various words, is employed about 27 times.

Another expression (used three times) which Jesus employed in His sermon connects His prophecy with the book of Daniel, and also connects the literal "war" of literal Rome against the Jewish nation and city with the spiritual "war" of spiritual Rome against spiritual Israel, the city of God. In Matt. 24: 19, the expression "those days" refers to the attack upon literal Jerusalem; in verses 22 and 29 the expression "those days" refers to the times of papal supremacy, when spiritual Israel was bitterly attacked by her spiritual enemy.

When Jesus predicted the coming of "the abomination of desolation" to destroy Jerusalem and to scatter the rejected nation of the Jews, He looked beyond the overthrow of literal Jerusalem. He saw more than the coming to Jerusalem of the literal Roman desolator. He saw the World-wide Papal Roman desolator attacking His spiritual Jerusalem, the church. He saw to the end of time, when all the cities of the rebellious world would be overthrown by the wrath of God.

The Jewish nation had been assured of the covenant blessing and protection of the Infinite on the condition of her obedience. All the promises to Israel were conditional. Notice the "if" in these promises. Ex. 19: 5; Deut. 28: 1, 2, 9, 13, 15, 58; 1 Kings 2: 4; Jer. 17: 24-27; Ezek. 43: 7-11; Zech. 6: 15. The blessings which God *would have* bestowed on literal Israel had they obeyed His voice, are expected by Futurists to be bestowed upon the literal Jews. They do not see that those promises, which were based upon an "if," cannot now be fulfilled to literal Israel, which, as a nation, came to its end in A.D. 70. The church has inherited the promises to Israel. "Prophets and Kings," p. 22, states:—

"A goodly *remnant* to whom are to be fulfilled *all the covenant promises*— this has been the theme of God's messengers to His *church* throughout the centuries that have passed."

Because of their sins, Christ could not cover literal Israel with His wings (Matt. 23: 37); but He will gather His spiritual Israel under His wings in the time of the world-wide slaughter of "Armageddon."

In His second advent sermon, Jesus has given us the principle to be applied in the understanding of the book of Daniel and other prophecies: the principle of the transition from the local to the world-wide; from the literal to the spiritual; from literal to spiritual Israel, and from literal to spiritual Rome.

CHAPTER XIX.

THE PRINCIPLE OF THE "DOUBLE," "SPIRITUAL" APPLICATION REVEALED IN THE BOOK OF DANIEL—SHOWING THE TRANSITION FROM THE LOCAL AND LITERAL TO THE SPIRITUAL AND WORLD-WIDE.

As already mentioned, the prophets of God saw a "double" view—the local and near at hand, and the world-wide in the last days. The book of Daniel, written in the days of types—at a time when national Israel and her experiences were *typical* of the experiences of *spiritual* Israel—contains prophecies which commence with the *literal* and *local*, but which automatically pass to the *spiritual* and *world-wide* when the Jewish *nation* ceased to be God's chosen people, and the *typical* days ceased.

The New Testament teaches that the church is now "the Israel of God." Gal. 6: 16, etc. But, while there is a change in the chosen people of God—the change from national to spiritual Israel —there is *no change* made in the *language* describing "Israel." The church inherits the phraseology of national Israel: *the same words and designations refer to both*—to national Israel in regard to the past, and to spiritual Israel from the time of the rejection of the Jewish nation. The prophecies and blessings which at one time referred to national Israel now refer to spiritual Israel. Failure to grasp this divinely-revealed truth has resulted in confusion and error among Bible students. Futurists, not guided by the New Testament teaching that spiritual Israel—the church—has taken the place of national Israel, still build their doctrines and their hopes for the world upon a belief in a *literal, Palestinian* fulfilment of the prophecies pertaining to Israel. Thus Schofield's Bible, on p. 1226, comments: "The promise of the kingdom to David and his seed, and described in the prophets (2 Sam. 7: 8-17, refs.; Zech. 12: 8) *enters the New Testament absolutely unchanged* (Luke 1: 31-33)." (Italics mine.) Unchanged so far as the *terminology* is concerned, but *positively* changed regarding the people to whom those prophecies and designations apply. The New Testament and Spirit of Prophecy teach the *spiritual*, world-wide application of the promises and prophecies concerning Israel.

Because we are creatures of responsibility, and are capable of understanding, the Lord has written the Bible in a way which calls for us to "*search* the Scriptures" (John 5: 39) with "an honest and good heart." Luke 8: 15. The Word of God is not written as an argument, but as a declaration of truth. The Bible contains no laboured argument to prove Gods' existence, because it is such a self-evident fact. Beliefs such as the virgin birth of our Lord are not discussed; they are declared a few times for the honest hearts that will accept them, and other portions of the Scriptures just take for granted the acceptance of these truths. The same procedure applies to principles of prophetic interpretation, for they are not often repeated. It is left with the sincere searcher to apply truths and principles already declared, wherever the occasion requires. As stated in my "Christ Conquers," p. 77: "When symbols are employed in the Bible, we are not informed in every instance where the same symbol is used regarding the symbolic interpretation. In fact, in numbers of instances there is nothing to directly indicate that a symbol or type is employed. In most instances, when once or twice our attention has been drawn to the interpretation of any symbol, we are not directed to the fact again, for it is left with us to apply the principle whenever we come to the same setting."

Having been shown that national Israel was rejected finally and that the church is now "the Israel of God," we are to apply this New Testament teaching when interpreting the many prophecies and promises concerning Israel. As the Revelation was written after the rejection of the Jewish nation, there should be no difficulty in understanding its basic principle, namely, that the church is now the Israel of God, and, therefore, all the things of Israel are applied therein in a spiritual, world-wide sense. The Revelation is "the Spirit of Prophecy"—"the testimony of Jesus"— by which the Lord shows us *"how"* (Luke 10: 26) to interpret the book of Daniel and other Old Testament prophecies concerning Israel. The prophecies of Daniel can be understood only by the principle that the literal and the local of the past pre-figure the spiritual and the world-wide of the last days. The transition takes place automatically, for the change from the literal and local to the spiritual and world-wide is a *principle operative in all prophecies pertaining to Israel and her enemies.* The prophecies of Daniel, and other Old Testament prophecies, do not explicitly declare the change from the literal and local to the spiritual and world-wide. It is not necessary for this "double," "spiritual" application to be directly pointed out in the Old Testament, for the New Testament makes it perfectly clear that the things of Israel, which exclusively belonged to national Israel before her rejection, now belong to the church, and that *wherever* the things of Israel are applicable to New Testament times, they are to be undertsood *spiritually* in relation to the Messiah's *spiritual* kingdom. Only by this transition from the literal and local to the spiritual and world-wide, can the prophecies of Daniel, and the Master's own prophecy, recorded in Matt. 24; Mark 13; and Luke 21, be rightly understood. The transition from the literal and local to the spiritual and world-wide is the *invariable plan followed by all the prophecies*—whether they are continuous prophecies (such as Daniel, Matt. 24, etc.), or whether they pass over the centuries and have their distinct "double" fulfilment in the last days.

In the chapter dealing with the Principle of the First and the Last, it is shown that the prophecies of Daniel are designed upon the principle that the local and national, which are first mentioned, provide imagery applicable to spiritual Israel and her enemies, at the endings of his prophecies. The book of Daniel commences with the historic reference to the invasion of Judea and the overthrow of Jerusalem, the destruction of the temple of God, and the taking of the vessels from the house of God to the house and service of the gods of Babylon. Later prophecies in Daniel—and prophecies in other portions of the Word of God—show that the things done by *literal* Babylon to the *literal* Jews and *literal* Jerusalem, to the *literal* temple and vessels employed in God's service, are also done, in a spiritual sense, by *spiritual* Babylon in her *spiritual* "war" against *spiritual* Israel. Thus the "double," "spiritual" application of the first few verses of Daniel lays the foundation for the "double" application of the prophecies which follow.

The prophecy of the second chapter of Daniel is of the continuous type. By the light shining from the New Testament, the "double" application—the transition from the literal to the spiritual —may be seen. Beginning with Nebuchadnezzar, the king of *literal* Babylon, the prophecy continues down to the time of *spiritual* Babylon, centred in Europe—the cradle of nominal Christianity. The position of absolute monarch occupied by the king of *literal* Babylon (Dan. 2: 38) will be duplicated, in a *spiritual* sense, when the Papacy, through the enforcement of *her* "Sunday" by the nations of Christendom, will be exalted among the people and shall say (in the pride of Nebuchadnezzar who boasted of the *"great Babylon"* he had built—see Dan. 4: 30) "I sit a queen, and am no widow, and shall see no sorrow." Rev. 18: 7. The expression *"great Babylon,"* in Dan. 4: 30, forms the basis of the Revelator's description of *spiritual Babylon.* See Rev. 14: 8; 19: 18; 17: 18; 18: 2, 10, 16, 18, 19; 19: 3.

The enforcement of the Babylonian "Sun-day" will bring spiritual Israel into great distress and imminent danger. God's people will face the threat of destruction, but the Lord will "deliver" *His people* (see Dan. 12: 1) from the hands of their spiritual Babylonian enemies. See E.W., pp. 282-285, "The Time of Trouble;" G.C., chapter 40, "God's People Delivered."

The "double," "spiritual" application of the book of Daniel is clearly seen when studied in the light of other portions of God's Word. As the *first* chapter of Daniel describes literal Babylon's attack upon literal Israel, her city and temple, so the *last* chapter brings us to the final attack to be made by *spiritual* Babylon upon God's *spiritual Israel*—the spiritual city and temple.

The experiences of the three Hebrews, who would not bow down to the *literal* image king Nebuchadnezzar had set upon the plains of Babylon, foreshadow the final struggle of the church when the spiritual king of Babylon endeavours to force all to worship the *spiritual* image—"the image of the beast," see Rev. 13, etc.—on the plains of *spiritual* Babylon. God's servant has declared that "the conflict that is right upon us will be the most terrible ever witnessed." 6T. 407. The Spirit of Prophecy is always in harmony with Bible principles. The book of Daniel teaches that "there shall be *a time of trouble, such as never was* since there was a nation even to that same time: and at that time *thy people* shall be *delivered*, every one that shall be found written in the book." Dan. 12: 1. "The burning, fiery furnace," heated "seven times more than it was wont to be heated," will have a "double," world-wide, *spiritual* application in the experiences of spiritual Israel, who will be plunged into unprecedented, fiery trials.

In his rage at being frustrated of complete dominion, Nebuchadnezzar boastingly said to the *three* faithful Hebrews, who typify the people of the Third Angel's Message: "Who is that God that shall *deliver* you out of my hands?" Dan. 3: 15. The faithful three trusted in the God of Israel to *deliver* them, and the covenant-keeping God of Israel walked with them in the fiery furnace, and *"delivered"* them. The "double" application of this experience refers to the last days, when the people of God—the people of the Third Angel's Message who refuse to bow down to the *spiritual* image to the beast (Rev. 13, 14, etc.)—will be thrown into times of unparalleled peril; but Jesus, by His angels, will walk with them in the world-wide, *spiritual*, fiery furnace and will *"deliver"* them from their *spiritual* Babylonian enemies. Thus we see the connection between the *deliverance* of the three Hebrews, brought to view in Dan. 3, and the *deliverance* of God's world-wide, spiritual Hebrews, mentioned in Dan. 12: 1.

The pride and boasting of Belshazzar's feast, when they praised the gods of Babylon (Dan. 5), will have a "double" application when spiritual Babylon, through the enforcement of her Sunday by the law of the land, is exalted among the nations. When literal Babylon was exultant and boasted of security through her gods, God wrote the close of her probation upon her festive walls. And "in *that night* was Belshazzar, the king of the Chaldees, slain." The last hours and doom of *literal* Babylon foreshadow the last hours and doom of *spiritual* Babylon. By enforcing the false Sabbath (using the vessel of God in the service of Babylon), spiritual Babylon will look for a time of "peace and safety": instead, "sudden destruction [as in the night of Belshazzar's feast] cometh upon them . . . and they shall not escape." 1 Thess. 5: 3. "The time of trouble" mentioned in Dan. 12: 1 has reference to the "double," or world-wide application of the record in Dan. 5 of the disaster which came to literal Babylon, following her hour of apparent security.

The plot of Daniel's enemies to persuade the king to pass a law necessitating a choice between obedience to God's law or the law of the State (see Dan. 6), will have its "double" application when the apostate churches seek government aid to enforce Sunday laws. As the king did not see the subtlety behind the request of Daniel's enemies, so many law-makers will not discern the cunning behind the appeal to the State to pass laws which will bring spiritual Israel into times of extreme peril. After passing through a night of supreme trust in God, Daniel was *"delivered"* (see Dan. 6: 14, 16, 20, 27) from his peril: similarly, spiritual, world-wide Israel, after being plunged into a period of affliction and distress necessitating implicit trust in their God, will be *"delivered"* (Dan. 12: 1) at the time of the 6th plague.

Daniel 7 commences with *literal* Babylon, and passes on to *spiritual* Babylon, headed by the little horn. Satan led this little horn to make *"war* with the saints" (Dan. 7: 21, 25; Rev. 13: 7) in the dark ages. The final phase of the *"war"*—the controversy between Christ and Satan—is referred to in Rev. 12: 17: "The dragon was wroth with the woman and went to make *war* with the remnant of her seed."

In the introduction to the symbol of the Papacy in Rev. 13, the prophet passes from the leopard (Grecia) and the bear (Medo-Persia) to the lion (Babylon). See Rev. 13: 2, and compare with Dan. 7; see also Rev. 17. Thus there is a definite connection between the *literal* Babylonian lion and the *spiritual* Babylonian beast. By this transition from *literal* to *spiritual* Babylon, the Holy Spirit illustrates the principle to be followed in the study of the book of Daniel.

The transition from the literal to the spiritual is also seen in relation to the two phases of Rome. Verses 23-25 of Daniel 8 use the same words to picture both pagan and papal Rome. What literal Rome did nationally, spiritual Rome did, and does, in a spiritual sense. To the Hebrews, the *literal* Romans spoke in "dark sentences" (compare Dan. 8: 23 with Deut. 28: 49), and *spiritual* Rome, by adhering to the Latin tongue in her services, also speaks in "dark sentences." To *spiritual* Hebrews their *doctrines*, also, are *"dark."* See Ps. 119: 105, etc. "His power shall be *mighty*, but not by his own power," is equally true of literal and spiritual Rome. Rome dominated most of the world; spiritual Rome's power is great. "He shall destroy wonderfully": both pagan and papal Rome have destroyed wonderfully. 50,000,000 martyrs testify to the "double" application of this passage in relation to *spiritual* Rome. The words "shall prosper, and practice, and shall *destroy the mighty and the holy people*" fit both literal and spiritual Rome. Pagan Rome invaded the typical land, and destroyed many Jews, their city and temple. Spiritual Rome invaded the spiritual land of Israel, and destroyed millions of the members of spiritual Israel—the spiritual city and temple of God. The transition from literal to spiritual Rome automatically takes place, in harmony with the established Bible principle.

This transition is also seen when comparing Dan. 12: 7 with Dan. 8: 24. In Dan. 12: 7 we read: "When they have made an end of breaking in pieces the power of *the holy people*." R.V. The reference to the destruction of "the holy people" has its origin in Dan. 7: 25 and 8: 24. That papal Rome, in addition to pagan Rome, is described in Dan. 8: 24 is evident from the fact that, in Dan. 12: 7, this work of destroying *"the holy people,"* is said to occur during the 1260 years of Papal supremacy. When Jesus, in Matt. 24, quotes from the prophecy of Daniel regarding the coming of "the abomination of desolation"—the Roman armies (Luke 21:

20; G.C. 21, 26)—to "destroy the city and the sanctuary" (Dan. 9: 26, 27; Luke 21: 20), and then passes, without a break in His sermon, to depict the destruction of the saints during the dark ages (Matt. 24: 15-20 and notice 21, 22), He is following the principle used in the book of Daniel itself. Dan. 12: 7 speaks of papal Rome having power to *"scatter* the power of *the holy people,"* or, as given in the Revised version, *"breaking in pieces* the power of *the holy people."* The "breaking in pieces" and scattering of the literal Jewish nation, referred to by Jesus in Luke 21: 24; Matt. 21: 43, 44, etc., was the *literal* fulfilment: but in the dark ages occurred the *spiritual* fulfilment, when papal Rome attacked the spiritual city and temple—the church.

In the days of the New Covenant, the expression *"thy people"* (Dan. 12: 1) refers to spiritual Israelites, who "are *now the people of God"* (see 1 Peter 2: 9, 10)—spiritual Israelites in the antitypical land of Israel, preaching God's judgment-hour message based upon the *antitypical* application of the Palestinian sanctuary services of the old covenant. *"The holy people"* mentioned in Dan. 12: 7 are the people of *spiritual* Israel. The angel informed Daniel that his last vision concerned "what shall befall *thy people* in the latter days." Dan. 10: 14. Concerning the final events of this long prophecy we read: "And at that time shall Michael stand up, the great Prince which standeth for the children of *thy people* . . . and at that time *thy people* shall be delivered." Dan. 12: 1. While the expression "thy people" of Dan. 10: 14 referred to the Jewish nation at the downfall of *literal* Babylon, that of Dan. 12: 1 has reference to *spiritual* Israel at the time of the downfall of *spiritual* Babylon. The change from *literal* to *spiritual* Israel is taught in the New Testament, where the rejection of the Jewish nation, for its infidelity to God, is declared. God's "chosen" people with whom He keeps covenant are those who keep His commandments. Deut. 7: 9. As "the kingdom of God" has been "taken from" the Jewish nation "and given unto a *nation"* (Matt. 21: 43)—the church, which is "a *spiritual* house . . . an holy nation" (1 Pet. 2: 5, 9)—"to whom are to be fulfilled all the covenant promises" (P.K. 22, 703, 713-715), the promise of deliverance to God's "people," in Dan. 12: 1, is for spiritual Israel—the church.

With the transition from *literal* to *spiritual* Israel, in the prophecies of Daniel, we also pass from *literal* to *spiritual* Rome, and from *literal* to *spiritual* Babylon.

This transition from the *national* to the *spiritual enemies* of "Israel" occurs *because God's chosen people have changed from national to spiritual Israel.* When the church became "the Israel of God," *everything* in the Scriptures pertaining *to Israel and her enemies* automatically passed from the national and local to the spiritual and world-wide.

As mentioned in chapter 17, the Third Angel's Message is based upon the belief that the 2,300 days, of Dan. 8: 14; 9: 24-27, commences with the literal Jewish nation being called out of Babylon to rebuild the temple and city of Jerusalem, but ends with the call of spiritual Israel from spiritual Babylon to rebuild the spiritual temple and city of God. Rev. 11: 1, 2, etc. The use of the "double," "spiritual" application in connection with the 2,300 days is representative of the many instances in the Scriptures where the application of this basic Bible principle proves that our denominational interpretation of the Third Angel's Message is correct.

The "double" application of the account of the last hours of literal Babylon, recorded in Dan. 5, is connected with the prophecy of Dan. 10 to 12. While the Babylonians were praising their gods, Cyrus and his army, having sufficiently deflected the waters of the Euphrates from their course, entered, and overthrew the city of Babylon. The prophecy of Dan. 10 to 12 *commences* with Cyrus (Dan. 10: 1)—Israel's deliverer, and the destroyer of her Babylonian oppressors. See Jer. 50: 33, 34; Isa. 45: 13, etc. The "double" application of the overthrow of Babylon by Cyrus refers to the coming of Jesus, the Almighty "Cyrus," the Shepherd-King (see regarding Cyrus in Isa. 44: 28), the Lord's Anointed (see also Isa. 45: 1), the Deliverer of Israel (Dan. 12: 1; Isa. 45: 13), the One Who bids God's people go free (Luke 4: 18) to worship their God (Isa. 44: 28; 2 Chron. 36: 22, 23; Ezra 1: 1-8). Daniel 12: 1 points forward to the time when spiritual Babylon will oppress spiritual Israel, and the waters of the Euphrates that have been a bulwark and a glory to Babylon will be "dried up." Rev. 16: 12. The 6th plague falls upon the "multitudes"—the waters which support the great spiritual Babylonian whore. Compare Jer. 51: 13 and Rev. 17: 1, 15; 16: 12. Jesus comes to *"deliver"* His people from their Babylonian oppressors. And spiritual Israel will worship God in her native land—the eternal Canaan.

There is no suggestion of a great battle to be fought among nations as the climax of Daniel' prophecies. Dan. 12: 1, 2 points to: (1) the close of probation (a world-wide event) for the spiritual

Babylonian world, typified by the close of probation for literal Babylon, when God declared to them: "Thou art weighed in the balances, and art found wanting" (Dan. 5: 27); (2) the standing up of Michael (affecting the whole world): the completion of Christ's *priestly* ministry in the heavenly temple, and the commencement of His reign (Rev. 15: 8; 11: 15-19, etc.); (3) the deliverance of God's people—spiritual Israel, in the spiritual *world-wide* land of Israel; (4) the partial and general resurrections which will be *word-wide*. Dan. 12: 1 makes no reference to a literal conflict to ensue in Palestine. The events outlined in this verse concern the deliverance of the church and the destruction of her enemies in the *world-wide*, antitypical land of Israel.

The following outline briefly illustrates the principle of the transition from the literal and Palestinian to the spiritual and world-wide, in the prophecies of Daniel.

RELATING TO LITERAL, PALESTINIAN ISRAEL AND HER ENEMIES.

Dan. 1: 1, 2; 2 Chron. 36: 17-20; Dan. 9: 17, 18. The Babylonians invaded Israel's land, destroyed the temple, and took the vessels of God for use in the service of the gods of Babylon.

Dan. 1: 2; 6: 2, 3; 9: 16-19, etc. *Literal* temple and city.

Dan. 9: 2. Israel in Babylonian captivity. Jer. 29: 10.

Dan. 9: 24, 25. Israel liberated from Babylon.

RELATING TO SPIRITUAL, WORLD-WIDE ISRAEL AND HER ENEMIES.

Rev. 13: 6; 2 Thess. 2: 4. *Spiritual* Babylon attacks God's sanctuary services by substituting false worship and using the spiritual vessels of God's temple for use in the services of a false system of worship. Israel's enemies attack God's sanctuary. See Isa. 63: 18.

Rev. 11: 1, 2; G.C. 266; T.M. 17; 7T. 219. *Spiritual* temple and city— the church. See also 1 Cor. 3: 16, 17; 6: 19; 2 Cor. 6: 16; Ephes. 2: 20-22.

"God's church on earth was as verily in captivity during this long period [1260 years of Papal supremacy] of relentless persecution, as were the children of Israel held in captivity during the period of the exile." P.K. 714.

"His church is no longer in bondage. To *spiritual* Israel have been restored the privileges accorded the people of God at the time of their deliverance. . . . No longer have the hosts of evil power to keep the church captive . . . to *spiritual* Israel is given the message, 'Come out of her, My people.'" P.K. 714, 715.

Literal Palestinian Israel.	Spiritual World-wide Israel.
Dan. 9: 24, 25. Israel came out of Babylon, and returned "to restore and to build Jerusalem."	"The work of *restoration* and reform carried on by the returned exiles . . . presents a *picture* of a work of *spiritual restoration* that is to be wrought in the closing days of this earth's history . . . every divine institution is to be *restored.* The breach made in the law at the time the Sabbath was changed by man is to be *repaired.* God's remnant people . . . are to be *repairers* of the breach, the *restorers* of paths to dwell in." P.K. 678.
Dan. 9: 25. "The street shall be built again, and the wall, even in *troublous* times."	"As the time of the end draws near, Satan's temptations will be brought to bear with greater power upon God's workers. He will employ human agents to mock and revile those who 'build the wall.' " P.K. 659. The work will be completed during "troublous times." See 5T. 463, etc.
Dan. 9: 25. The 2,300 days *commenced* with the return of *literal* Israel to the *literal* land to do a *literal* work of repairing and rebuilding.	Rev. 14: 6, 7. The 2,300 days *end:* spiritual Israel to come out of spiritual Babylon (Rev. 14: 8; 18: 1-4, etc.) to "repair" (Neh. 3 and Isa. 58: 12-14) and to rebuild the *spiritual* walls of Jerusalem.
Dan. 9: 24. "Seventy weeks are determined upon *thy people* and upon *thy holy city"*: literal Israel to prove worthy of being God's *"people."*	Luke 19: 41-44. Jews' probation closed. G.C. 21, etc.; Matt. 23: 38. Temple to be desolate—no longer God's "Naos," or dwelling-place. God's wrath "to the uttermost." 1 Thess. 2: 16; Matt. 21: 43; 1 Pet. 2: 5, 9, 10; Ephes. 2: 21, 22, etc. Church now God's "people": God's "Naos," or "temple," His "city." Rev. 11: 1, 2; G.C. 266, etc.
Dan. 8: 13; 9: 17, 18, 26, 27; 11: 31; 12: 11. The *literal* Roman desolator.	Dan. 12: 7. The *spiritual* Roman desolator.
Dan. 8: 9-14; 9: 26, 27. *Literal* Rome's invasion of Palestine: the destruction of many Jews, the temple and Jerusalem. See Christ's application in ,Matt. 24: 15; Luke 21: 20.	Rev. 11: 1, 2; G.C. 266. Applied by Jesus to *spiritual* Rome's work in attacking the *spiritual* city and temple—the church.

Dan. 8: 24. *Literal* Rome's *literal* "war" on the *literal* Jewish nation.

Dan. 9: 26, 27; Luke 21: 20. *Literal* Jerusalem was "*trodden down* of the Gentiles": by *literal* Romans, etc.

Dan. 8: 10. *Literal* Rome trampled under foot many *literal Jews.* Luke 21: 24.

Dan. 8: 13. "*How long* shall be the vision . . . to give both the sanctuary and the host to be *trodden under foot?*"

Dan. 8: 24. *Literal* Rome would "destroy the mighty and *the holy people.*"

Dan. 8: 24; 9: 15, 16, 19, 20, 24; 10: 14; 11: 14." "The holy people," "thy people," "my people Israel"—all refer to *literal* Israel.

Dan. 8: 14. "Unto 2,300 days; then shall the sanctuary be cleansed."

Dan. 8: 13; 9: 17, 18, 26, 27; 11: 31; 12: 11. The "desolations" of the "desolator."

Rev. 13: 7; Dan. 12: 7. *Spiritual* Rome makes *spiritual* "war" on *spiritual* Israel.

Rev. 11: 1, 2. Concerning *spiritual* Jerusalem—the church—we read: "And the holy city shall they ['the Gentiles"—*spiritual* Romans] *tread under foot* forty and two months." G.C. 266.

Rev. 11: 2. *Spiritual* Rome trampled under foot many *spiritual* Israelites.

Dan. 12: 6, 7. "*How long* shall it be to the end of these wonders? . . . it shall be for a time, times, and an half." Rev. 11: 2: "The holy city shall they *tread under foot* forty and two months"—that is, 3½ prophetic "times," or years. Rev. 6: 10. In the description of the period when spiritual Rome was treading "underfoot the holy city," or "the true church" (G.C. 266), the martyrs are pictured as crying to God: "*How long,* O Lord?"

Dan. 12: 7; 7: 25; Rev. 13: 7. *Spiritual* Rome would "scatter the power of *the holy people*" ("Breaking in pieces the power of *the holy people.*" R.V.).

Dan. 12: 1, 7. "Thy people," "the holy people"—refer to *spiritual* Israel.

Rev. 14: 6, 7. In 1844 the 2,300 days ended: the Investigative Judgment commenced in heaven, and upon earth God's spiritual temple began to be cleansed of the pollutions of sin and Babylonian errors.

Dan. 12: 7, 11. The "desolations" of the spiritual Roman "desolator" would cease. In 1798 came the end of "breaking in pieces the power of the holy people." The ending of the 2,300 days (Dan. 8: 14), or the 1,335 days (Dan. 12: 12), brought the time for the ending of the desolations of the spiritual Babylonians and Romans: spiritual Israel to be fully liberated from the errors of spiritual Babylon.

Dan. 11: 14. "The robbers of thy people . . . shall fall." *Literal* Rome was to "be broken without hand." Dan. 8: 25.

Dan. 11:45;12: 7. *Spiritual* Rome, which had spoiled and robbed God's people, would lose her power to "scatter" or break "in pieces the power of the holy people" and, eventually, would be destroyed. Dan. 7: 11; 2 Thess. 2: 3-8, etc. Matt. 24: 21. *Spiritual* Rome will never again be able to *destroy* the church as she did in the dark ages. Spiritual Rome's power to *destroy* the *church* was "finished" in 1798 (see Dan. 12: 7), and after 1844 she could not deceive true Israelites who accept God's last-day message. Compare Dan. 12: 7, 12 with Rev. 10: 5-11; 11: 1; 14: 6-14, etc.

Dan. 9: 26. *Apostate* Israel came to her "end . . . with a *flood*" of Romans. See also Dan. 11: 22, and compare with such passages as Isa. 8: 7, 8; 28: 2, etc.

Rev. 12: 15, 16. In the dark ages, *spiritual* Rome attacked the church by means of a "*flood*"—destroying millions of spiritual Israelites. In the last days *spiritual* Babylon will again endeavour to drown *spiritual* Israel in the "flood" waters of the Euphrates (Rev. 17: 1, 15; 16: 12), but, by the 6th plague, "the water thereof" will be "dried up." God's spiritual Israel will be "*delivered*." Dan. 12: 1. For fuller reference, see chapter "The River Euphrates and the Kings of the East."

Dan. 12: 7. "He held up his right hand and his left hand unto heaven, and *sware by Him that liveth for ever* . .. all these things shall *be finished*."

Rev. 10: 5-7. "Lifted up his hand to heaven, and *sware by Him that liveth for ever and ever* . . . that time should be no longer . . . mystery should be finished."

In Dan. 12: 7, the oath was uttered in connection with the work of the *spiritual* Roman desolator, the scatterer, the breaker of God's people. The question asked in Dan. 8: 13: "*How long* shall be the vision concerning . . . the transgression of *desolation* [margin, "making desolate"], to give both the sanctuary and the host to be *trodden under foot?"* is not only answered in v. 14, but also in Dan. 12: 7 and Rev. 10: 5-7. In 1798 spiritual Rome lost her power to scatter, break and rob God's people. Since 1844 God's last-day message has brought light and power to spiritual Israel, enabling her to come out of Babylon to do the work of rebuilding and restoring the spiritual temple and city of Jerusalem, in the spiritual land of Israel. The oath uttered in Dan. 12: 7, and mentioned in Rev. 10: 5-7 in connection with the rise of God's last-day message calling spiritual Israel out of spiritual Babylon to her own land, connects up with the oath God made to Abraham that his seed would inherit the land. See Gen. 15: 7-18; Jer. 34: 18, 19; Gen. 12: 1-7; Acts 7: 1-5, etc. "If ye be *Christ's*, then are ye *Abraham's seed*, and heirs according to *the promise*." Gal. 3: 29. God has sworn to spiritual Israel (Heb. 6: 13-20) that they shall inherit the land of Israel: (1) the *spiritual* land of Israel with the Euphrates as one of its boundaries (see chapter on the river Euphrates); (2) the glorified new earth. Rom. 4: 13. Since 1844 spiritual Israelites have been heeding the call of God to "come out" of spiritual Babylon, and they have been spiritually *gathering* to the land of Israel. See Isa. 11: 11, 12. In "Early Writings," pp. 74-76, God's servant makes a *spiritual* application of the prophecy of Isaiah which states "the Lord . . . shall *assemble* the outcasts of Israel, and *gather together* the dispersed of Judah from the four corners of the earth." God's servant also warns against Satan's device of persuading God's people to turn to *literal* Jerusalem.

In its spiritual application, the land of Israel means the place where's God blessings are fully bestowed. "The Lord shall greatly *bless thee in the land* which the Lord thy God giveth thee for an inheritance to possess it." Deut. 15: 4. To spiritual Israel is given the promise: "Now will I . . . have mercy upon the *whole* house of Israel. . . . *When I have brought them again from the people*, and *gathered* them out of their enemies' lands. . . . Then shall they know. . . . I have gathered them unto their own land, and have *left none of them any more there*." Ezek. 39: 25-29. When "the whole house of Israel" shall have come out of spiritual Babylon to the *spiritual* land of Israel, Satan will stir up the hatred of all people of all nations to unite, or "gather together," against His people. See Ezek. 38; 39; Joel 3; Zech. 12; 14; Rev. 16: 12-16; 17: 14; 19: 11-21; Isa. 54: 15, etc. After *literal* Israel came out of Babylon, and the "work of restoration had begun, and a remnant of Israel had already returned to Judea, Satan was determined to frustrate the carrying out of the divine purpose, and to this end he was seeking to move upon the *heathen nations to destroy them utterly."* P.K. 583. "As he influenced the heathen nations to destroy Israel, so in the near future he will *stir up the wicked powers of earth to destroy the people of God."* P.K. 587, 588. When the enemies of spiritual Israel gather together against God's people they will perish on "the mountains of Israel," "without the city." See Ezek. 38, 39; Joel 3; Rev. 14: 20, etc. "There shall be *a time of trouble,* such as never was since there was a nation even to that same time: and at that time *thy people shall be delivered."* Dan. 12: 1. The expression *"thy people* shall be *delivered"* refers to the *deliverance* of *spiritual* Israel from her *spiritual* enemies. The enemies of the church will never again be able to deceive or *destroy* the true Israel of God. In the dark ages, Satan was permitted to destroy millions of God's people, but in the closing scenes of the controversy, though bitterly persecuted, the remnant *church* will be preserved to meet the Lord without seeing death.

In "Early Writings," pp. 282-285, in the chapter "The Time of Trouble," God's servant refers to the *deliverance* of God's people mentioned in Dan. 12: 1:—

"The wicked rushed upon the saints to slay them; but angels . . . fought for them. Satan wished to have the privilege of destroying the saints . . . but Jesus bade His angels watch over them. God would be honoured by making a covenant with those who had kept His law, in the sight of the *heathen* [this is an inspired comment on Ezek. 38: 16, 23; 39: 7, 23, 28; Joel 3, etc.] round about them; and Jesus would be honoured by translating, *without their seeing death,* the faithful, waiting ones who had so long expected Him. . . . God would not suffer His name to be reproached among the *heathen.* . . . He was to manifest His mighty power, and gloriously *deliver* His saints. For His name's glory He would *deliver* every one of those who had patiently waited for Him, and whose names were written in the book [this is a definite reference to Dan. 12: 1] . . . the people of God who had faithfully warned the world of His coming, would be *delivered."*

The book of Daniel closes with the promise that Daniel would stand in his "lot at the end of the days." Dan. 12: 13.

The Hebrew word for "lot" is found 76 times in the Old Testament. Dr. Strong says of this word: "A portion or destiny (as if determined by lot)." See examples in Lev. 16: 8, 9, 10; Num. 26: 55: 33: 54; 34: 13; Prov. 16: 33; Esther 3: 7; 9: 24, etc. Two *main* uses of this word are brought to view in the Old Testament: *(1) dividing the land by lot; (2) deciding which of the two goats employed in the service of the day of atonement should represent Christ or Satan.* See "Messiah in His Sanctuary," p. 142, by F. G. Gilbert; "The Great Second Advent Movement," p. 83, by J. N. Loughborough; "Daniel and Revelation," p. 317; TM. 115; PK. 547. These authors show that the term is associated with the *last message at the time of the judgment—the antitypical day of atonement—* prior to Israel entering into *the everlasting land of Canaan.*

"When Israel was about to enter into the promised land, the lot was cast, and the possesion of each tribe was assigned. The tribes thus stood in their respective 'lots' long before they entered upon the actual possession of the land. *The time of the cleansing of the sanctuary corresponds to this period of Israel's history.* We now stand upon the borders of the heavenly Canaan, and decisions are being made, assigning to some a place in the eternal kingdom, and barring others forever therefrom. In the decision of his case, Daniel's portion in the celestial inheritance will be made sure to him. And *with him all the faithful will also stand.*" "Daniel and Revelation," p. 317.

The prophecies of Daniel were not given to describe events to happen in Palestine in the last days, but to describe the experiences of spiritual Israel in all the world—the spiritual land of Israel—just before they enter into their eternal Canaan.

All Scripture points to the fact that the Hebrew prophets took the *literal* things of Palestine and the Jewish nation and their enemies to be *types* of the world-wide in relation to *spiritual* Israel—the church.

A general survey of the prophecies of Daniel clearly shows the principle of the "double," "spiritual" application operating throughout the book: the transition from the literal and local, in the commencement of the book and of the individual prophecies, to the spiritual and world-wide.

CHAPTER XX.

THE SIGNIFICANCE OF THE "FIRSTS" AND THE "LASTS" OF SCRIPTURE.

An experienced miner seeking gold knows by "outcroppings" or certain indications on the surface of the earth that the precious metal will be found by digging below the surface. Similarly, he who searches the Scriptures will know by the "outcroppings," which the Holy Spirit has designedly and conspicuously placed in the general structure of Holy Writ, that patient digging into the mine of truth will bring to view more precious things from the Word of God.

In our next chapter we will deal with the law of the first and the last mention which is employed in conjunction with the laws of repetition and enlargement, and of type and antitype. In this chapter we wish to draw attention to the significance of the "firsts" and the "lasts" of Scripture used in a general way without direct reference to the law of type and antitype.

By drawing our attention to the significance of the "firsts" and the "lasts" of the Bible the Holy Spirit leads us on to continue our searching until we see that a definite law or principle of interpretation exists in the Scriptures themselves.

As the shape of a leaf often indicates the general shape of the tree, so the design of each book often indicates the design of the whole of the Bible.

It could be pointed out that in most books of the Bible there are definite and important connections between their commencements and their endings. These "firsts" and "lasts" are some of the "outcroppings" seen in the structure of the Scriptures.

The first and the last books of the canon of Scripture stand together vitally related; they are like a golden clasp that binds in one book all the other books between. The first themes written in Genesis—because Jesus is "the first and the last"—foreshadow the last themes in the last book, Revelation. Things appearing in the first chapters of Genesis re-appear on a grander scale in the last chapters of Revelation.

IN THE FIRST PART OF GENESIS.	IN THE LAST PART OF REVELATION.
"In the beginning."	At the end.
God created the first heaven and the first earth.	God creates a new heaven and a new earth.
All things new.	"I will make all things new."
Satan enters and first deceives.	Satan cast out and deceives no more.
Man first fears, and hides from God.	Man no more fears or hides from God.
Man communed openly with God until the first sin, and then the Divine face was hidden.	After sin is destroyed there will be open communion as there was before sin came. "And they shall see His face."
Banished from the tree of life.	"Have right to the tree of life."
Eden lost—exiles from God's garden.	Eden restored—inheritors of Paradise.
The gates shut.	The gates shall never be shut.
Water ran from Eden.	Water runs from God's throne.
Garment of light lost.	Garment of light restored.
Earth cursed.	"No more curse."
The first pains, sorrows, tears, death, etc.	The last pains, sorrows, tears, death, etc.
Satan tempts.	No more temptation.
Satan apparent victor.	Satan positively defeated forever.
Satan's first success.	Satan's complete failure.
Sentence pronounced upon Satan.	The sentence executed upon Satan.
The first Adam—father of a sin-cursed race.	The last Adam—the father of a sinless race.
Adam married to Eve.	Christ married to His Church.
Husband and wife.	The Lamb and His bride—the Church.

We read concerning the first two brothers mentioned in the Old Testament that Cain murdered his brother—*he took his life from him.* Gen. 4: 8. In contrast, we read in the sacred narrative of the first two brothers brought to view in the New Testament, that Andrew sought out Simon, not to kill, but *to lead him to the Life-Giver.* John 1: 35, 41, 42.

In Gen. 3: 9 we read that God sought fallen man with the question: "Adam . . . where are thou?" In the first question asked sinful man God was seeking to woo him back. The first question asked in the Book of Matthew is: "Where is He that is born King of the Jews?" Matt. 2: 2. Thus, there is a balance between the *first* question of Gen. 3: 9 and the *first* question recorded in Matt. 2: 2. In the first question in Gen. 3: 9 *the Saviour sought fallen man to save him;* but in the first New Testament question *fallen men are seeking salvation and enquiring where they could find the Saviour.* As stated in 1 John 4: 19: "We love Him, because He *first* loved us." We seek Him (Acts 17: 27) because He *first* sought us. John 4: 23. The right understanding of the firsts and the lasts of Scripture points us to Jesus the Saviour from sin, and the Destroyer of evil.

In the history of New Testament times the *first* mention of "the Lamb of God" is that He "taketh away the sin of the world." John 1: 29. The *first* mention of the Lamb in the Revelation is where Jesus is represented as "a Lamb as it had been slain." Rev. 5: 6. Only by His death could Jesus take away our sin. The *first* recorded words of Jesus were: "Wist ye not that I must be about *My Father's* business." Luke 2: 49. The *last* words spoken by Jesus before He returned back to heaven after His resurrection were: "I ascend unto *My Father,* and your Father, and to My God, and your God." John 20: 17.

Jesus, the Creator-Redeemer, is brought to view in the *first* verse of Genesis, and He is also mentioned in the *first* verse of Matt. 1. The Old Testament closes with the word *"curse."* Mal. 4: 5. Sin brought about the curse. See Rom. 5: 12-21, where Paul explains how Adam's sin brought the *curse* of sin and death into the world, and how, by Christ's righteous life and atoning death, *grace* enables the believer in Jesus to obtain eternal life. Hence, while the Old Testament ends with the word *curse,* the last verse of the New Testament (Rev. 22: 21) reads: "The *grace* of our Lord Jesus Christ be with you all."

Genesis is the book of beginnings—of the world, and all things in it; of life, sin, death, races of men, wars, etc. Genesis *commences* with "the *living God, which made* heaven, and earth, and the sea, and all things that are therein" (Acts 14: 15), and *ends* with a *dead man* in a coffin. Gen. 50: 26.

The *first* promise in the Old Testament (Gen. 3: 15) is that Jesus would come the first time. The *last* promise in the New Testament is that Jesus will surely come the second time. Rev. 22: 20.
"This is the book of the generations of Adam." (Gen. 5: 1.)

This is the *first* time this expression occurs in the sacred writings. The *last* occasion this expression occurs is in the first verse of Matt. 1: *"The Book of the generation of Jesus Christ."* In every conceivable manner in the Scriptures the Holy Spirit has glorified the work of the Creator-Redeemer.

"The *first* Adam" married to Eve is set forth as a type of "the *last* Adam"—Christ and His Church. (See Ephes. 5: 22-33.) "The *first* Adam, the sinful father who bequeathed a legacy of *death* to his children, is set forth in contrast to "the *last* Adam . . . a *quickening* spirit . . . The first man is of the earth, earthy; the second man is the Lord from heaven." (See 1 Cor. 15: 45-49.) "For as *in Adam* all *die,* even so *in Christ* shall all be made alive." (v. 22. See also Rom. 5: 14-19.) Adam *received* his mortal life from his Creator—he "was *made* a living soul." But Jesus, "the last Adam," was a *life-giving* spirit. "The *first* Adam" takes his children with him into the grave; "the *last* Adam," being the Creator, possesses in His nature and essence the fountain of life. (See John 1: 4; 5: 21; 10: 10; 12: 24; 1 John 5: 12.) Glorious truths are learned when one heeds the laws of the interpretation of Scripture set forth by Christ Himself.

"This is the book of the generation of Adam." In the table of Adam's genealogy which follows these words—the *first* time they occur in Scripture—we read *eight* times: "And he *died."* (See Gen. 5: 5, 8, 11, 14, 17, 20, 27, 31.) Following the *last* time that phrase is employed in Holy Writ—"The book of the generation of Jesus Christ," the repeated word is *"begat."* The 40th birth is that of Jesus. Forty is 5 times *8.* The number 5 is used by the Holy Spirit in the Bible for *grace,* and 8 is the number representing life from the dead—the resurrection number. By the grace of Jesus Christ the dead will be resurrected at His second coming. (Rev. 22: 20-21.) "The *first* Adam's" genealogy *ends in death;* "the last Adam's" genealogical table ends with the begettal of a *new life*— and the assurance of *eternal life* beyond the tomb through the *grace* of Jesus Christ.

Other wonderfully gripping truths are learned by a further study of the genealogical tables of the Bible when the principle of the first and the last is applied to them. But we must turn from ancestries to books. The Book of Exodus opens with God's people being oppressed and learning the ways of the heathen; it closes with the people re-learning the ways of God by means of the sanctuary service set up in their midst. See Ps. 77: 13. The

Psalms (1: 1) *begins* with God blessing man, and *ends* with *man blessing and praising God.* (Ps. 150.) The last five Psalms begin and end with "Praise ye the Lord."

The book of Proverbs commences with the kingly man, and ends with the queenly woman. (Prov. 31: 10-31.) Ecclesiastes begins with the king's statement that "all is vanity" (1: 1, 2), and ends with the king's advice to shun all vanities because of the coming judgment. (12: 14.) Matthew (1: 1) begins by declaring that Jesus is the King of Israel; it ends with the King's command and promise to His spiritual Israel—the church—to go in His power to preach the gospel; and His promise to be with His followers till the end of the world. (Matt. 28: 18-20.) Mark commences with the ministry of John the Baptist, the forerunner of Jesus, who opened up the Master's ministry; and it ends with the ascension of our Lord. The ascension closed His personal service upon the earth, and commenced the work of the Disciples as His representatives. In this capacity they went forth with great power, "the Lord working *with them,* and confirming the word with signs following." Mark 16: 20.

The gospel of Luke opens, after the preamble (which was designedly included for another reason which cannot be explained now), with the birth of John the Baptist. John was born in answer to the *prayers of his parents.* (Luke 1: 13.) John's priestly father burnt the incense upon the *prayer altar* (v. 9), and it was at the time the *people were praying* (v. 10) that the angel of the Lord appeared unto Zacharias "on the right side of the *altar of incense."* (v. 11.) Thus the commencement of Luke's Gospel brings to our attention the prayer altar in the temple. This book closes with the promise of the *Holy Spirit* Who would *come in answer to prayer.* (See Luke 24: 49, and compare with Luke 11: 13.) Thus the prayer altar and the temple in the first chapter are mentioned in the last verses—and also the gladness of heart which comes to those who pray. Luke 24: 53.

The gospel of John commences: "In the beginning"—before the birth of any human being, and before the worlds were created. John takes up the pen of inspiration to prove that Jesus is the Almighty Son of God, and his book opens with the explicit declaration that Jesus Who came in human form was God's Son. (John 1: 1-3, 14.) John's gospel ends with what otherwise would be an unnecessary hyperbole if Jesus is not the Son of God. For as Creator of the vast, illimitable universe (which John (1: 1-3, 14) declared Jesus to be) all that He has done could never be recorded in all the books in the world. From the first words to the last of his gospel John reveals Jesus as the eternal Son of God, possessor of infinite power.

Moses was a type of Christ (Deut. 18: 15-18)—Deliverer, Leader, Law-Giver, etc. Through Moses' ministry the *first* plague fell upon the Egyptians—water was turned into blood. (Ex. 7: 14-20.) Jesus' *first* miracle was the turning of water into wine (John 2: 1-11), and Jesus used wine as a symbol of His shed blood. (Matt. 26: 27-29.) Water was turned into blood in the *first* Egyptian plague; the *last plague* brought death to all the first-born who were not protected by the blood of the passover Lamb, which was slain for their salvation. See Ex. 12.

In the first book in the Sacred Canon of Scripture (Genesis) the question of numbering the stars, if we are able (which, of course, we are not able to do), is brought to our notice (Gen. 15: 5); the last book, Revelation, urges us to "count the number of the beast." (Rev. 13: 18), which, of course, we can do. As we are thus directed to the thought of counting in the first book and again in the last book of Scripture we take notice of this indication that within the Bible will be found a numeric system. Jesus is "Palmoni, the numberer of secrets, or, the *wonderful Numberer*." (See Dan. 8: 13, margin.) And those who follow the Master's injunction to heed the numeric system of Holy Writ will learn some amazing and helpful things.

Gen. 14: 4 brings to view for the first time the number twelve, when harmony existed among the nations brought to our notice in that verse. The last occasion the number 12 is employed in Scripture is when there is harmony among all people in the kingdom of Christ. (Rev. 22: 2.) The twelfth time the number twelve is mentioned in the Word of God is where the breastplate of judgment worn by the High Priest is first brought to view. This breastplate had upon it twelve precious stones, practically the same as the twelve foundation stones of the New Jerusalem. (Compare Ex. 28: 17-20 with Rev. 21: 19-20.) The breastplate was "Foursquare" (Ex. 28: 16) just as the Holy City, also, is said to be "Foursquare." (Rev. 21: 16.) The precious stones were arranged "in four rows" with three in a row; even as the future capital of Christ's kingdom has four sides with three gates to each side. (See Rev. 21: 12-13.) From the first time twelve is mentioned, when the nations were in harmony, we are pointed all through the Divine Book, by the use of

155

the number twelve in so many different ways, to the time when harmony will once more prevail among all people in the everlasting kingdom of the "Prince of Peace."

The *first* time the *number 13* is mentioned is when we read: "Twelve years they served Chedorlaomer, and in the thirteenth year they *rebelled*." (Gen. 14: 4.) From that first mention of the number 13 in connection with a rebellion that number is associated in Scripture with *the rebellion against God*. Hence the dragon (the designation used in the Revelation for Christ's adversary, Satan) occurs 13 times in the Revelation. See Rev. 12: 3, 4, 7 (twice), 9, 13, 16, 17; 13: 2, 4, 11; 16: 13; 20: 2.

But the rebelling forces of evil eventually will be overthrown —the final conflict in which Satan and his hordes will be vanquished is given the *symbolic,* or *antitypical,* name of "Armageddon." (Rev. 16: 16.) As *Megiddo* is brought into the picture in the *final con-flict between the forces of good and evil* we are not surprised to see that it is mentioned *13 times* in the Scriptures. See Josh. 12: 21; 17: 11; Judges 1: 27; 5: 19; 1 Kings 4: 12; 9: 15; 2 Kings 9: 27; 23: 29, 30; 1 Chron. 7: 29; 2 Chron. 35: 22; Zech. 12: 11; Rev. 16: 16. The numbers employed in the Revelation are used in con-nection with *Christ and His Church—and their enemies*—and are *not national* numbers.

It is an erroneous conception to interpret "Armageddon" as a battle between nations at Megiddo. Such a belief is not sustained by any of the laws of interpretation given by the Holy Spirit in the Scriptures themselves. As we shall show in our next chapter, there is a definite connection between the first and the last in the Scriptures. In the interpretation of last-day prophecies we must be sure to heed the Divinely-given principle of going back to the first recorded events, places, persons, names, etc. By this principle alone—and there are other principles of interpretation, all of which are in perfect harmony with the one we are considering—we know that the *last,* which is the thirteenth, reference to Megiddo (Rev. 16: 16) will be the world-wide, spiritual counterpart of the *first* typical conflict fought at Megiddo, recorded in Judges 4 and 5.

By the principle of going back to the first mention to understand more fully concerning the last mention we know that the things of Israel, which form the basis of the Third Angel's Message, and which are mentioned so frequently throughout the Revelation, are rightly applied by us in a world-wide, spiritual sense.

CHAPTER XXI.

THE LAW OF THE FIRST AND THE LAST ASSOCIATED WITH THE LAW OF TYPE AND ANTITYPE.

Like the books of the Bible, and the various features of Divine truth, the laws governing the understanding of the Bible are definitely connected and at times interwoven. Thus the law of the first and the last mention is connected with the law of repetition and the law of enlargement. The enlargement comes by the repetition, and the repetition repeats that which is first mentioned—and, naturally, the enlargement and the repetition are found in the last mention, for it is in the last mention that things are enlarged to their fullest sense, and it is there that the last repetition occurs. The laws of Biblical exegesis, like the glorious colours of the foundation stones of the New Jerusalem, blend together in wonderful harmony, revealing the exquisite handiwork and the faultless wisdom of the infinite Creator.

As in the human anatomy all the nerves lead from the extremities to the brain, so, in the Bible, all the threads of truth, all the laws of interpretation, meet in one splendid union in the Book of Revelation. The writer has often marvelled at the Creator's handiwork revealed in the almost endless weaving of a warp and woof of Old Testament types and shadows in an antitypical application until all the truths of divine revelation are woven into each other until they become one perfect, complete pattern incorporating all the laws governing Scriptural interpretation, and all the divine arts and sciences of instruction in the ways of righteousness. We cannot include in this book all that could be written in demonstration of the fact that the book which closes the sacred canon of Scripture is, indeed, "The *Revelation* of Jesus Christ," as the opening words of the Book declare it to be. Jesus is revealed therein in all the capacities in which He appears all through the Bible—Creator, King, Redeemer, Lamb, Lion, Destroyer of Evil, the Saviour of His people, the Leader of His people, the High Priest, the Mediator, etc. The use of numbers, colours, the meaning of names, the law of type and antitype, the principle of the world-wide symbolized by the local, the laws of repetition and enlargement, of the first and the last, etc., all of these laws and principles governing the interpretation of Scripture that are brought to view in other parts of the Bible are employed in the Apocalypse to reveal Christ in all His wisdom, honour, and glory.

Jesus said of Himself: "I am Alpha and Omega [the first and the last letters of the Greek Alphabet], the beginning and the end, the first and the last." Rev. 22: 13. In this verse we see that in three different ways Jesus has drawn our attention to the importance of the first and the last *as they pertain to Him.* As the whole Bible is a "Revelation of Jesus Christ"—and the book of Revelation reveals that fact, for it is impossible to understand the Revelation without first knowing the preceding books of Holy Writ—we know from the Master's re-iteration of the importance of the first and the last that herein is revealed one of the principles upon which is established the true interpretation of the Scriptures. The fact that our Lord, in three different ways, has drawn our attention to this guiding principle of studying His Word brings to view another principle of interpretation inseparable from the law of the first and the last, namely, the use of the number three throughout the Scriptures.

A complete understanding of the prophecies of the Bible comes to us only as we apply, not merely their "double," but also their "triple" application. A study of the first and the last, in conjunction with other laws of interpretation, makes this fact stand out very clearly. Jesus—the First and the Last—is the Revealer of the Trinity.

In the beginning of Revelation (as at its end) Jesus says: "I am Alpha and Omega, the beginning and the ending, saith the Lord, which *is,* and which *was,* and which *is to come,* the Almighty." Rev. 1: 8. Throughout the Revelation Jesus keeps before us the fact that He is the first and the last. See Rev. 1: 8, 11, 17; 2: 8; 21: 6; 22: 13. Jehovah, in His relation to the three divisions of time—the past, present, and future—is mentioned three times. Rev. 1: 4, 8; 4: 8. The Revelation, like the rest of Scripture, is "from Him which *is,* and which *was,* and which *is to come.*" The name Jehovah signifies God's eternal existence—"from everlasting to everlasting thou art God"—"The I AM" of the past, "The I AM" of the present, "The I AM" of the future. See Ex. 3: 14. "Jesus Christ the same *yesterday,* and *to-day,* and *forever.*" Heb. 13: 8. A study of the first and the last reveals Jesus as He was "*yesterday*" in His dealings with *national* Israel and their literal sacrificial services, "*to-day*" (see Heb., chapters 3 and 4) in His dealings with *spiritual* Israel until He completes His heavenly ministry and returns to claim His own, "and forever," in His eternal kingdom.

The connection between the first and the last and the number three is further demonstrated in the chapter dealing with "The Triple Application of the Prophecies." For the present we point out that the *first* mention of a thing in Scripture is its *literal* setting. All Bible symbols have literal, familiar things as a basis.

They are first mentioned in a literal, or "natural" way, whereas in their second, or "double," application they are to be applied symbolically, or spiritually. The "double" application (employed throughout the New Testament) is not in the same *literal* and *national* way as the *first* mention. By not heeding this principle grievous, last-day errors regarding the literal Jews and Palestine have been taught.

In harmony with other inspired writers, Paul directs us to the law of the first and the last. He says: "The *first* man Adam was made a living soul; the *last* Adam was made a quickening spirit." In connection with his mention of the first and the last Paul draws our attention to a principle governing the employment of spiritual interpretations. He shows that the *literal comes first, and afterward the spiritual application, when made, is based upon the first mention which is literal.* Paul says: "Howbeit that was *not first* which is *spiritual,* but that which is *natural;* and afterward that which is *spiritual.*" 1 Cor. 15: 45-49. Spiritual interpretations must not in any sense deny the literality or historicity of that which is first mentioned in a "natural" way. The literalness of the past must be the solid foundation upon which rests the spiritual interpretation. Care must be exercised in *"rightly dividing* the word of truth." 2 Tim. 2: 15. There is a place for the literal or the historical—that which is mentioned first—recorded in the Old Testament. There is a place for the spiritual application in this "dispensation of the Holy Spirit." (T.M., p. 511.) "Even the Spirit of truth; Whom the world cannot receive, *because it seeth Him not."* John 14: 17.

In the days of literal Israel things were on a literal, local, national basis. The dispensation of the literal and national ended when Jesus came literally and visibly to the literal Jews in the literal land of Israel. His death on Calvary terminated the typical sacrificial services. This was shown when "the veil of the temple was rent in twain from the top to the bottom." Matt. 27: 50, 51. The literal things—priests, offerings, temple, city, nation, land, promises and prophecies, etc.—which went with the literal sacrifices, the New

Testament writers apply in a "double" or world-wide, spiritual application in connection with spiritual Israel.

He who studies diligently into the Scriptures will notice that the laws of Repetition, the First and the Last, Type and Antitype, etc., are frequently used by the prophets. One thing is common to these laws—*the enlargement of the first mention.* The "double" application comprehends so much more than the original word, phrase, or sentence. The *first* occasion represents the *local* and *literal* pertaining to some historical incident; the *repetition,* or the *antitype,* represents the *world-wide* which is applied to the realms of the kingdom of Christ and the enemies of His church. In the musical world the octave illustrates the principle of the first and the last. The octave brings us back to begin again—but an octave higher—on the same note. This note, which is eight above the same note below, has so many more vibrations. And the repetitions and the antitypes of prophetic imagery are always magnifications of the historical basis upon which they rest. In His "Sermon on the Mount" Jesus proclaimed the first of the beatitudes: "Blessed are the poor in spirit: *for theirs is the kingdom of heaven."* He does not repeat "for theirs is the kingdom of heaven" until He comes to the *eighth* beatitude: "Blessed are they which are persecuted for righteousness' sake: *for theirs is the kingdom of heaven."* Matt. 5: 3-10. For a further study of the significance of the number eight in the Scriptures, see my "Christ Conquers," pp. 123-139.

In the prophecy of chapters 10-12 of Daniel eight kings, commencing with Cyrus, are said to "stand up"—the eighth being *Jesus* commencing His reign in His eternal kingdom. See Dan. 12: 1. Thus we have *Cyrus at the commencement* of this prophecy, and *Jesus at its ending.* Cyrus, "the shepherd king" (Isa. 44: 28) overthrew Babylon by drying up the waters of the Euphrates, liberated Israel from their Babylonian bondage, and gave the first decree for their return to their promised land to rebuild and restore the city and temple at Jerusalem. Cyrus, the *first* king in this prophecy, God's "anointed," or "messiah" (see Isa. 45: 1), is a type of the *last* king in the prophecy—Jesus "the Shepherd King," God's "Anointed" or "Messiah"—Who will come to overthrow spiritual Babylon by first drying up her symbolic waters, and will bring deliverance to His people and enable them to go to their land of promise and to the worship of God in His holy temple.

Here we have an example of "the first and the last." Cyrus, the *first* or *typical* king, was a literal, limited, national king; Jesus, the *last* or *antitypical* King, is the spiritual King, unlimited in power and glory. Thus the *last, or the antitype,* repeats in a *spiritual, world-wide* sense that which was *literal* and *national* in regard to the first.

In the prophecy of Dan. 8 and 9 we find the same principle brought to view. This prophecy came to Daniel during the last year of Babylon's reign—just before the coming of Cyrus, who issued the first decree for the return of the Jews from *literal* Babylon to Jerusalem to do their God-appointed task of rebuilding and repairing the temple and city. The 2,300 days of this prophecy were to *commence* "from the going forth of the commandment to restore and to build Jerusalem." Dan. 9: 25. Thus the *first* part of this prophecy referred to the literal return of literal Israel from literal Babylon to literal Jerusalem to rebuild and restore the literal temple and city of Jerusalem. The *last* portion of the prophecy pertains to spiritual Israel coming out of *spiritual* Babylon and spiritually returning to spiritual Jerusalem to rebuild and repair the *spiritual* temple, city, and walls of *spiritual* Jerusalem, which the spiritual Babylonians had destroyed in their day of power. The *last* is the repetition of the *first,* but always in a *spiritual,* world-wide sense.

The *first* part of the 70 weeks allotted to the Jewish nation pertained to the Jews returning to rebuild their temple and city. The 70 weeks—or the 490 years—*ended* the Jews' national probation. The destruction of the temple and city of Jerusalem by the Romans in A.D. 70 was the inevitable result—coming after God had given them an extended period of probation—of their failure to accept God's plan for them. See Dan. 9: 24-26, margin. The events occurring both at the *commencement,* and also following the *ending* of the 70 weeks of Dan. 9: 24-27, are typical of the experiences of spiritual Israel. Spiritual Israel comes out of spiritual Babylon to spiritually rebuild the temple and city and, later, in the final scenes, the spiritual Romans (the Revelation shows that the religion of ancient Babylon was transferred to Rome) will endeavour to destroy the spiritual temple and city of God—the church. (See 2 Cor. 6: 16; Ephes. 2: 20-22; Rev. 11: 1, 2, etc.) In 5T., p. 451, God's servant states:—

"As the approach of the Roman armies was a sign to the disciples of the impending destruction of Jerusalem, so may this apostasy [Protestant nations enforcing the keeping of the old Babylonian-Roman-Papal Sunday] be a sign to us that the limit of God's forbearance is reached, that the measure of our nation's iniquity is full, and that the angel of mercy is about to take her flight, never to return. The people of God will *then* be plunged into those scenes of affliction and distress which the prophets have described as the time of Jacob's trouble. . . . The cries of the faithful, persecuted ones ascend to heaven. . . . The mark of *deliverance* will be set upon the men who keep God's commandments, who revere His law, and who refuse the mark of the beast or of his image."

In the days of literal Rome, God could not protect the disobedient and rejected Jewish nation but, in the last days, obedient, spiritual Israel, God's chosen remnant, will not be destroyed by their enemies.

The book of Daniel *commences* with reference to the destruction of the literal temple at Jerusalem and the vessels of the house of the Lord being taken by the Babylonians over into the house of their false god. Dan. 1: 1, 2.

The last time the Babylonians used the vessels of God's temple in connection with their false system of worship was on the occasion of Belshazzar's feast. "Then they brought the golden vessels that were taken out of the temple of the house of God which was at Jerusalem. And the king, and his princes . . . drank in them . . . and praised the gods . . . In the same hour came forth fingers of a man's hand, and wrote over against the candlestick upon the plaister of the wall of the king's palace" (Dan. 5: 2-5), in living letters of fire, the announcement of the close of their national probation and their impending doom. Vs. 7-17, 24-28. Within the impregnable walls of their city the Babylonians felt secure, but disaster quickly followed. Cyrus led his conquering armies into the heart of Babylon via the bed of the Euphrates—the waters of which had been turned aside from their accustomed channel. "Sudden destruction" came upon Belshazzar who, but a few hours before, had praised his gods and felt secure from danger.

In my "Christ Conquers," pp. 99-107, I have shown that the prediction of the conditions prevailing in literal Babylon before and at the time of her overthrow is also a prophecy concerning the same experiences before and at the time of the overthrow of spiritual Babylon. Basing his prediction concerning spiritual Babylon in the last days upon the experience of literal Babylon (see Isa. 47, etc.), Paul declares that when the spiritual Babylonians also "say,

162

Peace and safety; then *sudden destruction* cometh upon them . . . and they shall not escape." 1 Thess. 5: 3. When spiritual Babylon "saith in her heart, I sit a queen, and am no widow, and *shall see no sorrow* . . . her plagues come in one day, death and mourning." Rev. 18: 7, 8.

The last prophecy of Daniel (10-12) brings us down to the close of probation—typified by the events recorded in Dan. 5—when Jesus, the great High Priest, ceases His ministry in the heavenly sanctuary on behalf of spiritual Israel. Then "there shall be a time of trouble, such as never was since there was a nation even to that same time; and at that time thy people shall be *delivered* [as literal Israel was delivered when Cyrus overthrew Babylon and freed them from their Babylonian oppressors, and caused them to return to their own land], every one . . . written in the book." Dan. 12: 1. This prophecy begins and ends with the Deliverer and the deliverance of God's people: their deliverance is associated with the *overthrow of Babylon.* The book of Daniel *commences* with literal Babylon's attack upon literal Israel—destroying the temple and city—the *last* chapter brings us to the time when the spiritual Babylonians will make war upon God's spiritual temple and city—the church—but, because spiritual Israel is obedient, God will deliver His people and destroy their oppressors.

A deeper insight into Daniel's first prophecy (chapter 2) will also reveal the same principle of the literal in the first, or historical, mention, and the spiritual at the end of time. Nebuchadnezzar, the first king of Babylon, represents the spiritual, world-wide rulership of spiritual Babylon. As Nebuchadnezzar was supreme ruler over his vast dominion (see Dan. 2: 37, 38) so spiritual Babylon will, for a time, gain full control in the last days of earth's history. Nebuchadnezzar's proud words: "Is not this *great* Babylon that I have built" (Dan. 4: 30) are used to describe "that *great* city"—spiritual Babylon. See Rev. 14: 8; 16: 19; 17: 18; 18: 2, 10, 16, 18, 19; 19: 2.

The Book of Revelation, being the last book in the sacred canon of Scripture, illustrates the application of the laws of interpretation which are revealed in previous books of Holy Writ. This book is "the Revelation." It can be rightly understood only in the light of such laws of interpretation as those of Repetition, Type and Antitype, and the First and the Last. Its references to Old Testament historical pictures are applied in a much vaster conception than the original incident which provided the prophet with his descriptive imagery. Failing to apply these laws has caused some to literalize some of the imagery employed by Christ in the Revelation—that is, the application is again applied to the local and literal as in its first historical mention in the Old Testament, instead of, according to the laws of repetition and enlargement, etc, to spiritual, world-wide Israel and their enemies. The historical records of the early books of the Bible are the seed thoughts which grow into matured plants in the later books—the Book of Revelation reveals those plants in their fuller growth. Those things that are brought to view in the Revelation are the magnification of earlier things mentioned in the Scripture. What was local and national in the Old Testament is lifted into the realm of the world-wide and the spiritual. Therefore, to fully understand each particular in the imagery of the Revelation it is necessary to trace that particular right through the Scriptures from its first mention and obtain all "the testimony of Jesus" concerning the Revelator's imagery.

In Gen. 14: 18 we *first* read of "the *priest* of the most high God." This first priest of God mentioned in the Sacred Book was "Melchizedek, *king* of *Salem*." Salem, later, was called Jerusalem. In Heb. 7: 1, 2 we are given the meanings of the names Melchizedek and Salem: "*Melchisedec*, king of *Salem* . . . first being by interpretation *King of righteousness*, and after that also *King of Salem*, which is, *King of Peace*."

The first mention of "the *priest* of . . . God" was a king who reigned at Jeru-salem—a king-priest. The record of this priest-king of Salem, who blessed Abraham after his triumph over his enemies, provides the local setting which (in harmony with the plan upon which the whole of the Bible is written) is enlarged upon by succeeding Bible writers. When God called Israel to be His peculiar people He said to them: "And ye shall be unto Me a *kingdom of priests*, and an holy nation." Ex. 19: 6. God commanded that the nation of Israel—the kingdom of priests—was to have Jerusalem—the city of Peace—as its national centre, where the priests of God were to officiate in the temple built according to God's explicit directions. In Ps. 110: 4, the Psalmist records the oath which God made to His Son: "The Lord hath sworn, and will not repent, Thou art a *priest* for ever *after the* order of Melchizedek." Melchizedek, the King-priest of Jerusalem, the city of Peace, is magnified into the kingly priesthood of the entire nation of Israel centred in Jerusalem; then, again, into the greater ministry of Jesus, "the *King* of Israel" (John 1: 49, Matt. 27: 11)—"a *priest* upon His *throne*"

(Zech. 6: 13), "the *throne* of *grace*" (Heb. 4: 16) in "the heavenly Jerusalem." Heb. 12: 22.

The New Testament writers apply the names and designations of national Israel to the church—the spiritual Israel. The things which first belonged to national Israel in Palestine are lifted out of their national and local Palestinian setting into the larger fulfilment —the antitypical—which is world-wide in connection with the church. The *last* application is definitely connected with the *first* application—except that it is *not limited in the old national sense, but is as extensive as Christ's spiritual kingdom—the world.* Thus *the church* is now said to be "a spiritual house, an holy *priesthood, to offer up spiritual sacrifices. . . . Ye are a chosen generation, a royal priesthood,* an holy nation." 1 Pet. 2: 5, 9.

Anyone, anywhere, who joins Christ's spiritual kingdom inherits the promises made to national Israel. National Israel was "the *kingdom* of *priests";* the church is now said to be "an holy *priesthood,"* a *"royal priesthood,* an holy *nation."* John declares that Jesus "hath made us *kings and priests* unto God." Rev. 1: 6. Pointing to people redeemed from this earth (resurrected and taken to heaven at the time of Christ's resurrection—see Matt. 27: 50-53 and Ephes. 4: 8-10, margin), who are assisting Christ in His heavenly ministry as the king-priest on the throne of grace, John says: "And they sung a new song, saying Thou art worthy . . . for Thou wast slain, and hast redeemed us to God by Thy blood out of every kindred, and tongue, and people, and nation; and hast made us unto our God *kings and priests;* and we shall *reign* upon the earth." Rev. 5: 9, 10. Later, after the second advent, the saved of all ages "shall be *priests* of God and Christ, and shall *reign* with Him a thousand years." Rev. 20: 6.

Thus the king-priest reigning in Salem, mentioned in Genesis, forms the basis of later references to king-priests, and is carried right through the Scriptures until the close of the Revelation and the events of eternity. To briefly summarise regarding Melchizedek: we learn that the *first priest* was a *king* who reigned at Jeru-salem; the *first* time *kingdom* is mentioned is in connection with a *nation of priests.* The *first* mention of priests in the Revelation is when the saints are said to be *"kings and priests."* The *last* occurrence of *priests* in the Revelation states that the church "shall *reign* with" Christ. Rev. 20: 6. The last time priesthood is mentioned in the Bible is when the church is said to be "a *royal priesthood,* an holy *nation."* 1 Pet. 2: 9. Thus, in the sacred Scriptures, "the *first* and the *last"* are definitely linked—the *first* foreshadows the *last;* the *last* is the enlargement of the *first.*

After the fall of Adam and Eve "the Lord God" made "coats of skins, and clothed them." Gen. 3: 21. Afterwards, in the economy of Israel, God commanded the priests to wear "fine linen" called the "holy garments" (Lev. 6: 10; 16: 4, 32; Ezek. 44: 17, 18). Isaiah declared: "He hath clothed me with garments of salvation; He hath covered me with the robe of righteousness." Isa. 61: 10. The Revelator speaks of believers now possessing "white robes." Rev. 6: 11. "White robes"—spiritual garments—are now worn by the saints. Rev. 3: 4, 5. Those assisting Christ in "the New Jerusalem temple" ("A Word to the Little Flock," pp. 11, 12) are "clothed in white raiment." The saved will wear white robes throughout eternity. Rev. 7: 9, 13. Thus, throughout Scripture, from Genesis where Eden is lost, to Revelation where Eden is pictured as being restored, the thought of God providing a covering for His people is kept before us.

Esau was born "red, all over like an hairy garment; and they called his name Esau." Gen. 25: 25. Esau sold his birthright for some *"red* pottage . . . *therefore* was his name called *Edom, that is, Red."* Gen. 25: 30, margin. Throughout the Scriptures, from this reference to the book of Revelation, there is a play upon the meaning of the name of *Edom* (the name of the man who despised his birthright and who hated Israel) in describing the fate of those who, like Esau, lightly esteem salvation and hate God's people. As shown in the chapters dealing with the meanings of Bible names "Edom," meaning *"red as blood,"* and "Bozrah" (the capital of Edom's land), meaning *"a vintage,"* are employed throughout the Bible in a symbolical way to describe the bloodshed in the world-wide "Armageddon," "the mountain of slaughter," which is likened to the treading of the red wine from the grapes in "the winepress of the wrath of God." Thus the *first* mention of *Edom* with its significant meaning is definitely connected with the *"blood"* which "came out of the winepress of the wrath of God" described by the Revelator in Rev. 14: 18-20; 19: 15.

From the time God gave Abram his new name "Abraham," meaning *"Father of a great multitude"* (Gen. 17: 4, 5, margin), we can trace throughout the Bible, firstly, the literal seed (see Gen. 13: 16; 15: 5; 22: 17; 28: 14; Deut. 1: 10; Jer. 33: 22; Heb. 11: 12, etc.), and then, the spiritual seed of Abraham until, in Rev. 7: 9, we read of *"a great multitude,* which no man could number, of all nations, and kindreds, and people, and tongues"—the *spiritual* children of Abraham—*"the father of all* that believe." Rom. 4: 11.

From the time that God gave Jacob, the Supplanter, his new name "Israel," meaning "A prince of God"—having prevailing power "with God and with men" (Gen. 32: 28, margin)—the name "Israel" stands for those who, like Jacob, wrestle with God in prayer until their natures change into the divine similitude. In Gen. 32: 28, the *first* mention of "Israel" concerned one man: in Rev. 7: 4 ; 21: 12, the *last* references to "Israel" apply to world-wide, spiritual Israel—the church of Jesus Christ.

And so we could go through the Revelation and notice that *there* is found the *last* mention, in a *world-wide, spiritual sense* in connection with the church, of those themes, persons, places, names, etc., coming *first* into the Old Testament Scriptures in connection with some *literal* historical incident. *This is a definite law of interpretation employed throughout the Revelation,* and to interpret it correctly—especially in its prophecies of the closing scenes of earth's history—this law must be heeded.

The name "Nimrod" means "Rebellious." From the time Nimrod the "rebellious" one founded Babylon (Gen. 10: 8-10, margin) we can trace Babylon in the Scriptures as the kingdom of rebellion until she comes to her end in the battle of Armageddon (Rev. 16: 16), which is the 13th (the Bible number for rebellion) time Megiddo, meaning "slaughter" or "destruction," is mentioned in the Bible. Armageddon, meaning "the mountain of slaughter," is the symbolical name for the world-wide destruction of those who, like Nimrod, are "rebellious" against the Commandments of the Lord by heeding the commandments and worship of Babylon.

Many hundreds of the expressions employed by the Revelator are quotations from the Old Testament. In the Old Testament those passages were used to describe national Israel and the overthrow of their national enemies. When the Revelator makes use of those same texts he lifts them out of their literal and local setting and gives them a world-wide and antitypical meaning. In the Old Testament they described literal factors in connection with God's national people, and their national enemies. The Revelator employs those Old Testament *pictures of the conflicts of national Israel and her enemies to provide* the descriptive imagery of the *conflicts of the Church of Jesus Christ with her foes.*

The doom of old, literal Babylon is clearly forecast in Isa., chapters 13 and 14. Isa. 14: 12-14 sets forth Lucifer as the invisible ruler of ancient Babylon. Babylon was overthrown because it had become the seat of Satan's worldly dominion. In describing the overthrow of spiritual, or the antitypical, Babylon, the Revelator employs imagery obtained from the prophetic pictures given in the Old Testament of the overthrow of ancient Babylon.

The Babylonians destroyed Jerusalem, burned down the magnificent Temple of Solomon, which was the centre of their religious and national life, and took the national people of God into captivity. Lucifer, the invisible king of spiritual Babylon, unites his forces to attack and destroy the *church*—God's temple. (See 2 Cor. 6:16; Ephes. 2: 20-22; Rev. 11: 1-2, etc.) The type and the antitype must never be lost sight of in the study of the Apocalypse, or the meaning of the symbols will not be understood in their proper sense.

When Jeremiah was chosen to proclaim to the rebellious Jewish nation that unless they repented the Babylonians would come to destroy them, their city and temple, God encouraged him with the glorious fact that God was first on the field of action. Before committing to this sorrowful prophet his stern messages of denunciation the Lord showed him the "rod of an *almond* tree." (Jer. 1: 11.) "Then saith the Lord unto me, Thou hast seen well: for I will *hasten* my word to perform it." (V. 12.) The meaning of the Hebrew word for *almond,* according to Dr. Strong, is: "to be alert, i.e., sleepless; hence be on the lookout . . . *hasten,* remain, wake, watch (for) . . . the *almond* tree as being the *earliest* in bloom."

As is so often the case in the prophetic descriptions, there is a play upon the meaning of a word. Before Jeremiah was informed of the coming depredatory invasion of Israel by the Babylonians, God showed by the *almond* tree that He was the *first* on the battlefield. Nothing could happen to His people, but what He knew all about it; and His enemies would never find Him unwatchful, or asleep. The *almond* tree, blossoming *first* of the trees, was a horticultural symbol that He was *first* on the scene of action, and that He would *"hasten"* to perform His word.

The same thoughts are expressed in the predictions given by God to Isaiah. Isaiah 39 brings before us the proud and foolish act of Hezekiah in showing to the representatives of Babylon all his treasures. Isaiah foretold the invasion of Palestine by the Babylonians to obtain possession of the wealth Hezekiah had shown them. (See Isa. 39: 3-6.) As usual, God did not leave His people to be fearful of the coming scourge. He immediately cheered them with the words: "Comfort ye, comfort ye, My people, saith your God." (Isa. 40: 1.) The Lord then told them of His almighty power. (Isa. 40: 12-26.) By His wonderful providences He would cause the kings of the east to come against Babylon and destroy these oppressors of His people, and thus bring about their deliverance from the hands of the Babylonians. (See Isa. 41: 2, 25; 46: 11.) "The Lord hath raised up the spirit of the kings of the Medes: for His device is against Babylon, to destroy it, because it is the vengeance of the Lord, the vengeance of His temple." (Jer. 51: 11.) "Prepare against her the *nations* with the *kings* of the Medes, the captains thereof, and all the rulers thereof." (V. 28.) "Many kings . . . against thee, O daughter of Babylon." (Jer. 50: 41, 42. See also Isa. 13: 17; Dan. 8:20.) Because Babylon was overthrown by kings from the east the Revelator, in describing the overthrow of spiritual Babylon, speaks of the coming of the kings of the east. Rev. 16: 12. "The kings of the east" can have reference only to the enemies of Babylon. To apply these kings of the east, in the description of the overthrow of Babylon, to Japan or China reveals a failure to grasp the setting of the prophecy.

In bringing down ancient Babylon Cyrus dried up the waters of the Euphrates. (See Isa. 44: 27, 28; 45: 1; Jer. 50: 38; 51: 32, 36.) Hence the mention of the drying up of the waters of the Babylonian Euphrates in the Revelator's description of the overthrow of modern Babylon. Rev. 16: 12; 17: 1, 15.

When Isaiah predicted the coming of the Babylonians, God *hastened* to comfort His people by reminding them of His almighty power. (Isa. 40.) Through the exercise of that power He would raise up Cyrus, the anointed, meaning the Messiah—the type of Christ—who would lead other kings from the east in the destruction of Israel's Babylonian oppressors. See Isa. 41: 2, 25; 44: 28; 45: 1, 13.

It was at the commencement of this message of the coming deliverance from the hands of the Babylonians by Cyrus and the kings from the east, that the God of Israel said: "I, the Lord, the first, and with the last; I am He." (Isa. 41: 4.) This comforting truth is repeated in Isa. 43: 10; 44: 6; 48: 12. "Thus saith the Lord, *the King of Israel,* and His *Redeemer,* the Lord of hosts; I am the *first* and I am the *last.*" (Isa. 44: 6.) "Hearken unto Me, O Jacob and *Israel, My called; I am He; I am the first, I also am the last.*" Isa. 48: 12.

These are the verses *Jesus quotes* in the Revelation *when referring to Himself as "the first and the last."* In Isaiah, the Son of God speaks of Himself as "the first and the last" when *encouraging His people* with the promise that He would *overthrow their Babylonian enemies* and bring them *deliverance.* In the Book of Revelation He again refers to Himself as "the first and the last" to encourage *His Church* that He will *overthrow the antitypical Babylon* and bring about *their eternal deliverance.*

The Bible commences with: "In the beginning *God,*" and ends with "The grace of our *Lord Jesus Christ,* be with you all. Amen." (Rev. 22: 21.) Jesus, the Almighty Son of God, is the One Who created all things. Thus the *first* and the *last* verses of the Bible itself *show that our Creator is our Redeemer.* This, of course, is plainly taught in such passages as Isa. 41: 14; 43: 1, 3, 11, 15, etc. It is in this very message, found in these comforting verses of Isaiah, that the *Creator-Redeemer refers to Himself as "the first and the last".* (Isa. 41: 4; 43: 10; 48:12.) Thus the actual construction of the whole canon of Scripture agrees with the internal teaching. That is, the *beginning* and the *ending,* the *first* and the *last verses of the Bible teach the same as the verses in which Jesus, the Creator-Redeemer, claims to be the first and the last.* To draw our attention to the fact that He is "the Author (or the Originator, or *Beginner)* and *finisher* of our faith." (Heb. 12: 2); and "the first and the last," Jesus repeatedly emphasised the importance of the first and the last.

As Israel's God early in His message of comfort to national Israel termed Himself "the first and the last," so this same expression is given at the commencement of "the Revelation of Jesus Christ," which is a message of comfort to His Church. As in Isaiah, the Redeemer-King of Israel repeated His designation several times in outlining Babylon's doom, so in the Revelation, which gives an outline of the final doom of spiritual Babylon, He repeats several times that He is "the first and the last." In the Revelation we are informed of the superiority of Jesus Christ over His enemies, who are couched under the symbolic term "Babylon." He is first on the field of battle against the army of wickedness—He is the "Almond" among the trees—He *"Hastens"* to perform His Word to save His people and to destroy evil. He will be the last on the field of conflict, for He will destroy His enemies and deliver His people. *This is the message of the Book of Revelation.*

In Rev. 1 there is employed an Epanados, which serves to illustrate the law of repetition, whereby the last comes back to the first only on a higher note, or greater number of vibrations if we regard it in the terms of the octave. Of course, these things are always used to exalt Jesus—for it is "The Revelation of Jesus Christ." In Rev. 1 eight quotations from the Old Testament are used in exalting Jesus as the destroyer of His enemies and the Deliverer of His people. These eight texts are so employed that the first text is quoted from the same Old Testament book as the eighth, and keeping before us the principle of "the first and the last," we note that the second Old Testament quotation is from the same book as the second to last; the third from the same book as the third from last; and the central ones—the fourth from the first and fourth from the last—are from the same Old Testament book. The following sets forth this Epanados, employed in Rev. 1 to declare Christ's Lordship:—

  (1) V. 5. *Isa. 55: 4.*
    (2) V. 7. Dan. 7: 13.
      (3) V. 7. Zech. 12: 10.
        (4) V. 8. Isa. 41: 4; 44: 6; 48: 12.
        (4) V. 11. Isa. 41: 4; 44: 6; 48: 12.
      (3) V. 12. Zech. 4: 2.
    (2) V. 13-15. Dan. 7: 9, 13, 22; 10: 5, 6.
  (1) V. 16. *Isa. 49: 2.*

Our Lord, in setting forth the truth that He is "the first and the last," employed this Epanados as one of the means of arresting our attention so that we would study further such laws of Scriptural interpretation as the law of repetition, the law of types and antitypes, the law of the first and the last—all of which laws are on an ascending or an enlarged scale—which bring to view Christ's Lordship over His people in their deliverance, and His Lordship over His enemies by their destruction.

The *first* quotation in this Epanados, like the eighth—which is the last—is from the book of Isaiah. The *first* text from Isaiah (55: 4) says that the Messiah would be "a Leader and a Commander to the people." The eighth—the last—quotation in this Epanados, in bringing us back to Isaiah (49: 2), shows *how* the Lord proves Himself to be the "Leader and Commander to the people."

"Out of His mouth went a sharp two-edged sword." (Rev. 1: 16.) The destruction of His enemies by the sword of His mouth.

referred to in Isa. 49: 2, which is the *8th text* quoted in the Epanados of Rev. 1, is again repeated (according to the law of repetition, which is the law of explanation) in Rev. 19: 15, 21: *"Out of His mouth goeth a sharp sword,* that with it He should smite the nations." Christ destroys His enemies at His second coming— that coming and that destruction will affect *the whole world.*

In the comforting message given in Isaiah concerning the over- throw of ancient Babylon, and the deliverance of His people, Jesus, the Almighty Son of God, repeatedly referred to Himself as "the first and the last." He encouraged Israel with the prophecy that Cyrus, the anointed, the messiah—the type of Jesus—would come with other kings from the east and overthrow their enemies, and would bring about their deliverance. By drying up the waters of the River Euphrates, Cyrus led his hosts into the heart of Babylon and brought about its complete destruction. According to the laws of Repetition, of the First and the Last, and of Type and Antitype, this is all to be repeated on a *world-wide scale.* Hence the allusion in Rev. 16: 12-16 to the drying up of the waters of the Euphrates and the overthrow of spiritual Babylon (v. 19) by the kings of the east. At His second advent the "Leader and Commander" of the forces of righteousness will overthrow the forces of evil in the *antitypical conflict of Megiddo.* (See Rev. 16: 16.) This final conflict is enlarged upon in Rev. 19: 11-21. The "sharp sword" in Isaiah's prophecy (49: 2) mentioned in the 8th quotation in the Epanados of Rev. 1, v. 16, is here seen in action (Rev. 19: 15) in the *antitypical* "Armageddon," which results in the complete de- struction of spiritual Babylon.

The *first mention* in the Scriptures has a *definite relation to the last.* The first is a promise of what may be expected in the last. *The first is a prophecy of the last,* though the last is on a larger scale. History repeats itself. (Eccles. 1: 9; 3: 15.) "For *whatsoever* things were written aforetime were written for our learning, that we through patience and comfort *of the Scriptures* might have hope." (Rom. 15: 4.) As we read in the Old Testament of the way God overthrew the evil forces which sought to destroy His people in days gone by we can see how God will overthrow those now who seek to destroy His church. "Now *all* these things happened unto them for ensamples [*types,* margin]: and they are written for our admonition, *upon whom the ends of the world are come."* (1 Cor. 10: 11.) This is speaking specifically of the events which befell national Israel—*one of which was the first battle fought at Megiddo.* This event, like the others, comes under the clearly-stated category of a *type* to have *its antitype in the experience of the church.* **When** the inspired writer says: "Now *all* these things happened unto them for types," wisdom urges us to heed this Divinely-given statement.

To understand what is to transpire at the last battle of the *antitypical Megiddo* we must go back to the *first*—the *typical*—battle fought at Megiddo. In the typical setting God's enemies *"mightily oppressed* the children of Israel." (Judges 4: 3.) God's anger is kindled when those led on by Satan persecute and harm His people. "He that toucheth you toucheth the apple of His eye." (Zech. 2: 8.) "Whosoever shall gather together against thee shall fall for thy sake." (Isa. 54: 15, 17.) "Inasmuch as ye have done it unto one of the least of these, My brethren, ye have done it unto Me." (Matt. 25: 40, 45.) It is when their enemies attack Israel that God's anger is manifested. (Ezek. 38: 18, 19.) Ancient Babylon was destroyed by the might of Israel's God because the Babylonians *"oppressed"* "the children of Israel and the children of Judah." (See Jer. 50: 33, 34.) Spiritual Babylon's doom will be sealed when the machinery for persecution is once more set up ready for operation. It is *the attempt* to destroy *the church that brings about Armageddon,* just as the *first* battle fought at Megiddo came when God's people were *"oppressed"* by their enemies.

Israel's oppressors and enemies were led by the "spirits of devils." (See Deut. 18: 9-14.) Hence the reference to this feature in Rev. 16: 14. "The stars [the angels of God—see Isa. 14: 13, etc.] in their courses fought against Sisera." Judges 5: 19-21. In the *antitypical*—Megiddo conflict—"Armageddon"—the angels destroy those who seek to harm Christ's faithful people. (Joel 3: 11; Rev. 19: 11-21, etc.)

Of the results of the *first* Megiddo battle we read: "And there was *not a man left."* (Judg. 4: 16.) In the *last*—the antitypical—battle of Megiddo all the enemies of Christ and His church will be destroyed. (Luke 17: 27-30; 2 Thess. 1: 7-9; 2 Thess. 2: 8; Rev. 6: 14-17; Rev. 16: 12-21; Rev. 19: 11-21, etc.)

When Jesus refers in Rev. 16: 12-16 to the conflict at Megiddo He does so according to the laws of repetition, of type and antitype, of the first and the last, etc. The historical account of the *first* battle at Megiddo shows that it was a *conflict between demon-led forces against the people of God.* God intervened—sending the angels to execute His wrath upon Israel's, and, hence, His enemies. Thus Israel was delivered. The *last* conflict at Megiddo (Rev.

16: 16) *must be world-wide, according to the laws of interpretation* so abundantly illustrated throughout the Apocalypse; and *that battle must be between God and the evil forces led* by "the spirits of devils" attempting to persecute the people of God. They meet their doom because God intervenes to *deliver* His people. (Dan. 12: 1, etc.) Any other interpretation ignores not only the law of "the first and the last" but every other Biblical law of interpretation.

CHAPTER XXII.

THE LAW OF THE SIGNIFICANCE OF BIBLE NAMES.

A decided connection exists between the proper names of the Bible and its history and doctrines. The meaning of proper names throws much light on the Scriptures. In his "Bible Handbook," p. 185, Dr. Angus states:—"Nearly all the names in Hebrew are significant, and a knowledge of their meaning throws a light upon the context."

Sometimes important aspects of prophetical understanding depend upon the meaning of a name. For instance, in the interpretation of the prophecy of the 2,300 days, or years, of Dan. 8: 14; 9: 24-27, we need to know the meaning of the word "Messiah." This time period commenced with the decree of Artaxerxes, in B.C. 457. See Ezra 7: 6-28; 6: 14. In Dan. 9: 25, we are told to count "seven weeks, and three-score and two weeks" "from the going forth of the commandment to restore and build Jerusalem *unto the Messiah* the Prince." Sixty-nine weeks represent 483 literal years. Four hundred and eighty-three years from mid-way through B.C. 457 (when the decree began to be executed in Palestine, see Ezra 5: 8, 9) brings us to A.D. 27. It is obvious that Jesus was not *born* in A.D. 27. The key is in the *meaning* of the word Messiah, which is given in John 1: 41, margin: "We have found the *Messiah*, which is, being interpreted, the *Christ*, or the *Anointed*." At His birth, our Lord was given the name "Jesus." Matt. 1: 21. Jesus did not become "Christ"—"the Messiah," or "the Anointed"—until the time of His baptism in A.D. 27. See Luke 3: 21-23. In A.D. 27 Jesus declared: "The *Spirit* of the Lord is upon Me, because He hath *anointed* Me." See Luke 4: 1, 14-18. In A.D. 27, "God *anointed Jesus* of Nazareth with the Holy Ghost" (Acts 10: 38), and Jesus, referring to the prophecy of Daniel, proclaimed: "the *time* is fulfilled." Mark 1: 9-15. Thus was fulfilled the prophecy of Daniel, which declared that "the Messiah," or "the Anointed"—"the Christ"—would commence His work of confirming the New Covenant (Dan. 9: 27), which, as also prophesied in Dan. 9: 27, He ratified by the shedding of His blood 3½ years later. The true interpretation of this prophecy, also the proof that Jesus fulfilled it, depends upon the meaning of the word "Messiah."

GOD'S NAME IN THE SCRIPTURES.

The following texts show the significance in the Scriptures of God's name. When Moses requested of God: "I beseech thee, shew me Thy *glory*," God "proclaimed the *name* of the Lord . . . merciful and gracious, long-suffering," etc. Ex. 33: 18; 34: 5, 6. God's character is always associated in Scripture with His name. Isa. 42: 8; 48: 11. "The *name* of the God of Jacob defend thee." Ps. 20: 1. To trust in the *name* of the Lord means to trust His character. V. 7. "Save me, O God, by Thy *name*." Ps. 54: 1. "I will wait on Thy *name*." Ps. 52: 9. "The *name* of the Lord is a strong city: the righteous runneth into it, and is safe." Prov. 18: 10. "They that know Thy *name* will put their trust in Thee." Ps. 9: 10. "I will set him on high, because he hath known My *name*.' Ps. 91: 14. These verses are representative of many which teach that to love and trust the name of God means to have a knowledge of His character. In His prayer on the night of His betrayal, Jesus said: "I have manifested Thy *name*, and will declare it." John 17: 6, 26. In His teaching of the Gospel, Jesus brought a revelation of the character of God. The teaching of the truth of God is a declaration of His character, His nature, His attributes. By false teaching Satan gives an erroneous idea of God's nature and character. Thus the false system of worship centred in the Papacy blasphemes God's *"name and His tabernacle."* Rev. 13: 6. Throughout the Old Testament there is a constant repetition of God's name in association with the sanctuary or temple. 1 Kings 8: 16, 17, 18, 19, 20, 29, 41, 42, 43, 44, 48 illustrates many other passages where the name of God and His revelation of the Gospel in the sanctuary services are invariably connected.

MEANINGS OF NAMES WHICH REVEAL GOD'S CHARACTER AND TEACH THE GOSPEL.

Gen. 22: 14, margin: "And Abraham called the name of that place *Jehovah-jireh*, i.e., *The Lord will see, or, provide.*" God provided Abraham with a sacrifice to die in his son's stead. The story of our redemption is taught in the experience of Abraham offering his *"only son, Isaac"* (Gen. 22: 2, 12), whom he loved so dearly, and in whom all his hopes were centred. The amazing love of God provided not only a sacrifice for Abraham but, on Calvary, a sacrifice for the world. Thus the story of salvation is wrapped up in the meaning of the name *"Jehovah-jireh"*—*"the Lord will provide."* And God is our Provider in so many other ways. See

Phil. 4: 19; Ps. 23: 1; Matt. 6: 31-33, etc. Ex. 17: 15, margin: "And Moses built an altar, and called the name of it *Jehovah-nissi, i.e., The Lord my banner.*" God defended Israel when the Amalekites attacked His people. The defeat of Amalek is typical of the defeat of all the enemies of God's people. See also Num. 24: 20, margin. With the name "Jehovah-nissi" as our banner, we can fight the battles of the Lord, knowing that our enemies will be defeated. Those who trust Him are those who know His name. Ps. 5: 11; 9: 10. "God is . . . a very present help in trouble." Ps. 46: 1.

Judges 6: 24, margin: "Then Gideon . . . called it *Jehovah-shalom, i.e., The Lord send peace.*" This was Gideon's response to the words of the Lord: "Peace be unto thee; fear not." V. 23. In the midst of tumult and trouble God gives His people peace. Isa. 32: 17-19; 48: 14; John 16: 33.

Jer. 33: 16, margin: "And this is the name wherewith she [Jerusalem, or the church] shall be called, *The Lord our Righteousness*, Heb. *Jehovah-tsidkenu.*" Our righteousnesses are as filthy rags. Isa. 64: 6; Phil. 3: 9; Rev. 3: 14-18. Our eternal salvation depends upon the imputed and imparted righteousness of Jesus our Saviour.

Ezek. 48: 35, margin: "And the name of the city from that day shall be, *The Lord is there*, Heb. *Jehovah-shammah.*" God's presence is constantly with His earth-born children. Jesus said: "Lo, I am with you alway, even unto the end of the world." Matt. 28: 20. "The Lord working with them." Mark 16: 20. The companionship of Jesus in life's battles is one of the most comforting and necessary truths. All Christians need to practice the presence of Christ, to hold hourly, conscious communion with Him. As John Wesley exclaimed on his death-bed, "The best of all is, God is with us." Wherever God's people are it can be said: "The Lord is there—Jehovah-shammah."

WITH THE HEBREWS THE MEANING DETERMINED THE NAME.

The Hebrews attached great importance to the meaning of proper names—the meaning determined the name—a fact which must be remembered when studying the Scriptures, for often there is a deliberate play upon the meaning of a word. To the Hebrews a name represented not merely a sound, but more particularly a meaning. In Neh. 12: 11, 22, 23 we find two names, Jonathan and

Johanan, given to the same person. Both names have a similar meaning: "Jehovah hath graciously given." In 1 Chron. 25: 4, 18 we have a similar instance, where a person is called both Uzziel, meaning "strength of God," and Azareel, meaning "God hath helped." In 2 Kings 15: 1, 13, 30, King Azariah is given his other name Uzziah. Notice the marginal references; also 2 Chron. 26: 1, margin. Note the play upon the meaning of his names in 2 Chron. 26: 7, 8, 15, 16: God *helped* him and he became *strong*. This use of synonymous names shows the importance attached to their *meaning*.

Jehoshaphat was born after the triumph of Judah over the hosts of the Ethiopians. His name means "Jehovah hath judged, or is Judge." Hence the play upon the meaning of his name in connection with the coming *judgment*—in the *symbolic* "valley of Jehoshaphat"—of all outside the Israel of God. See Joel 3: 2, 12. Nehemiah was born during the captivity, and his parents gave him a name which expressed their joy in their new-born child and also their trust in God. Nehemiah means "the consolation of Jehovah."

THE MEANINGS OF THE NAMES OF THE PROPHETS WERE FREQUENTLY KEYS TO THEIR BOOKS.

"Isaiah" means "salvation of Jehovah." The term salvation is more frequently used in his book than in other prophetic books. He is known as the gospel prophet. "Daniel" means "God is Judge." His book describes: (1) the judgment upon Babylon. Dan. 5: 26-28. (2) The judgment in the heavenly sanctuary. Dan. 7: 9, 10. (3) The time prophecy concerning the hour of God's investigative judgment. Dan. 8: 14: 9: 24-26. (4) The close of the investigative judgment. Dan. 12: 1. "Jeremiah" means "whom Jehovah launches forth." The references to him being sent of God are a play upon the meaning of his name. See Jer. 1: 7; 19: 1-3; 22: 1, 2, etc.

"Hosea" means "saviour," or "salvation." The theme of the book of Hosea is God's love for backslidden Israel, and the salvation of spiritual Israel. "Joel" means "the Lord is God," and in the book of Joel the supremacy of God is shown in His blessings bestowed upon His people, and His judgments poured upon their enemies. "Amos" means "weighty, burden." Throughout the book of Amos various nations—and especially Israel—are charged with being weighted down by sin; they have not carried their heavy responsibilities in the fear of God. God's judgments are predicted to fall heavily upon the transgressors of His law—especially in the last days. Amos 2: 13; 8: 2, 3, 11, 12. "Obadiah" means "servant of the Lord." In his book we learn who are, and who are not, the true servants of the Lord. The Edomites, the descendants of Esau, carried hatred in their hearts toward their brethren the Jews, and at every opportunity distressed the people of God. God's servants have love, not only for their brethren, but also for their enemies. "Jonah" means "dove." When David was distressed, he said, "Oh that I had wings like a *dove!* for then would I fly away, and be at rest. Lo, then would I wander far off." Ps. 55: 6, 7. Jonah sought to flee from his distressing task of extending the message of mercy to Israel's enemies. If we stay by the task we shall see results, as Jonah did. Someday, God's messengers will "fly away" from the scene of strife, "and be at rest." "Micah" means "Who is like unto the Lord." Micah 7: 18 is a play upon the meaning of the name "Micah." Though Israel had become corrupt, God would pardon His repentant people and save them. The Saviour would be born (Micah 5: 1, 2) and, through Him, Israel would inherit the eternal kingdom. "Nahum" means "consolation," and in the book of Nahum we see the goodness of God manifested toward those "that trust in Him" (Nah. 1: 7), and the destruction of the enemies of His people. "Habakkuk" means "a wrestler." In his book we see evidence of Habakkuk wrestling with doubts until his faith is established in God, even when everything seems to go wrong. See Ch. 3: 17-19; 2: 4. "Zephaniah" means "hid of the Lord," and in his book, which depicts the terrible judgments of God upon the violaters of His law, we are assured: "ye shall be *hid* in the day of the Lord's anger." Zeph. 2: 3. "Haggai" means "festival of the Lord." The burden of his book is the completion of the unfinished temple—the centre of the Lord's festivals. Zerubbabel (mentioned in Hag. 1: 1, 12; 2: 2, 4, 21) was one of the leaders in the work of rebuilding the temple. "Zerubbabel" means "born in Babylon;" but the people of God were then called, as now, to "come out of her My people" to complete the restoration of the temple and its services, which the Babylonians had destroyed. "Zechariah" means "God remembers," and this thought is the one emphasized by the prophet. "Malachi" means *"messenger* of the Lord." In Mal. 3: 1 we read: "I will send My *messenger* . . . and the Lord, whom ye seek, shall suddenly come to His temple, even the *messenger* of the covenant." The book of Malachi, which is written for those who profess to be God's messengers, closes (4: 5, 6) with God's assurance that He will send a messenger to warn the world of the coming day when He will "smite the earth with a curse."

The meanings of the names of Bible writers are key-words to the main purpose of their books.

GOD IS THE AUTHOR OF THE LAW OF THE SIGNIFICANCE OF BIBLE NAMES.

Going back to the commencement (to the first mention), where our Biblical research on any subject should begin, we notice that God named the man He had created "Adam." Gen. 5: 1, 2. The meaning of Adam, according to Cruden, is *"earthy,* taken out of red earth." Paul, in harmony with other Bible writers, directs us to the law of "the first and the last" employed in the Bible. He says: "The *first* man Adam was made a living soul; the *last* Adam was made a quickening spirit." In contrasting the two Adams—the first and the last—Paul makes a play upon the *meaning* and the *history* of the origin of the name Adam. He says: "The *first man* is of the *earth, earthy;* the second man is the Lord from *heaven."* 1 Cor. 15: 45-47.

Eve thought that the first child was the promised Seed Who would bruise the serpent's head. Gen. 3: 15. Naming him Cain, which means "gotten, or, acquired" (see margin), she exclaimed, "I have gotten a [or *"the,"* as in Spurrell's trans.] man from the Lord." But, alas, instead of the hoped-for Saviour, Cain proved to be a murderer. "Abel" means *"breath, vapour"*—something transient. Surely this name was prophetic of this life, cut off in its youthfulness. Writing in the Ecclesiastes of the "vanity" of earthly things, Solomon refers to "the days of the life of his [man's] *vanity* which he spendeth as a shadow." Eccles. 6: 12, margin. The word *"vanity"* comes from the same word as "Abel." "For what is your life? It is even a *vapour,* that appeareth for a little time, and then vanisheth away." Jas. 4: 14. Abel's brief life and sudden death are employed to represent the brevity of this present life. In Gen. 4: 25 we are told the reason Eve named her next son *"Seth* [margin, *appointed*]: For God, said she, hath *appointed* me another seed instead of Abel." Gen. 4: 25. When Noah was born, his father, Lamech, "called his name *Noah,* that is, *rest* or *comfort,* saying, This same shall *comfort* us." Gen. 5: 29, margin. Noah is a type of Him, Who later said "Come unto Me . . . and I will give you *rest."* Matt. 11: 28, 29. By his faith and works "Noah . . . prepared an ark to the *saving of his house."* Heb. 11: 7. By His shed blood and His spiritual ministry Jesus saves *"His own house."* Heb. 3: 6. As indicated by the meaning of Noah's name, Jesus gives His people *rest* and *comfort*. See also Isa. 66: 13. Jesus referred to the Holy Spirit as "another *Comforter*" (John 14: 16), "the *Comforter*" (John 14: 26; 15: 26). Noah sacrificed time and effort to prepare a shelter for believers from the storm of God's wrath. Christ's infinite sacrifice provides His children with shelter —through His blood, shed and applied. The destroying angel passes over when he sees the "blood." Ex. 12, etc.

The significance of the meaning of Bible names has impressed Bible students for many centuries. The Reformer Urinus, author of the Heidelburg Catechism, is credited with being the first to draw attention to the teaching of the Gospel in the meanings of the names of the ten antedeluvians mentioned in the genealogical table of Gen. 5, which takes us from Adam to the flood. Taking these names as they appear in the genealogical line, and reading down their meanings to make one connected line of thought, we read:—

Adam	......	...... Man,
Seth	......	...... Placed or appointed;
Enos	......	...... Wretched, fallen man,
Cainan	......	...... Lamenting.
Mahalaleel	......	...... The Blessed God
Jared	......	...... Shall descend, or come down.
Enoch	......	...... Teaching, dedicated, disciplined (obedient unto death).
Methusaleh	......	...... His death shall bring
Lamech	......	...... Power,
Noah	......	...... Rest and comfort.

In many instances in Scripture, once the meaning of the name is understood, spiritual truths and doctrines are constantly associated with it. The name Abraham means "the *father* of height, or high *father*." God had changed Abram's name, saying, "Neither shall thy name any more be called Abram, but thy name shall be Abraham (margin, i.e., "*Father* of a *great multitude*") for a *father of many nations* have I made thee." Gen. 17: 4, 5. The New Testament makes a play upon the meaning of Abraham's name when it refers to him as "the *father* of them that believe . . . the *father* of circumcision to them who are not of the circumcision only . . . the faith of our *father* Abraham . . . the heir of the world . . . who is the *father* of us all . . . the *father* of many nations." Rom. 4: 11-18. "We have Abraham to our *father*." Matt. 3: 9. "*Father* Abraham." Luke 16: 24, 27, 30. The New Testament applies the spiritual meaning of the name. See Gal. 3: 7-29: Rev.

21: 24; 7: 9. Sarah's name was changed from Sarai (Gen. 17: 15, 16) for reasons similar to those which gave Abram the name of Abraham.

Abraham, "the *father* of them that believe," is a type of "the everlasting Father." Abraham offering his only rightful son—"thine *only son* Isaac, whom thou *lovest*" (Gen. 22: 2, 12)—illustrates his typical character. The *"great multitude"* of the saved, seen in Rev. 7: 9, are the spiritual children of Abraham, for his name means *"father* of a *great multitude."*

The name of Hagar's child was chosen by God. "Ishmael," as stated in the margin of Gen. 16: 11, means "God shall *hear."* "And the angel of the Lord said unto her . . . shalt bear a son, and shalt call his name *Ishmael; because* the Lord *hath heard* thy affliction." The meaning of that name shows God's compassion for the afflicted and the destitute. Abraham pleaded with God to make Ishmael His choice for the progenitor of the Messiah. Knowing the meaning of the name Ishmael to be that God has *heard,* we can see the play God makes upon the meaning of the name Ishmael in Gen. 17: 20: "And as for Ishmael, I have *heard* thee." When, finally, Abraham was obliged to send Ishmael from the camp, Hagar in her wanderings ran out of water and wept bitterly. Once again there is a play upon the meaning of the name Ishmael: "And God *heard* the voice of the lad; and the angel of God called to Hagar out of heaven, and said unto her, What aileth thee, Hagar? fear not; for God *hath heard* the voice of the lad where he is." Gen. 21: 17.

When promised a child, "Abraham fell upon his face, and *laughed,* and said *in his heart,* Shall a child be born unto him that is an hundred years old? and shall Sarah, that is ninety years old, bear? . . . And God said, Sarah, thy wife, shall bear thee a son indeed; and *thou shalt call his name Isaac."* Gen. 17: 17-19. The name Isaac means "he *laughs,* shall *laugh,* or there is or shall be *laughter."* The Lord told Abraham to name the child Isaac. In Gen. 18 we see the play upon the meaning of the name Isaac. When the Lord came to Abraham to repeat the promise of the child, Sarah was in the tent, and heard the promise repeated. The record says: "Therefore Sarah *laughed* within herself. . . . And the Lord said unto Abraham, Wherefore did Sarah *laugh?* Vs. 12, 13. "Then Sarah denied, saying, I *laughed* not; for she was afraid. And He said, Nay, but thou didst *laugh."* V. 15. When Isaac was born, "Sarah said, God hath made me to *laugh*, so that all that hear me will *laugh* with me." Gen. 21: 3, 6.

Throughout the writings of the New Testament, we see the *spiritual* application of the Old Testament persons, places, etc. Paul points out that Isaac is a type of christians: "Now we, brethren, as Isaac was, are the children of promise." Gal. 4: 28. The meaning of Isaac's name, as we have shown, suggests joyous laughter. Joy is the second fruit of the Spirit. See Gal. 5: 22. Thus the meaning of Isaac's name suggests joy now, and also points us to the joy of the ransomed of the Lord. David declared: "In Thy presence is *fulness of joy;* at thy right hand there are pleasures for evermore." Ps. 16: 11.

In the Scriptural account of the birth of Esau and Jacob we see the significance attached to the giving of names among ancient people of the east. *Because* the first boy was born *"red*, all over like an *hairy garment*, they called his name *Esau,"* and *because* the second twin *"took hold on Esau's heel*, his name was called *Jacob."* Gen. 25: 25, 26. The word Jacob means "He taketh by the heel." The verb is figuratively used to denote the action of deceiving or defrauding, which is expressed also by the English word supplant. In Gen. 27: 36, margin, we see how Esau, in lamenting his loss of the birthright at the hand of the shrewd Jacob, made a play upon the meaning of the word Jacob: "And he [Esau] said, Is not he rightly named *Jacob*, that is, *Supplanter?* for he hath *supplanted* me these two times: he *took away* my birthright and, behold, now he hath *taken away* my blessing." When Jacob's character was changed God changed his name: "Thy name shall be called *no more, Jacob*, but *Israel, that is, a prince of God: for as a prince* hast thou *power* with God and with men, and *hast prevailed."* Gen. 32: 27, 28, margin. Being the first occasion this name is given in the Scriptures, it is the *historical basis* for the spiritual use of that name in the New Testament when referring to events subsequent to the rejection of the Jewish nation. The name "Israel" now stands for those who, like Jacob, have wrestled with God in prayer until their characters have become changed into the divine similitude.

Jacob poured out his soul before God at the brook Jabbok. Gen. 32: 22-30. *"Jabbok"* means *"emptying, pouring out."* "And Jacob called the name of the place *Peniel: for I have seen God face to face*, and my life is preserved." A true Israelite knows from experience what it means to pour out the soul before God, clinging to Him and trusting in His love and mercy. By "emptying," or "pouring out," one's heart before God a true Israelite, even now, with spiritual vision, sees the face of God, and is spiritually preserved. Thus the name of the place where Jacob wrestled with God, and also the meanings of the names Jacob and Israel, are given in the Scriptures because of their spiritual significance. As Jacob received a new name when he overcame, so each overcomer is promised "a new name" (Rev. 2: 17) which will express his character. The book of Revelation is written with significant emphasis upon the spiritual meaning of names, etc.

Losing sight of the *spiritual* significance God has attached to the meaning of names, etc., Futurists see only the literal Jewish nation and Palestine in the many references to the things of Israel contained in the book of Revelation. The Revelation can be rightly undestood *only* when Old Testament historical events, persons, names, numbers, colours, etc., are applied *spiritually* in connection with *Christ and His church.* Jesus is "the King of Israel." See John 1: 49. And "the King of Israel," Who knows His children, said to Nathaniel (who had spent time with His God in prayer in the secrecy of an overhanging fig tree): "Behold an *Israelite indeed,* in whom is *no guile."* John 1: 47-49. "The remnant of Israel" (Zeph. 3: 13) will be those of whom it is said: "in their mouth was found *no guile."* Rev. 14: 5.

GOD SELECTED THE NAMES OF THE CHILDREN OF SOME OF HIS PROPHETS.

God does nothing in vain. The meanings of the names He chose for the children of some of His prophets carried messages for the professed people of God in their days, and also for subsequent years.

In the days of Hoshea, Israel had departed from the ways of God to follow the ways of the heathen. The Lord proclaimed messages by the meanings of the names of Hoshea and his children. "Hoshea" means "saviour," or "salvation." Throughout his book runs the theme of salvation from sin and its consequences. See Hos. 6: 1-3; 14: 1-7, etc. Before proclaiming messages of judgments to come, God gave a message of hope in the name of Hosea's first child. Concerning the first child, God commanded: "Call his name Jezreel." Vs. 3. 4. By that name God conveyed the thought that after His judgments came upon Israel for her idolatrous sun-worship, she—and particularly spiritual Israel—would be *"sown* of God."

Jezebel, who fostered sun-worship in Israel, was slain at the place called Jezreel. See 1 Kings 21: 19-23; 2 Kings 9: 36, 37. The destruction which came to Jezebel in Jezreel pre-figured the destruction awaiting the northern ten tribes of Israel because of their persistent practice of heathen worship. "The valley of Jezreel" became a typical place for the destruction of those who depart from the God of Israel to follow Satan's system of sun-worship. The waters which drained part of the valley of Jezreel ran into "the river Kishon . . . the waters of *Megiddo*" (Judges 5: 19, 21)—that typical place of the destruction of Israel's enemies, to which reference is made in the symbolic word Armageddon of Rev. 16: 16.

Of Hosea's second child we read: "And God said unto him, Call her name Lo-ruhamah, that is, *not having obtained mercy:* for I will have *no more mercy* upon the house of Israel; but I will utterly take them away." Hos. 1: 6, margin. Thus the termination of the kingdom of Israel was foretold by the meaning of the name "Lo-ruhamah." When the prophet's third child was born God said: "Call his name *Lo-ammi,* that is, *not My people:* for ye are not My people, and I will not be your God." V. 9, margin. The rejection and, later, the restoration of the northern ten tribes are taught in the meanings of the names of the prophet's children. The prophecy of Hos. 1: 10, 11 is based upon the meanings of these names. In Rom. 9: 22-28, Paul presents the spiritual interpretation of Hosea's prophecy: through Gentiles accepting Christ, "the number of the children of Israel shall be as the sands of the sea." "Jezreel" means "he will be *sown of God,* that is, *have a numerous progeny.*" See Cruden. God's prophesied judgments fell upon the northern 10 tribes, but the prophecy also declared: "*great shall be the day of Jezreel.*" Hos. 1: 11. "They shall hear *Jezreel.* And I will *sow her* unto Me in the earth." Hos. 2: 22, 23; see also Jer. 31: 27. In Hos. 2: 23 there is a play upon the meanings of the names of Hosea's three children. To-day, *spiritual* Israel have "obtained mercy," and are God's "people," and are "sown of God" "in the earth." Rom. 9: 6-8; Gal. 3: 29, etc.

THE SIGNIFICANCE OF THE NAMES OF ISAIAH AND HIS CHILDREN.

Because His people were departing from Him, God inspired Isaiah to warn them of coming judgments: the land would be desolated and they would go into captivity (Isa. 6: 11, 12, etc.), but a *remnant would return.* Isa. 6: 13, etc. God used the meanings of the names of Isaiah and his children as messages to His people. The name of Isaiah's son "Shear-jashup" means *the remnant shall return.*" See Isa. 7: 3, margin. When Ahaz was troubled with forebodings of national disaster, "then said the Lord unto Isaiah, Go forth now to meet Ahaz, *thou,* and *Shear-jashup thy son . . .* and say unto him . . . fear not, neither be fainthearted." God's command that *Isaiah* (whose name meant *"salvation of Jehovah')* take his son, whose name meant *"the remnant shall return,"* indicates God's desire to encourage the trembling king with a message of hope: though God would permit their enemies to afflict them, yet through His *salvation, a remnant would return.* Ahaz was invited to ask "a *sign* of the Lord . . . but Ahaz said, I will not ask. . . . Therefore the Lord Himself shall give you a *sign;* Behold, a virgin shall conceive, and bear a son, and shalt call His name *Immanuel."* Isa. 7: 10-14. The meaning of "Immanuel" is given in Matt. 1: 23: "And they shall call His name *Emmanuel,* which *being interpreted* is, God with us." The angel also commanded: "Thou shalt call His name JESUS (margin, "Saviour"): for He shall save His people from their sins." Matt. 1: 21. The meanings of the names Jesus, Immanuel and Shear-jashup teach that the trusting believer will triumph over threatening disaster. Through the work of "Jesus"—the "Saviour," "Emmanel"—"God with us," we can be confident that "Shear-jashup"—*"the remnant shall return."* "The God-man" will turn apparent defeat into complete victory. In connection with the significant references to the meanings of the names Immanuel, Isaiah and Shear-jashup, Isaiah prophesied the coming of the Assyrians, likening the invasion to the overflowing of the river Euphrates. See Isa. 7: 14, 20; 8: 7, 8. But the waters which threatened to destroy the people of God were dried up by the intervention of the "Saviour," "Immanuel"— "God with us." See chapters 24 and 25 for the last-day anti-typical application of this historic incident. To His people in peril, Immanuel was, and will be, their Saviour, and the Destroyer of their enemies. The meaning of the name *"Shear-jashup"* contains the assurance *"the remnant shall return,* even the *remnant* of Jacob, unto the mighty God. For though Thy people shall be as the sand of the sea, yet a *remnant* of them *shall return."* Isa. 10: 20-22; Rom. 9: 27; Joel 2: 32; Rev. 12: 17. By God's instruction, Isaiah gave his second child the name "Maher-shalal-hash-baz"—the longest name in the Bible—the meaning of which contained a pro-phecy that Syria and Israel would soon be subdued by the Assyrians. See Isa. 8: 1-4, margins. That Isaiah knew the significance of his own and his children's names is obvious by his declaration in Isa. 8: 18: "Behold, *I and the children* whom the Lord hath given me are for *signs* and for wonders in Israel *from the Lord of hosts,* which dwelleth in Mount Zion."

THE SIGNIFICANCE OF THE NAME SOLOMON.

God informed David that he would have a son "who shall be a man of *rest;* and I will give him rest from all his enemies round about: *for* his name shall be *Solomon* (margin, *Peaceable*), and I will give him *peace and quietness* unto Israel in his days. He shall *build an house* for my name; and he shall be *my son,* and I will be *His father;* and I will establish the *throne of his kingdom over Israel for ever."* 1 Chron. 22: 9, 10. In his righteous days, and in the full glory of his reign, Solomon was a type of Jesus. This is evident from the meaning of his name, and from the fact that he was to build God's "house," and was to reign "over Israel *for ever."* Solomon's throne was said to be "the throne of the Lord." 1 Chron. 29: 23. Christ is building God's house—the temple of the Lord. See Matt. 16: 18; Zech. 6: 12, 13; 1 Cor. 3: 16; 2 Cor. 6: 16; Ephes. 2: 21; 1 Tim. 3: 15, etc. Jesus spoke of "Solomon in *all his glory,"* and of the Queen of Sheba coming "from the uttermost parts of the earth to hear the wisdom of Solomon; and, behold, *a greater than Solomon is here."* Matt. 12: 42.

During Solomon's reign "he had *peace* on all sides round about him. And Judah and Israel *dwelt safely, every man* under his vine and under his fig tree, from Dan even to Beersheba, *all the days of Solomon."* 1 Kings 4: 24, 25. The peaceful state of his kingdom was expressed in the meaning of his name. The title at the heading of Ps. 72 reads: "A Psalm for *Solomon."* Notice the expressions "The mountains shall bring *peace* to the people . . . *abundance of peace* so long as the *moon endureth."* Vs. 3, 7. These words refer to the kingdom of Jesus Christ, typified by Solomon's peaceful kingdom, which reached to the borders (to the river Euphrates, see Gen. 15: 18) of the typical land promised by God. Someday, Christ's eternal kingdom will stretch from pole to pole, and then there will be "abundance of *peace so long as the moon endureth."* God's promise "He shall be My son, and I will be his Father" (1 Chron. 22:10) is quoted in Heb. 1: 5 and applied to Jesus. God's Spirit revealed to David that the promises concerned not only his son Solomon, but referred, more particularly, to "a greater than Solomon." See Acts 2: 30-36.

The Lord gave Solomon a second name: "He sent by the hand of Nathan the prophet; and He called his name Jedidiah, because of the Lord." Jedidiah means *"Beloved of the Lord."* See margin, 2 Sam. 12: 25. When Jesus was baptized God declared: *"This is my beloved Son,* in Whom I am well pleased." Matt. 3: 17. Rightly understood, the whole Bible is "The Revelation of Jesus Christ."

NAMES OF PLACES ASSOCIATED WITH JESUS.

Jesus, Who was born at Bethlehem (Micah 5: 2; Matt. 2: 1, 6), "the house of bread," is "the Bread of life" (John 6: 35, 41, etc.). He was "brought up" in Nazareth (Luke 4: 16), "the place of shrubs or sprouts": He is "the Branch of the Lord" (Isa. 4: 2), "a righteous Branch" (Jer. 23: 5; Zech. 3: 8), "THE BRANCH" (Zech. 6: 12), the tender shoot "out of the stem of Jesse." See Isa. 11: 1; 53: 2. Nazareth also signifies "separated or sanctified": Christ lived a sanctified life. John 17: 19. He agonised at Gethsemane, "the oil press." He trod "the winepress alone; and of the people there was none with Me" (Isa. 63: 3). He was crucified at "the place which is called Calvary," (margin) "the place of a skull." Luke 23: 33. "He bearing His cross went forth into a place called the place of a skull, which is called in the Hebrew Golgotha." John 19: 17. "The skull," or the place of death, is a fitting name for the place where Jesus died to save us from sin and death.

JORDAN AND SILOAM.

When Namaan, the Syrian, sought healing by the God of Israel, he was commanded to "go and wash in *Jordan* seven times . . . and thou shalt be clean." 2 Kings 5: 10. He had to forsake pride and *descend* to this humble act. "Jordan" means "descender" —referring to the fall of several thousand feet in the comparatively short distance from its source to the Dead Sea. In John 9: 1-7 we have another passage in which the interpretation of a watering place is given to point out the *spiritual lesson* to be learned from the *name.* To the man born blind Jesus said: "Go, wash in the pool of Siloam (which is by interpretation, *Sent).* He went . . . and washed, and came seeing." Thus the Lord teaches that humble obedience to His Word brings *spiritual* sight. Many instances in Scripture show the *spiritual* significance of the meanings of names of places, rivers, hills, valleys, etc.

JESUS GAVE NAMES BECAUSE OF THEIR MEANINGS.

In Mark 3: 16, 17 we read: "And Simon He surnamed Peter; and James . . . and John the brother of James; and He surnamed them *Boanerges, which is, The sons of thunder.*" The Lord gave Simon a name which expressed his character: "And when Jesus beheld him, He said, Thou art Simon the son of Jona: thou shalt be called *Cephas,* which is by interpretation, A *stone* (margin, or, "Peter"). John 1: 42. Peter, the movable *"stone,"* is not the foundation of the church. Jesus, Whom Peter acknowledged to be "the Christ, the Son of the living God" (Matt. 16: 16)—He Who is known throughout the Old Testament as "the *Rock* of Israel" (2 Sam. 23: 3; 22: 2, 32; Deut. 32: 4, 15, 18; Isa. 17: 10; Ps. 18: 2, etc.) is the immovable *"Rock"* upon Whom the church is built. Matt. 16: 18. "Built upon *the foundation* of the apostles and prophets, *Jesus Christ Himself* being the chief corner-stone." Ephes. 2: 20; 1 Pet. 2: 5-8. The right interpretation of the name for Peter, and a knowledge that throughout Scripture the Son of God is said to be the *"Rock of Israel"* would prevent many from being deceived by Papal assumptions.

The fact that Jesus gave names according to their meanings shows that a full understanding of the Scriptures depends upon applying the Law of the Significance of Bible Names.

CHAPTER XXIII.

THE LAW OF THE SIGNIFICANCE OF NAMES IN THE REVELATION.

The book of Revelation, as the *name* indicates, is a *"Revelation of Jesus Christ"* in His work of redemption, from the commencement of the controversy between the forces of good and evil until the establishment of the everlasting kingdom. The Revelation bears the message of "the *everlasting* gospel" (Rev. 14: 6) and reveals the *same principles* which the Lord employed in the writing of the preceding books of the Bible. As in these earlier books of Scripture, the meaning of names employed in the Apocalypse assists considerably in understanding its true teachings.

In chapter 19 we have shown that the Revelation is a message from Christ, "the King of Israel" (John 1: 49), to spiritual Israel. Jesus communicated His Revelation through *"John* to the seven churches." Rev. 1: 4. In the Hebrew, John, or Johanan, means "Jehovah hath granted grace" or "shown favour." The name John is found five times in the Revelation: 1: 1, 4, 9; 21: 2; 22: 8. Throughout Scripture, five is employed as the number representing *grace. John,* a recipient of *grace,* whose name meant "Jehovah hath granted *grace,"* closed the Revelation with the words: "the *grace* of our Lord Jesus Christ be with you *all."* Rev. 22: 21. The Revelation was written for spiritual Israelites (see Rev. 7, etc.): spiritual "Jews" (Rev. 3: 9). In Rom. 2: 28, 29 Paul makes a play upon the meaning of the word Jew, which is an abbreviation of Judah: "he is a *Jew . . .* whose *praise* is not of men, but of God." The giving of the name Judah and the significance of its meaning, "praise," is recorded in Gen. 29: 35, margin. See also Gen. 49: 8. "Israel" (mentioned 3 times in the Revelation: 2: 14; 7: 4; 21: 12) means "a prince with God" having *"power* with God and with men" (Gen. 32: 28)—an overcomer. The name Jesus, mentioned 14 times in the Revelation, means "Jehovah is salvation," or "Jehovah Saviour." "Christ" means "the Anointed." Thus the meanings of the names Jesus Christ, John, Israel and Jew teach that "the Revelation" is the message from "the Anointed" "Jehovah," Who is "salvation" (see Matt. 1: 21) to those who wrestle in prayer and find "grace" and the "praise . . . of God," and thus become "princes with God" (Gen. 32: 28).

Moses altered the name "Oshea," meaning "to save—save thou," to "Jehoshua" (Joshua), meaning "Jehovah is salvation." See Num. 13: 2, 16; 14: 6, etc. Joshua encouraged Israel to possess the land, saying *"Jehovah* is with us." Num. 14: 9. Moses encouraged Joshua to lead Israel into the land with the words: *"Jehovah* thy God is with thee." Josh. 1: 5, 9; 3: 10. In the pronunciation of the Alexandrian Jews, the word Jeshua, or Joshua (Neh. 8: 17) was altered into Jesus. Hence Jesus is read for Joshua in the Greek of the New Testament and retained in our version in Acts 7: 45 and Heb. 4: 8, margin. Joshua, by his work and the meaning of his name, is a type of Jesus. Literal Israel was led into the land of promise, not by Moses, whose name means "drawn" (see Ex. 2: 10, margin), but by Joshua: spiritual Israel is led into the eternal Canaan by "Jehovah Saviour." "Jerusalem," meaning "foundations of *peace,"* is mentioned three times in the Revelation. Rev. 3: 12; 21: 2, 10. Melchisedec, the king of Salem (or Jerusalem), is definitely stated in the Scriptures to be a type of Jesus. See Ps. 110: 4; Heb. 7, etc. In Heb. 7: 1, 2 Paul makes a play upon the meanings of the names of Melchisedec and Salem: "For this *Melchisedec,* king of *Salem* . . . first being by interpretation *King of righteous-* ness, and after that also King of *Salem,* which is, King of *peace."* Jerusalem, the city of "the Prince of *Peace"* (Isa. 9: 6), is presented in the Revelation as the seat of the Messiah's *spiritual* kingdom— spiritual Israel, the church—and also the capital of the eternal king- dom. The names written on the gates of this city are "the names of the twelve tribes of the children of *Israel."* Rev. 21: 12. Like Melchisedec, spiritual Israelites are said to be *"kings* and *priests."* Rev. 1: 6; 5: 10; 20: 6. Throughout Scripture, Jerusalem, the city of *peace,* is presented as the centre of the great controversy between the forces of good and evil—between the principles which are the foundations for everlasting peace and the principles which create strife and "war." Every time the word "war" or "battle" is em- ployed from Rev. 12: 7-9 to Rev. 20: 8-9, the reference concerns Satan's "war" against the *"foundations of peace"* or God's "war" or "battle" against Satan's kingdom.

In the vivid description of the commencement of the great controversy between Christ and Satan, given in Rev. 12: 7-9, the names "Michael" and "Satan" are employed. "Michael" means "the One like God," and is revealed in Scripture as Jesus our Lord. Compare Jude 9; Dan. 10: 13, 21; 12: 1; 1 Thess. 4: 16-18. In

Rev. 12: 7 He is mentioned as being at the head of the angelic hosts. They were created by Him, and are referred to as "*His* angels." Heavenly beings having "El" as part of their names are designated as belonging to God: Michael, the One like God; Gabriel, God is my strength.

"El," expressed in its English form "God," is the first of the three primary names of Deity. In Matt. 27: 46 we are given the meaning of "El": "Jesus cried with loud voice, saying, *Eli, Eli . . .* that is to say, My *God*, My *God*, why hast thou forsaken me?" "El" signifies "strength, or the strong One." Jesus had placed all His hopes upon "El," "the strong One," and in His dying agonies, when human strength failed, He committed Himself to the almighty strength of His Father's never-failing arm.

All Hebrew names commencing or ending with "El" have meanings linking them with God, as Dani*el, God* is my Judge; Ezeki*el,* the strength of God; *El*ijah, *God* the Lord; *El*imelech, my *God* is king; Emmanu*el, God* with us, etc. The name which God will give to each of the redeemed will convey to each person God's knowledge of his character: "A new name written, which no man knoweth saving he that receiveth it." Rev. 2: 17. These character names were "written in the book of Life from the foundation of the world." Rev. 17: 8. Each must permit God to fit him to obtain the character expressed in the meaning of the "new name." God does not predestinate *persons,* but He does predestinate *character.* The privilege of each is to co-operate with God to obtain the character predestinated to measure up to the meaning of the name written in the book of life from the beginning. The redeemed will also bear names which designate them as belonging exclusively to God. "Him that overcometh . . . I will write upon him the *name of My God,* and the *name of the city of My God,* which is New Jerusalem . . . and I will write upon him *My new name.*" Rev. 3: 12.

"Satan" means "Adversary." See Zech. 3: 1 , margin. Satan's heavenly name "Lucifer" meant "Day Star." See Isa. 14: 12, margin. The word "devil" means "a slanderer": Satan slanders and accuses God's people. Rev. 12: 10-12. The word "dragon" suggests his ravenous desire to devour the saints of God. When designated as the "serpent," his cunning and his deceptive powers are referred to. See Rev. 12: 4, 9; 20: 2, etc.

THE MEANINGS OF THE NAMES OF "THE TRIBES OF ISRAEL." Rev. 7: 4-8.

God recorded details associated with the giving of the names of Jacob's sons, and pointed out why they were called by their respective names. As these names are mentioned in the book of Revelation (Chap. 7), where the completion of the work of God on earth is brought to view—the sealing "of all the tribes of the *children of Israel*" (Rev. 7: 1-8)—these names and their meanings must be significant to the remnant church. In the following verses and their margins the history of the giving of the names of Jacob's sons, and also the meanings of these names, are found, set forth *in order of birth:*—

Gen. 29:32	Reuben	......	See a son
,, 29:33	Simeon	......	Hearing
,, 29:34	Levi	......	Joined
,, 29:35	Judah	......	Praise
,, 30:6	Dan	......	Judgment
,, 30:8	Naphthali	......	My wrestling
,, 30:11	Gad	......	A troop or company
,, 30:13	Asher	......	Happy
,, 30:18	Issachar	......	An hire
,, 30:20	Zebulon	......	Dwelling
,, 30:24	Joseph	......	Adding
,, 35:18	Benjamin	......	The son of the right hand

When dying, Rachel gave her new-born son the name of "Ben-oni, that is, the *son of my sorrow;* but his father called him *Benjamin*, that is, *the son of the right hand.*" Gen. 35: 18, margin. Benjamin was born in Bethlehem (see v. 16-19), and is a type of Jesus Who was also born in Bethlehem. Jesus was born into this world to be "a man of *sorrow*" (Isa. 53: 3), but, later, to sit "on the *right hand* of the throne of the Majesty in the heavens." Heb. 8: 1. Thus both names given to Benjamin—"the son of sorrow" and "the son of the right hand"—apply to Jesus. All those who are redeemed, like their Lord, will know from their own experiences what it means to be sons of sorrow; but "if we *suffer*, we shall also *reign* with Him" (2 Tim. 2: 12) and be sons of His right hand.

Turning to the names of the tribes of Israel as given in Rev. 7, we observe that the name of Dan is not included among the twelve tribes. The meaning of Dan indicates "judging," and Jacob, in Gen. 49: 16, 17, pictures Dan as a *"serpent* by the way, an *adder* in the path, that *biteth* the horse heels, so that his rider shall fall backward." Dan represents those in the professing church who criticize and "judge" their fellow-believers, backbiting as they pass along life's highway, causing those they slander to "fall backward." The Dan-ites will not be counted among the tribes of Israel. Manasseh, meaning *"forgetting"*—representing those who forgive and forget—replaces Dan in the list of the tribes of Israel given in Rev. 7.

In Gen. 41: 51, 52 we are given the names and their meanings of the two sons of Joseph. "And Joseph called the name of his firstborn Manasseh [margin, "forgetting"]: for God, said he, hath made me *forget* all my toil . . and the name of the second called he Ephraim [margin, "fruitful"]: for God hath caused me to be *fruitful* in the land of my affliction." Ephraim represents those who are "joined to idols" (Hos. 4: 17): those who have "mixed" (Hos. 7: 8) with the world and have not sufficiently valued their eternal life to earnestly seek the things of God. Hos. 6: 8-11. His name does not appear in Rev. 7.

The *order* in which the names of the tribes of the children of Israel are given in Rev. 7 is significant. Having noted the names which do not appear in the list of the tribes of the children of Israel in Rev. 7, we now note the order in which they appear. They are *not given in the order of their birth.* Not only because Judah was the kingly tribe through which Jesus was born, or because the tribe of Judah during the encampment of Israel was located to the east of the sanctuary, is the name of Judah, the *fourth* child born to Jacob, mentioned *first,* but also because the name means *"praise."* In the days of Jehoshaphat, the king of *Judah,* the people of God were faced with perils. The king of *Judah* "appointed singers unto the Lord (margin, *"praisers")* that should *praise* the beauty of holiness, as they went out *before* the army, and say, *Praise* the Lord . . . and when they began to sing and to praise, the Lord" gave them the victory over their enemies. 2 Chron. 20: 21-24.

Setting out the names *in the order in which they are given in Rev. 7* we see that, by this arrangement of the names *according to their meanings* and *not according* to their *order of birth,* we have *God's message of assurance to those who are sealed among the tribes of Israel.*

(Read *meanings* down as a connected sentence.)

	Name		Meaning
Rev. 7: 5	Judah	......	"Praise" (Israelites enter God's spiritual Jerusalem through the gates called "Praise." See Isa. 60: 18.)
	Reuben	.....	"A son" (John 1: 12; Rom. 8: 14-17, etc.)
	Gad	......	"A company" (Rev. 7: 9; 19: 1, 6, etc.)—*of sons, redeemed and*
v. 6	Aser	.....	"Happy" (John 13: 17, etc.)—*after*
	Nepthalim	.....	"Wrestling" (Gen. 32: 24-30, etc.)—*in prayer*
	Manasses	.....	"Forgetting" (Phil. 3: 13; Isa. 65: 17)—*self, and the past*
v. 7	Simeon	......	"Hearing" (1 Sam. 3: 10: "Speak, for Thy servant heareth.")—*God's Word*
	Levi	......	"Joined" (John 15: 1-7; Acts 2: 47)—*to God as*
	Issachar	.....	"Servants" (Rom. 6: 16-22, etc.)
v. 8	Zabulon	......	"Dwelling" (Ps. 91: 1; Isa. 33: 14, etc.)—*with*
	Joseph	......	"Added" (2 Pet. 1: 2, 5-11, etc.) —*joys and special blessings as*
	Benjamin	......	"Sons of the right hand" (not "sons of sorrow"). "In Thy presence is fulness of joy; at *Thy right hand* there are pleasures for evermore." Ps. 16: 11.

CHAPTER XXIV.

THE SIGNIFICANCE OF THE MEANING OF NAMES MENTIONED IN CONNECTION WITH THE GREAT BATTLE OF ARMAGEDDON.

From the dawn of creation God has employed the meaning of names by which to teach His children. The intelligence test which the Creator gave Adam was that of giving appropriate names to each species of life. "Out of the ground the Lord God formed every beast of the field, and every fowl of the air; and brought them unto Adam to *see what he would call them:* and whatsoever Adam called every living creature, that was the name thereof." Gen. 2: 19, 20. The names given were indicative of the characteristics or purpose. We also read: "Adam called his wife's name Eve [margin, i.e., Living], *because* she was the mother of all *living."* Gen. 3: 20. Turning to the Revelator's description of the enemies of the remnant children of the *"last* Adam," we see that God has appealed to our intelligence to consider the meaning of "the *name* of the beast" and *"the* number of his *name."* "Here is wisdom. Let him that understanding count the number of the beast: for it is the number of a man; and his number is six hundred three-score and six." Rev. 13: 17, 18. The Pope's accustomed title, "Vicarius Filii Dei," meaning "Vicar of the Son of God," numbers 666 in the Latin numerals. Because the Papal system of worship has brought into the professing Christian Church false conceptions of the worship of God, has outwardly changed God's Law of the Ten Commandments, and has introduced a false system of prophetic interpretation, the Revelator declares that this power has blasphemed God's *"name,* and His tabernacle." Rev. 13: 6. By its erroneous system of salvation by meritorious works and an earthly priesthood, the Papacy does injustice to the *name* of Jesus—"Jehovah is salvation"—for Jesus is our only Saviour.

Spiritual truths present spiritual intelligence tests. The more we love the Lord, obey His Word, and follow the Holy Spirit's leading, the more discerning becomes our spiritual perception. Adam possessed the discernment to give appropriate names to all living things. God would have His children spiritually in tune with Him, to be able to readily discern the *spiritual* meaning of the names He has employed throughout the Scripture—particularly in the description of the final conflict.

"ARMAGEDDON": A SYMBOLIC "PLACE."

Before giving the symbolic meaning of the word "Armageddon," we shall briefly deal with the word "place." Some students of Scripture have thought that the word "place" mentioned in Rev. 16: 16 definitely determines that "Armageddon" must refer to a *literal* conflict of nations to be fought in the literal place Megiddo. This is an extraordinary conclusion when a number of *places* are mentioned in the book of Revelation *only* because of their *symbolical* import. Jerusalem and Babylon—both literal places—are *not* mentioned in reference to literal things, but to *spiritual*.

Chapters 1-3 of the Revelation apply the spiritual meaning of the seven candlesticks of the sanctuary to the world-wide church throughout the Christian dispensation. There is a *"spiritual"* priesthood (1 Pet. 2: 5, 9) associated with *spiritual* Jerusalem. Jerusalem and Babylon, and all that was anciently associated with them, are brought into the prophecies of the Revelation in a world-wide, *symbolical* sense in connection with the great controversy between Christ and Satan. The latter fact is sustained by the law of Bible numbers. The word "place" (from the Greek "topos") is found seven times in the Revelation: 2: 5; 6: 14; 12: 6, 8, 14; 16: 16; 20: 11. The sixth use of the word "place" in Revelation is in ch. 16: 16. The number 6, as shown in my "Christ Conquers," pp. 113-122, stands for Satan's *spiritual* kingdom. In Rev. 13: 18 attention is called to this numbering system in connection with Satan's false system of worship—the "number of a *man*," 666 (man was made on the 6th day)—known in the Apocalypse as Babylon. The word Babylon is found 6 times in the Revelation. See Rev. 14: 8; 16: 19; 17: 5; 18: 2, 10, 21. It is the 6th plague which brings us to the time of the slaughter of Armageddon, and the 6th mention of the *word* "place" in the Revelation is in connection with Armageddon. The number 6 is used in the Revelation for Satan's *spiritual* kingdom: it is not employed as a national number. In the Revelation, the numbers, names, etc., have a *world-wide* significance, and cannot be limited to Palestine: they have a *spiritual*, and not a national significance. The first occurrence in the Apocalypse of the word "place" is in connection with the 7 churches. Their *world-wide*, *spiritual* significance is recognized by all. "The seven churches" are represented by "the seven candlesticks" (Rev. 1: 20) of the old sanctuary services. These candlesticks were all on the one "shaft" (Ex. 25: 31-37): they were all placed, or grouped, together. The first mention of the word "place" in the Apocalypse is in connection with the *first* of "the seven churches." To the church in Ephesus the warning was given, "repent, and do the first works; or else I will come unto thee quickly, and will remove thy candlestick out of his *place*, except thou repent." Rev. 2: 5. As each of the churches has a candlestick, the *symbolic* "place" of each respective candlestick is as follows: Ephesus, Smyrna, Pergamos, Thyatira, Sardis, Philadelphia, and Laodicea. Rev. 2 and 3. These are the names of cities that existed in Asia Minor—not far distant from Megiddo! The whole book of Revelation was written for "the seven churches which are *in* Asia." Rev. 1: 11. The cities enumerated and stated definitely to be "in Asia" were the *places* in which the "seven candlesticks" were located. But these, the first seven places mentioned in the prophecies of the Revelation, are used in a world-wide, symbolical sense.

The reader's attention is directed to Uriah Smith's "Daniel and the Revelation," pp. 345-383, where this writer has given the meanings of the seven names of the cities "in Asia," fully explaining their prophetic significance throughout the Christian dispensation.

After pointing out a number of churches to whom John could have written, Uriah Smith asks: "Why, then, were the seven particular churches chosen that are mentioned? For the reason, doubtless, that *in the names* of these churches, *according to the definition of the words*, are brought out the *religious* features of those periods of the gospel age which they respectively were to *represent*.

"For these reasons, 'the seven churches' are doubtless to be understood to mean *not* merely the seven *literal* churches of Asia which went by the names mentioned, but seven periods of the Christian church, from the days of the apostles to the close of probation." p. 329. (Italics mine.)

A. W. Anderson, in his instructive book "The World's Finale," pp. 13, 14, points out the *symbolic* use the Apocalypse makes of these places:—

"A glance at the accompanying map of Asia Minor reveals that these seven cities are situated on an old Roman road which traversed the country in an irregular circular direction, connecting all these cities in the order named, with Ephesus, which was the main seaport of that province in ancient times. It must be obvious that *these seven churches are used symbolically* of all the churches, for it is self-evident that Christ could not represent Himself as standing in the centre of these seven *literal* churches, and holding in His right hand the angels of only these seven churches . . . the seven churches in Asia Minor were *chosen to symbolise* the seven periods of church history, because the *names* of these seven *cities* and the *characteristics* of their citizens were *admirably fitted to represent the whole gospel church in seven divisions.* What a wonderful tribute to the divine prescience of Jesus is here unfolded! From His throne in the heavens He could look down upon a section of *Asia Minor,* and *there* trace the outworking of the whole Gospel age in seven periods, by simply following the meandering of an old Roman road which connected the cities of the province of Asia with the seaport of Ephesus; and then to select seven of those cities through which this road passed, *the definition of whose names,* together with *the characteristics* of their respective citizens, exactly *typified* the seven periods of church history . . . seven ancient cities, whose names even were *typical* of the period *symbolized."* (Italics mine.)

On p. 16 the meanings of the names of the 7 cities are given, showing their *symbolic* significance to "the 7 periods of church history."

"The *names* of the seven churches are *symbolic* of the church in different periods of the Christian era." A.A., p. 585.

Let us apply the principle. *There is not the slightest mention that these actual cities were to be symbolically understood.* These definitely named cities Rev. 1: 11 says "are *in* Asia." The cities were literal, and Asia is literal. Yet *they are used in a symbolic, world-wide sense.* As the *first* time the word "place" is employed in the Revelation it *is used in a world-wide, spiritual sense* in connection with *world-wide symbolic cities,* and as the *names* of the seven *cities* are chosen *because of the significance of their meanings,* associated with the *"topographical and historical features"* of these cities, Scripture and logic demand that the *same principles* be recognized and followed when interpreting "place" and "Armageddon" of Rev. 16: 16. As the *"history"* of the people and cities was coupled with the *meaning* of the *names* of those cities and used in a *symbolic sense,* so, also, when, in the same book of *symbols,* we read of *"a place called in the Hebrew* tongue *Armageddon"* the *same principle* of associating the *history* of the place with the *meaning of the name* must be followed. Megiddo is introduced in the Bible, in Judges 4 and 5, as the place where Israel fought against devil-led enemies. Subsequent Old Testament references also show it as the place of conflict between the forces of good and evil. The history of the "place" Megiddo, like that of the 7 places, or cities, in Asia, must be taken into account in understanding its *symbolical* use in Rev. 16: 16. Writing of the *symbolical* nature of the names of the Revelation, Isbon T. Beckwith, Ph.D., D.D., in his "The Apocalypse of John," p. 25, says:—

"The use of proper names and designations calls for special notice here. . . . Even the *names* of the church . . . are really intended to be *typical* of the whole church. Abaddon, Armageddon, Gog and Magog belong solely to apocalyptic language; and in our book, Babylon, Jerusalem, Jezebel, Sion, and Sodom have a *typical sense only."*

If "Armageddon" referred to a specific locality, it would be the *only prophetic* name in the Revelation used in its *literal* sense.

Again, on p. 648, Dr. Beckwith says:—

"Rev. 16: 16, Harmageddon. The name here given to the place where Satan's hosts are gathered, and where doubtless the battle of Rev. 19: 11 is conceived to occur *is unquestionably purely mystical.* . . . It is *unknown to Hebrew literature,* and it would be *contrary to the Apocalyptist's use of proper names to identify it,* in its eschatalogical application, *with any place so called.* . . . It is an *imaginary name* for designating the scene of the great battle between Antichrist and the Messiah. . . . The designation 'Mount Megiddo,' thus derived, is open to the objection that the region is not a mountain, but a vast plain."

Then this noted author connects up the word "mountain," mentioned in the prophecy of Ezek. 38, 39, with the word "Armageddon" (Rev. 16: 16), which contains a reference to "Megiddo," "famed in Israel's history as the *place where Jehovah's enemies perished."*

"The great battle of the Messiah with the Antichrist. Rev. 19: 11-21. This prelude (vs. 17, 18) to the battle is suggested by Ezekiel's prophecy of the assault of the nations *upon God's people in the last days,* and the overthrow of Gog with his hosts upon the *mountains* of Israel." Ibid., p. 734.

Henry's Commentary declares:—

"Armageddon . . . it should now be the field of *the last battle in which the church . . . shall be victorious."*

There is no *literal* place called "Armageddon." Megiddo, of course, is in John's mind, but he coins the word (see my "What is Armageddon?" pp. 12-17) when referring to the slaughter of *spiritual* Israel's enemies on the antitypical *"mountains of Israel."*

THE MEANING OF "ARMAGEDDON."

Rev. 16: 16 definitely directs us to "the *Hebrew* tongue" for our understanding of the word "Armageddon." In Rev. 9: 11 we also find reference to a "name in the *Hebrew tongue."* Uriah Smith, in his "Daniel and Revelation," page 479, says that it is "evident that the *character,* rather than the name of the power, is intended to be represented." This conclusion applies with equal force to the term "Armageddon."

If one interprets the word "Armagedddon" as *"Mount* Megiddo," the meaning of *merely the first part* of the word is applied, namely, "Har," meaning "Mount." We are not instructed to notice merely the "Har" portion of the word, for it does not give the *complete* meaning of the word. "Mageddon," or

"Megiddo," comes from a Hebrew root "gadad," meaning "to cut off, slaughter." The noted Hebraist, Dr. William Gesenius, in his lexicon, defines this word "gadad": "to cut into, to cut, to prune a vine, to cut cloth from the loom, to penetrate, to break in upon; Ps. 94: 23 from the idea of cutting off . . . to cut oneself, to make incisions on one's skin, as in mourning, Jer. 16: 6; 41: 5; or as afflicting the body for any cause. Deut. 14: 1."

In Dr. Strong's Hebrew Dictionary, Megiddo is shown to come from a root word meaning ". . . to *gash* . . . *cut* selves . . . to *cut* down; *hew down.*" Dr. Strong declares that "Armageddon" is "a *symbol* name."

Christopher Wordsworth says: "Armageddon or Harmegedon is formed from two Hebrew words, the one 'har,' signifying a mountain, the other a cutting to pieces; and thus it means the mountain of excision or slaughter. The word Armageddon then signifies a mountain of slaughter, like the valley of decision or cutting off described by Joel (3; 14), and is a figurative expression similar to that in the same prophet, namely, the valley of Jehoshaphat (Joel 3: 2, 12) or Judgment of God. The word Armageddon seems also designed to signify a defeat and slaughter, such as that of the kings of Canaan at Megiddo in the reign of Galilee, wrought by miraculous interposition of Almighty God discomforting the vast and terrible army of Sisera and his confederates."

Other authorities giving the meaning of "Armageddon" as "The Mountain of Slaughter" or "The Mountain of Destruction" are The New Testament Pocket Commentary from Henry, Doddridge, Burkitt, and other writers; Schofield's Bible; Dr. Scott's Commentary; Wilson's Emphatic Diaglott; Weymouth; Dr. Young, etc.

The symbolic word Armageddon is employed in Rev. 16: 16 because of the *meaning* attached to its *name* and because of the Old Testament *history* associated with Megiddo.

"THE VALLEY OF JEHOSHAPHAT" THE SYMBOLICAL VALLEY OF "GOD'S JUDGMENT."

The principles by which we interpret one part of Holy Writ determine the interpretation of other portions of Scripture. The belief that Rev. 16: 12-16 prophesies a literal conflict of nations at Megiddo has caused some expositors to declare that Joel 3 refers to the same conflict. Joel 3 does predict the same events as those prophesied in Rev. 16: 12-16; Ezek. 38, 39; Zech. 14, etc., but while a logical examination of these passages reveals the error and incongruities of a literal interpretation in relation to warring nations, complete harmony exists in the spiritual interpretation in relation to the Israel of God and her enemies.

Joel 3 pictures a gathering of *"all* nations" outside Jerusalem, *in* the valley of Jehoshaphat. In verse 2 God declares: "I will also gather all nations, and will bring them *down into* the valley of Jehoshaphat." In verses 11, 12 God also says: "Assemble yourselves, and come, *all* ye *heathen* [Heb. Goyim, nations, Gentiles], and gather yourselves together round about [Jerusalem]: thither cause Thy mighty ones to come down, O Lord. Let the heathen [nations, gentiles] be awakened, and come up to the valley of Jehoshaphat: for *there will I sit* to judge *all* the heathen [nations, gentiles] round about [Jerusalem]." We are also informed in v. 14: "Multitudes, multitudes *in* the valley of decision (margin, concision, or threshing): for the day of the Lord is near *in* the valley of decision. . . . The *Lord* also shall roar *out of Zion,* and utter His voice *from Jerusalem;* and the heavens and the earth shall shake: but the Lord will be the hope of His people, and the strength of the children of Israel."

In Rev. 16: 14-16 we are informed that "the kings *of the earth* and of the *whole world"* will be "gathered together *into a place* called in the Hebrew tongue Armageddon." It is impossible for "the kings of *the earth* and of the *whole world"* to *all* gather together at the "place" Megiddo, for Megiddo is not large enough to accommodate them, and the valley of Jehoshaphat is only a small valley to the east of Jerusalem. It is impossible for "the kings of the earth and of the *whole* world" to be literally gathered at Megiddo and, at the *same time,* be "*all*" brought "*down into* the valley of Jehoshaphat." How could they "*all*" be "*in the valley* of Jehoshaphat" and at the same time be at *mount* Megiddo, about 70 miles away? Armageddon, as we have shown, is employed because of the symbolical meaning of the word.

The literal application of Joel 3 to the warring nations in the valley of Jehoshaphat brings to view many incongruities. Christ will not literally *"sit"* (Joel 3: 12) *in* "the valley of Jehoshaphat" to judge the nations supposed to be literally gathered there, for that would be a contradiction of the Master's own use of this very passage of Scripture (Matt. 25: 31, 32). It would also mean that Jesus would do *the very thing against which He warned when referring to the coming of false christs and false prophets.* The sign of being counterfeit is the appearing in certain localities. He declared that His coming would not be to any earthly locality, but would be seen by all (Rev. 1: 7); and His saints would "be *caught up* . . . to meet" Him *"in the air."* See Matt. 24: 23-27, 30, 31; 1 Thess. 4: 16-18. Christ will not descend to the *earth* until at the end of the millennium.

By adhering strictly to the principle that the church is now the Israel of God and that Jerusalem, the ancient seat of the Lord's kingdom, is now the Scriptural *symbol* of the dwelling place of the Lord in His church, the contradictions so apparent in the literal interpretation do not exist. In Joel 2: 32 deliverance from the foes which have gathered *without* the city of God is promised to "the remnant" *within* Jerusalem. "For *in mount Zion* and *in Jerusalem* shall be *deliverance,* as the Lord hath said, and in the remnant whom the Lord shall call." In the final struggle between the forces of good and evil, deliverance will be found *"in* Mount Zion and *in* Jerusalem." Zion is definitely interpreted in the New Testament to refer to the church. Compare Joel 2: 32 with Rom. 10: 13; Isa. 28: 16 with 1 Pet. 2: 6-8; Isa. 59: 20 with Rom. 11: 26, etc. The remnant who are said in Joel 2: 32 to find deliverance are the same remnant referred to in Rev. 12: 17 as the special objects of Satanic hatred in the final conflict (or "war" or "controversy") over the law of God. In Rev. 14: 1 this remnant is pictured as being *"with"* the "Lamb . . . *on* Mount Zion." When the earthly powers "give their power and strength unto the beast" (Rev. 17: 13) and gather, or unite, together to attack Jerusalem (the church of the living God), and thus "make *war* with the Lamb," this "remnant" of the church will stand loyally *"with* the Lamb." "They that are *with* Him are called, and chosen, and faithful." Rev. 17: 14. They will stand on Mount Zion with their Lord when the forces of evil make *"war* with the Lamb." The Christian church is portrayed by the beautiful imagery of the vision of the great temple and city in the "holy oblation" in "the land of Israel . . . upon a very high mountain." Ezek. 40: 2; 43: 12.

The enemies of spiritual Israel will "unite," or "gather" their forces around Jerusalem—the spiritual dwelling-place of the Lord—and there, "in the valley of Jehoshaphat," meaning "the valley of God's Judgment," spiritual Israel's enemies will be cut in pieces in one vast "mountain of slaughter." In other places we have shown how the Revelator refers to the valley of Jehoshaphat (compare Joel 3: 13 with Rev. 14: 15-20; 19: 15) in a world-wide sense. The harvest of wheat and the harvest of grapes, mentioned in Joel

3: 13, 14 as being reaped "in the valley of Jehoshaphat" (margin, "valley of decision, or concision, or threshing"), can refer only to the harvest of the righteous and the harvest of the evil of *all the world*. In the parable of the wheat and the tares Jesus explicitly declared: "The field is the *world* . . . the *harvest* is the end of the *world*; the reapers are the angels." Matt. 13: 38, 39. In Matt. 25: 31, 32 Jesus points to His second advent as the time when *"all the heathen, or nations,"* mentioned in Joel 3, shall be gathered before Him to receive God's judgment: "then He shall *sit* [not in the *literal* valley of Jehoshaphat. Note the word *"sit"* is taken from Joel 3: 12] upon the throne of His glory: and before Him shall be gathered *all nations:* and He shall separate them one from another, as a shepherd divideth his sheep from the goats." Thus Jesus gives the interpretation of "the valley of Jehoshaphat," mentioned in Joel 3, to be the symbolical valley "into" which "all nations" would be "gathered" before Him; the valley in which would take place the harvest of the wheat and the tares, the dividing of the sheep and the goats: He applies the valley of Jehoshaphat (in harmony with the meaning of the name—"the valley of God's Judgment") in a world-wide, symbolical sense. Rev. 14: 14-20 pictures the second advent, when the Master will come with His sickle "and reap: for the time is come for Thee to reap; for the harvest of the earth is ripe." Thus the harvest, pictured in Joel as being *"in* the valley of Jehoshaphat," is said in Revelation to be "the harvest of *the earth."* The reference in Joel 3: 13 to the *treading* (see Variorum Bible) of the winepress—the wrath of God upon the "multitudes, multitudes *in* the valley of concision, or *threshing"*—is given a world-wide application in Rev. 14: 18-20: "And the angel thrust in his sickle into *the earth,* and gathered the vine of *the earth,* and cast it into the *great* [world-wide—not the *small*, literal valley of Jehoshaphat] winepress of the wrath of God. And the winepress was trodden without the city [Jerusalem, the church], and blood came out of the winepress, by the space of a thousand and six hundred furlongs." Thus the *gathering* of "all the nations" "into the valley of Jehoshaphat"—the reaping of the harvests of wheat and grapes, the cutting, or threshing, of "multitudes, multitudes in the valley of decision"—outside Jerusalem is interpreted in the New Testament to mean the world-wide scenes of judgment at the second coming of Christ. *"In* Mount Zion and *in* Jerusalem [that is, the church] shall be deliverance, as the Lord hath said, and in the remnant whom the Lord shall call," while the winepress is "trodden *without the city"*—the church. There will be a literal application of these verses at the end of the millennium, as explained in another chapter.

The Revelation often takes several local, *literal* things mentioned in the Old Testament and blends them into one picture describing the final world-wide scenes. If applied *literally*, contradictions would appear; but when the Revelation blends them into one *symbolical* picture, all the incongruities of a literal interpretation do not exist. When applied symbolically, Jehoshaphat, meaning "the valley of God's judgment," and Armageddon, meaning "the mountain of slaughter," refer to the *same* event: both refer to the judgment of God, which results in the utter destruction of all His enemies and the enemies of the church. In the Commentary by Jamieson, Fausset and Brown, we read that "the valley of Jehoshaphat" "may be used as a general term for the theatre of God's final judgment on *Israel's foes.*" "The valley of Jehoshaphat" is symbolical of the slaughter of "Armageddon," when God arises to slay the last foes of spiritual Israel of whom Tyre, Edom, Egypt and Philistia, mentioned in Joel, were but types.

Ezek. 38, 39; Joel 3; Zech. 14; Rev. 16: 12-16, etc., do not describe a battle to be fought between nations in Palestine, but a world in rebellion against God, seeking to destroy His church: a rebellious world which is slaughtered in the world-wide valley of "God's judgment."

The following extracts are representative of what many commentators have expressed concerning the symbolical, world-wide application of the prophecies of Joel, etc. Cruden says:—

"Jehoshaphat, in Hebrew, signifies the judgment of God. And it is very probable that the valley of Jehoshaphat, or God's judgment, mentioned in Joel 3, is symbolical."

Christopher Wordsworth says:—

"Multitudes, multitudes in the valley of decision . . . or in the valley of *cutting to pieces.* like sheaves crushed on the summer threshing floor by the sharp-toothed instrument which was formed with revolving cylinders and by which they were threshed.
"The valley of Jehoshaphat. or Judgment of God, *is the world's threshing floor;* and rebellious men and nations are compared to sheaves that have been reaped in the *world's harvest,* and are cast on the floor to be threshed—as Mercer well says, 'However numerous they may be in multitude, however furious the uproar they make in their bold and blasphemous insurrection, raging against God (Ps. 2: 1-2), yet He will gather them all together into *the threshing floor of His judgment,* and cast them down prostrate there.' "

Dr. W. Smith's Bible Dictionary comments concerning "the valley of Jehoshaphat":—

"The passage is one of great boldness, abounding in verbal turns in which Hebrew poetry so much delights, and in particular *there is a play between the name given to the spot*—Jehoshaphat, i.e., 'Jehovah's judgment'—and the 'judgment' there to be pronounced. . . . The name may be only an *imaginary* one conferred on a spot which *exists nowhere* but in the *vision of the prophet.* Such was the view of some of the ancient translators."

Matthew Henry's Commentary says:—

"A challenge given to all the *enemies of God's kingdom,* to do their worst; to signify to them that God is *preparing war against* them, they are called upon to prepare war against Him. Vs. 9-11. When the hour of God's judgment is come, effectual methods shall be taken to gather all nations to the *battle of that great day of God Almighty,* Rev. 16: 14. It seems to be here spoken ironically: *'Proclaim ye this among the Gentiles,'* let all the forces of the nations be summoned to join in confederacy against God and His people. . . . Thus does a God of almighty power *bid defiance* to all the opposition of the powers of darkness; let the *heathen rage,* and the *kings of the earth take counsel together* against the Lord and His Christ; let them assemble and come, and gather themselves together; but He that sitteth in the heavens shall laugh at them. . . . Jehoshaphat signifies, the judgment of the Lord. Let them come to the place of God's judgment, which perhaps is the chief reason for the using of the name here, but it is put together as a proper name for the sake of allusion to the place so called, which we observed before; let them come thither where God will sit to judge the heathen, to that throne of glory before which shall be gathered all nations, Matt. 25: 32. . . .

"The valley of threshing; so the margin, carrying on the metaphor of the harvest (V. 13). . . . *The proud enemies of God's people* will then be crushed and broken to pieces, and made as the dust of the summer threshing floors. Innumerable multitudes will be gathered together, to receive their final doom in that day. As in the destruction of Gog we read of the valley of Hamon-Gog, and the city of Hamonah (Ezek. 39: 15, 16), both signifying the multitude of the vanquished enemies; it is the word here used [in Joel 3: 14], Hamonim ["multitudes"] . . ."

Dr. Scott's Commentary on Joel 3 says:—

"We may suppose the word *'Israel'* to comprehend the *faithful of all ages:* and then we may observe that the judgments denounced against the *church's enemies* are chiefly for their hatred and cruelty towards *God's servants.* . . .

"*This is a challenge,* publicly proclaimed, *to the enemies* of Israel, and of the church, to excite themselves and each other to a combined assault. . . . Let all the heathen collect all their forces *to battle against the worshippers of Jehovah.* . . . But the Scriptures, referred to (Ezek. 38-39, etc.), show that almost all the prophets foretell the same *final victory of the church* over all *nations* that oppose it. . . .

"'Sanctify war.' From this expression many conclude that the war spoken of will be engaged in on *religious pretexts,* and be a kind of proclaimed crusade, or *holy war, for* the extirpation of restored *Israel, and of the true church of God.*"

Christ chose the valley of Gehenna (Mark 9: 43-45), south of Jerusalem, to symbolize a world-wide annihilation of the wicked after the millennium. Rev. 20. Similarly, the valley of Jehoshaphat, east of Jerusalem (maps at back of Bibles; Philip's Handy General Atlas, etc., place the valley of Jehoshaphat between Jerusalem and the Mount of Olives. See also G.C. 33), is used to symbolize the world-wide judgment at the second advent.

As explained in my "What is Armageddon?" pp. 16, 17, the measurement mentioned in Rev. 14: 20 in connection with the treading of the winepress of God's wrath is taken from Ezekiel's vision of the temple, city and "the oblation." See Ezek. 40-48.

One thousand six hundred furlongs is equivalent to 200 miles, which is the circuit of "the Holy oblation" in which, in Ezekiel's vision, the church is pictured under the figures of a mighty temple and city on the "very high mountain" "in the land of Israel." In the Apocalypse, Ezekiel's visions concerning Israel are given their spiritual meaning, and Ezekiel's "oblation," and all it contained, are referred to as God's city—the world-wide church—outside of which the enemies of the church perish in Armageddon's world-wide slaughter.

THE MEANING OF "GOG" AND "MAGOG"
(Rev. 20: 8).

The inspired interpretation of Ezek. 38, 39 is given in the book of Revelation. Rev. 20: 8 distinctly states that Gog and Magog are "the nations [or Gentiles, people] which are in the *four quarters of the earth* . . . the *number* of whom is as the sand of the sea." As in the case of *all* other Old Testament prophecies brought into the Revelation, a world-wide application is made of the great army of Gog and Magog: we are directed to the *vast numbers* in Gog's army. God's Word does not indicate Gog's army to be Russia, but, to the contrary, distinctly says that Gog's army is "in the *four* quarters of the *earth.*" As we have shown elsewhere, the number four is employed in the Scripture for the whole world. The prophecy of Ezek. 38, 39 does not concern merely Palestine, but is a prophecy comprehending *the whole world.* All the Hebrew prophets present the *world-wide* scenes of the last days in a Palestinian setting and, as shown in another chapter, the Revelation employs the local scenes of the Old Testament in predicting the world-wide events of the last days. This is one of the basic principles upon which depends the true understanding of the prophecies of the Old Testament.

At the end of the millennium, how would the armies of Gog be found in *all* parts of the *world if* they were all killed in Palestine at the second advent? When resurrected at the end of the millennium, they will be in all parts of the world (Rev. 20: 8) because they were a world-wide army—"in the four quarters of the earth"—slain in all parts of the world at the second advent. Satan wishes to confuse the people of God on this issue: by his counterfeit interpretation—that Gog's armies attack the *literal* Jews in Palestine—he seeks to obscure the true interpretation that Gog's armies attack *spiritual,* world-wide Israel and Israel's sign of allegiance to God. Ex. 31: 13-17; Ezek. 20: 12, 20; Rev. 7: 1-4, etc. The New Testament shows the spiritual application in relation to the church of those things in the Old Testament which belonged to national Israel. The *literal* application of Ezek. 38, 39, Joel 3, Zech. 14, Rev. 16: 12-16, etc., in relation to Palestine is *opposed to the principles of interpretation revealed throughout the New Testament: principles upon which rests God's last-day message.*

The prophecy of Joel 3 refers to *"multitudes, multitudes in the valley of decision."* We have shown that these "multitudes" represent the great hosts of the unsaved who are destroyed at the second advent. Gog's armies, described in Ezek. 38, 39, are the same "multitudes" who are slaughtered in "Armageddon . . . the battle of the great day of God Almighty." The prophecy of Ezek. 38, 39 prominently brings to view the *great number* comprising Gog's army, to which Rev. 20: 8 also directs us. Notice the following passages in the prophecy: "Thus saith the Lord God: Behold, I am against thee, O Gog. . . . I will bring thee forth, *all* thine army . . . *all* of them clothed with *all* sorts of armour, even *a great* company with bucklers and shields, *all of them* handling swords: Persia, Ethiopia, and Libya *with* them; *all of them* with shield and helmet: Gomer, and *all his* hands; the house of Togarmah of the north *quarters* [those not of the house of Togarmah come from the other three *quarters,"* making up the *"four quarters* of the earth" mentioned in Rev. 20: 8], and *all his* bands: and *many* people with thee. Be thou prepared, and prepare for thyself, thou, and *all* thy company that are assembled unto thee." Ezek. 38: 2-7. To further the graphic portrayal of the *great multitudes* ("Multitudes, multitudes in the valley of decision") in Gog's world-wide army, the prophecy declares: "Thou shalt be like a *cloud* to cover the land, thou, and all thy bands, and many people with thee." Writing as a believer in the literal interpretation of this prophecy in relation to Palestine and the literal Jews, R. T. Naish, in his "The Last Call," p. 117, says: "The reference to 'a storm' and 'cloud,' may refer to the great fleet of aeroplanes darkening the sky, which will accompany the huge host of the Red armies." This, of course, is a man-made, or "private interpretation" against which we are warned. 2 Pet. 1: 20. Looking to the Word of God for guidance, we turn to Heb. 12: 1, where reference is made to Christians being "encompassed about with so great a *cloud* of *witnesses.*" The myriads of angelic hosts who accompany Christ at His second advent are referred to as "the clouds of heaven." Dan. 7: 13; Matt. 24: 30, etc.

Thus we have Scriptural testimony for the belief that the *cloud* to which the army of Gog is likened refers, not to aeroplanes, but to the *vast numbers* led by Gog. This fact is definitely taught in Ezek. 38: 15, 16: "And thou shalt come from thy place out of the north parts [many of Israel's ancient enemies—such as Babylon, etc.—came from the north], thou, and *many* people with thee, *all* of them riding [not in aeroplanes] upon horses, a *great company,* and a *mighty army:* and thou shalt come up against my people of Israel, *as a cloud* to cover the land." Thus the cloud represents the great number in Gog's army: as stated in Rev. 20: 8, *"Gog and Magog . . . the number* of whom is as *the sand of the sea . . .* the nations which are in the four quarters of the earth."

Other references in the Apocalypse to portions of Ezek. 38, 39 also clearly reveal that the prophecy of Ezek. 38, 39 refers to the great multitudes of the people of the world who are in the army of Satan, whose earthly, visible ecclesiastical representative is the Papacy. Study Ezek. 39: 4. 17-20 in the light of Rev. 19: 11-19.

"The New Testament Pocket Commentary," compiled from Henry, Scott, Doddridge, Burkitt, and other Writers," comments on Rev. 20: 8:—"Gog and Magog: *figurative personifications of the enemies of God's people.* Magog was the son of Japeth, Gen. 10: 2, from whom the nations formerly called Scythians, and in modern times, Tartars, are said to be descended. The Scythian kings went by the name of Gog. Gog is said to mean 'covered,' alluding to the deceitful character of those who bore his name. Ezek. 38: 2; 39: 1."

Thus "Gog" is a fitting name for that false system of worship which, under the guise of Christian nomenclature, continues, in the professedly Christian church, the old Babylonian mysteries associated with sun-worship. It is a deceitful form of worship, for it counterfeits the true: it "covers" "the truth in unrighteousness," and "changes the truth of God into a lie." Rom. 1: 18, 25. Spiritual Babylon of the Revelation is the rival of Jerusalem, the spiritual home of God's people; but many of God's children are still within Babylon, not knowing that its system is condemned by God. The Lord calls His people to come out of Babylon to Jerusalem, the city of truth and peace. Rev. 18: 4. Though the head of that false system professes to be "the vicar of the son of God," the Scriptures define him as "that *man of sin . . . the son of perdition;* who opposeth and exalteth himself above all that is called God, or that is worshipped; so that he as God sitteth in the temple of God [the pro-

fessing church of Christ], shewing himself that he is God."
2 Thess. 2: 3, 4. Verses 6 and 8 show that "Gog," the "covered"
one, would be "revealed": "then shall that Wicked be revealed."

How true are the footnotes of Brown's Bible concerning Ezek.
38, 39: " 'Gog and Magog,' both signifying 'covered, concealed,'
which, read in the light of 2 Thess. 2: 3, 6, 8, where 'that man of
sin,' 'that wicked,' is as yet to be revealed—to be uncovered, as it
were—and deprived forever of that mask of hypocrisy, that assumption of Christianity behind which is concealed his idolatry—his
heathenism."

The Rev. A. Jones, in the "List of the Proper Names in the
Old and New Testaments" at the back of Cruden's Concordance,
gives the meaning of "Gog" as "roof, covering, extension."
"Magog," according to the same authority, means "place of Gog or
expansion, that is, increase of family." Thus we see the play upon
the meanings of the names "Gog and Magog" in the description
of the leaders and multitudes of those who are deceived by Satan.
In heaven Lucifer covered up his real intentions. Under the pretext
of bettering the lot of the angels, he led them into rebellion against
their Maker. In the garden of Eden he employed the same deceitful
tactics, promising our first parents that, by following him, their
eyes would be opened to be as gods knowing good and evil. See
Gen. 3: 1-6. By deceiving them to believe that they would be
better off in rebellion against God than in serving Him, Satan
succeeded in wooing the third of the angels, our first parents, and
the majority of the people of this world. He has always "covered"
his real intentions, being "a liar" and a deceiver: so subtlely does
he lead that many do not know that they are going contrary to
God's will. The Revelator describes the devil as "Satan which
deceiveth the whole world." Rev. 12: 9. Satan has succeeded in
deceiving many to believe that prophecies of "the final conflict"
pertain to a conflict of nations in Palestine, with Russia coming
from the north, Japan and China from the east, etc. The Papacy
has fostered this system of interpretation which "covers" them by
diverting the attention of Bible students to some national interpretation in relation to the literal Jews in Palestine, instead of
applying the prophecies in relation to spiritual Israel and her
enemies. "Magog," meaning "expansion," refers to the world-wide
extension of Satan's false system of worship, which has "cast down
the truth to the ground; and it [has] practised and prospered."
Dan. 8: 12, 24, 25. Error will so prosper that "all that dwell upon
the earth [except the remnant church, Rev. 12: 17, etc.] shall wor-

ship the beast." Rev. 13: 8. "Magog," also meaning *"increase of family,"* represents the vast numbers in the armies of Gog: the vast *"multitudes"* of the unsaved. In Ezek. 39: 11 we read: "And there shall they bury Gog and *all his multitude;* and they shall call it the valley of *Hamon-Gog."* The margin gives the meaning of this name as *"the multitude of Gog."* See also v. 15. The third use of the word *Hamon* is in v. 16, where the name is given of the city which was to have been built in commemoration of this wonderful victory for Israel: "And also the name of the city shall be *Hamonah.* . . ." The margin gives the meaning of the name: "that is, *multitude."* Fenton's Translation says: "And the city also will be named Hamonah. Note:—'Hamonah' means *'Mob-town.'* " Dr. Strong says of Hamon-Gog: "The *multitude* of Gog; the fanciful name of an *emblematic* place in Palestine." The reference to "Gog and his *multitude"* in the play upon the meanings of the names Hamon and Magog is obvious. No city of that name has ever been built (see Dr. Scott's Com.). *If* the prophecy of Ezek. 38, 39 were to have a *literal* fulfilment, then, after the battle of Armageddon, the victorious Jews would build a city near Megiddo and call it "Hamonah," to commemorate the slaughter of Gog's *multitude* in Armageddon! But, as the Bible teaches the utter destruction of *all* the wicked at Armageddon (including the unbelieving Jews), it is very evident that Ezek. 38, 39 will not now have a *literal* fulfilment. Gog, therefore, cannot refer to Russia, and the actual fulfilment will not be Palestinian, but world-wide. Gog's "multitude" (see also Rev. 17: 15; G.C. 635, 636), which seek to slay spiritual Israel, are brought to view as being destroyed in the world-wide slaughter of Armageddon. See my "What is Armageddon?" pp. 14, 15, for further reference to the modern name of Megiddo—Legio, now Lejun. "Legio corresponds to the great multitude."

Referring to the burial place of God's army, Hengstenberg's Commentary says: "The valley of Megiddo is in no doubt meant, to which the description eminently applies." After giving particulars concerning the location of the grave of Gog and his multitude, he says: "All the three marks which the prophet gives suit Megiddo. In all probability, Legio, now Lejun, the modern name of Megiddo, is derived from our passage. *Legio* corresponds with the great *multitude* here."

When Jesus asked the evil spirit his name, "he answered, saying, My name is *Legion,* for we are *many."* Mark 5: 9; Luke 8: 30. Evil spirits, which are very *many,* will lead to their doom the *multitudes* of the enemies of God and Israel, in the antitypical Megiddo slaughter.

It is interesting to notice the spiritual application given in Brown's Bible of the prophecy of Ezek. 38, 39: "Then borrowing from one prophecy the light derived from another, it appears from Rev. 20: 8, that 'Gog and Magog' represent the devil deceived nations which are in the four quarters of the earth, and who, according to Ezek. 38: 16 and Ezek. 39: 7, 21, 23, 28, are 'the heathen,' 'the enemies' (Ezek. 39: 27)."

The Spirit of Prophecy (see E.W., p. 284) uses the term "the heathen" (see Ezek. 38, 39) as representing "the enemies" of the truth. Many of the old godly commentators stated that Ezek. 38, 39 portrayed the combination of Satanic forces arrayed against the church. Brown's Bible comments thus: "There will never be wanting *multitudes to assemble against Christ's church.*"

"The Annotated Paragraph Bible" says:—

"*The triumphs of the church of Christ, and the overthrow of its enemies,* are represented by the destruction of vast armies from the extreme north and south . . . the consummation of the *great conflict* . . . *between the kingdoms of God and of Satan in the world.*"

In his "The Book of Revelation," pp. 352, 353, T. W. Christie, B.A., says:—

"But what are those simple truths of those chapters of Ezek. 38, 39, and embodied in the spiritual vision of John? . . . They are those *figurative illustrations* of spiritual truths *relating to the church of God and its enemies,* down to the *last conflict.* . . . Ezekiel, as a prophet of Israel, used the enemies of the nation Israel as *typical* of the *foes of the spiritual Israel.*"

Hengstenberg's Commentary on Ezekiel, p. 330, says:—

"The Apocalypse destroys the appearance of a historical character, inasmuch as it at once identifies Gog and Magog with the *heathen* in the four ends of the earth. . . . This is explained only when under Gog and Magog are concealed the *enemies of the community of God.*"

From "The Scripture Gazeteer" we quote:—

"The terms Gog and Magog are used *figuratively* as representing the *vast hordes of the Lord's adversaries led by Satan.*"

Isbon T. Beckwith, Phd., D.D., in his "The Apocalypse of John," p. 288, says:—

"Gog and Magog, in which are embraced under a *symbolic* name *all the tribes of men hostile to God.*"

See also the "Bible Handbook," by Dr. Angus, p. 288.

THE SIGNIFICANCE OF THE MEANINGS OF "EDOM" AND "BOZRAH" IN RELATION TO ARMAGEDDON.

The arresting prophecy of Isa. 34 depicts a great slaughter, which expositors generally agree is the coming Armageddon. Schofield's Bible, representing the futuristic view that Armageddon refers to a literal conflict of nations at Megiddo, says: "The day of the Lord: Armageddon." This statement is enlarged in his notes on Rev. 19, which read:—

> "Armageddon (the ancient hill and valley of Megiddo, west of Jordan in the plain of Jezreel) is the appointed place for the *beginning* of the great battle in which the Lord, at His coming in glory, will *deliver the Jewish remnant* besieged by the Gentile world-powers under the Beast and False Prophet (Rev. 16: 13-16; Zech. 12: 1-9). Apparently the besieging hosts, whose approach to Jerusalem is described in Isa. 10: 28-32, alarmed by the signs which precede the Lord's coming (Mt. 24: 29, 30), have fallen back to *Megiddo*, after the events of Zech. 14: 2, where their *destruction begins; a destruction consummated* in Moab and the *plains of Idumea* (Isa. 63: 1-6)."

Another writer, in a recent article entitled "Notes on Prophetic Interpretation of Rev. 16: 12-16," also expresses his belief in the futuristic conception of Armageddon. He says:—

> "In Isa. 34 and 63 it is suggested that the final scenes stretch from the extreme south of Palestine, the land of Edom, of which Bozrah was the capital . . . it would indicate that the centre of this last great struggle is in the land of Palestine from the Arabian peninsular in the south, or the country of Edom or Idumea, of which Bozrah was the capital, to the northern extremity covering the plain of Esdraelon, and embracing the valley of Jehoshaphat."

We have already pointed out the impossibility of the literal, military, futuristic application of Joel 3 and Rev. 16: 14-16. As we have shown, "the valley of Jehoshaphat" and "Armageddon" are mentioned because of their *symbolical* meanings, and for this same reason Edom, or Idumea, and Bozrah are brought into the prophetic description in relation to "Armageddon," "the mountain of slaughter." The Scripture Gazeteer, p. 330, in its comments on Isa. 34, says:—

> "The original sense of these words aptly applies to a place of slaughter. *Edom*, signifying *red as blood*, and *Bozrah*, a *vintage*, which, in prophetic language, *often denotes God's vengeance upon the wicked.*"

In the Scriptures wine is a symbol of blood. When inaugurating the Lord's Supper, Jesus selected wine as a *symbol* of His blood. He said: *"This is My blood* of the new testament, which is shed for many for the remission of sins. But I say unto you, I will not drink henceforth of *this fruit of the vine,* until that day when I drink it new with you in My Father's kingdom." Matt. 26: 27-29. Jesus did not actually say that the wine was a *symbol* of His blood, nor the bread a *symbol* of His body. Roman Catholics teach that when Jesus said "This is My body . . . this is my blood" He intended us to take His words *literally,* and not symbolically. Protestants rightly maintain that, though Jesus did not say the bread and the wine were *symbols,* He certainly meant them to be understood as such. This belief is based upon the fact that, in the Old Testament, God had already employed bread with which to symbolize the Saviour. The manna—the "bread from heaven" (Ex. 16: 4)—is applied by Jesus, in His spiritual sermon to the literally-minded Jews, as a type of Himself. The Jews, not seeing the *spiritual* application of the manna, said: "Our fathers did eat manna in the desert; as it is written, He gave them bread from heaven to eat. Then Jesus said unto them . . . My Father giveth you the *true bread from heaven. For the bread of God is He which cometh down from heaven,* and giveth life unto the world . . . *I am the bread* of life." John 6: 31-35.

The Futuristic teaching, which applies the prophecies concerning Israel and her enemies in a literal, Palestinian and militaristic sense, belongs to the same system which erroneously applies the bread and wine of the Lord's Supper in a *literal* sense instead of interpreting them *spiritually.* Futurism declares that Armageddon is a literal conflict of nations because Rev. 16: 12-16; Joel 3, etc., do not state that they are to be *symbolically* understood. Thus reason the Roman Catholics regarding the bread and wine of the Lord's Supper.

Jesus did not need to state that the bread and wine were symbols, for the manna, and the bread which was placed in the ancient sanctuary were already employed in the Scriptures as symbols of "the true Bread from heaven," and wine is shown in Scripture as a symbol of blood.

The names Edom, Idumea and Bozrah are employed in Isa. 34 and 63 because of their *symbolical* meanings. Christ's application of *"blood . . . the fruit of the vine"* is in harmony with the meanings of "Edom," "red as *blood,*" and "Bozrah," "a *vintage.*" In Isa. 63: 1-6, Christ is represented as coming "from Edom, with *dyed* garments. . . . I that speak in righteousness, mighty to save." When the *fruit of the vine* was picked, it was thrown into a vat and the juice was squeezed from the grapes by men in naked feet stamping and jumping on the fruit. The men would often shout, and would splash their garments with the wine as they pressed down the bunches of grapes by stamping and jumping. When Jeremiah pictured the world-wide slaughter of Armageddon, he said: "The Lord . . . shall *give a shout, as they that tread the grapes,* against *all* the inhabitants of *the earth."* Then follows a description of the "slain of the Lord . . . at that day *from one end of the earth even unto the other end of the earth."* Jer. 25: 30-33. Thus Jeremiah applies the passages in Isa. 34 and 63 to the slaughter of the wicked in the entire world, using the winepress in Edom and Bozrah as a descriptive symbol.

We have already shown that Joel 3: 13, 14 pictures a "full" winepress—full of "multitudes, multitudes" of unrighteous people "in the valley of Jehoshaphat." Rev. 14: 14-20 applies this to the world-wide destruction of the unprepared at the second coming of Christ. See also Rev. 19: 15. In Rev. 14: 19, 20, the "fully ripe ' grapes—with their *red* juice ripened by the summer suns of "the harvest"—are pictured as thrown "into the great winepress of the wrath of God. And the winepress was trodden without the city, and blood came *out of the winepress."* Thus we are definitely given the *symbolical* interpretation of the meanings of Edom and Bozrah: the grapes and their juice—"the fruit of the vine" trodden out in the winepress—represent the blood of the multitudes who have not made Jesus their Saviour, and so must suffer the wrath of God.

In Isa. 63: 2, the Saviour, Who is represented as coming from Edom and Bozrah, is asked: "Wherefore art thou red in thine apparel, and Thy *garments like him that treadeth in the winefat? I* have trodden the winepress alone; and of the people there was none with Me." When Jesus suffered the wrath of God because He bore our sins, He suffered alone, and His holy garments were dyed with His blood. He went alone into the winepress of God's wrath, and there shed His precious blood, which is typified by the *wine.* As the spiritual interpretation of the passages in Isa. 34 and 63 made it unnecessary for Jesus to state that the wine used in the Lord's Supper was a *symbol* of blood, so these, and other passages of Scripture relating to the final conflict, made it unnecessary for John to stress that his description of Armageddon is couched in symbolic language.

Having paid the price for man's redemption by staining His raiment with *His* own blood, Jesus says of those who reject His loving sacrifice: "I will *tread* them in mine anger, and *trample* them in My fury; and *their* blood shall be *sprinkled upon My garments,* and I will *stain all My* raiment. For the day of vengeance is in my heart . . . and I will *tread* down the *people* in mine anger." Isa. 63: 1-6.

Isa. 34, itself, clearly shows the world-wide, *symbolical* nature of the picture presented in connection with Edom, or Idumea, and Bozrah. At the heading of chapter 34 of Isaiah we read: "The judgments wherewith God revengeth His *church*. The desolation of *her enemies*." It was the custom of Bible writers to name some of the *national* enemies of *national* Israel when predicting the calamities to come to the *spiritual* enemies of *spiritual* Israel. Thus the Edomites, or Idumeans, are employed in this chapter as *symbols* of the *enemies* of the *church*. The Edomites, or the Idumeans, were descendants of Esau, the twin brother of Jacob. Because at birth Esau was "*red* all over like an hairy garment, they called his name Esau." When Esau sold his birthright for "*red* pottage . . . his name was called *Edom,* that is, *Red.*" Gen. 25: 25, 30, margin.

Once persons, events, etc., are mentioned in the Scriptures, subsequent writers frequently keep them before us, and then the book of Revelation gives them a spiritual, world-wide application. From the first time the name "Israel" was given by God to repentant, overcoming Jacob, the Bible keeps before us the children of "*Israel*." The book of Revelation enlarges upon the main features of the history and prophecies concerning "the tribes of the children of *Israel*" and applies them in relation to the *church*. Only when interpreted in relation to the church and *her* enemies can the true meaning be obtained concerning the final conflict in "a place called in the *Hebrew* tongue Armageddon."

To rightly understand the application made throughout Scripture concerning Edom, or Esau, it is necessary to trace from the beginning the history of Esau and his descendants. Esau, who so lightly exchanged his birthright for some "red pottage," is a type of those who are called to be heirs of a heavenly birthright in Christ, but who, like Esau, relinquish it for some pleasure which appeals for the moment. Notice Paul's *spiritual* application: "Follow peace with all men, and holiness, without which no man shall see the Lord . . . lest there by any fornicator, or profane person, *as Esau,* who *for one morsel* of meat sold his birthright." Heb. 12: 14-17.

The Scripture says: "And Esau hated Jacob. . . . I will slay my brother Jacob." Gen. 27: 41. Here we see typified the hatred which is in the heart of some toward their more spiritual brothers. Jacob fled from the wrath of his brother, but after an absence of twenty years (Gen. 31: 38), decided to return to the promised land, though fearful of his brother's anger. "And Jacob sent messengers before him to his brother unto the land of Seir, the country of

Edom." Jacob was so afraid that his blood would be shed by a man whose name meant "red as blood," that he sent presents to appease Esau's wrath. But Esau, still nursing hatred for his brother, set out with "four hundred men" to slay Jacob. Jacob's prayer of anguish by the brook Jabbok brought to him his new name, "Israel," and God's assurance of blessing and protection. In this experience we see the type of God's blessing and protection upon all who, like Jacob, wrestle in prayer and become "children of Israel."

The experience of Jacob (whose name "Israel" means "a prince of God") with Esau, or Edom (whose name means "red as blood") has its world-wide application in the last days. As stated in "The Great Controversy," pp. 616-622:—"Jacob's night of anguish, when he wrestled in prayer for deliverance from the hand of Esau, *represents* the experience of God's people in the time of trouble. . . . As Satan influenced Esau to march against Jacob, so he will stir the wicked to destroy God's people in the time of trouble." Thus God's servant refers to Esau as a *type* of those who will endeavour to slay God's people in the last days: thus showing the principle by which Isa. 34 and 63 should be interpreted. Edom, Idumea, and Bozrah are no more to be understood literally than Esau or Jacob, but are to be interpreted in a symbolical, world-wide sense. Within Isa. 34, itself, we are shown that Edom, Idumea, and Bozrah are brought into the picture because of their symbolical meaning in describing world-wide events. Notice to whom this chapter is addressed:—"Come near . . . let the *earth* hear, and *all* that is therein; the *world,* and *all* things that come forth of it. For the indignation of the Lord is upon *all* nations, and His fury upon *all* their armies . . . and the mountains shall be melted with their *blood* [remember the meaning of "Edom" and "Bozrah"] . . . for My sword shall be bathed in heaven: behold, it shall come upon Idumea, and upon the *people* of my curse [*literally,* the Edomites *no longer exist*]. . . . The sword of the Lord is filled with *blood* . . . for the Lord hath a sacrifice in *Bozrah,* and a great slaughter in the *land of Idumea* [prophecies concerning 'the land of Israel' are applied in the New Testament in a world-wide sense, and, similarly, 'the land of Idumea' stands for the world, where dwell the *antitypical* Esaus who will seek to slay their brother Israel] . . . their land shall be soaked with *blood* . . . for it is the day of the Lord's vengeance." The play upon the meaning of the names Edom, or Esau, and Bozrah is apparent.

The Idumeans, the descendants of Esau, are mentioned, in various parts of Scripture, as having *hatred and enmity against Israel.* They are mentioned as *types* of those who hate and war against spiritual Israel. Obadiah 18 foretold their national end, which is used as a type of the destruction of all those who are enemies of spiritual Israel. As recognized by most Bible commentators, the Revelator draws his imagery of the destruction of all the wicked from Isa. 34. Compare Isa. 34: 4 with Rev. 6: 13, 14; Isa. 34: 10 with Rev. 14: 11; 18: 18; 19: 3, etc. See the following chapter of this book, where, in the study of the book of Isaiah in relation to the river Euphrates, further facts are presented showing that Edom, or Idumea, and Bozrah are mentioned in the prophecies of Isa. 34 and 63 because of their *symbolical* meaning in connection with the *world-wide* slaughter of the wicked.

"THE MOURNING OF HADADRIMMON IN THE VALLEY OF MEGIDDON." Zech. 12: 11.

The historical background forming the basis for Zechariah's prophecy concerning the last days and the mourning and slaughter of the wicked in the antitypical valley of Megiddo, is the death of King Josiah who, as an ally of Babylon, was slain "in the valley of Megiddo" (see 2 Chron. 35: 20-22)—"and all Judah and Jerusalem mourned for Josiah." Vs. 24, 25. The death of Josiah, which occasioned such lamentation among "all the families," or "tribes," of the chosen nation, was, as Geikie says, "the ruin of the kingdom." Geikie, in his "Hours with the Bible," Vol. 5, pages 274, 275, writes: "Tradition says that he (Josiah) adhered to his resolution to fight, in spite of the earnest entreaties of Jeremiah. Even Necho himself, indeed, tried to restrain him, but he rushed to his fate. . . . Their (Israel's) hopes as a nation had perished with him. *Never before had there been such a deep or universal lamentation."* See 2 Chron. 35: 25.

Jesus and John, employing Zechariah's reference to the mourning which followed Josiah's death in the valley of Megiddo, direct our attention to the destruction which will surely come to those who ally themselves with spiritual Babylon in "the final conflict" concerning the Sabbath. The mark of spiritual Babylon's power is the observance of Sunday, the first day of the week, instead of the Sabbath. For a fuller study concerning spiritual Babylon's mark of power in relation to the final conflict, see my "Christ Conquers, or Why Christ Rose on Sunday: the Vital Relation to the Battle of Armageddon."

It is interesting to notice the word "Hadadrimmon," found in Zech. 12: 11: "In that day there shall be a great mourning in Jerusalem, as in the *mourning of Hadadrimmon* in the valley of Megiddon." Concerning "Hadadrimmon in the valley of Megiddon," the Rev. Alfred Jones, M.A., in his list of the meanings of Bible names, in Cruden's Concordance, says: "*Rimmon* was a *god of the Syrians; the invocation of the god Rimmon.*" In their apostasy before they went into captivity, the professed people of God worshipped the gods of the surrounding nations—including the Syrian sun-god. In vain the devotees of the sun-god invoked his protection.

The first day of the week was devoted to the honour of the sun-god—in reality, Satan, whose heavenly name "Lucifer" meant "Day Star" (Isa. 14: 12, margin). As light had been created on the first day of the week of creation, and as Satan determined to make himself "first" in his contest against the God of heaven, he chose as his day the first day of the week, calling it Sunday, in contrast to the seventh day which God said was His Sabbath. "Hadad," according to the Rev. Alfred Jones, M.A., means "Chief, most eminent, a title of the kings of Syria. The god Rimmon was styled Adad. It was originally a *title of the sun.* It signified The FIRST."

Not only is "Hadad," the "chief," "the first"—"a title of the kings of Syria"—significantly employed in the prophecy, but the name "Syria" is significant, for it means "the highland," "highness," "magnificance," "to be elevated." In his covetous ambition to be "first," Lucifer desired "to be *elevated.*" He said: "I will *ascend* . . . I will *exalt* my throne: I will sit also *upon the mount* . . . I will *ascend* above the *heights.*" Isa. 14: 12-14. In describing that period of church history when Satan was laying the foundations for the Papal apostasy, through which he designed to reach the ascendancy in the professing church of Jesus, the Lord gave it the name of "Pergamos." "The word Pergamos signifies *height, elevation.*" "Daniel and the Revelation," p. 355, 356, by Uriah Smith.

Hence we can see the significance of the prophetic language—"the mourning of *Hadadrimmon* [Rimmon was a god of the Syrians] in the valley of *Megiddon*"—in describing the slaughter of the Babylonian world which elevates Satan by endeavouring to force all Christendom to exalt Sunday, the *first* day of the week.

In the chapter "The Principle of the World-wide Symbolized by the Local," we show that the mourning of "all tribes, or kindreds," mentioned in Matt. 24: 30; Rev. 1: 7, occurs at the second advent of Christ when, in the slaughter of Armageddon, those fighting against God and His church are destroyed. Jesus, in His second advent sermon (Matt. 24: 30) and in the Revelation (1: 7), refers back to the prophecy of Zech. 12: 11-14, which reads: "In that day there shall be a great *mourning* in Jerusalem, as the *mourning* of *Hadadrimmon in the valley of Megiddon*. And the land shall *mourn,* every *family* apart, the *family* of the house of David . . . the *family* of Shimei . . . *all the families . . . every family."* The Hebrew for "family"—"mishpachah"—according to Dr. Strong, means "kindred, tribe." Thus Jesus (in Matt. 24: 30; Rev. 1: 7) applies Zech. 12: 11-14, which predicts the *mourning* of *all the tribes, or kindreds, "in the valley of Megiddon,"* to the world-wide *mourning* of the unsaved at the second advent. He applies *"the valley of Megiddon"* in a world-wide sense. God's last-day message goes to these same tribes, or people (see Rev. 14: 6), and their *mourning* "in the valley of *Megiddon,"* or "the valley of *destruction, or slaughter,"* is the result of their rejection of God's message concerning the seventh-day Sabbath, the sign of His creatorship. Rev. 14: 7; Ex. 31: 13-18; Ezek. 20: 12, 20, etc.

THE SIGNIFICANCE OF THE MEANING OF THE WORD "EUPHRATES."

As shown in the following chapter, the river Euphrates is *not* employed to represent a nation or nations occupying the territory through which it runs, but *is* employed, *throughout the Scriptures,* as a symbol of *invading forces, rushing to destroy.* In Rev. 8 and 9 the powers symbolized are mentioned because they destroyed the Roman Empire. *Because* the Ottoman Empire did this *invading, destroying work,* she was symbolized by the river Euphrates. It would be illogical to turn to Rev. 9 to prove the theory that the Euphrates in Rev. 16: 12 represents the downfall of Turkey or other nations occupying the territory adjacent to the Euphrates, for the Euphrates is *not* employed in Rev. 9—or *anywhere in God's Word*—as a symbol of a power that *diminishes until it is defunct*— "dried up." The Euphrates is employed to symbolize *only* a strong, vigorous, *invading force*—never to symbolize a stationary or dying nation.

There is always harmony between the meaning of a name employed and its setting in the prophecy. According to Dr.

Strong, the meaning of the word "Euphrates" is: "to break forth; *rushing.*" The Bible records reveal a wonderful harmony between the *meaning* of the name and the significantly-written Bible history relating to the Euphrates.

In Rev. 16: 12; 17: 1, 15 (compare with Jer. 51: 13), the waters of the Euphrates symbolize the "multitudes" of Babylon who "break forth" and *"rush"* to destroy God's people.

CHAPTER XXV

THE "TESTIMONY OF JESUS" REVEALS THE INTER-
PRETATION OF THE DRYING UP OF THE WATER OF
THE EUPHRATES AND THE COMING OF "THE KINGS
FROM THE SUN-RISING." Rev. 16: 12.

CONTENTS:

"The Testimony of Jesus" is the united testimony of the *whole* of the Word of God. Not by isolated texts, but by comparing Scripture with Scripture, we arrive at the full revelation of God upon any theme. If we would know the true interpretation of the Euphrates in Rev. 16: 12 we should investigate the significance of the meaning *in other portions of the Scripture* of this ancient Biblical river.

We are not saved by heeding an isolated verse or two, neither are we to build our beliefs upon isolated verses of Scripture. Jesus says, *"Search* the Scriptures" (John 5: 39). He also says: "If ye *continue* in My *word,* then are ye My disciples indeed." John 8: 31. The reason so many erroneously interpret the Scriptures, and particularly the prophecies, is because they do not *"continue"* in *searching* the Word of God.

This chapter illustrates how the Holy Spirit leads us in the study of the Word of God. Our present study of the river Euphrates illustrates how we should "search the Scriptures" to obtain "the Testimony of Jesus" upon any Biblical subject. As we follow certain words through the Scriptures we are led to analyse the contents of various books. We are led to see that there is an indissoluble link between certain books. In this way we are trained by the Spirit of God to take a more comprehensive view of the books of the Bible, and to notice the similarity of contents. Our decisions then become founded upon unshakable faith because we *know* that our beliefs are supported by so *much* Scriptural testimony. *Continuing* in Christ's Word in order to obtain His "testimony" on the understanding of the river Euphrates in Rev. 16: 12 we go back to the Old Testament (where we should commence our study of any theme in the Book of Revelation) and see the way the Holy Spirit has inspired the writers to bring the river Euphrates into the sacred narratives.

(1). THE RIVER EUPHRATES IN BIBLICAL HISTORY: THE BOUNDARY OF THE LAND OF ISRAEL.

The river Euphrates is mentioned 21 times, or 3 times 7, in the Bible. See Gen. 2: 14; 15: 18; Deut. 1: 7; 11: 24; Josh. 1: 4; 2 Sam. 8: 3; 2 Kings 23: 29; 24: 7; 1 Chron. 5: 9; 18: 3; 2 Chron. 35: 20; Jer. 13: 4-7; 46: 2, 6, 10; 51: 63; Rev. 9: 14; 16: 12. In 7 of these references the Euphrates *is definitely* said to be the *boundary of the promised land.* See Gen. 15: 18; Deut. 1: 7, 8; 11: 24; Josh. 1: 4; 2 Sam. 8: 3; 1 Chron. 5: 9; 1 Chron. 18: 3. These facts show that the Holy Spirit superintended the writing of the records of Scripture and employed the Euphrates in the sacred Book in a significant manner. Therefore, as we study the Scriptures, the Holy Spirit will reveal to us the full significance of the use of the Euphrates in Rev. 16: 12, which is the *last* occasion the word is found in Holy Writ.

The Holy Spirit has seen fit to emphasise that the Euphrates is the boundary between the two centres which are brought so prominently before us in the study of the Book of Revelation— namely, God's house in *Jerusalem,* in the land of Israel; and "the synagogue of Satan" (Rev. 2: 9) in *Babylon.* That the Euphrates is brought to view in Rev. 16: 12 as *Babylon's river* will become apparent as we continue to search the Scriptures for its significance in the Bible.

In addition to the 21 times, or 3 times 7, that the Euphrates is mentioned in the Bible, and the 7 times it is definitely stated to be the boundary line of the land of Israel, the fact of it being the boundary is repeatedly kept before us even in those passages where the *name* Euphrates does not occur (but about which there cannot be the slightest doubt that the Euphrates is meant) and also in these texts where the word appears *without the boundary aspect being definitely stated.* Notice the following verses which, for the sake of brevity, are quoted in the fewest possible words:—*"From the river* unto the land of the Philistines, and unto the land of Egypt." 1 Kings 4: 21. *"From the river* even unto the land of the Philistines, and unto the border of Egypt." 2 Chron. 9: 26. "All the region *this side of the river* . . . over all the kings on *this side of the river."* 1 Kings 4: 24. *"To the river Euphrates."* 2 Kings 23: 29. "From the river of Egypt *unto the river Euphrates."* 2 Kings 24: 7. "Unto the entering in of the wilderness *from the river Euphrates."* 1 Chron. 5: 9. "And David smote Hadarezer King of Zobab unto Hamath, as he went to establish his dominion *by the river Euphrates."* 1 Chron. 18: 3. "The Syrians that were *beyond the river"* (1 Chron. 19: 16)—the context shows that the Euphrates is the river referred to. See 1 Chron. 18: 3; 19: 6, etc., etc.

"Solomon in all his glory" (Matt. 6: 29) was a type of Jesus the "greater than Solomon" (Matt. 12: 42). Particularly in the early part of Solomon's reign, when heavenly wisdom was revealed and peace prevailed everywhere, we see *typified the eternal and glorious reign of the Lord Jesus.* From this, and the other typical teachings associated with Israel's typical land and the Euphrates as the boundary of that land, we see the significance of the inspired statement that Solomon reigned over the whole land of Israel reaching to the Euphrates: "For he had *dominion over all* the region on *this side the river* . . . over *all* the kings on *this side the river:* and he had *peace on all sides* round about him. And Judah and Israel *dwelt safely, every man* under his vine and under his fig tree, from Dan even to Beersheba, *all the days of Solomon."* 1 Kings 4: 24, 25.

Throughout Scripture constant mention is made of the land God gave Israel for an inheritance, and some invaluable instruction in the understanding of the Scriptures is to be found in noting the significant manner in which the Holy Spirit has caused the Bible writers to draw our attention to these illuminating statements. However, it would take us far beyond the scope of this present book if we were to include all of interest and importance regarding "the land of Israel." It is sufficient for our present purpose to point out that God said: "I will remember the land." Lev. 26: 42. He called it "My land." 2 Chron. 7: 20; Isa. 14: 25; Jer. 16: 18; Ezek. 38: 16; Joel 1: 6; 2: 18; 3: 2. It is said to be the land of *"Immanuel"* (Isa. 8: 8), "a land which the Lord thy God careth for." Deut. 11: 12. In contrast to "the land of Egypt . . . the house of bondage" (Ex. 20: 2, etc.). Israel's land was to be the land of liberty in the service of God. The importance of the land in the Scriptures is seen by the fact of it being included in the fifth Commandment— "the first Commandment with promise." Ephes. 6: 2, 3; Ex. 20: 12. God's eyes were to be "always upon it, from the beginning of the year even unto the end of the year." Deut. 11: 12. And in this land Israel was to be blessed: "the Lord shall greatly bless thee *in the land* which the Lord thy God giveth thee for an inheritance to possess it." Deut. 15: 4; 28: 8, etc.

Because of the disobedience of His professed people God declared that He would "root up Israel *out of this good land* . . . and shall scatter them *beyond the river."* 1 Kings 14: 15. In fulfilment of this threatened judgment God's people were removed from the promised land to the land of their Babylonian captivity beyond the Euphrates. The historical narrative recorded in 2 Kings 17: 18-23 states, three times, that when Israel was removed from their land of promise and taken beyond the river Euphrates God had *"removed them out of His sight."* See 2 Kings 17: 18, 20, 23. In the study of the Book of Jonah we also notice a similar expression, stated three times, namely, that Jonah "fled *from the presence of the Lord."* Jonah 1: 3, 10. God's shekinah glory was manifested between the cherubim above the mercy seat in the temple at Jerusalem, in the land of Israel—the boundary of which is clearly stated (in the texts previously given) to be "from the river of Egypt unto *the great river, the river Euphrates.*" Gen. 15: 18. It is not without reason that the heathen people referred to Israel's God as "*the God of the land.*" This expression is found three times—see 2 Kings 17: 26, 27.

God's blessings to national Israel were associated with their national existence in the land of promise. Jonah fled from God's presence manifested in the promised land. Israel was removed from God's sight beyond the boundary of the promised land, namely, the Euphrates. We know, of course, that actually God's presence and His sight were not limited to the territory within the river of Egypt and the river Euphrates, for Jonah, and Israel in captivity, were sustained by the presence of the Lord, though out of the promised land. Much more could be said in regard to these facts in relation to the vital subject of the sanctuary and God's plan of salvation, but we can pause only to point out that these things were significantly recorded in the manner in which they appear in the Old Testament because of their *typical* teachings. To obtain God's blessing we are not to go over to the land of the enemy, but we are to stay by the bleeding Lamb of God whose redemption is wrought out for us in connection with the ministry in the sanctuary in the land of promise. Other antitypical lessons could be pointed out, but we cannot digress any further to discuss them in our present study of the significance of the use of the river Euphrates in the Scriptures.

As we have shown in the chapter dealing with the meanings of Bible names, Esau's descendants—the Idumeans—are mentioned in the Scriptures as the enemies of Israel. Esau nursed a spirit of hatred against Jacob, and his descendants also bore enmity against the children of Israel. They had refused to permit the Israelites to pass through their land to the land of promise—see Num. 20: 14-21—and represent those who are opposed to the progress of the Israel of God to the heavenly Canaan. The Edomites joined in with the Babylonians in destroying Jerusalem—see Ps. 137: 7, 8; Obad. 10-18—and are typical of the enemies of Israel who ally themselves with Babylon. Thus the prediction of the burning of the land of Idumea (see Isa. 34: 5-11) is employed as the basis of the imagery used by the Revelator in describing the destruction of those who are allied to Babylon and oppose the remnant of spiritual Israel. See Rev. 14: 9-11; 19: 3; 20: 10. The destruction of the

Edomites typifies the annihilation of the unsaved. Obad. 18, etc. Thus the Edomites, in Mal. 1: 4, are said to be "the people against whom the Lord hath indignation for ever."

God ordained that Israel's land should have for its boundaries the river Euphrates and the land of Babylon at one end, and, at the other end, the land of Edom. See Num. 34: 1-3. The Israelites were not to have "not so much as a foot breadth" of Esau's land. Deut. 2: 5. ' In God's denunciation of the Edomites He declared that the Israelites would refer to the Edomite boundary adjoining the land of Israel as "The *border* of wickedness, and the people against whom the Lord hath indignation for ever. And your eyes shall see, and ye shall say, *The Lord will be magnified from the border of Israel.*" Mal. 1: 4, 5. Thus God's blessing is said to rest upon the land of Israel, while His curse rested upon those lands wherein dwelt the enemies of Israel. The land of Israel is the place of God's blessing; outside it rests the curse of God. As it was *typically* in the days of national Israel, so it is in a spiritual sense to-day—God's blessing rests everywhere His obedient people dwell.

The first time the Euphrates is mentioned *in connection with the typical land* it is stated to be *the boundary of "the land* of Israel." See Gen. 15: 18. Rom. 4: 13 interprets the promise regarding *"the land"* to mean *"the world."* As "the land of Israel" is world-wide in its present spiritual application *so, likewise, must its boundary* to-day have a *world-wide spiritual significance.* The following extract from Ellicott's Commentary on Revelation, pp. 127, 128, 195, shows how this fact has been somewhat realized, though not properly applied, by some Bible students:—

"The whole tenor of the Apocalypse keeps before us Jerusalem, the temple, and its surroundings (chap. 11: 1, 8), and Babylon, with its might and opulence, as two opposing cities; and it is out of all scriptural analogy to interpret Jerusalem allegorically, and Babylon allegorically, and then to claim the privilege of understanding Euphrates literally. In fact, the inconsistency and arbitrariness of interpreters is tested by these *three names, Babylon, Jersusalem, Euphrates.* Some will have Jerusalem to be literal, and Babylon and Euphrates mystical; others will have Babylon mystical; and Jerusalem and Euphrates literal. Surely those who hold all three to be literal are more consistent. But if Babylon be mystical and Jerusalem mystical, it is hard to see why Euphrates should not be so also. . . .

"It is in this *war between the mystical Jersualem and the mystical Babylon that the great river Euphrates is to play an important part. . . . Babylon is the great foe of Israel* and *the Euphrates* was the great river or flood which formed a natural boundary between them. 'The other side of the flood' (i.e., Euphrates) was the phrase which pointed back to the early life of Abraham before he had entered upon the life of pilgrimage and faith; the Euphrates was the rubicon of his spiritual history. The Euphrates was the great military barrier also between the northern and southern nations; it occupied a place similar to the Rhine and the Danube in modern history. The advance of the Egyptian army to the banks of `the Euphrates threatened the integrity of the Assyrian empire (2 Kings 23: 29). The battle of Carchemish established the supremacy of the Chaldean power to the west of the Euphrates (2 Kings 24: 7); such a preponderance of Babylonish influence threatened the safety of Jerusalem. . . . The drying up of the Euphrates signifies the annihilation of the protecting boundary. Such a frontier line between the spiritual city and the world city does in practice exist. . . . *In the great age-long struggle between the kingdoms of Christ and the world the Euphrates represents the great separating boundary between the two kingdoms,* as the literal Euphrates formed the barrier between Israel and the hostile northern and eastern kingdoms."

When in Babylon, Abraham was on "the *other* side of the *flood*" or the Euphrates. He had to come across, or leave the region of, the Euphrates, in order to live in the *typical* land. Abraham is a type of the faithful. His coming out of Babylon and crossing the Euphrates to the land of Israel is the initial type of the Third Angel's Message, which calls people out of spiritual Babylon. Rev. 14: 8; 18: 4, etc. As Babylon, the land of Israel, and Jerusalem are typical in connection with spiritual Israel and her enemies, so the *Euphrates must have a spiritual significance when employed in relation to Jerusalem, Israel, and Babylon.* And this *is* the setting in which the Euphrates is employed in *Rev. 16: 12.*

Jerusalem and Babylon are both spiritually employed in the Apocalypse in a world-wide sense. The Euphrates, which, in Gen. 15: 18, is introduced in Scripture *in connection with the boundary of Israel's land,* is employed in its *last* reference (Rev. 16: 12) in *as wide a symbolic sense* as "the land of Israel," "Jerusalem," or "Babylon."

The call out of Babylon of Abraham, the father of the faithful, is a type of the call out of Babylon of all God's children. The

228

crescendo plan which appears in Scripture-truths is seen in this. Centuries later, when the Israelites came out of Babylon, they were duplicating the experience of their father Abraham—only in a much larger way. The call out of Babylon to-day is larger still, and now comprehends the people of God from all sections of error in the *world-wide* Babylon.

The books of Ezra and Nehemiah—the books setting forth the restoration of the temple service in Jerusalem and the rebuilding and repairing of the walls of Jerusalem after their Babylonian captivity—illustrate, in a *physical* way, the work which *spiritual Israel* will accomplish after its call out of *spiritual Babylon*. These facts are so fully dealt with in the Spirit of Prophecy and accepted among us that there is no need for me to labour to prove anything further in relation thereto. But the point to which the reader's attention should be turned is that the Euphrates is referred to as "the river" over which those called out of Babylon had to cross to return to the land of Israel.

The expression *"this side the river"* occurs 8 times in Ezra. See Ezra 4: 10, 11, 16; 5: 3, 6 (twice), 6:13; 8: 36. The number 8, as shown in my "Christ Conquers," pp. 123-139, is the number for the new life in Christ—the resurrection life. "This side the river" illustrates the new life in Christ—the new world—in which one lives with Christ the King of Israel, in the land of Israel. Those on *the other side of the Euphrates* are those born of the flesh, who "war" or persecute those on *"this side the river."* Facts given elsewhere concerning the new life, the new birth, the new world, and the use of the number 8 in Scripture, show conclusively the correctness of the application made here of the 8 times "this side the river" occurs in the book of Ezra. The Spirit of Prophecy applies the historical pictures of Israel's work of rebuilding Jerusalem and there restoring the service of God as types of our work to-day, after we have come out of spiritual Babylon into the spiritual land of Israel, after passing over the boundary—the spiritual Euphrates.

The term *"beyond the river"* occurs 7 times in Ezra. See 4: 17, 20; 6: 6 (twice), 8; 7: 21, 25. Seven is the number for completion, or continuity to the end, and Babylon will exist till the end. There will be a "beyond the river"—the place of the worship of false gods—until Babylon is overthrown in the final destruction of Armageddon.

There are three historical books which come prominently to view in regard to Israel and deliverances in connection with the

Babylonian captivity—namely, Ezra, Nehemiah, and Esther. There were three calls out of Babylon away from the river Euphrates. Zerubbabel and Joshua headed the first return to Jerusalem (Ezra 1 and 2); Ezra led the second (Ezra 7); and Nehemiah the third.

The experiences of Israel coming out of Babylon, from the Euphrates into the land of Israel—and what they did, or did not do, in Palestine—is applied by the Scriptures and the Spirit of Prophecy in an antitypical way to our work in all the world—the antitypical land of Israel. Babylon and Israel's land are constantly kept before us in the Book of Revelation and in the Spirit of Prophecy. We need to remember that it is in this setting that the Euphrates is mentioned in Rev. 16: 12.

(2) THE RIVER EUPHRATES IS REFERRED TO AS THE "FLOOD."

The first time the Euphrates is referred to as "the flood" is in Joshua 24. Dr. Strong's definition of the original word here translated "flood" is "a stream (including the sea, especially the Nile, Euphrates, etc., flood, river)".

No one doubts that the "flood" mentioned in Joshua 24: 2, 3, 14, 15 means the Euphrates. But we need to note the significance of the fact that these verses describe the Euphrates as the boundary line between Israel's land—the land of the worship of the true God—and Babylon—*that land of false gods and false worship*. Notice how this fact is significantly emphasised by the Holy Spirit in the first time the Euphrates is introduced in Scripture as "the flood." God says: "Your fathers dwelt on *the other side of the flood* in old time, even Terah, the father of Abraham, and the father of Nachor: and *they served other gods*. And I took your father Abraham from *the other side of the flood*. . . . Put away the gods which your fathers served on *the other side of the flood* . . . and serve ye the Lord . . . choose ye this day whom we will serve; whether the *gods which your fathers served* that were on *the other side of the flood*. . . ."

The first time the Euphrates is mentioned in Scripture it is said to be the *fourth* river emerging from Eden—the *world-wide* significance of this fact will be shown later. The second time the Euphrates is mentioned by name is in Gen. 15: 18, which is the *first of the 7 times* it is explicitly stated to be the *boundary* of the promised land of Israel. The law of first mention, operating both in its connection with the number 4—the world-wide number—and also in its connection with the boundary of the land of Israel, shows that the world-wide symbolical application of the Euphrates is that which is the proper, or *normal, antitypical one.*

The promise of the land given in Gen. 15: 18 where the Euphrates is *first* mentioned as the *boundary* of the promised land, is the *third time* that promise was given to Abraham. The previous promises are found in Gen. 12: 1-7; 13: 14-17.

It is interesting to note that the last occasions the word "flood" occurs in the Scriptures are the only 3 times the word occurs in the Apocalypse. See Rev. 12: 15 (twice), 16. The Variorum Bible, the Revised Version, Dr. Strong, etc., have "river, stream" for "flood" in Rev. 12: 15, 16—the same meaning that Dr. Strong gives for "flood" ("the flood" is the Euphrates) in Josh. 24.

As we all know, Rev. 12: 15-16 pictures the hateful work of Satan when he tried to drown the church in the waters of persecution. What was done in the "war" against the saints in the dark ages (Dan. 7: 21; Rev. 13: 7) illustrates the kind of "war" with which earth's final scenes will be characterised. As the "war" with the saints was pictured by a mighty "flood" with which Satan hoped to sweep the church away in complete destruction, so the final phase of the same "war" (Rev. 12: 17) is likened to a "flood." And as the river Euphrates is first introduced as a "flood" in Josh. 24—as the dividing line between the land of the true worship and Babylon the land of false worship; the line of demarcation between Israel's God and the gods of Babylon—so, when the final "flood" or "war" against the saints, or the remnant, takes place, the Euphrates is chosen to represent that flooding of the antitypical land of Israel.

The action of Satan's assault on the church in the dark ages is described: "that he might cause her to be carried away of the *flood."* Rev. 12: 15. Dr. Strong says of the Greek word for "flood": *"overwhelmed* by a stream—carried away of the flood." In Josh. 24 the Euphrates is said to be "the flood"—and there it is the boundary line between Israel's land and Babylon's land. When the "flooding" takes place it is from Babylon *over the land of Israel.* As the "flood" of Dan. 9: 26 referred to the invasion of Palestine by the Romans, and their destruction of the temple, Jerusalem, and the Jewish nation, so the final "flood" will be when *spiritual Babylon,* with its *centre* in the territory of *literal Rome,* makes "war" (which is the other word employed for the "flood" of persecution in the dark ages) on the remnant church. But the river upon which *literal*

Babylon was built was the *literal* Euphrates: *spiritual* Babylon is built upon the *spiritual* Euphrates.

(3) OTHER SCRIPTURAL REFERENCES TO THE *FLOODING* OF THE RIVER EUPHRATES.

The river Euphrates was not only the divinely-prescribed boundary for the land of Israel (Gen. 15: 18, etc.), but it was that river which so many of their northern enemies crossed in order to invade Israel's land and attack God's people. In Gen. 14; Judges 3: 8; 2 Kings 15: 19 etc., we see that Palestine had, for many ages, been subject to invasion by formidable hosts from the region of the Euphrates, which is so often presented in Scripture as the scene of battle. See 2 Sam. 8: 3; 2 Kings 23: 29; 24: 7; 1 Chron. 18: 3; 2 Chron. 35: 20; Jer. 13: 4-7; Jer. 42: 2, 6, 10. Jeremiah had predicted that destruction would come to Judah and Jerusalem from the north. See Jer. 1: 13-15; 4: 6; 6: 1; 25: 9, etc. This "north country" was *"by the Euphrates."* See Jer. 46: 2, 6, 10, 20, 24; 47: 2; 25: 9; 1: 15. The synopsis at the heading of Jer. 13 reads: "In the type of a linen girdle, God pre-figureth the destruction of His people." In this chapter trouble is pictured as coming from the Euphrates, and in fulfilment of this prophecy the literal Babylonians did come from the Euphrates and wrought destruction upon God's literal Israel because they were not keeping the covenant with their God.

Thus we see that the *invasion of the land of Israel* and the attack upon the people of God is *likened to the flooding of the land of Israel by the waters of the Euphrates.* See Jer. 46: 6-10; Jer. 47: 2; 25: 9-11, 15-26. Jer. 25: 27-33 couples up the destruction of the Jewish nation and all the other surrounding nations by the hand of the Babylonians (and, later, the destruction of the Babylonians themselves) with the final slaughter of the Lord at Armageddon, when the wicked will be slain from one end of the earth unto the other end. This passage of Scripture—Jer. 25: 27-33—is quoted in G.C. 655, 656, in connection with the destruction of all the wicked at the end of the world—the false "shepherds" of Jer. 25: 34-38 are applied in the Spirit of Prophecy to the preachers who have deceived their flocks over the Sabbath. So we see that this prophecy ends where the other predictions concerning Israel and her enemies end, namely, in the *final conflict over the Sabbath* versus the mark of the beast, *which is not a Palestinian matter* but something which *affects every person upon the entire globe.*

232

"Who is this that cometh up as a *flood*, whose *waters are moved as the rivers? Egypt* riseth up *like a flood,* and *his waters* are moved like the rivers." In this way Jeremiah described the movements of the Egyptian army which threatened to overthrow the Babylonians. But they were to be destroyed "in the *north country by the river Euphrates.*" See Jer. 46: 2-10. The rest of the chapter shows that overwhelming destruction awaited the Egyptians —from the greater overflowing—the waters of the mighty Euphrates would be greater than their "flood."

Then, Jer. 47-49 outlines the overthrow of various nations by the Babylonians. Chapters 50-51 portray the doom of Babylon after she had brought disaster to Israel and the other nations.

From chapter 45 Jeremiah outlines, in detail, the destruction of the various nations which he has already enumerated in chapter 25. The reader will notice that they are the same nations—and given in much the same order. Judah and Jerusalem and the surrounding nations were to suffer calamities from a Babylonian invasion of their countries. Jer. 13: 4-14 (where the name Euphrates is employed three times) shows that the destruction awaiting Israel (and the surrounding nations) would come from the *Euphrates.* Jer. 46: 2-10 (where the word Euphrates is again mentioned three times) speaks of "the north *by the river Euphrates.*" Vs. 6, 10. The coming of the Babylonians from *"the north by the river Euphrates"* to bring destruction upon Israel and the surrounding nations is likened, in Jer. 47: 2, to a "flood"; "Behold, *waters* rise up *out of* the north [the "river Euphrates"], and shall be *an overflowing flood,* and shall *overflow the land.*" Thus, rebellious Israel, and the nations surrounding her, were to be destroyed by the Babylonian overflowing of the Euphrates.

These pictures of the overflowing of the Euphrates by the Babylonian invasion should be kept in mind when interpreting the Euphrates—Babylon's river—in Rev. 16: 12. In Rev. 16: 12 the reference to the Euphrates (which throughout Scripture is the boundary line between Israel's land and Babylon) in connection with the overthrow of spiritual Babylon has for its background Isa. 8: 7, 8; 7: 20 in regard to the Assyrians coming from the Euphrates to destroy Israel in Jerusalem; and Jer. 13: 4-14; 25: 1-26; 46: 2-10; 47: 2 in regard to the Babylonians coming against Israel (and other surrounding nations) at the commencement of the Babylonian captivity. The drying up of the waters of the Euphrates when Cyrus marched along the drying up river-bed of the Euphrates into the heart of Babylon to bring about its final doom and thus deliver Israel from Babylon (Isa. 44: 27; Jer. 50: 38; 51: 36; 50: 33, 34) forms the historical basis for the drying up of the water of the Euphrates mentioned in Rev. 16: 12.

As Babylon's invasion of the land of Israel and destruction of Jerusalem and the Jewish nation in the time of Nebuchadnezzar was represented by the "flood"—the overflowing Euphrates —so the Roman invasion of Israel's land, and their destruction of the temple, Jerusalem, and the Jewish nation—finally and irretrievably—was predicted in Dan. 9; 26: "shall destroy the city and the sanctuary; and the end thereof shall be *with a flood."*

In the last days spiritual Israel—the church (God's dwelling place and holy city)—will be threatened with overwhelming disaster by the flooding of the spiritual (Babylonian) Euphrates. God could not dry up the waters of the Euphrates overflowing Israel's typical land in the days of the Babylonians, and at time of the Roman invasion, because the Jews had then departed from God. God did dry up the waters of the Assyrian invasion and attack upon Jerusalem because, led by Hezekiah, *the people sought God* to avenge them against their enemies. The helpless woman—the widow—of Christ's parable (Luke 18: 1-8) represents the church in the last days—without any earthly husband to support her (without any support from the state, or any kindly power on earth), crying to God for help. "Shall not God avenge *His own elect,* which cry day and night unto Him, though He bear long with them? I tell you that *He will avenge them speedily.* Nevertheless, *when the Son of Man cometh,* shall He find faith on the earth?" Vs. 7, 8.

In the final flooding of the Babylonian-Roman Euphrates the waters will be dried up (Rev. 16: 12) by the King of glory—the great antitypical Cyrus, the shepherd king, the liberator of Israel— coming from the east with all His royal retinue to deliver His people from Babylon's grasp. The remnant of Israel will be pure (Zeph. 3: 13; Rev. 14: 3-5; Matt. 25: 1-13, etc.), and so God will be able to manifest the fulness of His almighty power in the deliverance of His faithful, spiritual Israel, who will be in all the world—the spiritual land of Israel.

The Holy Spirit's superintendence over the writing of the Bible is apparent in many marvellous ways—the deeper one studies the more apparent this becomes.

To the deep student of Holy Writ there is such a blending of all the prophecies into one complete pattern that one stands amazed at the wonder of it all.

(4) THE EUPHRATES IN REV. 16: 12 IS NOT A SYMBOL OF A NATION THROUGH WHOSE TERRITORY IT RUNS.

Our study of the Euphrates clearly reveals that it is not a symbol representing the Turkish or Mohammedan nations living near it, nor is it a symbol of the nation through whose territory it runs. We have seen that in its geographical setting it is the boundary between the land of Israel and the land of Babylon, and it is employed as a symbol of Babylonian armies *flooding over the land of Israel,* threatening to destroy the people of God. This, we have seen, is the *constant* use which is made of the Euphrates throughout the Old Testament Scriptures, and its last use in Rev. 16: 12 must, according to laws of interpretation previously dealt with, be a *world-wide,* spiritual application in connection with the *invasion of the antitypical land of Israel* by the waters of the Euphrates (the "multitudes" who support the Babylonian whore— see Rev. 17: 1, 15; G C. 635, etc.) threatening to destroy the people of God. Even in Rev. 9: 14, where the Euphrates is employed in a *limited, national* setting, it directs us to the Ottoman Empire which *invaded* the territory of the Roman Empire and thus brought the final extinction of the remnant of that empire. Even in Rev. 9: 14 it refers to an *invading, destroying* force—it is not mentioned in order to point out that the Ottoman Empire occupied territories through which the Euphrates ran but to point out this nation (which emerged from the region of the Euphrates) as the *invader* of Roman territory and the *destroyer* of the last portion of the Roman Empire.

In the Old Testament the Euphrates was *not* employed to represent Assyria and Babylon as nations occupying the territory through which it ran, but they were symbolized by it ONLY WHEN THEY BECAME INVADING, DESTROYING NATIONS—*the enemies of Israel.*

The history of the Euphrates in the Bible proves to be in harmony with the *meaning of its name*—"to break forth; *rushing"*— Dr. Strong. Isaiah, who has likened the invasion of the land of Israel to the rushing of the waters of the Euphrates, describes the woes of Israel's enemies: "Woe to the multitude of many people . . . and the *rushing* of nations, that make a *rushing* like the *rushing* of mighty waters! The nations shall *rush* like the *rushing* of *many waters* [Isa. 8: 7 refers to the Assyrians' invasion as "the *waters* of the river (Euphrates), strong and *many*"]: but God shall rebuke them." Isa. 17: 12, 13. As shown elsewhere, at the time of the out-pouring of the 6th plague, God's "rebuke" dries up the *rushing,* persecuting waters of the *Euphrates*—the enemies of spiritual Israel.

(5) THE EUPHRATES—A SYMBOL OF *INVADING* FORCES.

The figure of flooding waters is often used in Scripture to picture the invasion of a country, or an assault on certain people. Water is a symbol of "peoples, and multitudes, and nations, and tongues." Rev. 17: 15. "The wicked are like the troubled sea." Isa. 57: 20. Dan. 11: 22 says, "And with the arms of a *flood* shall they be overflown before him." David said, "When the *waves* of death compassed me, the *floods of the ungodly men* made me afraid." 2 Sam. 22: 5. David prayed: "I am come into *deep waters,* where the *floods* overflow me. Let me be delivered from *them that hate me,* and out of the deep waters. Let not the water-flood overflow me, neither let the deep swallow me up." Ps. 69: 1, 2, 14, 15.

When God pictured the *invasion* of the territory of the *northern ten tribes of Israel* by the armies of the *Assyrians* coming from the region of the Euphrates, He said: "The Lord hath a mighty and strong one [to punish Ephraim for his pride and sin], which as a tempest of hail and a destroying storm, *as a flood of mighty waters overflowing,* shall cast down to the earth with the hand." Isa. 28: 1, 2.

When God pictured the *invasion of Judah* He likened it, also, to the overflowing of "the *waters of the river* [Euphrates], strong and many, even the king of Assyria." Isa. 8: 7, 8.

When God foretold the end of the Jewish nation and the downfall of Jerusalem in A.D. 70 He said: "And the end thereof shall be with a *flood.*"

Thus we see that the employment in Rev. 16: 12 of the waters of the Euphrates as the symbol of the "peoples, and multitudes, and nations, and tongues" who, under Babylonian instruction, seek to overwhelm the people of God in the final struggle between the forces of good and evil is that which is the *normal* application running throughout all the Scripture.

A correct reading of the Spirit of Prophecy shows that this interpretation is the one which is given in the writing of the servant of God. For further reference see my "What is Armageddon?" pp. 45-53.

(6) TO UNDERSTAND ANY SUBJECT GO BACK TO THE BEGINNING.

Bible students recognize the significance of the first mention in the Bible of a place, name, number, etc. The last time it is mentioned brings to view a fuller significance of the first occasion. For instance, things appearing in the first chapters of Genesis re-appear on a grander scale in the closing chapters of Revelation. (See previous chapters for a full consideration of this principle.)

The first time the number 13 occurs is in Gen. 14: 4: "And in the *13th* year they *rebelled.*" From then, the number 13 is associated with the great rebellion against God. As we have shown in "Christ Conquers," pp. 116-118, Megiddo occurs 13 times in Scripture—the 13th is given (Rev. 16: 16) in the description of the final rebellion against God, and the subsequent slaughter of Armageddon. The last, or 13th, time Megiddo occurs is thus seen to definitely repeat—but in connection with a *world-wide* rebellion—the significance of the first time the number 13 is used in Scripture—it describes the slaughter of those who have *rebelled* against the authority of God by joining with Satan in his great *rebellion.*

In the same manner the key to the understanding of the *last* time the Euphrates occurs in Scripture is found in the *first* time it is mentioned in the Bible, namely, Gen. 2: 14, where we read:— "And the *fourth* river is Euphrates."

(7) THE SIGNIFICANCE OF THE NUMBER FOUR IN SCRIPTURE.

The number four is used throughout Scripture as the number for the world:—

There are 4 kingdoms in this world—mineral, vegetable, animal, spiritual.

On the 4th day the material world was created—on the fifth day God began the creation of animal life.

There are 4 regions of earth—4 main points of the compass—north, south, east and west.

There are 4 seasons of the year—spring, summer, autumn, winter.

The 4th book of the Bible—Numbers—gives the history of Israel in the wilderness, and is a type of the Christian in the world, marching to the evergreen Canaan.

Gen. 13: 14—North, south, east, and west are interpreted in Rom. 4: 13 to be the world.

1 Cor. 15: 39—There are 4 kinds of flesh in the world—man, beast, fish, birds.

Rev. 7: 1—Four angels, four corners, four winds, mean the whole world—therefore, those who limit the sealing of the twelve tribes of Israel, brought to view in Rev. 7, are out of harmony with the use the Holy Spirit makes of the number 4 as the symbol number for the whole world. The troubles to come, represented by the four winds coming from the four corners of the earth, are not Palestinian troubles, but world-wide disasters.

Gen. 9: 13, 14, 16; Ezek. 1: 28—The rain "bow" sign which God gave to Noah—and to us—that He would never again destroy the world by *water* is found 4 times in the Old Testament.

Matt. 13: 4—There are 4 kinds of soil—wayside, stony, thorny, good—in the field, which is the world. V. 38.

Daniel's book has 4 Gentile kings mentioned therein—Nebuchadnezzar, Belshazzar, Darius, Cyrus.

Dan. 2—Four world empires—and only 4—would rule the earth.

Dan. 7—Four winds, 4 beasts—only 4 universal empires to rule the earth.

Rev. 1: 1—God's last message, which is for the whole world—and not, as Futurists affirm, merely for the literal Jews in Palestine—comes from *God, Jesus Christ, His angel, to John.* Four rivers emanated from Eden to water the earth, and there are 4 avenues through which the waters of life flow to the *world.*

Matt. 1: 3, 5, 6—Four women come into Christ's genealogy—He is the Saviour of the *world.*

John 14: 16, 26; 15: 26; 16: 7—Four times, in His last discourse, Christ spoke of the coming of the Comforter—the Paraclete—who would have charge of the *world-wide* work of the church.

Four Gospels explain to the world about God's love and Christ's life, work, death, and resurrection. They also depict 4 sides of Christ's life.

Rev. 1: 4; 3: 1; 4: 5; 5: 6—Four times the 7 Spirits of God are mentioned in Revelation.

Rev. 5: 11, 12—When the heavenly angels give ascription of praise to the Deity, it is sevenfold—power, riches, wisdom, strength, honour, glory, and blessing.

Rev. 5: 13—But when earthly beings give an ascription of praise, it is fourfold—blessing, honour, glory, and power.

Rev. 5: 8-10—The "four and twenty elders" were redeemed from the earth.

Rev. 2 and 3—In each of the messages to the churches, the Word says,—"He that hath an ear, let him hear what the Spirit saith to the churches," but in 4 of them the promise of the reward comes *before* this injunction to "hear." In the other 3 the *injunction* comes *before* the promise of the reward. For the 3 with the *injunction preceding* the *promise* of reward. See Rev. 2: 7, 11, 17. For the 4 in the reverse, see Rev. 2: 26-29; 3: 5, 6; 3: 12, 13, 21, 22. A close study of the churches will reveal that 4 of them—the last 4—are presented as yielding to the world. While Philadelphia does not appear to be blamed yet she has only "a little power." In the messages to the last 4 churches, the second coming of Christ is brought to view. Rev. 2: 25; 3: 3, 11, 20.

Often in the Apocalypse the number 4 is conspicuous in such prophecies as the 4 horsemen of Rev. 6; the 4 trumpets and the 3 woe trumpets, etc.

In the Lord's prayer, there are seven factors—three pertaining to God, and *four concerning man on earth.*

1. Hallowed be Thy name.
2. Thy kingdom come.
3. Thy will be done.

1. Our daily bread.
2. Forgive us our trespasses.
3. Lead us not into temptation.
4. But, deliver us from evil.

Then follow another 3 things belonging to God—Kingdom, Power, Glory.

238

The bottomless pit is mentioned 7 times in Revelation—3 times in reference to the Arabian desert—Rev. 9: 1, 2, 11—and 4 times in reference to the arsenal of Satan—the world—Rev. 11: 7; 17: 8; 20: 1, 3. From the numeric measure we can see that the bottomless pit is this earth.

Rev. 20: 2—When Satan is chained to this earth, called here the bottomless pit, he is given a four-fold description—-dragon, serpent, devil, satan.

Mark 13: 35—When Christ spoke of the unknown hour of His second advent to the earth, he gave 4 times—even, midnight, cockcrowing, morning.

Mark 13: 3—When Christ gave His sermon concerning His coming to earth again, there were 4 disciples present—Peter, James, John, Andrew.

Acts 1: 8—When Christ commanded His church to take the Gospel to the world, He used 4 places—Jerusalem, Judea, Samaria, and the uttermost parts of the earth.

Rev. 19: 1, 3, 4, 6—In their triumph over the world, the reedemed say "Alleluia" four times.

Rev. 19: 1—The redeemed use a four-fold ascription of praise to God—Salvation, Glory, Honour, and Power unto the Lord our God.

Rev. 20: 8—Gog and Magog come from the 4 quarters of the earth. This in itself shows that the invasion of the land of Israel (Ezek. 38-39) by Gog's army (which is supposed, by some, to refer to Russia) cannot possibly be restricted to Palestine. Only a world-wide application will meet the requirement of the numeric system which operates throughout Scripture.

The 4th clause in the Lord's prayer is the one which mentions the "earth."

The 4th Commandment, by the numeric system of the Bible, is definitely a command which is for the whole world—not merely for the Jews or Palestine, as some have taught.

Gen. 10: 5, 20, 31—In the account of the peopling of the earth, a four-fold description is given—different terms may be employed on each occasion, but only 4 are used at a time.

Rev. 5: 9; 7: 9; 10: 11; 11: 9; 14: 6; 17: 15—The Revelation uses the same four-fold description as given in Genesis. Nothing but a world-wide application of the things in the Apocalypse pertaining to Israel will fit the numeric standards of Scripture.

The Apocalypse uses expressions occurring in Genesis, as illustrated in the above four-fold description of the peoples of the whole earth. In the same way we notice that the tree of life is mentioned 3 times in the Book of Genesis—Gen. 2: 9; 3: 22, 24. The tree of life occurs 3 times in the Book of Revelation—Rev. 2: 7; 22: 2, 14. A balance of thought is noticeable. In the same way the river Euphrates occurs twice in Genesis (Gen. 2: 14; 15: 18), and it also occurs twice in the Apocalypse—Rev. 9: 14; 16: 12. The first time it is mentioned in the Scriptures is in connection with the rivers which commenced in Eden and wended their ways to water the earth: "The fourth river is Euphrates." Gen. 2: 14.

There are words, phrases, etc., which are significantly mentioned 4 times in different ways in Scripture, but the simple instances which have been given will serve the purpose we have in mind in connection with the river Euphrates, which is introduced in the Bible as the fourth river. In the study of the numeric system operating throughout Scripture, we learn to note the world-wide implication of the *first*—and also the *last* time—the Euphrates comes into the sacred Record, for the number 4 is the number for the *world*.

In this connection it is interesting to note that the second time this river occurs in the Bible, it is used in reference to the promise to Abraham regarding the land promised him and his seed:—"In the same day the Lord made a covenant with Abram, saying, Unto thy seed have I given this land, from the river of Egypt unto the great river, the river *Euphrates*." Gen. 15: 18. The Divine comment, or interpretation of this promise, is given in Rom. 4: 13, "For the promise, that he should be *heir of the world*, was not to *Abraham*, or to his *seed*, through the law, but through the righteousness of faith."

In the original promise God had said:—"Unto thy seed will I give this land" (Gen. 12: 7). In Gen. 13: 14 the fulness of this promise is seen:—"And the Lord said unto Abraham . . . Lift up now thine eyes, and look from the place where thou art *northward*, and *southward*, and *eastward*, and *westward*: for all this land which thou seest, to thee will I give it, and to thy seed for ever." The four points of the compass mentioned in this promise to Abraham are taken in Rom 4: 13 to mean the *whole world*. And the third time this promise is made to Abraham the Euphrates is mentioned as the boundary of the promised land. The *typical* land had the river *Euphrates as its boundary*. and the *antitypical land of Israel* also has the *Euphrates for its boundary*—in all *the world*.

In its *final* use (the 21st, or 3 times 7) in Scripture (Rev. 16: 12), in connection with the great battle between good and evil, the Euphrates (mentioned 7 times as the boundary of Israel's land) is definitely linked with the Third Angel's Message, the centre of which is the 7th day Sabbath.

There are other factors which establish the truth that the *Euphrates* is employed in Rev. 16: 12 in a *spiritual, world-wide* sense, just as *Babylon*, which was anciently seated upon the Euphrates, is employed in a *spiritual*, world-wide *sense*.

The Euphrates—"the *fourth* river" (Gen. 2: 14)—is the symbol of the *world-wide* forces of *Babylon*, as, similarly, "the *valley*" of Jehoshaphat, mentioned 4 times in Joel 3: 2, 12, 14, symbolizes the *world-wide* valley of God's judgment in which those forces of Babylon meet their doom.

(8) THE NECESSITY OF STUDYING THE CONTEXT AND ASSOCIATION.

Every passage of Scripture has to be studied in the light of its context and association. Care needs to be exercised that the symbols of Scripture be interpreted according to Biblical rules. For instance, a lion in Holy Writ is used to represent the Assyrians (Nah. 2: 11-13), the kingdom of Babylon (Dan. 7), the princes of Israel (Ezek. 19: 2-7), Satan (1 Pet. 5: 8), Christ (Rev. 5: 5), the righteous (Prov. 28: 1), etc. But the contexts show why the same symbol is fittingly employed to represent entirely different persons or kingdoms. See my "What is Armageddon?" pp. 57-60, for further instances where the same symbols or illustrations are employed in different ways. The association and the context indicate the use in each case—this is true of any part of the Bible, but is especially true of the book of Revelation. As God's servant has written of the Apocalypse: "This book demands *close, prayerful study,* lest it be interpreted according to the *ideas of men,* and *false construction* be given to the sacred word of the Lord which, in its *symbols* and *figures,* means so much to *us.*"

A woman in Bible symbols represents a church. But it would not do to *assume* that the woman of Rev. 12 represents the same church as the woman of Rev. 17. The setting of the prophetic outline in each case reveals that the woman of Rev. 12 is not the same as the woman of Rev. 17. Similarly, the factors involved show that the Euphrates of Rev. 16 is not to be interpreted in the same national, restricted way, as in Rev. 9.

In the Apocalypse stars represent: "The seven stars are *the angels of the seven churches*" (Rev. 1: 16, 20; 2: 1); Jesus (Rev. 22: 16; 2: 28); the twelve Apostles of the Christian church (Rev. 12: 1); Satan working through Mahomet (Rev. 9: 1, 11); the angels of God (Rev. 12: 4); political lights in the Roman heavens (Rev. 8: 12). After obtaining the interpretation of any one of these examples of the use of "stars" we are not to *assume* that the same interpretation will apply to the others. Each time the same symbol is employed we must examine the context and the association to discover the true interpretation.

Rev. 9: 1 and Rev. 12: 4 both refer to the falling of stars unto the earth. By the contexts we know that those stars refer to persons. Rev. 6: 13 also says: "And the stars of heaven fell unto the earth." Because of the use of stars in the other passages referred to above some expositors have maintained that these falling stars mentioned in Rev. 6: 13 also refer to people—that is, they interpret these falling stars symbolically, and not literally.

The belief that Rev. 6: 13 predicts the literal meteoric showers which have fallen within recent centuries is not founded upon supposition, but is supported by the context, the right understanding of which is based upon such Old Testament passages as Zech. 6: 1-7; Ps. 45: 3-5; Joel 2: 30-31; Matt. 24-29, etc. The context and the association show why the falling stars in Rev. 6: 13 refer to *literal* meteoric showers, whereas the stars mentioned in Rev. 12: 4, where we read that "the third part of the stars of heaven" were "cast to the earth," refer to the coming to this earth of the angels who had joined with Lucifer in his revolt against God.

To illustrate the importance of observing the laws of context, association, and type and antitype, attention is directed to the earthquake mentioned in Rev. 11: 13. This is to be *symbolically* interpreted because it is definitely grouped with "*the city,*" or spiritual Babylon. See Rev. 16: 19; 17: 18; 18: 10, 16, 18, 21. But it was not a world-wide earthquake, for it is limited by the expression "and the *tenth part* of the city fell."

Similarly, by the laws of context and association we know why the sun in Rev. 6: 12 and Rev. 16: 8 refers to the *literal* sun, but in Rev. 8: 12; 12: 1 to a *symbolic* sun; why a *literal* earthquake is referred to in Rev. 6: 12 and Rev. 16: 18, but a *symbolic* earthquake in Rev. 11: 13; why the waters in Rev. 12: 15, 16; 13: 1; 16: 12; 17: 1, 15 are *symbolic*, but the waters in Rev. 16: 3, 4 are *literal;* why the moon of Rev. 8: 12 does not have the same symbolic meaning as the moon in Rev. 12: 1; why the "bottomless pit" of Rev. 9: 1, 2, 11 is limited to the regions of the Arabian desert, but in Rev. 20: 1-3 refers to the *whole world;* why the waters of the second and third plagues (Rev. 16: 3, 4) are *literal,* and the water of the Euphrates in the 6th plague is symbolic. The teaching that the water of the Euphrates in Rev. 16: 12 represents Turkey or other nations is a symbolic interpretation. The teaching that the water of the Euphrates in Rev. 16: 12 represents the people of spiritual Babylon is also a symbolic interpretation—the difference being that the former applies it in connection with purely national events of a restricted character, whereas the latter applies it in connection with the world-wide conflict between Christ and Satan. Thus there is agreement that, although the waters of the second and third plagues are to be understood *literally,* the water of Rev. 16: 12 is to be understood *symbolically*. But Biblical laws of interpretation show that the water of the Euphrates in Rev. 16: 12 does not symbolize a nation or nations adjacent to the Euphrates.

It should be noted that, although the plagues are *literal*, the *people* of Babylon who are affected thereby are mentioned under *symbols*. Notice the following symbols brought to view in the seven last plagues: the mark of the beast, his image, the dragon, the beast, the false prophet, the waters of the Euphrates, Armageddon, great Babylon. The dragon in Rev. 16: 13 represents the "kings, and rulers, and governors" who enforce Sunday laws. See T.M. 39, 62. The seven last plagues fall upon spiritual *Babylon* (Rev. 16: 19), and the *symbols* employed in picturing the plagues which bring about her doom *represent the people and things of Babylon*. As Babylon is *world-wide*, so, also, the people and the things symbolized in *connection with Babylon* are, in their widest sense, world-wide.

This interpretation is sustained by the law of association in the Book of Revelation itself, but it is primarily supported by the fact that the things mentioned in the Old Testament concerning the overthrow of literal Babylon have a world-wide spiritual application in the Apocalypse. By the law of type and antitype, the allusion in Rev. 16: 12 to the overthrow of ancient Babylon by Cyrus, who employed the strategy of drying up the waters of the Euphrates, has a world-wide, symbolical application. The water of the Euphrates definitely symbolizes the people of spiritual Babylon. See Jer. 51: 13, which is quoted in Rev. 17: 1, 15.

(9) NOT ALL THE SEVEN LAST PLAGUES WILL BE UNIVERSAL.

That the plagues will be *world-wide* is evident from the fact that they fall upon those who worship the beast in the homage paid to it by the observance of Sunday. Rev. 14: 9-11 contains the warning of the Third Angel's Message against the "beast" (the adherents of which are scattered throughout the world) "and his image" (i.e., wherever church and state unite in enforcing Sunday laws), and "whosoever receiveth the mark of his name" (i.e., all who wilfully persist in observing the false sabbath—Satan's day)— these will be found in all parts of the globe.

It is true that GC. 628 says:—"These plagues are *not universal*, or the inhabitants of the earth would be *wholly* cut off. Yet they will be the most awful scourges that have ever been known to mortals."

Perhaps Webster's definition of the word "universal" will assist us to understand the use which the Spirit of Prophecy makes of that word:—Universal: *"Extending to, including, or affecting, the whole number, quantity, or space, unlimited, general, all-reaching, all-pervading."*

If the plagues were *universal* every one, *without exception,* would receive the plagues. As these terrible scourges will result in vast numbers of deaths, it would mean that the first plagues would destroy so many that there would be few, if any, left to receive the plagues that follow. But not all the unrighteous of the world will be *simultaneously* afflicted with the plagues "or the inhabitants of the earth would be *wholly* cut off." The plagues will be world-wide, for the Third Angel's Message is world-wide. Rev. 14: 6-14, 7: 1-4, etc. That message warns the world regarding the coming of God's wrath in the plagues—the world would not be warned if the world was not to suffer the plagues. 6T. 18 informs us that:—"As America, the land of religious liberty, shall unite with the Papacy in forcing the conscience and compelling men to honour the false sabbath, the peoples of *every country on the globe* will be led to follow her example." This means that in *"every country on the globe"* the beast and his image will be worshipped and the mark of the beast enforced—against which the Third Angel's Message warns. , Consequently, the plagues will fall upon "every country on the globe," for there "the image of the beast" and "the mark of the beast" will operate. We need to draw a distinction between "world-wide" and "universal." Because "every country on the globe" receives the plagues, we speak of them as being *world-wide,* but some are *not universal* in regard to each *individual* of "every country on the globe." GC. 627 speaks of these plagues as *"extensive* judgments which are to *fall upon the world* before the final deliverance of God's people."

The Spirit of Prophecy differentiates between world-wide and universal. Notice the following extract taken from P.K., p. 171: "Yet this apostasy, *widespread* as it has come to be, *is not universal. Not all in the world* are lawless and sinful; *not all* have taken sides with the enemy." In this extract the servant of the Lord refers to *"widespread"* apostasy which, as yet, "is not universal" because *"not all in the world* . . . have taken sides with the enemy."

Elsewhere, we have pointed out that "the false prophet" refers to more than the United States of America for "the false prophet" symbolizes apostate Protestantism which is led in the work of

244

enforcing Sunday laws by the example set by the United States:— "The Sabbath question is to be the issue in the great final conflict in which *all the the world will act a part."* 6T. 18, 19. "The substitution of . . . Sunday in place of the Bible Sabbath is the *last act in the drama.* When this substitution *becomes universal,* God will reveal Himself, He will arise in His majesty to shake terribly the earth." 7T. 141.

(10) THE PLAGUES WILL BE LITERAL.

The seven last plagues will be literal. However, although the plagues themselves are to be literal, *symbols* are employed to represent or to distinguish the *people who receive them.*

That symbols are used in the prophecy concerning the plagues is very evident when we remember that the first plague is poured out upon "the men which had the *mark* of the *beast,* and upon them which worshipped his *image."* The fifth plague is poured out upon the "seat of the *beast."* Then, in the events associated with the 6th plague, the *dragon,* the *beast,* the *false prophet,* the *water of the Euphrates,* and *Armageddon,* are mentioned. Other symbols are brought to view in Rev. 16: 19: "And the great *city* was divided into *three parts* . . . and great *Babylon* came in remembrance before God to give unto *her* the *cup* of the *wine* of the fierceness of His wrath." "The beast," "his image," "the dragon," "the false prophet," "the water" of the "Euphrates," "the great city," "Babylon," symbolize the *people* of the three sections of spiritual Babylon. The "mark of the beast," "cup," "wine," and "Armageddon," are symbols associated with the *people of Babylon.* The mark of the beast is the sign of allegiance to Babylon; the cup and wine denote the wrath of God to be poured out upon the *people of Babylon.* Thus, all the *symbols* in the seven last plagues either represent, or are associated with, the *people* of *Babylon.* *Literal* plagues fall upon *people* or organizations who are *symbolized* in the prediction. The plagues are *literal,* though the *people upon whom the plagues fall* are represented in the prophecy under *symbols.*

Regarding the *symbols* given in the description of the seven literal plagues one feature which deserves our close attention is the *world-wide nature of all of them.* "The beast," "his image," "his mark," "the great city" with its "three parts," "the dragon," "the false prophet," the "water" of the "Euphrates," "Armageddon," "Babylon," the "cup" of the "wine" of God's wrath, are *all symbols of world-wide import.* Most of the interpretations give the drying up of the water of the Euphrates a *symbolical meaning.* Some say it refers to the ending of the Turkish nation; others, to the ending of the Mohammedan peoples living in, or adjacent to, the territory drained by the Euphrates. But to take the river Euphrates from *among* the other symbols which are recognized as being *world-wide* in character and give it a *regional* meaning is to conspicuously *force it to have a limited, regional, and national application in contrast to the other symbols.*

There is a similarity—though they are not identical—between some of the seven last plagues and some of the plagues which fell upon Egypt. God's servant says:—"The plagues upon Egypt . . . were *similar* in character to those more *terrible* and *extensive* judgments which are to fall upon the *world* just before the final deliverance of God's people." G.C. 627. These *similar* plagues will be *world-wide* in harmony with the Biblical law that the *local* in the Old Testament is *world-wide* in the Apocalypse; but these are not to be interpreted *spiritually* because, in the Old Testament, there is no mention of them in connection with the overthrow of Babylon. Those things which are mentioned in the Old Testament *regarding the downfall of literal Babylon* are brought into the Revelator's *spiritual imagery* depicting the *overthrow of spiritual Babylon.*

The symbols employed in the description of the plagues are to be interpreted *spiritually because they are Babylonian;* whereas the other features are literal because nowhere are they said to be Babylonian. When things are definitely linked with Babylon they, too, become spiritual and world-wide. The Euphrates is spiritual Babylon's river. To apply the Euphrates in the plagues to something of a *military* nature—a *non-Babylonian feature*—is out of alignment with the fact that all the other *symbols* mentioned in the plagues are definitely *Babylonian symbols*—it would be the *only* feature in the plagues which would be interpreted militarily, and the *only symbol not a Babylonian one.*

It is evident that both the Euphrates and Armageddon are employed as symbols of world-wide import in connection with the people of Babylon. A great slaughter follows the drying up of the Euphrates. That slaughter is *real,* though the events that lead to or are associated with it are symbolized by the drying up of the Euphrates. That slaughter is *real,* though it is pictured under the symbolic name of Armageddon.

(11) THE INTERPRETATION OF THE EUPHRATES IN REV. 16: 12 NOT TO BE DETERMINED BY REV. 9:14.

Some of the expositors of Holy Writ who lived before the rise of the Advent movement in 1844 (and others who have unthinkingly followed their expositions) thought that, because the Euphrates in Rev. 9 symbolized the Ottoman Empire, the Euphrates in Rev. 16: 12 must have the same meaning. They did not apply the laws of context and association, or of type and antitype, but merely *assumed* their interpretation that the Euphrates in Rev. 16: 12 symbolized the Ottoman Empire which they thought must be dried up to enable the Jews to return to Palestine. As the Ottoman Empire no longer exists, and as it does not hinder the return of the Jews to Palestine (whose return to Palestine, of course, is not God's plan), it is impossible, *even along this line of reasoning,* to give the Euphrates in Rev. 16 *exactly the same* meaning as in Rev. 9.

In my "Armageddon—The Time of Spiritual Israel's Deliverance," pp. 3, 4, I summarized as follows: "There are *some* similarities between the seven trumpets (Rev. 8, 9) and the seven plagues (Rev. 16), and it was because of this outward similarity that some of the earlier commentators *assumed* that the same things were meant in both prophecies. Thus the Euphrates in the Plagues was given the same meaning as in the Trumpets, but the analysis of the features brought to view in the Trumpets and the Plagues shows the error of this interpretation. In prophetic understanding all the facts must harmonize.

"The trumpets present the overthrow of the *literal* Roman Empire; the seven plagues deal with the overthrow of the *spiritual* Roman Empire—Babylon. The sun, moon, and stars mentioned in the trumpets are there employed as *national* symbols of a *very restricted* character. The bottomless pit of Rev. 9: 1, 2, 11 also has a *limited application* because of the *national* setting; whereas in Rev. 20: 1-7 it refers to the whole world, which is the territory of *spiritual* Babylon. There are other factors—the earth (Rev. 8: 7), the sea (Rev. 8: 8), rivers and fountains of water (Rev. 8: 10), the Euphrates (Rev. 9: 14)—mentioned in the trumpets which are *limited* (because *national*) in their application which, when applied in Rev. 16 in connection with the overthrow of *spiritual* Babylon, have a world-wide meaning." For a fuller presentation see my "What is Armageddon?" pp. 57-60.

To obtain the interpretation of the Euphrates in Rev. 16: 12 we should not merely look to Rev. 9. We should examine this question in the same manner as we prove the truth concerning the Sabbath or any other theological question, namely, go back to the commencement of the Bible and trace the subject through the "testimony of Jesus" until we are positive that we have the truth. We should enquire, "Before its occurrence in Rev. 9 is the Euphrates used in a significant manner? Are there earlier uses in the Old Testament which reveal the principles governing its interpretation?"

It cannot be too strongly emphasised, in this connection, that Rev. 9 is neither the first occasion the Euphrates is symbolically employed in the Scriptures, nor is it given the full application of that river as a symbol: therefore it is not to be taken as the complete guide for its after use in Rev. 16: 12. In Rev. 9 the Holy Spirit draws from His own armoury—the Word of God—and uses in a *limited* application this symbol which *otherwise* is employed in its full application in a *world-wide capacity*. In Isa. 8 the Euphrates is used as a symbol of the Assyrians *invading the typical land of Israel*—its *antitypical* application is a *world-wide* one. The "double" application is never limited as in its *typical* use; the *antitypical* application is *world-wide*. The use of the Euphrates as a symbol in Rev. 9 is that of an accommodated, *limited* use of that which *otherwise has a world-wide symbolical meaning*.

The use of the river Euphrates in Rev. 9: 14, which is applied there to the Ottoman Empire (G.C. 334) in connection with the destruction of the *literal* Roman Empire, should not guide us when considering the downfall of *Babylon, the spiritual* enemy of the church. The Ottoman Empire has no *Old Testament* imagery and, therefore, *no typical significance*. Babylon not only is mentioned in the Old Testament, but is *there* presented also, as in the Revelation, as the rival city of Jerusalem: the place of captivity for Israel: the city of confusion and error, in contrast to Jerusalem the city of peace and truth. *As things associated with old Jerusalem had a typical world-wide meaning, so the things linked with ancient Babylon likewise have a spiritual, world-embracing application.* Hence, in the Revelator's description of the *overthrow of Babylon* (Rev. 16: 19) *the river Euphrates* (Rev. 16: 12), the seat of ancient Babylon, must refer to something *world-wide* in character. Unfortunately, expositors have been guided by the use of the Euphrates in Rev. 9—there used in connection with a power having no Old Testament imagery and without an Israel-Old Testament association—in their understanding of the *river Euphrates in Rev. 16, where it is associated with Babylon, which has abundant Old Testament typical meaning.* Babylon in the Old Testament is definitely connected with Israel in a *typical* way. The Ottoman Empire was not connected with Israel, and thus has no *typical* value. In other words, the river Euphrates in Rev. 9: 14 is used in a different sense from that in Rev. 16: 12 where *its use associated with Babylon gives it as wide an application as modern, mystical Babylon itself.*

(12) THE ASSYRIAN INVASION OF JUDEA SYMBOLIZED BY THE OVERFLOWING OF THE EUPHRATES.

When interpreting the meaning of the Euphrates in Rev 16 some quote Isa. 8· 7, 8 in an endeavour to prove that a nation or people living near the Euphrates is referred to by this symbol. But such a position is based upon false premises. It would be incongruous to restrict the interpretation of the Euphrates in Rev. 16: 12 to Turkey—a small *nation*—and then give Babylon, *built upon that river*, a world-wide, *spiritual* meaning. We should notice the use made in Isaiah 8 of the river of the Assyrians. This is one of a number of instances when the Euphrates is not *named* (perhaps for the numeric reason of restricting the use of that name to 21 times— or 3 times 7—in the Bible), but commentators agree that the Euphrates is the river referred to. In Isa. 8: 7, 8 the reference to the River Euphrates is that of the Assyrians *coming from their own parts and invading Israel and Judah.* "The Lord bringeth *upon them* the *waters of the river, strong and many*, even the king of Assyria, and all his glory; and he shall *come up* over all his channels, and go *up over all his banks.* And he shall pass through *Judah; he* shall *overflow and go over;* he shall reach *even to the neck;* and the stretching out of his wings shall *fill the breadth of thy land*, O Immanuel."

Thus the Euphrates is employed to represent the Assyrians, not because they possessed the territory through which it ran, but it is employed to represent the Assyrians *invading* Israel and Judah. The Assyrians were represented by the *overflowing* of the Euphrates—"the waters of the river"—because they were "strong and many."

"The Assyrians are called *the waters of the river*, because they came from the river Euphrates in great multitudes, and wasted and destroyed the nations and the countries whithersoever they came. V. 8. The Assyrian army ravaged the whole of the land of Judea in a rapid and resistless manner (where Immanuel was born, lived, and died), up to Jerusalem the capital." *Brown's Bible.*

"The waters of the Euphrates, great, rapid, and impetuous; *the image of the Babylonian empire,* which God threatens to bring down *like a mighty flood* upon all these apostates of both kingdoms." Dr. Clarke.

In the synopsis of Isa. 8, Dr. Clarke's commentary states:— "Israel . . . is threatened to be *overflowed* by the great river of Assyria, manifestly alluding by this strong figure to the conquests of Tiglath-pileser and Shalmaneser over that kingdom. V. 5-7. The *invasion* of the kingdom of Judah by the Assyrians under Sennacherib foretold. V. 8."

Dr. Clarke's comment on "He shall reach even unto the neck" is: "He compares Jerusalem, says Kinchi, to the head of the human body. As when the waters come up to a man's neck, he is very near drowning (for a little increase of them would go over his head); so the king of Assyria coming up to Jerusalem was like a flood reaching to the neck—the whole country was overflowed, and the capital was in imminent danger. Accordingly, the *Chaldee* renders *'reaching to the neck'* by *'reaching to Jerusalem'.*"

Under Sennacherib the Assyrians invaded the whole of the typical land, and were about to destroy Jerusalem when they met their doom. See 2 Chron. 32; 2 Kings 18, 19. (Similar pictures regarding Israel's enemies are presented in such prophecies as Ezek. 38-39; Joel 3; Zech. 14 and Rev. 16: 12-16; 20: 8, 9.) It was through "Immanuel," Isa. 8: 8; 7: 14—"God with us," Matt. 1: 23 (given in the Var. Bible on Isa. 7: 14: "God (is) with us")—that Jerusalem and its inhabitants did not fall before the "strong and many" murderous Assyrians. The destruction of Sennacherib's army resulted from God's intervention. The Assyrians trusted in their gods to crush the people of God in Judah.

Said God at the time of the crisis, "And the *remnant* that is *escaped* of the house of Judah shall yet again take root downward, and bear fruit upward. [PK. 22, 703 applies similar passage to *mean the church*]. For out of *Jerusalem* shall go forth a *remnant,* and they that escape out of *Mount Zion.* . . . For I will defend this city to save it for mine own sake." Isa. 37: 31-35; 2 Kings 19: 28-34. The figure of the overflowing of the Euphrates representing the invasion of the hosts of the enemies of God's people can be carried to its full meaning: God stopped the *invading waters of the Euphrates;* He did more; *He dried them up by the destruction of the army* by the angel of the Lord.

The remarkable deliverances in the experiences of the Jews are typical of the experiences of the remnant church. Joel 2: 32: "For in Mount Zion and in Jerusalem shall be *deliverance* . . . and in the *remnant* whom the Lord shall call." In EW., p. 142, 143 (and in other publications), this verse is interpreted to *refer to the remnant church in the final struggle,* and is coupled with Rev. 12: 17 where the dragon is pictured as making "war with the *remnant*" of the church. This application, that Joel 2: 32 refers to the deliverance of the remnant church, must also be made to Isa. 37: 32 and 2 Kings 19: 31, for the three texts each refer to the deliverance of the *remnant* in connection with Jerusalem.

The experiences of the people of God when the *Assyrians came as the flooding of the Euphrates to bring destruction to the children of the Most High* are typical of what will be the experiences of the *remnant* against whom Satan will make war. The literal city, Jerusalem, or Zion, of the Old Testament is interpreted in the New Testament to mean the church in all the world, around which the battle will rage between God and His angels and Satan with his angels assisted by evil men. The winepress will be trodden "without the city" (Rev. 14: 20) the church.

Commenting on the *Assyrian invasion,* in Prophets and Kings, p. 339, the servant of God has written that it was "to be *demonstrated before the nations of the world whether the gods of the heathen were finally to prevail.*"

It was to be a *test of power between God and Satan.* Thus it will be in the last great battle—Satan determined to slaughter the remnant, but God determined that they shall be preserved. Around the church will be waged this warfare: the winepress will be trodden "without the city." God will triumph, and His church with Him.

Sennacherib, king of Assyria, sent this message by Rabshakeh: "Thus saith the king . . . neither let Hezekiah make you trust in the Lord, saying, *The Lord will surely deliver us:* this city shall not be delivered into the hand of the king of Assyria. . . . Hath any of the gods of the nations delivered his land out of the hand of the king of Assyria? . . . Who are they among all the gods of these lands, that have delivered their land out of my hand, that *the Lord should deliver Jerusalem out of my hand?*" Isa. 36: 13-20. When Sennacherib heard the decision of the Jews to trust in their God to deliver them he wrote "letters to rail on the Lord God of Israel, and to speak against Him, saying, As the gods of the nations of

251

other lands have not delivered their people out of mine hand, *so shall not the God of Hezekiah deliver His people out of mine hand."* 2 Chron. 32: 17.

"When the king of Judah received the taunting letter (2 Kings 19: 10-13), he took it into the temple, and 'spread it before the Lord,' and prayed with strong faith for help from heaven, that the nations of the earth might know that the God of the Hebrews still lived and reigned. The *honor of Jehovah was at stake; He alone could bring deliverance." PK., p. 355.*

And the decisive way in which God demonstrated His care and protection over Jerusalem then is typical of how He will care for His tried remnant when surrounded by those led on by demons to destroy them. *As the angel of the Lord slew the hosts of the Assyrians, so the hosts that try to kill God's remnant church will be destroyed by angels executing the divine command.* As the *overflowing* of the Euphrates of Isa. 8: 7-8 represented the *invasion* of Judea by the Assyrian hosts, so their *destruction* was the *drying up* of those waters.

That the drying up of the waters of the Euphrates has an application to the remnant church becomes obvious when we study the rest of Isa. 8. Verses 7-8 prophesied the invasion of the Assyrians under the figure of the overflowing of the Euphrates, but the remaining portion of the chapter plainly points to the last days. 6T. 17; TM. 463; 7T. 153; 5T. 691; GC. 452; 6T. 332; GC. 593, 559; EW. 59, etc., give ample proof of our belief that *Isa. 8 contains messages for the remnant church.* "Bind up the testimony, seal the law among my disciples" (verse 16) is the sealing message of Rev. 7: 1-4. Isa. 8: 17 shows that verse 16 refers to the people who are waiting for the coming of Christ. Verses 19-20 *predict the work of evil spirits in leading men away from the law and the sealing message.* Verse 20 tells us to test the spirit-possessed miracle workers by "the law" and "the testimony." Verses 9-12 prophesy concerning the last-day confederacies, 6T. 17; TM. 463; 7T. 153, etc. It is the combination of spiritualism with these confederacies which brings about the overflowing of the Euphrates in its allegorical meaning in relation to the people of God in the last days. Hence the association of the Assyrians, under the figure of the overflowing of the Euphrates, with the remainder of the chapter dealing with the enemies of the remnant church.

The Lord's people were nearly drowned by the waters of the Euphrates—only their heads remained out of the water. Only a slight rise of the inundating river and they would have perished. But Israel's God took complete charge of the situation; the Assyrians were destroyed—the waters of the river, "strong and many," were "dried up."

In harmony with the laws governing the interpretation of the typical imagery used in Old Testament prophecies, the river Euphrates *employed in Rev. 16 in connection with Babylon must* have a *world-wide,* antitypical application. It must, in the last days, refer to an attack by spiritual Babylon upon spiritual Jerusalem. The people of that antitypical, spiritual region of the Euphrates are to overflow their banks and to inundate the land of Israel and surround Jerusalem (the church). As spiritual Babylon is world-wide, so the symbolic Euphrates *("the image of the Babylonian empire"—Dr. Clarke)* must likewise be world-wide. As the in-vading flood of Assyrian troops was dried up—destroyed—by the miraculous intervention of Immanuel ("God (is) with us"), so the antitypical waters of the Euphrates—the hosts emerging from the region of Babylon to destroy the remnant in Jerusalem (the church) —will be "dried up" by that Immanuel Who will save His people from the designs of Satan and the hordes of Babylon. Just as God intervened at the last moment to save Jerusalem falling before the invading Assyrians, so God's intervention will come at the *last moment* to save His remnant church. This fact is clearly taught in the Spirit of Prophecy.

From the foregoing it is clearly seen that *ancient Babylon situated on the literal river Euphrates* has its counterpart in the spiritual, world-wide Babylon on the *symbolical world-wide* Euphrates. With Rev. 17: 1 compare Jer. 51: 13.

(13) CYRUS A TYPE OF THE MESSIAH.

It is generally accepted that the outstanding personalities of the Bible—such as Adam (1 Cor. 15: 45-49), Melchizedek (Heb. 7: 1-21), Isaac (Gen. 22: 2-18; Gal. 3: 16; 4: 28), Joseph (Acts 7: 9-13), Moses (Heb. 3: 2-6; Deut. 18: 15-18; Acts 3: 22; 7: 37-40), Aaron (Ex. 28: 1; Heb. 5: 4, 5), David (Matt. 1: 1; Luke 1: 32), etc.— in their characteristics or in the work which they accom-plished typified the Messiah.

Because of his work of overthrowing Babylon and of liberating God's people from their captivity Cyrus is also presented in the

Scriptures as a *Messianic type.* Notice the significant words of the prophecy: "Thus saith the Lord . . . That saith of Cyrus, He is *My shepherd,* and shall perform *all* My pleasure: even saying to *Jerusalem,* Thou shalt be built; and to the *temple,* Thy foundation shall be laid. Thus saith the Lord to *His anointed,* to Cyrus, whose right hand I have holden, to subdue nations before him." Isa. 44: 24-28; 45: 1.

In Brown's Bible, under the heading "A collection of the names and titles given to Jesus Christ," the name of Cyrus appears and Isa. 45: 1 is quoted for proof. In overthrowing Babylon Cyrus prefigures what Christ will do in the destruction of modern Babylon.

Isa. 41: 2 declares that God "raised up the righteous man *from the east."* (See also v. 25; 46: 11, etc.) The Annotated Paragraph Bible, commenting on Isa. 41: 2, says:—"Heb., 'who raised up righteousness,' meaning the instrument of righteousness. The deliverances which God achieves for His people are called 'His righteousness.' See Isa. 45: 8; 46: 13; Rom. 3: 21, 22. Cyrus might be thus described as God's agent for *punishing idolaters* and for *delivering Israel.* See Isa. 44: 27, 28; 45: 1-7. But the connection (see Isa. 42: 1-7) *forbids us to restrict the application to him."*

The overthrow of idolatrous Babylon and the liberation of the Jews *prefigured the final overthrow of spiritual Babylon and the glorious liberation of God's people at the end of human history.*

In Dr. Clarke's commentary the synopsis at the commencement of Isa. 41 reads:—

"The prophet, having intimated the *deliverance from Babylon,* and the *still greater redemption under it,* resumes the subject."

Isaiah's use of the destruction of Babylon and the liberation of Israel by Cyrus to picture "the still *greater redemption* couched under it" is the normal way all the prophets have written. It was the custom of the prophets to employ local, literal, national events in a "double" application in picturing world-wide, spiritual events.

(14) WHO ARE "THE KINGS FROM THE SUN-RISING" MENTIONED IN REV. 16: 12?

Throughout the Scriptures Christ is said to be the "Dayspring," or "Sun-rising." See Luke 1: 78, margin; Mal. 4: 2, etc. He is declared to be "the Light of the world." See John 9: 5; 1: 5,

9; 3: 19; 8: 12; 12: 35, 46; Ephes. 5: 14; 2 Pet. 1: 19; Rev. 2: 28; 22: 16; etc. These oft-repeated, explicit statements should guide Christ-loving Bible students when interpreting Rev. 16: 12.

When interpreting Rev. 16: 12, expositors of Holy Writ should not heed Japan's blasphemous claim to be "the light of the world" —the Japanese or the Chinese are not "the kings from the sun-rising," even though some may think that their national emblems may be taken as an indication that they are. Actually their flags do not show a sun *rising*, but a sun *risen*. Jesus is "the Sun-rising" mentioned in the Bible. Japan is not even referred to in Scripture. The Scriptural way to prove an interpretation is not by comparing a verse of Scripture with a nation's flag, but by "comparing *spiritual* things with *spiritual*." (1 Cor. 2: 13.) "In the mouth of *two* or *three* witnesses shall *every* word be established." The use of only one Scriptural or other kind of witness is not sufficient, according to the Word of God. See Num. 35: 30; Deut. 17: 6; 19: 15; Matt. 18: 16; John 8: 17; 2 Cor. 13: 1; Heb. 10: 28. We should follow the pen of inspiration from Genesis to Revelation in order to know the teaching of God's Word.

THE "EAST" IN RELATION TO ISRAEL SINCE JERUSALEM CEASED TO BE GOD'S CENTRE.

We must not *assume* that the kings of the "east" mentioned in Rev. 16: 12 refer to nations to the *east of Jerusalem*. Since the rejection of Jerusalem as God's centre no prophet has written a prediction with the directions of the compass centring in Jerusalem. Jerusalem is brought into the Revelation *always* in a *symbolical* setting (except at the end of the 1,000 years: this exception—an important key in the understanding of the Revelation—is explained in a later chapter) and, consequently, the *literal* directions of the compass cannot literally apply in relation to a *symbolical* city. For a fuller consideration see my "What is Armageddon?" pp. 61-70.

In the Revelation, in describing *pre-adventual* events, the "east" is the *only point of the compass* mentioned by John. As shown in a later chapter, the second advent terminates "the dispensation of the Holy Spirit" (T.M. 511)—the dispensation when the "things" (1 Cor. 2, etc.) of Israel are spiritually applied. But even in describing post-adventual events the geographical directions in Rev. 20: 8; 21: 13 are mentioned only as they pertain to Israel.

255

The word "east" occurs three times in the Apocalypse—Rev. 7: 2; 16: 12; 21: 13. The first reference shows that the Sabbath Message comes from Jesus "the Sun-rising" (the Sabbath is the "sign" or "seal" between God and *Israel,* Ex. 31: 13-18); the second refers to the coming of Christ to deliver Israel from their Babylonian oppressors, and the third to the gates of the New Jerusalem through which "the Israel of God" will pass into their everlasting rest in the promised land. The words "Israel" (Rev. 2: 14; 7: 4; 21: 12) and "Jerusalem" (Rev. 3: 12; 21: 2, 10) are also mentioned three times in the Apocalypse. In the Revelation the Lord employs the word "east" *only in connection with spiritual Israel.*

The Revelation applies in a *spiritual* sense to the church the experiences of ancient Israel. The "east" played an important part in Old Testament history and in the economy of literal Israel. When God prepared the earth for man He "planted a garden eastward in Eden; and *there* He put the man whom He had formed." Gen. 2: 8. When Adam yielded to the great deceiver God "drove out the man; and He placed at the *east* of the garden cherubims . . . to keep the way of the tree of life." Gen. 3: 23, 24. Driven from the "garden *eastward* in Eden" our first parents and their children worshipped God "at the *east* of the garden of Eden." God commanded that the sanctuary be erected facing the east. See Ex. 26: 16-22, 35; Num. 2: 3, 10, 18, 25, 34. Thus, in the daily ministration of the sanctuary, priests who entered to serve came by way of the gate and the veil that faced the east; and the people in bringing their sacrificial offerings were also obliged to enter into the "court" by the "gate" that faced the east. Ex. 27: 9-16. But on the day of atonement the "east" came into added prominence by the fact that the blood of the sacrifices was to be sprinkled "upon the mercy seat *eastward.*" Lev. 16: 14, 15.

As the "east" was brought into prominence in the services of the Day of Atonement (the *last* of the yearly round of *typical* services) so, in the *antitypical* Day of Atonement (during the closing work of the heavenly ministry of Jesus, Israel's great High Priest), the "east" is brought prominently to view in the Revelator's description of God's *last-day* Message, which comes "from *the east*" (Rev. 7: 2) to "the tribes of the children of *Israel.*" Rev. 7: 4-8.

Before their Babylonian captivity, the children of Israel had so departed from the true worship of God that Ezekiel was shown the High Priest and his twenty-four associate priests "with their backs toward the temple of the Lord and their faces *toward the east;* and they *worshipped the sun toward the east."* Ezek. 8: 16. God had ordered the tabernacle to be built facing the east. To worship the *rising sun* (an important feature of sun-worship), therefore, meant to turn one's back upon the Lord. See Ex. 26: 18, 20, 22, 36; Ezek. 8: 16.

In Ezek. 10: 19; 11: 1, 22, 23, the glory of the Lord is said to have departed from the Lord's house by the way of *"the east gate."* Israel's sins had caused God to withdraw His presence from the temple, and as the "east" gate was the normal entrance to the sacred structure God, accordingly, withdrew His presence through the "east" gate. However, God did not leave His people without hope, but encouraged them with the thought that He would return. The promises concerning the magnificent temple brought to view in Ezek. 40-48 were provisional, and it is generally recognized that the proper interpretation of those chapters now relates to the Christian church. This is the interpretation given in the Spirit of Prophecy. The river of life which emerges "from under the threshold of the house *eastward:* for the *forefront* of the house stood *toward the east"* (Ezek. 47: 1-3) is applied by the Spirit of Prophecy to the work of the church proclaiming the Third Angel's Message. AA. 13-16; 7T. 24; 9T. 96, etc. The "east" of this temple is thus definitely connected with the proclamation of God's last-day Message. In Ezek. 44: 1-3 reference is made to "the gate of the outward sanctuary which looketh *toward the east* . . . the Lord, the God of Israel, hath entered in by it. . . . It is for the prince . . . he shall enter by the way of the porch of *that gate,* and shall go out by the way of *the same."* In Ezek. 46: 1-3 we read that "the inner court that looketh *toward the east* shall be shut the six working days; but on the *Sabbath it shall be opened,* and in the day of the *new moon* it shall be opened. And the prince shall enter by the way of the porch of *that gate* . . . and he shall worship at the threshold of *that gate* . . . *likewise the people* of the land shall worship at the door of this *gate* before the Lord in the *Sabbaths* and in the *new moons."* The importance of the "east" in the service and worship of the God of Israel on the *Sabbath* and the *new moon* is thus *clearly* emphasised. Referring to these important services, Isaiah points forward to the time in the new earth when "all flesh" will worship before the Lord "from one *new moon* to another, and from one *Sabbath* to another" (Isa. 66: 22, 23). God's last-day Sabbath Message (pictured in Rev. 7: 1-4 as coming from the *east* to the tribes of Israel) calling attention to the sanctuary services is inseparable from the "*east*," which was so definitely connected with the worship of God in *Israel's sanctuary* services (see Ex. 26: 18, 22, 35; 27: 9-16; Num. 2: 3, 10, 18, 25, 34; Ezek. 8: 16; 10: 19; 11: 1, 22, 23; 44: 1-3; 46: 1-3; 47: 1-3; etc.)—and, in a *special* manner, with the worship of God on the *Sabbath* (Ezek. 46: 1-3, etc.), and on the day of *Atonement*. Lev. 16: 14, 15.

In vision Ezekiel was shown God's return to His holy temple— from which He had withdrawn His presence, departing through the east gate. Ezekiel declares: "Afterward he brought me to the gate, even the gate that looketh *toward the east:* And, behold, the *glory of the God of Israel came from the way of the east* . . . and the *earth shined with His glory.*" Ezek. 43: 1, 2. These verses are applied *spiritually* in Rev. 18: 1, for there we read: "and *the earth was lightened with His glory.*" This, we know, describes the loud cry of the Third Angel's Message. Thus, at its commencement, God's last-day Message is said to come *from the east* (Rev. 7: 2) and, in picturing it being proclaimed with "great power" at its close, John applies Ezek. 43: 1, 2, which speaks of the glory of God *coming from the east.* The God of Israel is said to enter or depart from His temple by the east gate.

As shown elsewhere, the "things" of Israel which are spiritually applied in this "dispensation of the Holy Spirit" have a literal application when referring to the eternal kingdom established at the second advent. The *spiritual* east in the services and predictions pertaining to spiritual Israel becomes the *literal* east at the second advent.

In describing the second coming of Christ the servant of the Lord in E.W., p. 285, quotes Ezek. 43: 2: "The voice of God like many waters." The servant of the Lord also saw Christ's glory coming from the east. EW., p. 15; G.C., p. 640. Ezek. 43: 2 reads:—"The *glory* of the God of *Israel* came from the *way of the east:* and His voice was like a noise of many waters."

As I have pointed out in my book, "Christ Conquers," sun-worship was fostered through Satan's perversion of the Lord's Old Testament teaching regarding the importance of the east in the worship of God.

In the Old Testament times things concerning the worship and service of God were on the basis of the *literal:* literal nation, literal priests, literal temple, etc.—including the *literal east.* Since the rejection of the Jewish nation the things of Israel have their *spiritual* application, and, in the prophecies now applying to spiritual Israel, the "east" is to be regarded (until the second advent) as a *spiritual* east. The fact that in Mal. 4: 2 we read: "But unto you that fear my name shall the *Sun* of righteousness *arise* with healing in his wings," shows that a *spiritual* application of the *sun rising in the east* was made even in Old Testament times. As the literal sun arose in the east and scattered the darkness, so Jesus, spiritually, arises and shines upon our spiritual darkness, and gives us light. 2 Pet. 1: 19. Satan uses the things of Christ to deceive, and he caused the people to worship the *literal* sun in the *literal* east. Not content with the sun and the east as *symbols,* they became idolatrous and worshipped the sun, paying respect to the literal east. Mosheim says: "Nearly *all* the people of the east, before the Christian era, were *accustomed* to worship with their faces directed *toward the sun rising.*" Then he proceeds to state that *Christians* in the early church *"retained"* this custom.

"How extensive and comprehensive the Christian worship toward the east was, Dr. Dodgson shows in a note to Tertulian's Apology, chapter 16:—'*Christians prayed to the east,* as the type of Christ the Sun of Righteousness, whence also *in baptism* they *turned to the east* to confess Christ, and their *churches were towards the east.'* " "History of the Sabbath," p. 320. In my "Christ Conquers" other extracts are given showing the popularity of this custom, and also how Sun-day keeping more easily obtained an entrance into the Christian church because the sun and the east were regarded in a *literal* sense, instead of as God's *symbol* of light and truth. Papal and last-day errors—including the teaching of a Palestinian, military "Armageddon"—are based on exactly the same erroneous principle of applying literally, *instead of spiritually,* the things of Israel.

Cruden says: "The east is the first of the four cardinal points of the horizon, where the sun is seen to rise when in the equinoctial." In the appointment of the locations of the tribes around the sanctuary, which was erected "in the *midst* of the camp" (Num. 2: 17), God gave first consideration to the east. He appointed the tribe of Judah to pitch his "standard with the ensign [the lion] of their father's house . . . on the *east side* toward *the rising of the sun.*" Num. 2: 1-3. In the Revelation (5: 5) Jesus, the Son of David, is declared to be "the *Lion* of the tribe of Judah." As the tribe and standard of Judah were "on the east side toward *the rising of the sun,*" we know that the Revelator's reference to "the Lion of the tribe of Judah" keeps before us the connection of the *east* with Jesus, as "the Lion of the tribe of Judah" Who leads His people across the sands of the desert to the promised land. In the Scriptures the *lion* is employed as the *symbol* of *strength* to *destroy one's enemies,* and when Jesus comes the second time He is pictured as Israel's "strong Redeemer" (Jer. 50: 34) coming from the east—"from the *rising of the sun"*—like Cyrus (whose name meant "the sun") to liberate Israel from the bondage of Babylon. Jer. 50: 33; Isa. 41: 2, 25; 45: 1, 13; 46: 11.

JESUS, AND THE "EAST," OR "SUN-RISING," OF REV. 7: 2 AND REV. 16: 12.

The same Greek word for "east" ("anatole") is employed in Rev. 7: 2, and Rev. 16: 12. Dr. Strong gives the meaning of this word as "a rising of light, i.e., *dawn* (fig.); impli. the east (also in plur.):—*dayspring, east, rising."*

The same word "anatole" is also employed in Luke 1: 78, where Jesus is definitely termed "the Dayspring," or "Sunrising." Zacharias declared "The *Dayspring* [margin, *"Sunrising"*] from on high hath visited us, *to give light* to them that sit in *darkness* and in the shadow of death, to guide our feet into the way of peace."

At His first coming, Jesus was declared to be "the Sunrising from on high," and the prophet, in Rev. 16: 12, has employed the same word when writing of His second coming. "Anatole" is used also in Rev. 7: 2 in the description of the coming of the Sabbath Message from "the east," or "the sunrising." Malachi (4: 2) declared that "the *Sun* of righteousness" would *"arise* with healing in His wings." In the Sabbath Message "the *Sun* of righteousness" has arisen with "healing in His wings." The Third Angel's Message has come from the Source of light.

Jesus is the Source of spiritual light, comfort and growth of the soul as the sun is the source of the literal light, warmth and growth of all living things on this world. Without the light of the sun all earthly life would perish; without the light of Jesus all spiritual life would perish. This truth is well expressed in the words of the hymn written by John Wesley, "Christ, Whose Glory" (Advent Hymnal, No. 457); and in such hymns as "Sun of my Soul," "Jesus, the Light of the World," etc.

Christ is said to be "the light of men," "that light," "the true light." John 1: 4, 7, 8. John declares that "God is light." 1 John 1: 5. James states that God is "the Father of lights." James 1: 17. The Psalmist says: "The Lord God is a sun." Ps. 84: 11. Isaiah assures us that "the Lord shall be thine everlasting light, and thy God thy glory." Isa. 60: 20, 21. "The Lord is my light." Ps. 27: 1. "The light dwelleth with Him." Dan. 2: 22. Jesus came to be "a light to lighten the Gentiles." Luke 2: 32. "Christ shall give thee light." Ephes. 5: 14. "Come, let us walk in the light of the Lord." Isa. 2: 5. "And in Thy light we shall see light." Ps. 36: 9. "The saints in light." Col. 1: 12. "The light of the gospel." 2 Cor. 4: 4. "His marvellous light." 1 Pet. 2: 9. The gospel church is likened to "a woman clothed with the sun." Rev. 12: 1. "The law is light." Prov. 6: 23. "Thy word is a lamp, and a light unto my path." Ps. 119: 105. "The entrance of Thy words giveth light." Ps. 119: 130. "The path of the just is as the shining light." Prov. 4: 18. These are a few of scores of such expressions to be found throughout the Word of God. Christ's kingdom is depicted in the Scriptures as the kingdom of light (Luke 16: 8, etc.), and Satan's kingdom as the kingdom of darkness. Ephes. 6: 12; Col. 1: 13, etc. It should be emphasised that the light from Jesus, "the Light of the World," "The Sun of righteousness," comes to the believer *as the sun rising* in the *eastern skies,* scattering the darkness and giving light to those who previously were in darkness. "His going forth is prepared *as the morning."* Hos. 6: 3. "Then shall thy *light* break forth *as the morning."* Isa. 58: 8. "Until the *day dawn,* and the day star *arise in your hearts."* 2 Pet. 1: 19. "But unto you . . . shall the Sun of righteousness *arise."* Mal. 4: 2. "I am . . . the bright and *morning* star." Rev. 22: 16.

The blessings of the light of the gospel come from the spiritual east. "Arise, shine; for thy *light* is come, and the *glory of the Lord* is *risen* upon thee. For, behold, the darkness shall cover the earth, and gross darkness the people: but the Lord shall *arise* upon thee, and *His glory* shall be seen upon thee. And the Gentiles shall come to thy light, and kings to the brightness of thy *rising."* Isa. 60: 1-3. Upon a world of spiritual darkness the light of the Third Angel's Message is now shining. Commencing in the spiritual east (Rev. 7: 1-4), its glory is now being shed with increasing power throughout the earth. Soon "the earth" will be *"lightened* with His *glory."* Rev. 18: 1.

The spiritual light of the Sabbath Message precedes the *literal* light of the glory of the second advent. The law of the "triple application" of the things of Israel (dealt with in a later chapter) shows that things of the *literal* kingdom of glory have a *spiritual* application in "this dispensation of the Holy Spirit"—that is, the *spiritual* application precedes the *literal fulfilment.* Thus the Scriptures refer to the *spiritual* light of the Sabbath message coming "from the east" or "from the sunrising," and also refer to the *literal* glory of Christ coming "from the east" or "from the sunrising."

Speaking of the New Jerusalem, the Revelator says: "For the glory of God did lighten it, and the Lamb is the light thereof." Rev. 21: 23. "The Lord God giveth them light." Rev. 22: 5. The church, the spiritual Jerusalem, receives her spiritual light from God and the Lamb. And the remnant church received her message of the Sabbath from "the God of *glory*" (Acts 7: 2); from the "Dayspring," the "Sunrising."

The god of this world has worked through "Babylon the great" to exalt the sun-day anciently dedicated to the sun. According to Biblical laws of interpretation, the fact that "the Lord's Day" (Rev. 1: 10) is mentioned in the *commencement* of the Book of Revelation indicates that it is around this "seal" of the eternal king that "the final conflict" will rage in its fury. But before the King of Light comes to execute judgment upon the rejectors of His Sabbath, He sends the light of the Third Angel's Message: hence the same word to describe the origin of the Sabbath Message in Rev. 7: 2, and the coming of the Lord of the Sabbath in Rev. 16: 12.

The angel bearing God's message comes from the east (Rev. 7: 2)—the same place as the "kings" mentioned in Rev. 16: 12, namely, "from the sun-rising"—see Young's Literal Translation; Fenton's Modern English Translation; the Douay version; the American Standard version; Emphatic Diaglott; Rotherham, etc. God's message comes from Jesus in heaven—hence it is said to come "from the sun-rising," for every thing or person coming from heaven will, on account of the rotundity and rotation of the earth, appear to earth-dwellers to come from the east. After the Sabbath Message has been given (Rev. 7: 1-3), the Lord of the Message will come (Rev. 16: 12) "as the lightning cometh *out of the east, and shineth even unto the west.*" Matt. 24: 27. In Matt. 24: 27; Luke 1: 78; Rev. 7: 2; 16: 12 the same Greek word "anatole" occurs, and in each case it refers either to our Lord, His Message, or His coming.

The following extract (which is really an explanation of Rev. 7: 2) gives the words spoken by Sister White in a vision at the home of Brother Otis Nichols, near Dorchester, Mass., November 18, 1848. She said: "He [God] was well pleased when His law began to come up in strength. That truth [the Sabbath truth] arises, and is on the increase, stronger and stronger. It's the seal!

It's coming up! *It arises, coming from the rising of the sun,* like the sun, first cold, grows warmer, and sends its rays. When that truth arose, there was but little light in it; but it has been increasing. Oh, the power of these rays!"—"Questions on the Sealing Message," by J. N. Loughborough, page 15.

S, H. Lindt, of the Department of Oriental Studies in the Walla Walla College, Washington, U.S.A., in his "The Kings of the East. A Detailed Study of the Sixth Plague," states:—

"The Hebrew of the Old Testament has a word for sun-rising which is a close synonym of the Greek word referred to above. This Hebrew word occurs in the Old Testament a total of seventy-three times, and, like its Greek synonym, it is used in literal narrative frequently where its natural meaning is the east, or the sun-rising. The Hebrew word is pronounced *mitzrach.* It is also used a few times in symbolic prophecy, and in such instances it is applied to Christ just like the Greek word in the New Testament. Two sample verses illustrating this fact can be found in Isaiah 41, verses 2 and 25, where 'the righteous man from the east,' or 'from the rising of the sun,' can be no other than Christ Himself."

CYRUS, "THE SUN," A TYPE OF JESUS, "THE SUN OF RIGHTEOUSNESS."

The name "Cyrus" means *"the sun,"* and Cyrus in his work of destroying Babylon and liberating Israel typifies Jesus "the *Sun* of righteousness." Mal. 4: 2. To captive Israel Cyrus brought light and freedom; to His people in spiritual Babylon Jesus, the Light of the world, brings light and freedom from the bondage of sin. Thus we see that the references to Cyrus coming "from the east," "from the *rising of the sun,*" is a play upon the meaning of his name (as well as a reference back to the Lion of the tribe of Judah encamped "toward *the rising of the sun*"), just as there is a spiritual play upon the designation of Jesus as "the *Sun* of righteousness" Who *arises* "with healing in His wings." Peter declares that the purpose of prophecy is to lead us "out of *darkness into* His marvellous *light.*" 1 Pet. 2: 9. "Until the *day dawn,* and the *day star arise* in your hearts." 2 Pet. 1: 19. The name Lucifer meant, "Day Star." See Isa. 14: 12, margin. But Lucifer became "Satan" "the Adversary," the bringer of spiritual darkness. Jesus is the true "Day Star," "the Day dawn," "the Dayspring" or "the Sun-rising," "the Light of the world."

"The *Sun-rising* from on high" came "to give *light* to them that are in *darkness*." Luke 1: 78, 79, margin; Isa. 9: 2; 42: 6, 7.

At His second advent He will again come *"from on high"* and, *therefore,* will appear to come from the east.

Cyrus, whose name is explicitly stated, is called by God, "My *shepherd,* and shall perform all My pleasure. . . . Thus saith the Lord to His *anointed,* to Cyrus." Isa. 44: 28; 45: 1. In Isa. 41: 2 he is spoken of as "the righteous man *from the east,*" and in verse 25 we read: *"from the rising of the sun* shall he call upon My name." Isa. 46: 13 speaks of him as *the avenger of Israel* coming like a "ravenous bird *from the east,*" alighting upon and destroying Babylon. He would free the captives of Israel (Isa. 45: 13), and enable them to return to their own land to rebuild the temple and Jerusalem and enjoy the true worship of God. He would come "from a far country" (Isa. 46: 11) and would be given "the treasures of darkness, and hidden riches of secret places." Isa. 45: 3. Obviously these things concerning Cyrus typify the "greater redemption" to be wrought out by the greater Cyrus, the greater *"Shepherd-King,"* God's *"Anointed"* or *"Messiah,"* the Deliverer of spiritual Israel.

After having introduced Cyrus in Isa. 41, verses 1-7 of chapter 42, etc., outline the work of God's "servant"—the coming Messiah —who would "bring out the prisoners from the prison, and them that sit in *darkness* out of the prison house." Isa. 42: 7. As Cyrus, the Lord's "anointed" (Isa. 45: 1), set captive Israel free, so the greater Cyrus, the Lord's "Anointed" (Isa. 61: 1), would "proclaim *liberty* to the captives, and the *opening of the prison* to them that are bound." Isa. 61: 1. Isa. 43 points us to our Creator-Redeemer Who says: "I, even I, am the Lord; and beside Me there is no Saviour." V. 11. Thus the Messiah's work of redemption is described in connection with the prophecy concerning the work of Cyrus in liberating Israel from their Babylonian captivity.

The expressions "from the east" (Isa. 41: 2; 43: 5, 46: 11) and "from the rising of the sun" (Isa. 41: 25; 45: 6; 59: 19) are each employed three times in the book of Isaiah in connection with Israel's deliverance. The same Hebrew word, "Mizrach," is employed in these expressions "from the east" and "from the rising of the sun." Thus it occurs six times in connection with the coming of the destroyers of Babylon, whose number in Scripture is six. See my "Christ Conquers," pp. 113-122.

The first time the Hebrew word "Mizrach" is used in Isaiah's prophecies of Israel's deliverance it has definite reference to the coming of Cyrus to overthrow literal Babylon. Isa. 41: 2, 25; 45: 6; P.K. 557. The sixth reference (Isa. 59: 19) concerns the coming of Israel's King to overthrow spiritual Babylon, after probation has closed (Isa. 59: 16-18) and the time has come for Him to "put on the garments of vengeance." Isa. 59: 17. Then "He will repay, fury to His adversaries, recompense to His enemies." V. 18.

"When the enemy shall come in like a *flood*" then "His glory *from the rising of the sun*" (Isa. 59: 19) will be seen, and those who have sought to destroy the church will perish: the waters of the Babylonian Euphrates will be completely "dried up." Rev. 16: 12.

The star which heralded the first coming of Christ was seen in the east (Matt. 2: 1, 2, 9) by the wise men from the east. "The east" is mentioned three times in Matthew's narrative of this event. Just as the sign of the Saviour's first advent was seen in the east so, at His second advent, "the sign of the Son of man in heaven" (Matt. 24: 30) will also be seen in the east.

"Soon our eyes were drawn *to the east*, for a small black cloud had appeared, about as large as a man's hand, which we all knew was *the sign* of the Son of man." EW. 15.

"Soon there appears in the east. . . ." GC. 640. "For as the lightning *cometh out of the east*, and shineth even unto the west; *so shall also the coming of the Son of man be*." Matt. 24: 27.

Writing of the glory of the second coming of Christ being seen in the east, Ezekiel says: "And, behold, the *glory* of the God of Israel came *from the way of the east*: and His voice was like a noise of many waters: and *the earth shined with His glory*." Ezek. 43: 1, 2. At His second advent the whole earth will be ablaze with the fire of His presence. After directing us to the *east* for the first appearance of the glory of the second advent, the prophets *then depict the dazzling splendours* which will envelope the earth. In harmony with the prophets of the Bible. the servant of God turns our attention to the east for the first appearance of the glory of the second advent, and then describes the celestial brilliance of the Saviour's return to earth:—

"Soon our eyes were drawn to *the east*. . . . We all in solemn silence gazed on the cloud as it drew nearer, and became *lighter, glorious, and still more glorious*. . . . The bottom appeared like fire." EW. 15.

"Soon there appears in *the east* . . . Jesus rides forth a mighty conqueror . . . 'in righteousness He doth judge and make war.' And 'the armies in heaven follow Him.' . . . No human pen can portray the scene, nor mortal mind is adequate to conceive its splendour. 'His *glory* covered the heavens. . . . And His brightness as the *light.*' . . . His countenance outshines the dazzling brightness of the noonday *sun.* . . . The King of kings descends upon the cloud, wrapped in *flaming fire.*" GC. 640, 641.

"THE KINGS FROM THE SUNRISING." REV. 16: 12.

The plural expression the *"kings"* of the east (Rev. 16: 12) refers us back to the overthrow of literal Babylon. Cyrus, King of Persia, came from the east, leading other *"kings."* Predicting the downfall of ancient Babylon, Jeremiah said: *"Many kings* shall be raised up from the coasts of the earth." "The *kings* of the Medes . . . Prepare against her the nations with the *kings* of the Medes, the captains thereof, and all the rulers thereof." Jer. 50: 41; 51: 11, 28.

"The kings of the east" (Rev. 16: 12) are the *enemies of spiritual Babylon,* and bring about her downfall as Cyrus, coming from the east with other "kings" under his command, overthrew literal Babylon. This is the only interpretation which is in harmony with the principles of prophetic interpretation and the Spirit of Prophecy.

In his tract, "The Kings of the East," p. 14, S. H. Lindt states: "The kings of the east are set forth in contra-distinction to the kings of the earth in Rev. 16, indicating that they are a separate and a distinct group and cannot be considered a part of this world because the kings of the earth and the whole world are included in the words of verse 14."

One of the foremost scholars and writers of the Advent Movement says:—"It does seem reasonable that the 'kings of the east' must be the antagonists of 'the kings of the whole world'; for the latter are under the control of the evil spirits, and hence the former must be the ones on the Lord's side, and must be the ones employed for the destruction of the spirit-led enemies."

Other prominent Bible scholars and ministers loyal to the Message in Australia and other countries now believe that Rev. 16: 12-16 refers to the final conflict between the forces of good and evil, and the overthrow of spiritual Babylon.

After reaching my conclusions from a study of the Bible and the Spirit of Prophecy, it was interesting to discover that some of the most learned and spiritual men of the Christian church also taught that "the *kings* of the east" of Rev. 16: 12 refer to those on God's side in the spiritual conflict: some definitely taught that "the *kings* of the east" refer to the coming of Christ with His vast retinue of angels and saints.

Notice the following comment on Rev. 16: 12 from the "New Larger Type Edition Critical and Explanatory on the Whole Bible," by Robert Jamieson, D.D., A. R. Faussett, A.M., David Brown. D.D.: "The drying up of the Euphrates, I think, is to be taken figuratively, as *Babylon* itself, which is situated on it, is undoubtedly so (ch. 17: 5). *The waters of the Euphrates* (c.f. Isa. 8: 7, 8) *are spiritual Babylon's*, i.e., the apostate churches' (of which Rome is the chief, though not exclusive representative) spiritual and temporal powers. The drying up of the waters of Babylon expresses the same thing as the ten kings stripping, eating and burning the whore. The phrase 'way may be prepared for' *is that applied to the Lord's coming* (Isa. 40: 3; Matt. 3: 3; Luke 1: 78). *He shall come from the east* (Matt. 24: 27; Ezek. 43: 2); not alone, for His elect transfigured saints of Israel and the Gentiles shall accompany Him, who are *'Kings* and priests unto God' (ch. 1: 6). As the anti-christian ten kings accompany the beast; so the saints accompany as *Kings* the King of kings in the last decisive conflict.

"But as *Babylon* refers to the apostate church, *not to Mohammedanism*, the drying up of the Euphrates *(answering to Cyrus' overthrow of literal Babylon* by marching into it through the dry channel of the Euphrates) must answer to the draining off of the apostate churches' resources.

"The *Kings of the Earth* who are earthly (v. 14) *stand in contrast to the kings from the East, who are heavenly* . . .

"Working miracles—Greek 'signs'—go forth unto or 'for,' i.e., to tempt them to battle with Christ. 'Kings of the whole habitable world,' who are 'of this world' in *contrast to the 'Kings of (from) the East'* (the *sunrising*), v. 12.

"Battle—Greek 'war'—the final conflict for the Kingship of the world described in Rev. 19: 17-21, Rev. 16: 14. The gathering of the world-kings with the beast against the Lamb *is the signal for Christ's coming.*"

Notice the comment upon Rev. 16: 12 by Christopher Wordsworth, D.D., a devout and spiritual scholar: "And, as the great River, the River Euphrates, the *glory and bulwark of Babylon*, became a road for Cyrus and his victorious army when he besieged the city. . . .

"And so the drying up of that spiritual Euphrates will prepare a way for the *Kings of the East* (Rev. 16: 12, compare Isa. 44: 27, 28; 45: 1; Jer. 50: 38; 51: 36), *that is, for Jesus Christ, and for His children of Light,* who are faithful soldiers, and who will be permitted to *share in the royal splendour of the Mighty Conqueror, the King of Glory,* Who is the Dayspring from on high—the Light of the world—the Sun of righteousness, with healing in His wings (Luke 1: 78; John 8: 12; Mal. 4: 2). May all who read these lines be of that blessed company through Jesus Christ our Lord! Amen." "Miscellanies Literary and Religious," Vol. 1, p. 437, 438.

"The Pulpit Commentary" remarks concerning Rev. 16: 12:—

"The 'Kings of the East' are *certainly ranged on the side of God. Many writers see an allusion to Christ and His saints.* The sun is a frequent figure of Christ in the Scriptures (cf. Mal. 4: 2; Zech. 3: 8; 6: 12, LXX., Luke 1: 78, also Rev. 7: 2; 12: 1; 22: 16). *The Kings of the East may thus be identified with the armies of Rev. 19: 11-16.*"

T. W. Christie, B.A., in his "The Book of Revelation" (p. 273) says: "East is *ever connected with Christ and His children.* 2 Pet. 1: 19; Rev. 22: 16; Mal. 4: 2; Isa. 60: 20."

In his "The Book of Revelation," p. 269, W. Milligan, D.D., comments on Rev. 16: 12-16:—"We have also met at Rev. 7: 2 with the expression 'from the sunrising,' and it is there applied to the quarter from which the angel comes by whom the people of God are sealed. In a book so carefully written as the

Apocalypse, it is *not easy to think of anti-christian foes coming from a quarter described in the same terms.* These kings from the sun-rising are not said to be part of 'the kings of the whole inhabited earth' immediately afterwards referred to. *They are rather distinguished from them.* The 'preparing of the way' connects itself with the thought of Him whose way was prepared by the coming of the Baptist. The type of drying up the waters of a river takes us back, alike in the historical and prophetic writings of the Old Testament, *to the means by which the Almighty secures the deliverance of His people."*

Rev. 16: 12 contains a message of thrilling import to the church in its last great hour of peril. Soon Christ's faithful followers will meet the forces of Babylon in "the great conflict in which all the world will act a part." To encourage His people with the knowledge that the vast armies of heaven would come to their aid, and that He would deliver them, Christ inspired John to write Rev. 16: 12.

In song, the Advent people, for many years, have expressed their faith in this precious promise:—

"Watchman on the walls of Zion,
    What, O tell us, of the night?
Is the daystar now arising?
    Will the morn soon greet our sight?
O'er your vision
    Shine there now some rays of light?

"Light is beaming, day is coming!
    Let us sound aloud the cry;
We behold the daystar rising
    Pure and bright in yonder sky!
Saints, be joyful;
    Your redemption draweth nigh."
—Advent Hymnal, No. 608.

Christ is coming, "and all the holy angels with Him." Matt. 25: 31. In Rev. 5: 11 we are told that there are "ten thousand times ten thousand [100.000,000], and thousands of thousands" of angels. "An innumerable company of angels," declared Paul in Heb. 12: 22. One angel is as bright as lightning (Matt. 28: 2, 3)— who then can visualize the glory and the splendour which will burst upon the world from the eastern skies and then spread over the face of the heavens at the coming of Christ? "And then shall that wicked be revealed, whom the Lord shall consume with the spirit of His mouth, and shall destroy with the *brightness of His coming."* 2 Thess. 2: 8. See also 2 Thess. 1: 7-9.

The New Testament, alone, contains 318 references to the second advent. Every twenty-fifth verse, on an average, directs us to the return of Jesus: thus, *every twenty-fifth verse points us to the eastern skies* where the glory of the returning Lord will be seen. All the heavenly bodies appear to rise in the east because the earth rotates upon its axis from west to east. Therefore, as Christ descends from heaven, His coming will appear first in the east—from the place of sunrise. Just as our sun passes overhead and, because of the rotation of the earth, is seen by all the world, so Christ, with all His vast retinue, will be seen by all the world. "Behold, He cometh with clouds; and *every eye shall see Him.*" Rev. 1: 7.

Myriads of shining angels will accompany Christ, and with Him, also, will be those saints who were resurrected at His resurrection (Matt. 27: 50-53) and who went to heaven at the time of His ascension. See Ephes. 4: 8, margin; Ps. 24: 7-10; D.A. 833. These saints who are now assisting Christ in His mediatorial capacity, are distinctly said to be "kings" (see Rev. 1: 6; 4: 4; 5: 10), and are pictured as sitting on *thrones* ("seat" comes from the same original word as "throne"), "and they had on their heads *crowns of gold.*"

All saints are said to be "kings," Rev. 1: 6; "a *royal* priesthood." 1 Pet. 2: 9. "The Saviour invests them with the insignia of their *royal* state." G.C. 645. Study also Rev. 3: 21; 2: 26, 27; Ps. 149: 7-9. The saints share Christ's throne (Rev. 3: 21; 20: 4, 6) and His triumphs, and in this way, *only,* can it be said of *each* saint: *"He* that overcometh . . . to *him* will I give *power over the nations:* and *he* shall rule them with a rod of iron; as the vessels of a potter shall they be broken to shivers: *even as I received of My Father."* Rev. 2: 26, 27. Concerning Jesus, the Scriptures state: "And He shall divide the spoil with the strong." Isa. 53: 12. No doubt the "kings"—saints—now sitting on *thrones* and wearing *crowns* of gold and assisting Jesus in His heavenly ministry will accompany Christ, the "King of *kings*" (Rev. 19: 16), and His angels (who are also said to sit on *thrones*—see Isa. 14: 13—"as having *kingly* power"—Cruden) at His coming.

Daniel's last prophecy commences with Cyrus (Dan. 10: 1) who, leading other "kings" inferior in rank, came from the east and liberated God's ancient people from the oppression of literal Babylon. At the time the Babylonians were praising their gods (Dan. 5: 3-5), the judgment of God, working through Cyrus and his army from the east, was drying up the Euphrates preparatory to the utter downfall of that proud city.

The Revelator, in chapter 16, verse 12, points us to the time when spiritual Babylon will be boasting of her power (Rev. 18: 7, 8); but God's judgments will dry up the waters of the spiritual Euphrates (compare Jer. 51: 13 with Rev. 17: 1 and Jer. 50: 38 with Rev. 16: 12; 17: 1, 15), and, suddenly, Babylon's final destruction will come. Isa. 47: 11; 1 Thess. 5: 3; Rev. 18: 8, 10, 17.

Thanks be to God, Babylon's power is soon to be broken forever. Soon our Lord Jesus Christ will return to deliver His remnant people. But, before their deliverance, God's people must go through their time of trial. Rev. 3: 10, 11. The nearer we draw to the great hour of conflict, and particularly during "the time of Jacob's trouble" (Jer. 30: 7), God's people will more and more earnestly look for the coming of the great Deliverer Who will appear in glory in the eastern heavens, bringing complete destruction to Babylon, and everlasting salvation, joy and freedom to His waiting people.

"THOU ART COMING."

Thou art coming, O my Saviour,
Thou art coming, O my king!
Ev'ry tongue Thy name confessing,
Well may we rejoice and sing!
Thou art coming! *Rays of glory*,
Through the vail Thy death was rent,
Gladden now our pilgrim pathway,
Glory from Thy presence sent.

Thou art coming! Not a shadow,
Not a mist and not a tear,
Not a sin, and not a sorrow,
On that *sunrise* grand and clear:
Thou art coming! Jesus Saviour,
Nothing else seems worth a thought;
Oh, how marvellous thy glory,
And the bliss Thy pain hath bought!

Thou art coming, O my Saviour,
Thou art coming, O my King,
In Thy beauty all resplendent;
In Thy glory all transcendent;
Well may we rejoice and sing:
Coming! in the opening *East*
Herald brightness slowly swells;
Coming! O my glorious Priest,
Hear we not Thy golden bells?   —F. R. Havergal

(15) THE SPIRIT OF PROPHECY AND THE SEVEN LAST PLAGUES: THE TIME ELEMENT INVOLVED IN THE 6th AND 7th PLAGUES.

"The Great Controversy," pp. 627-644, deals with the seven last plagues. While giving only brief references to the first four plagues, God's servant dwells at great length on the events of the 6th and 7th. Pages 627, 628, describe the affects of the first, second, third, and fourth plagues. On page 635 reference is made to the literal *darkness* of the 5th plague which falls upon the beast and his *world-wide kingdom*: "A *dense darkness*, deeper than the *darkness* of the night, falls upon *the earth*." In Rev. 16: 10 we read: "And the fifth angel poured out his vial upon the seat of the beast; and his *kingdom* was *full of darkness*; and *they gnawed their tongues for pain*." This last clause is a reference back to Zech. 14: 12, which reads: "And this shall be the *plague* wherewith the Lord will smite all the people that have *fought against Jerusalem* [the church]; their flesh shall consume away while they stand upon their feet . . . and their *tongue* shall consume away in their mouth." The next verse (13) then describes the awful scenes of carnage when God pours out His final judgments upon the persecutors of His church: the false shepherds, then unmasked, will be slain by the people who, knowing that they are lost, turn with maddened fury upon each other.

In GC., p. 657, and EW., p. 289, the description of Zech. 14: 12, 13 is applied to the *very last* events occurring at the time of the second coming of Christ. Thus the 5th plague of darkness, when the false shepherds and people ("the beast and his kingdom") who "have fought against Jerusalem" (the church) will be "gnawing their *tongues* for pain," is poured out but a very short while before the second advent, and is associated with the events occurring at the coming of Christ. The fifth, sixth and seventh plagues, therefore, are really parts of one picture giving the final acts in the great drama. Apart from the fact that the darkness of the 5th plague falling "upon *the earth*" would prevent a literal gathering of nations to Palestine, the events of the 5th, 6th, and 7th plagues, as described by the Bible and the Spirit of Prophecy, occur within a *very short* space of time.

While the servant of God does not quote the 6th plague, yet her description of events following the first four plagues, and also before the commencement of the 7th, is undoubtedly the true inter-

271

pretation of the drying up of the waters of the Euphrates. (See earlier in this book; also "What is Armageddon?" pp. 45-52.) After describing the earlier plagues, the servant of the Lord describes the severe trial coming to the remnant people of God before the 6th plague brings them *deliverance* from their Babylonian persecutors, who are symbolized in Rev. 16: 12 by the *"rushing"* waters of the Euphrates.

In "The Great Controversy" we read:—

"Yet to human sight it will appear that the people of God must soon seal their testimony with their blood . . . it is a time of fearful agony. Day and night they cry for *deliverance.*" The angels "are waiting the word of their Commander to snatch them from their peril. But they must wait yet a little longer. The people of God must drink of the cup, and be baptized with the baptism." The death decree is about to be *executed.* "In all ages, God has wrought through the holy angels for the succor and *deliverance* of His people."

"With earnest longing, God's people await the tokens of their coming king . . . *Light is gleaming* upon the clouds *above the mountain tops* [the eastern horizon]. *Soon* there will be a revealing of *His glory* [coming "from the sun-rising"—like Cyrus, "the sun"]. The *Sun of Righteousness* is about to *shine forth.* . . . The heavens *glow* with the *dawning* of eternal day . . . the words fall upon the ear, 'Stand fast to your allegiance. Help is coming' . . . Glorious will be the *deliverance* of those who have patiently waited for His coming." GC. 630-632. "Soon there appears in the *east* . . . Jesus rides forth a mighty conqueror . . . 'in righteousness He doth judge and make war.' And 'the *armies* in Heaven follow Him.' . . . His *glory* covered the heavens . . . and His brightness as the *light* . . . His countenance outshines the dazzling brightness of the noon-day *sun.*" GC. 640, 641.

"The voice of God *turns the captivity of His people.*" GC. 653. "It is at midnight that God manifests His power for the *deliverance* of His saints. . . . Signs and wonders follow in *quick* succession. In the midst of the angry heavens is one clear space of indescribable glory, whence comes the voice of God like the sound of many waters, saying, *'It is done'* (Rev. 16: 17, 18)." GC. 636. Thus, in the description of the last few days of earth's history, given by the Lord's servant, we find that the Babylonian "multitudes" (the waters upon which the Babylonian whore sitteth, Rev. 17: 1, 15; Jer. 51: 13) are sweeping toward the people of God, threatening to engulf them in irretrievable ruin. "Evil men are about to *rush* [the meaning of the word "Euphrates" is "to break forth; rushing"] upon their prey, when, lo, a *dense darkness* deeper than the *darkness* of the night, falls upon *the earth* [the fifth plague is poured out]. . . . The angry *multitudes* are suddenly arrested" (G.C. 635, 636)—the sixth plague is poured out upon the persecuting waters of the Babylonian Euphrates, and the voice of God is heard saying, "It is done" (mentioned in Rev. 16: 17, 18 in connection with the 7th plague).

In bringing us down to the time when the remnant church will long for their deliverance, God's servant declares that the deliverance of the saints from the persecuting "multitudes" will be followed by the coming of Jesus—the rising of the "*Sun* of Righteousness" Who "is about to *shine forth*. . . . The heavens *glow* with the *dawning* of eternal day." Thus the Spirit of Prophecy, in describing the final scenes, presents what we have previously shown to be the interpretation of Rev. 16: 12: God's judgments in the 6th plague fall upon the waters of the Babylonian Euphrates—the persecuting "multitudes" "*rushing*" to destroy the people of God—bringing deliverance to His people; followed by the coming of the kings "from the sun-rising"—the coming of the "Sun of Righteousness" ("the Light of the world," "the Daystar," "the Dayspring") with all the kingly angels, and the royal children of the living God who have assisted Christ in His heavenly ministry.

The many details presented in the abovementioned pages of "The Great Controversy" are to be found in the Scriptures. The principles of interpretation which we have previously enunciated enable one to obtain these details from the Old Testament. "The written Testimonies are *not to give new* light, but to impress vividly upon the heart the *truths* of inspiration *already revealed*. . . . *Additional truth is not brought out;* but God has through the Testimonies simplified the great *truths already given*." 5T. 665.

By carefully studying *any* Bible theme *from Genesis to Revelation*, we shall see better that the writings of the servant of the Lord are in harmony with the Word of God, being definitely based upon the whole of the Bible. The Scriptural interpretation of the Revelator's description of the events coming under the 6th and 7th plagues is that which is also described in the pages of "The Great Controversy" given above.

A careful study of the description given in the Spirit of Prophecy, together with the true interpretation of the Scriptures, reveals that the last three plagues occur within a very short space of time, as *parts of one dramatic climax.*

In the "Order of Events in the Travels of the Advent People to the Holy City," drawn up by Pastor E. L. Pingenot and published by "The Signs Publishing Co.," he suggests from his reading of the Spirit of Prophecy, that "Events from 6 to 10" (on his chart) will occur "perhaps *within the compass of a few days.*" The first event Pastor Pingenot gives under number 6 is "the deliverance of the living saints." This, we have previously shown, occurs during the 6th plague, when the waters of the spiritual Babylonian Euphrates (Rev. 17: 1, 15)—"the angry *multitudes*" (GC. 635)—are "dried up" (Rev. 16: 12), as similarly, the waters of the literal Babylonian Euphrates were "dried up" (Jer. 50: 38) when Cyrus turned them out of their accustomed channel. Isa. 44: 27, 28, etc.; P.K. 531.

Pastor Pingenot places the deliverance of the saints at the "opening of the seventh plague." In a general sense this is true, because their deliverance is an introduction to the 7th plague, for the 6th plague quickly merges into the 7th. Very little time elapses between the outpouring of the 6th and 7th plagues, and the 6th plague does not terminate with the outpouring of the 7th, for, after "the angry *multitudes*" have been turned from their intention of slaying God's people, they turn and slay each other. See Zech. 14: 13; 1 Sam. 14: 15, 16; Judges 7: 22; 2 Chron. 20: 23; Ezek. 38: 21, etc.

"*After the saints had been delivered* by the voice of God, the wicked *multitude* turned their rage upon one another. The *earth* seemed to be deluged with blood, and dead bodies were *from one end of it to the other.*" E.W. 290. "The swords which were to slay God's people are now employed to destroy their enemies. *Everywhere* there is strife and bloodshed." "The work of destruction *begins* among those who have professed to be the *spiritual guardians* of the people. The *false watchmen* are the first to fall. There are none to pity or to spare. . . . 'And it shall come to pass in that day that a great tumult from the Lord shall be among them; and they shall lay hold every one on the hand of his neighbour, and his hand shall rise up against the hand of his neighbour' (Zech. 14: 12, 13). In the mad strife of their own fierce passions, and by the awful outpouring of God's unmingled wrath, fall the wicked inhabitants of the earth—priests, rulers, and people. . . . 'And the slain of the Lord shall be at that day from one end of the earth even unto the other end of the earth' (Jer. 25: 33)." GC. 655-657. "And the *remnant* were slain with the sword of Him that sitteth upon the horse." Rev. 19: 21. Thus the waters of the Babylonian Euphrates will be completely "dried up," and Babylon entirely destroyed.

The 6th and 7th plagues are parts of *one picture*—the final judgments which *complete* the destruction of *spiritual Babylon.* The events to transpire from "the deliverance of the living saints" by the outpouring of the 6th plague until the coming of the Lord, will all occur within a short period—"perhaps *within the compass of a few days."*

The belief of a Palestinian "Armageddon" requires considerable time to elapse between the outpouring of the 6th plague and the coming of Christ. But, as we have pointed out, after the outpouring of the 6th plague, there is not sufficient time for a literal gathering of the nations "of the whole world" (Rev. 16: 14) to Palestine. Writing of events after the outpouring of the first four plagues God's servant declares: "The end will come more quickly than men expect." GC. 631. A *simultaneous* gathering of all nations of "the WHOLE WORLD" (Rev. 16: 14) to Megiddo could be accomplished only by mutual agreement and assistance, and only after much planning and organization.

If the drying up of the Euphrates referred to the ending of Turkey (or other nations adjacent to the Euphrates)—a belief which is without support from the Word of God—and the gathering of the nations is to be caused by the *subsequent* scramble to gain possession of her territory, then the gathering would occur between the outpouring of the 6th and 7th plagues. Modern warfare requires a vast amount of materials, and though the preparation of these is a tremendous problem, the transportation of continuous supplies of guns, ammunition, vehicles, petrol, oil, food, medical apparatus, etc.—amounting to over 3,000,000 *separate* items, and weighing *millions* of tons—is a prodigious task. Before taking on an offensive in some near-at-hand sector, it takes time to build up huge supplies. What time, then, would be required to transport vast armies and enormous supplies of war materials to Megiddo *after* the ending of Turkey! *If* the drying up of the Euphrates is interpreted to mean the ending of Turkey (or other nations), "that the *way* of the kings of the east [*mis*-interpreted to mean Japan and China, etc.] *might be prepared,"* what time, then, would elapse before these and other distant nations—"the kings of the *earth* and of the *whole world"*—could gather to Megiddo!

A literal, "military," Palestinian interpretation of Rev. 16: 12-16 raises such problems as the transportation of large armies by sea when, by the second plague, the sea is rendered poisonous and thick, as "the blood of a *dead* man" (Rev. 16: 3), and is littered with the decaying carcasses of myriads of all forms of marine life. Transportation by huge 'planes would also present many problems. There would also be the problem of the gathering taking place in the literal, impenetrable darkness which "falls upon *the earth*" under the 5th plague (Rev. 16: 10)—"A *dense darkness, deeper* than the *darkness of the night.*" GC. 635.

Rocket bombs, atomic bombs, and the extensive battlefields of modern warfare out-date and further show the incongruity of the old belief of a literal *gathering* of nations to Megiddo.

There is no need for Seventh-day Adventists to wrestle with the many unnecessary problems the erroneous teaching brings to them. It is impossible to harmonize the truth of the Third Angel's Message with the fallacious teachings of Futurism, of which the Palestinian "Armageddon" is *definitely* a part.

The Third Angel's Message teaches that Christendom is to be the dominating force in the world in the last days. The prophecies show that the United States of America will lead the world in enforcing the Papal Sunday. "Every country on the globe will be led to follow her [America's] example." 6T. 18, 19. This shows that the nations of Christendom—not Japan, etc.—will have the power to influence and lead in world events. Only because they enforce the Papal Sunday are nations brought into the Revelator's portrayal of the final conflict: only because they are the enemies of the remnant church.

The teaching of the Spirit of Prophecy concerning "the final conflict" is also the "testimony" of the Bible.

(16) THE BOOK OR ISAIAH AND THE THIRD ANGEL'S MESSAGE.

As we further study the book of Isaiah we recognize that much of the language and imagery of Isaiah is employed in the Revelator's description of God's last-day Message: "And the *third* angel followed them, saying with a loud voice, If any man worship the beast and his image, and receive his mark in his forehead, or in his hand. the same shall drink of the *wine* of the wrath of God, which is poured out without mixture into the *cup* of His indignation; and he shall be tormented with *fire and brimstone* in the presence of the holy angels and of the Lamb; and the *smoke* of their torment *ascendeth up for ever and ever;* and they have no rest *day nor night,* who worship the beast and his image, and whosoever receiveth the mark of his name." Rev. 14: 9-11.

We notice that these verses giving the warning of the Third Angel contain four expressions taken from Isaiah:—

1. Drink the wine of God's wrath from the cup of His indignation.
2. Fire and brimstone in the punishment.
3. Smoke ascendeth up for and ever.
4. No rest day nor night.

As Isaiah's prophecy of the drying up of the Euphrates by Cyrus in his overthrow of literal Babylon—and the consequent liberation of national Israel—is used by the Revelator in describing the overthrow of spiritual Babylon and the time of spiritual Israel's *deliverance,* so these other expressions of Isaiah are employed in the Message of the Third Angel in describing the doom of those who reject that Message.

1. The *cup* containing the *wine* of God's wrath is for Babylon. This cup is mentioned 3 times in the Book of Revelation. Rev. 18: 6; 16: 19; 14: 10. It was at the time that Jeremiah prophesied the invasion of Judah and Jerusalem by Nebuchadnezar, king of Babylon (Jer. 25: 1-11), that God also predicted the overthrow of ancient Babylon (v. 12-14) and, later, the destruction of all worldly kingdoms. See vs. 15-33. That destruction was figured by the drinking of the *wine* of God's fury out of the *cup* of His anger—Jer. 25: 15-33. In Isa. 63: 6 we read. "And I will tread down the people in Mine anger, and make them *drunk* in *My fury.*" This picture of the wicked drinking of God's fury is mentioned here in connection with Edom and Bozrah and the treading of the winepress of God's anger. Isa. 63: 1-6. Thus the destruction of spiritual Babylon is associated with prophecies concerning Edom and Bozrah and the winepress there. Compare Isa. 63: 1-6; 34: 1-6 with Rev. 14: 18-20; 19: 15. (For further consideration, see chapter dealing with the meaning of Bible names mentioned in connection with Armageddon.)

2. The *"fire and brimstone"* of Rev. 14: 10 is taken from Isa. 34: 9, where the doom upon Edom, or Idumea, and Bozrah, is prophesied. See v. 5, 6, 9. Thus, once more, we see that the destruction of spiritual Babylon is couched in the Book of Revelation under imagery borrowed from Isaiah.

3. *"The smoke of their torment ascendeth up for ever and ever."* This statement in Rev. 14: 11 is taken from Isa. 34: 10: "It |the land of Idumea, v. 5, 6, 9] shall not be quenched night nor day; the *smoke* thereof shall *go up for ever:* from generation to generation it shall lie waste; none shall pass through it *for ever and ever."* The destruction of spiritual Babylon is set forth in Isaiah's pictures of the destruction of Idumea. Idumea was distant from literal Babylon. *Literally,* there is no connection between them, but John uses distant literal places and merges them into one spiritual imagery depicting the doom of spiritual Babylon. He uses the picture of the *smoke of Idumea* going up for ever in describing the *end of Babylon.*

Three times it is said to be "the smoke of *her* burning"—Rev. 18: 9; "the smoke of *her* burning," v. 18; "And her smoke rose up for ever and ever," 19: 3. The last reference connects up definitely with the "for ever and ever" of Isa. 34: 10. In this connection it may be helpful to point out that the literal land of Idumea has been lying "waste" "from generation to generation," as predicted by Isa. 34: 10. During the millennium this earth will likewise lie "waste." In the present desolation of Edom, or Idumea, is foreshadowed the state of the earth following the overthrow of *spiritual* Babylon.

We must always remember that the prophets saw the literal, near-at-hand, local settings of their predictions, and commingled these with forecasts having world-wide applications at the end of time. Therefore, when John quotes Isaiah's description of the desolation of Idumea in his prophecy of the overthrow of spiritual Babylon, we must avoid the exact literality of the actual wording as *it pertained to Idumea,* but must catch the *imagery* he uses. The desolation "from generation to generation," "for ever and ever," has reference, first, to the *literal* state of *Idumea,* which has existed down through the centuries. But from the fulfilment of Isaiah's prediction the Revelator saw the fate of the wicked. The fate which befell Idumea was certain and complete, and John declared that the destruction of the wicked will be just as certain and final. Isaiah, too, looked beyond Idumea's desolation to the fires of God's destruction, which seemed to him to be burning in the very land from whence, and about which, his local setting pertained. Hence there is a coupling together of the limited local pertaining to Idumea and the future world-wide. The Revelator borrows this picture which coupled the local and the world-wide and with it forecasts the end of spiritual Babylon. We must be careful to note how the local was fulfilled—Idumea has lain waste for generations, and this part of the prediction does not refer to the burning of the wicked from generation to generation, but refers to the desolations of the earth following the doom of spiritual Babylon, and also to the complete annihilation of the wicked after the fires of God's wrath have accomplished their work at the end of the millennium.

4. *"No rest day nor night."* This expression, found in Rev. 14: 11, is taken from Isa. 34: 10: "It shall not be quenched night nor day." The comments just given concerning the land of Idumea apply with equal force to the expression, "No rest day nor night." During the outpouring of the seven last plagues there will be no "rest" for those who have rebelled against God. Night and day the hand of wrath will rest heavily upon the world until the second advent. Since the land of Idumea was laid desolate it has lain waste night and day. The hand of God's curse has not been lifted from it for a day nor a night. During the millennium there will be no respite; no blessing for the earth during that long period. And when the wicked are eventually destroyed by the fires of wrath they will never be resurrected for a night nor a day. Their death will be endless. Isa. 34: 10 says of the burning of the land of Idumea, "It *shall not be quenched.*" This is the origin of the Saviour's statement found in Mark 9: 43-48. Isa. 66: 24 is also the source from whence the Lord quotes. Isa. 34: 10 introduces the expression; Isa. 66: 24 repeats it. In the Third Angel's warning of Rev. 14: 9-11 the expressions are drawn from the prediction of Isaiah concerning the destruction of the Idumeans. Jesus says 3 times, "Where their worm dieth not, and *the fire is not quenched."* See Mark 9: 44, 46, 48. In the New Testament *three* Greek names of places—Hades, Tartarus, Gehenna—are used in connection with the consequences of sin against God.

The Third Angel's Message warns the world of the final outcome of sin: the Book of Isaiah also points to the results of sin. The last 27 chapters of Isaiah are divided into three divisions, with nine chapters to each. The first section commences with Isa. 40: 1, which is a distinct break in the previous part of Isaiah—"Comfort ye, comfort ye, My people," and ends 9 chapters later with, "There is *no peace,* saith My God, to *the wicked."* Isa. 48: 22. The next portion opens with "Listen, O Isles, unto Me," and ends nine chapters later, "There is *no peace,* saith my God, *to the wicked."* Isa. 57: 21. The third division begins, "Cry aloud" (Isa. 58: 1), which is the third message (for each part has been introduced with a call from God, and each ends with the sad results of rejecting that message), and ends with the terrible fate of those who heed not the three messages which God in mercy has sent. See Isa. 66: 24. where we read: "their worm shall not die, *neither shall their fire be quenched."*

Thus, the Saviour's use *three* times, in Mark 9: 44-48, of the latter expression (which is the *third* of the 3 statements concerning the fate of the wicked found in the last 27 chapters of Isaiah, where the final overthrow of evil, and the misery of the wicked are depicted) is seen to be a reference to the 3 times Isaiah predicts the fate of the wicked. Isa. 48: 22; 57: 21; 66: 24. Isa. 66: 24 is connected up with Isa. 34: 10 which, in turn, is linked up with the Third Angel's Message of Rev. 14: 9-11. Three times Jesus spoke of Satan as "the Prince of this world." John 12: 31; 14: 30; 16: 11.

The end of the wicked is spoken of as "the second death." This term occurs 3 times, and refers to the destruction of the wicked at the end of the 1,000 years. Rev. 20: 6, 14; 21: 8. The *third* of these references states that sinners "shall have their part in the lake which burneth with *fire and brimstone."* The expression "fire and brimstone" also connects us with the Third Angel's Message for Isa. 34: 9, 10, from whence comes the expression regarding the "fire and brimstone," is the passage used in the Third Angel's warning. Rev. 14: 10, 11. *"Brimstone"* is mentioned six times in the Book of Revelation. Rev. 9: 17, 18; 14: 10; 19: 20; 20: 10; 21: 8. Thus Babylon, whose number is 6, is definitely associated, not only with the Third Angel's Message, but also with the predictions of Isaiah concerning the overthrow of Idumea, the land of the ancient enemies of Israel.

Three times the expression *"lake of fire* burning with brimstone" occurs. Rev. 19: 20; 20: 10; 21: 8. The first of these 3 references is connected with the Third Angel's Message, for it refers to the beast and the false prophet who reject that message of warning.

In obtaining the imagery employed in the Book of Revelation to describe the overthrow of spiritual Babylon, John quotes from Isaiah's predictions concerning the *three* enemies of Israel—the desolation of *Idumea,* or Edom; the invasion of the *Assyrians* under the figure of the overflowing of the River Euphrates; and the overthrow of *Babylon* by the drying up of the Euphrates by Cyrus.

When interpreting the Revelation never once should we fail to see the *source of its imagery.* Japan, China, Turkey, or the people living adjacent to the literal Euphrates are not the powers specified in Rev. 16: 12. These powers and people are entirely irrelevant to the book of Isaiah and should not appear in our consideration of the doom of spiritual Babylon.

Notice the following brief outline of some of the salient features of Isaiah:—

Isa. 7: 14—Virgin's son, Immanuel, to be born to troubled Judah.
Isa. 7: 17—Prediction of an *impending invasion of Judea.*
Isa. 8—Prediction of the *Assyrian invasion.*
Isa. 8: 7, 8—*Likened to the overflowing of the Euphrates.* 8: Immanuel again mentioned. *Israel's hope—"God with us."*
Isa. 9: 6—Israel to be delivered—a Divine Child to be born
Isa. 10: 5—The Assyrians coming.
Isa. 10: 20-23—The remnant escape.
Isa. 10: 24—"O My people that *dwellest in Zion,* be *not afraid of the Assyrian."*
Isa. 10: 25—"Mine anger in *their destruction."*
Isa. 10: 26—*The Assyrians to be destroyed* like the Amalakites, the first nation to attack liberated Israel. Ex. 17: 8-16; Num. 24: 20, margin. What God said of the first nation to attack Israel:—"I will utterly put out the remembrance of Amalek from under heaven" (Ex. 17: 14) applies likewise to the last nations to attack His people.
Isa. 11: 11—*The gathering of Israel*—impossible to be fulfilled literally now—being fulfilled spiritually. See E.W. 74-76, chapter "The Gathering Time," etc.
Isa. 11: 16—Jews not in Assyria now. The northern tribes went there after the Assyrian invasion. The God-fearing returned after the decrees of Cyrus, etc. But the prophecy speaks of them being there. God's people to-day are coming out of *spiritual* Babylon and *spiritual* Assyria.
Isa. 12: 2, 3—God is my salvation. "Salvation" used three times in this chapter.
Isa. 12: 6—"Cry out and shout, thou inhabitant of *Zion;* for great is the *Holy One of Israel in the midst of thee."*
Isa. 13—The *downfall of Babylon* by the Medes is foretold. The army of Cyrus, a type of the Lord's army in the day of God's wrath. See verses 3-19. The language of the prophecy shows that the prophet looked past the overthrow of the literal Babylon to the doom of world-wide Babylon. The doom and desolation of the city of Babylon is connected up with *the desolation of the entire world at the second advent.*
Isa. 14: 4—The doom of the king of Babylon foretold.
Isa. 14: 12-15—*Lucifer is the king of Babylon.*
Isa. 14: 18-23—Babylon is to be destroyed.
Isa. 14: 24-26—*Assyria to be destroyed in the land of Israel*—"I will break the Assyrian in My land, and upon My mountains tread him under foot." V. 24. In the same prediction both Babylon and Assyria are prophesied to be destroyed.
Isa. 31: 4, 5—"So shall the *Lord of hosts* come down to *fight for Mount Zion."* "The Lord of hosts will *defend Jerusalem;* defending also He will *deliver it;* and passing over will *preserve it."*
Isa. 31: 8—"Then shall the Assyrian fall with the sword." "Saith *the Lord,* Whose fire is *in Zion,* and His furnace is *in Jerusalem."*
Isa. 34—The land of Idumea to be desolate. Idumeans to be slain. The language used shows that more than Edom is intended. The destruction of the *Assyrians,* and *Babylon,* and *Edom* foretold in Isaiah forms the basis of John's imagery in the Book of Revelation. *These three enemies of Israel are brought to view by John in connection with the final scenes of the people of the Third Angel's Message.*
Isa. 36 ; 37 gives the account of the invasion of Judea by Sennacherib.

Isa. 37: 36 records the slaughter of the Assyrian army, which was planning to come against Jerusalem to destroy God's people. The historic record of the slaughter of Sennacherib's army is found three times in Scripture:—2 Kings 19: 35; 2 Chron. 32: 21; Isa. 37: 36. Thus is foreshadowed the destruction of those who seek to slay the people of the Third Angel's Message.

This brief outline of chapters 7 to 37 of Isaiah helps us to appreciate the *imagery* which John uses in the Book of Revelation regarding the overthrow of the *antitypical Idumeans, Assyrians, and Babylonians*—the 3 enemies of Israel whose end is predicted by Isaiah. But John does not refer to them as separate people. Idumeans, Assyrians, and Babylonians of the Book of Isaiah are grouped together as one people in the Book of Revelation. One name designates the three—namely, Babylon. And the references in Isaiah to these three enemies of Israel converge into one description by John. The burning of the *Idumeans* refers to the destruction of the wicked—the spiritual Idumeans, the spiritual Babylonians. The overflowing of the Euphrates at the time of the *Assyrian* invasion, and its consequent drying up by the intervention of God, form part of the typical background for the imagery employed in Rev. 16: 12 in connection with the overthrow of spiritual Babylon. Rev. 16: 19. And the destruction of literal *Babylon* (Isa. 47, etc.) forms a basis for the pictures in Rev. 18 of the overthrow of spiritual Babylon.

Continuing with the Book of Isaiah we see that chapter 38 records Hezekiah's sickness and recovery, which brought over the ambassadors from Babylon.

Isa. 39 describes how Hezekiah showed them all his precious things. Isaiah is then inspired to tell Hezekiah that the Babylonians would come and take these valuables, and that God's people would go into the Babylonian captivity. V. 4-7.

Commencing with Isa. 40 we are led to look beyond the captivity of Babylon to the restoration of Israel—to both the literal return from Babylon, and the spiritual deliverance to be wrought by Israel's Redeemer—"God with us." *This* deliverance was to come from the Deliverer Who *would dry up the waters of the Euphrates,* and thus bring about the final overthrow of Babylon. The Revelator uses "Babylon" as the general name for the three enemies of Israel. In John's descriptions of the final overthrow of *spiritual* Babylon the imagery pertaining to *Idumea, Assyria,* and *Babylon* blend into one—the Revelator uses Babylon as the general name for these three enemies of Israel. This blending into one is also seen in the Revelator's reference in Rev. 16: 12 to the drying up of the Euphrates which takes us back to the drying up of the flooding Assyrian Euphrates (Isa. 8; 7, 8), and the drying of the waters of the Euphrates by Cyrus at the time he entered into Babylon and brought about its downfall. Isa. 44: 27; Jer. 50: 38; 51: 36.

This same blending we have seen in the description of the destruction of Idumea by fire (Isa. 34: 9, 10) and the destruction of Babylon (Rev. 14: 10-11; 18: 9, 18; 19: 3), also concerning the winepress in Idumea and Bozrah (Isa. 63: 1-6) and the destruction of Babylon (Rev. 14: 18-20; 19: 15).

In Fenton's Bible, at the head of Isa. 40, we read, "Prophecies fortelling the *Restoration of Israel* and the *Coming of the Messiah.*" The heading of Isa. 41 in this translation reads:—"The Call of Cyrus." Isa. 45: 1 is translated, "Thus saith the *Lord to His Messiah,* to Cyrus."

Isa. 40 commences that part of the prophecies of Isaiah which deal with the coming of Israel's Almighty Saviour Who will redeem His people from the yoke of the oppressor and will destroy those oppressors.

The account of the overthrow of the literal city and empire of Babylon by Cyrus from the east was intended to be merely incidental to the main purpose of the prophecy, namely, the coming of the strong Redeemer of Israel who would completely overthrow Satan's Babylonian kingdom and bring "everlasting salvation" to His people.

Isa. 40 contains good news for Jerusalem. The Redeemer is coming! V. 1-9. This coming Messiah possesses almighty power. V. 12-31. Isa. 41 contains the prophecy of one *coming from the east to liberate Israel from Babylon,* coupled with assurances from the Redeemer that He will sustain His people and destroy their enemies. Isa. 42: 13: "The *Lord* shall go forth as a mighty man, He shall stir up jealousy *like a man of war.*" Isa. 43: 14 foretells the destruction of Babylon. The manner in which Babylon's destruction would be brought about, namely, by the drying up of the river Euphrates by Cyrus, whom God calls "My shepherd," "His anointed," or "Messiah," is forecast in Isa. 44: 27-28. Compare with Jer. 50: 38; 51: 36. Isa. 45: 1-6 foretells the entrance of Cyrus through the river-gates which led to the heart of Babylon. He reached these gates by the bed of the dried up river Euphrates. Verse 13 presents the liberation of Israel, and verse 16 the confusion of the Babylonian idolators. Verses 17 and 25 then state:

"But *Israel shall be saved* in the Lord with an *everlasting salvation;* ye shall not be ashamed nor confounded *world without end."* "In the Lord shall *all* the seed *of Israel* be justified, and shall *glory."*

We are not left to human conjecture regarding the coupling of the overthrow of Babylon and the deliverance of Israel by Cyrus with the glorious deliverance of the church from spiritual Babylon by the greater Cyrus, "that great Shepherd of the sheep" (Heb. 13: 20), for Isa. 45: 17, and verse 25 just quoted, are those referred to by Paul in Eph. 3: 21: "Unto Him be *glory* in the *church* by Jesus Christ throughout all ages, *world without end.* Amen."

The prediction of Isaiah concerning *Israel* Paul quotes in connection with the *church.* Isa. 46 predicts that the doom of Babylon would come because the gods of Babylon, Bel—another form of Baal, or sunworship—and Nebo, would not be able to save the Babylonians. Verse 11 again refers to the *coming of Cyrus from the east to overthrow Babylon.*

Isa. 47 is devoted to almost a complete picture of the doom of Babylon. Particularly from this chapter, and also from Jer. 50; 51, John, in Rev. 18, draws so much of his imagery in describing the overthrow of spiritual Babylon. See margins Rev. 18. See also my "Christ Conquers," pp. 104-109. Thus a survey of the prophecies of Isaiah relating to the coming of the Almighty Saviour of Israel to bring in "everlasting Salvation" and "the world without end" are linked up with Cyrus, the Lord's "Anointed" ("Messiah"), who destroyed literal Babylon. *Before that eternal world can come and Israel enjoy "everlasting salvation," Babylon must be completely overthrown.* That is the teaching of Isaiah, and that is also the teaching of the Revelator.

John obtained his imagery regarding spiritual Babylon from Isaiah's forecasts of the destruction of literal Babylon by Cyrus, who is the type of Christ. Brown's Bible, commenting on Isa. 41: 25 where Cyrus is predicted coming from the north, and "from the rising of the sun," says: "This has been interpreted as descriptive of Cyrus coming from Media. . . . But is it not *rather spoken of the Messiah?* . . . And *is it not prophetic of His coming as King,* in providential power and judgment, *to smite the nations for their rebellion against His authority?*—Ps. 2: 9-12."

The *order* of events in the Old Testament predictions of ancient Babylon, and the New Testament prophecies of spiritual Babylon deserve our attention:—

1. The call out of Babylon. Isa. 48: 20. Three calls out of Babylon are given. See Jer. 50: 8; 51: 6, 45.
2. The drying up of the river Euphrates, referred to 3 times in Jer. 50: 38; 51: 36, Isa. 44: 27.
3. The coming of Cyrus, leading "the *kings* of Media and Persia" from the east, Isa. 41: 2, 25; 45: 6; 46: 11; Dan. 8: 20: 5: 28. Jer. 50: 41; 51: 11, 28 speak of "many *kings*" who would be in the army of Cyrus who came from the east—hence the allusion in Rev. 16: 12 to the "*kings of the east.*" In the margin of Isa. 41: 2, the translators ask us to compare with Isa. 46: 11 and Rev. 16: 12.
4. The final doom of Babylon brought around thereby, Isa. 47.

In the New Testament the order is just the same:—

1. The call out of Babylon. Rev. 18: 4. Three calls out of Babylon are given in the three angels' messages. See Rev. 14: 6-12.
2. The drying up of the waters of the Euphrates, Rev. 16: 12.
3. The coming of the *antitypical* Cyrus, "that Great Shepherd of the sheep," the King of Kings, and Lord of Lords, leading down the eastern skies the angels, and "the *kings* and priests" unto God (Rev. 1: 6; 4: 4; 5: 10; 20: 4; 1 Pet. 2: 9)—the saints taken to heaven to assist Christ in His heavenly ministry. Ezek. 43: 2; EW. 15; GC. 640; Matt. 24: 27; Luke 1: 78 margin; Mal. 4: 2. Cyrus—"the sun"—came from the "sunrising"—Jesus, "the Light of the world," Himself, "the sun-rising from on high" (Luke 1: 78, margin), will appear in the east, the place of "the sunrising." Rev. 7: 2; 16: 12.
4. The final doom of Babylon brought around thereby. Rev. 16: 19; 18; 19: 11-21.

Examine it as we will there can be no doubt as to the imagery employed by the Revelator in his description of the overthrow of modern, spiritual Babylon. He draws all his pictures from the Old Testament predictions concerning the downfall of ancient Babylon, but *always gives those pictures a spiritual world-wide meaning.* To apply the Euphrates mentioned in Rev. 16 in the account of the destruction of *spiritual* Babylon to any locality or nation is to destroy the beautiful imagery employed all through Scripture and, particularly, in the Book of Revelation, regarding Israel and Jerusalem, and her enemies. Such application is entirely unscriptural.

The Annotated Paragraph Bible has this note on the drying up of the waters of the river Euphrates of Rev. 16: 12:—"*This figure seems to have reference to the fall of ancient Babylon; when Cyrus, at that time one of 'the kings of the east,' laid dry the bed of the Euphrates, and so obtained an entrance into the city. This drying up of the Euphrates. therefore, would seem to indicate the removal of some impediment in the way of the executioners of Divine judgment upon the spiritual Babylon.*"

It is evident, too, that the translators were of the belief that John used the drying up of the river Euphrates in the taking of ancient Babylon to obtain his imagery for the overthrow of spiritual

Babylon for, in the margin of Rev. 16: 12, they have placed Jer. 50: 38; 51: 36, which prophesied the drying up of the river Euphrates. And that they regarded the reference to the kings of the east as referring back to the overthrow of ancient Babylon by Cyrus is evident by the fact that they placed Isa. 41: 2, 25, which predicted the coming of one "from the east," "from the rising of the sun," in the margin of Rev. 16: 12. In Isa. 44: 24-28; 45: 1, Cyrus is set forth as a type of the Messiah. Cyrus overthrowing the literal, ancient Babylon after the drying of the Euphrates, is a type of Christ overthrowing spiritual Babylon after drying up the flooding, persecuting waters of modern Babylon by the manifestations of His "fury" (Ezek. 38: 18), which arrest the attempt of the murderous throngs to slay the remnant of Israel.

(17) ISA. 59: 12 AND THE PROMISE OF DELIVERANCE FROM THE FLOODING EUPHRATES.

The great Sabbath reform movement is brought to view in Isa. 58: 12-14. Isa. 59: 16-19 points us to the close of probation, the perils to the remnant because of their loyalty to God's Sabbath, and the promise of deliverance. We read: "There was no intercessor" "For He [Christ] put on righteousness as a breastplate, and an helmet of salvation upon His head [the warrior's garb for conflict]; and He put on the garments of vengeance for clothing [Rev. 19: 11-15; Isa. 63: 1-6] . . . according to their deeds, accordingly He will repay, fury to His adversaries, recompense to His enemies. . . . So shall they fear the name of the Lord [as did Sennacherib when his army was slain by the angel of God—PK. 361; Isa. 37: 36-38; 2 Chron. 32: 21] from the west, and *His glory from the rising of the sun. When the enemy shall come in like a flood,* the Spirit of the Lord shall lift up a standard against him." Notice— "no intercessor," "the garments of vengeance," "according to their deeds," "fury to His adversaries," *"His glory from the rising of the sun,"* "when the enemy shall come in like a *flood."* After the close of probation the enemy will come in like a *flood,* and *the glory of the Lord will come from the rising of the sun*—or *from the east.* The coming of the Assyrians was likened to the Euphrates flooding over the people of God; but God dried up that flood by the destruction of the hosts of Assyrian soldiers. The Book of Revelation, in describing the combined forces of evil against the remnant church, calls that combination, or confederacy (to use the term employed in Isa. 8), "Babylon." Babylon was built upon the Euphrates, the waters of which were predicted to dry up. Jer. 50: 38; 51: 36; Isa. 44: 27. *This prediction provides the Revelator with the expression which he uses in Rev. 16: 12 regarding the drying up of the waters of the Euphrates* to prepare the way of "the kings of the east"— or "the kings *from the sun-rising.*"

The expression "from the rising of the sun," which is employed in Isa. 45: 6 in reference to Cyrus (PK. 557), who is a type of Christ, is used in Isa. 59: 19 in prophesying of the coming of the Deliverer to deliver His people from spiritual Babylon "when the enemy shall come in like a flood." In E.W., p. 60, writing of the perils of the last days, God's servant says:—"God's watchful eye is ever over Israel for good, and He will protect and *save His people.*" Isa. 59: 19 is then quoted. Thus the Spirit of Prophecy definitely applies Isa. 59: 19 to the remnant church.

Bible themes are connected by a series of chain texts. Rev 12: 15 is one of the links connected with Isa. 59: 19. The references in the margins of these texts show that the translators recognized this connection. Rev. 12: 15-16 says, "And the serpent cast out of his mouth *water as a flood,* after the woman, that he might cause her to be carried away of *the flood.* And the earth helped the woman, and the earth opened her mouth, and swallowed up *the flood,* which the dragon cast out of his mouth." In various ways this was fulfilled at the time of the reformation. Satan tried to destroy the church by stirring up fierce persecution. Wave after wave of the waters of hate, cruelty, and blood-lust swept over the people of the living God. Millions were destroyed in the devastating *"flood."* Then political conditions in countries accepting the work of reformation, together with the discovery of, and migration to the shores of the New World, "helped the woman." By the destruction of the Spanish Armada, and political reverses among the nations supporting the papacy, "the earth helped the woman, and the earth opened her mouth, and swallowed up the *flood,* which the dragon cast out of his mouth." Both Isa. 59: 19 and Rev. 12: 15, 16 use the expression *"the flood."* But Isa. 59: 16-19 predicts specifically of the events after the close of probation, when there will be "no intercessor," and when Christ will don "the garments of vengeance," and "will repay fury to His adversaries." At that time "the enemy will come in like a *flood,*" and then "the Spirit of the Lord shall put him to flight," margin.

In Rev. 13: 7 and Dan. 7: 21, 25 we are informed that the persecution of the saints in the dark ages was a "war." This *"war* with the saints" is stated in Rev. 12: 15, 16 to be *"the flood."* As the "war" of Rev. 13: 7 is stated in Rev. 12: 15, 16 to be "the flood," so the term *"the flood"* would also be descriptive of the final phase of the *"war"* (Rev. 12: 17) over the Sabbath. The waters of the spiritual Babylonian Euphrates—*the waters upon which spiritual Babylon sits* (Rev. 17: 1, 15, compare with Jer. 51: 13)—will "flood" over the people of God as did the flooding of the Euphrates in the days of the Assyrians (Isa. 8: 7, 8). But, as then, God will deliver His people by destroying their persecutors.

The prophet Daniel predicted the downfall of the Jewish nation. He said: "And the people of the prince that shall come shall destroy the city and the sanctuary; and the end thereof shall be with a *flood"* (Dan. 9: 26). In giving the disciples the last sign before the destruction of Jerusalem, Jesus said: "And when ye shall see Jerusalem compassed with armies, *then* know that the desolation thereof is nigh." Luke 21: 20. As recorded in Matt. 24: 15 and Mark 13: 14 Jesus, when speaking of the coming of the Roman armies ("the flood"), referred to that which was *"spoken by Daniel the prophet."* God's servant has connected this "flood" of Roman soldiers surrounding Jerusalem with the enforcement of Sunday laws, which is to be the last sign before the close of human probation, followed by the destruction of the world, typified by the destruction of the Jewish nation and their capital city. See 5T., pp. 451, 464; G.C. 26, 37, 38.

Isa. 59: 16-19 refers to the events to take place after the close of probation when there will be "no intercessor." Then the enemy will come in "like a *flood"*—"as a flood of mighty waters overflowing," Isa. 28: 2 (which was predicted concerning the overthrow of the *northern ten tribes* of Israel by the Assyrians)—as in the Assyrian invasion of *Judea,* which was likened to the overflowing of the Euphrates. Isa. 8: 7, 8. As Isaiah had already written so much concerning the attack upon the people of God under the figure of the flooding of the Euphrates over the land of Israel we know that his reference, in Isa. 59: 19, to the "flood" must be concerning the overflowing of the waters of the Euphrates which are dried up under the sixth plague (Rev. 16: 12), when there is "no intercessor."

On account of a scarcity of rainfall the river Euphrates was essential to the existence and prosperity of Babylon. It was the occasion of their pride and added to their feeling of security. God's servant, in "Prophets and Kings," p. 523, mentions that Babylon was "*protected* by the river Euphrates." Christopher Wordsworth, D.D., wrote of "the river Euphrates, the *glory* and *bulwark* of Babylon." "Miscellanies Literary and Religious," Vol. I, pp. 437, 438. John wrote concerning the Babylonian whore "that *sitteth upon many waters.*" Rev. 17: 1, 5, 15. This is a quotation from Jer. 51: 13, which reads: "O thou that dwellest upon *many waters.*" In commenting on Jer. 51: 13, the Annotated Paragraph Bible says: "*the Euphrates* and its numerous canals, which passed through and near the city."

In Rev. 16: 12, the waters of the Euphrates are the symbol of the people who add to Babylon's glory by assisting her spiritually, as the literal Euphrates added to Babylon's prosperity and safety. Just immediately before the outpouring of the sixth plague the people who do the bidding of the Babylonian leaders will be about to destroy God's people. The crisis will come at the time of the sixth plague. The description in E.W. 283-285; G.C. 635-637 applies to the climax hour *just before the outpouring of the sixth plague* when "every appearance" will be against the church. "It is now, in the hour of utmost extremity, that the God of Israel will interpose for the deliverance of His saints." The sixth plague will then be poured out upon the Babylonian Euphrates—the "*multitudes*" (Rev. 17: 1, 15). The demonstration of the mighty power of God on behalf of His people turns the hostile crowds from their murderous intentions—"the angry *multitudes* are suddenly arrested" (see G.C. 635) —and they commence slaying each other. "And the *water thereof was dried up*" (Rev. 16: 12) is a quotation from Jer. 50: 38 and refers to the overthrow of Babylon.

The reference in Rev. 12: 15, 16 to the flooding of the Babylonian Euphrates in connection with the church in the dark ages and the reformation shows that Isaiah's picture of the "*national*" flooding of the Euphrates over *national* Israel is applied by the Revelator to the *persecution* of *spiritual* Israel by her *spiritual* enemies. Thus the Revelator shows us that the *flooding* of the Euphrates now means *persecution against the church;* and, consequently, the *drying up of the water* of the Euphrates (Rev. 16: 12) by the judgment of God (the sixth plague) is the intervention of God which causes *the persecution to cease* and brings deliverance to His people. This is the teaching of the Spirit of Prophecy. See G.C. 635, 636, etc. As the persecution of the church in the dark ages was likened to a flooding of the Babylonian Euphrates, and as the remnant is to go through a similar persecution, the same figure is continued. But there is an important difference. In the days of the reformation church, *"the earth helped* the woman, and the earth opened her mouth, and swallowed up the flood, which the dragon had cast out of his mouth." But in the days of the final flooding of Satanic wrath *the earth will not help the woman;* the earth will not open and swallow up the flood which the dragon will cast out of his mouth.

In the days of the Assyrian overflowing of the Euphrates, Judah and Jerusalem were without human help. In Prophets and Kings we read:—"The long-expected crisis finally came. The forces of Assyria, advancing from triumph to triumph, appeared in Judea. Confident of victory, the leaders divided their forces into two armies, one of which was to meet the Egyptian army to the southward, while the other was to besiege Jerusalem. *Judah's only hope was now in God. All possible help* from Egypt *had been cut off,* and no other nations were near enough to lend a friendly hand."

When the dragon casts out of its mouth *the final flooding of the Euphrates* the remnant will have the whole world against it. "Romanism in the Old World, and apostate Protestantism in the New, will pursue a similar course toward those who honour all the divine precepts." GC. 615. No Protestant countries to champion the cause of the remnant, no migrating to a new world away from persecution, as when the *dragon cast out waters as a flood in those days of the reformation church.* Without human support the remnant people of God will meet the final outpouring of Satan's anger— *the last great flood of the Euphrates, the river of Assyria and Babylon.*

But the promise of Isa. 59: 19 is for that day when there is "no intercessor," for the day of Christ's "vengeance" and *"fury"* (in this connection see Ezek. 38: 18: *"When Gog shall come against the land of Israel, saith the Lord, that My fury shall come up in My face"). "When the enemy shall come in like a flood,* the Spirit of the Lord shall put him to flight." God, Himself, will vindicate His authority and demonstrate His superiority over the gods of the "Assyrians."

In pointing to the time of the defeat and overthrow of the forces of spiritual Babylon who have sought to destroy spiritual Israel, Zechariah says: "In that day there shall be a great mourning . . . as the mourning of *Hadadrimmon* in the valley of *Megiddon."* Zech. 12: 11. Concerning this *"Hadadrimmon* in the valley of

Megiddon," the Rev. Alfred Jones, M.A., says: *"Rimmon was a god of the Syrians; the invocation of the god Rimmon."* "Hadad," according to the Rev. A. Jones, M.A., means: *"Chief, most eminent,* a title of the kings of Syria. The god of Rimmon was styled Adad. It was *originally a title of the sun.* It signified THE FIRST." Lucifer ,the "Day Star" (Isa. 14: 12), in his mad ambition to be THE FIRST in his controversy with the "Sun of righteousness," and in defiance of the explicit Commandment of God, exalted *Sunday* the *first* day of the week as the day dedicated to his honour. Hence we can see the significance of mentioning in connection with the great battle of Armageddon the mourning of those who, heeding not God's last-day Message, cling to the observance of Sun-day the first day of the week—the day dedicated to the worship of the sun by the ancient Babylonians and Syrians. Modern followers of the Syrian god Rimmon will, by the threat of death, seek to force spiritual Israel to keep Sun-day. But in vain will they call upon Lucifer, the once proud "Day Star," who endeavoured to be THE FIRST, to protect them from the wrath of God which falls upon those seeking to destroy His people. All their efforts to destroy the faithful remnant will come to nought:—"The time had nearly come when He was to manifest His mighty power, and gloriously *deliver His saints.* For His name's glory He would *deliver everyone* of those who had patiently waited for Him . . . God would not suffer the wicked to destroy those who were expecting translation, and who would not bow to the *decree of the beast or receive his mark.* I saw that if the wicked were permitted to slay the saints, Satan and all his evil host, and all who hate God, would be gratified. And oh, *what a triumph it would be for his satanic majesty,* to have power, in the last closing struggle, over those who have so long waited to behold Him Whom they loved." EW. 284.

The promise of Rev. 16: 12 is that at the time of the final flooding of the Euphrates, God will send His judgment upon "the flood"—"and the water thereof was dried up, that the way of the kings of the east might be prepared."

Just as the *drying up* of the Euphrates *prepared the way* of the kings of the east to *bring complete destruction to Babylon,* so the drying up of the waters of spiritual Babylon will prepare the way for the kings of the east to bring complete destruction to modern Babylon. And as the *drying of the flooding waters of the Euphrates in the days of Sennacherib meant the intervention by God and the subsequent destruction of the hosts about to attack Jerusalem, so* the sixth plague will terminate the attack on spiritual Jerusalem, the church, by God intervening and bringing destruction to the enemies of the remnant. Armageddon—"the mountain of destruction" or "the mountain of slaughter"—follows the drying up of the Babylonian Euphrates. As the wicked surround the church, God manifests His power to deliver His people. The Babylonian throngs are arrested in their murderous intent, God puts them to confusion, and they turn and slay each other. The angels of God —the divine executors—also slay the wicked who have sought to kill God's people. This is the Armageddon destruction, or slaughter, *which will follow the drying up of the Babylonian Euphrates* which has *rushed* (this is the meaning of the word Euphrates) "as a flood after the woman, that he [Satan] might cause her to be carried away of the flood." Rev. 12: 15.

As the valley of *Jehoshaphat* is used for the significant meaning of its name—the valley of *God's judgment;* as *Armageddon* is used for the significant meaning of the *Hebrew* name of the place—the *mountain of slaughter;* as *Jerusalem* is used because of the significance of it being the city of *peace and of truth* (Heb. 7: 1-2; Zech. 8: 2, etc.); as *Babylon* is used for the significant meaning of its name—*confusion,* Gen. 11: 9; so, also, *Euphrates* is mentioned because of the meaning of its name. Dr. Strong says of the Hebrew origin of the name Euphrates:—"From an unused root meaning to *break* forth; *rushing.*" The Euphrates, in Rev. 16: 12, meaning to *"break forth; rushing,"* is a fitting designation for the devil-led world which *breaks forth to kill God's people;* a fitting name to describe the people of Babylon who *"rush"* upon the remnant of *Israel to destroy them.*

In describing the actions of the "multitudes" who are represented by the Babylonian Euphrates (Rev. 17: 1, 15; 16: 12) the Spirit of Prophecy uses the very word which is the meaning of the name "Euphrates":—"The wicked *rushed* upon the saints to slay them; but angels in the form of men of war fought for them." E.W. 283.

The things pertaining to *national* Israel were recorded in the Old Testament to set forth *typically* the experiences of *spiritual* Israel. "For *whatsoever* things were written aforetime were written for our learning." Rom. 15: 4.

We should give full heed to the inspired declaration concerning the experiences of national Israel that *"all* these things happened unto them for ensamples [or *types*, margin]: and they are written for our admonition upon whom the ends of the world are come." 1 Cor. 10: 11. See also v. 6, margin.

A close study of the Scriptures reveals that a belief in God's last-day Message, including the Spirit of Prophecy, is based upon the irrefragable foundation of the *whole* Bible.

But the point which must again be emphasised is that the things which occurred in the land of Israel have their spiritual counterpart *in all the world*. Thus the Euphrates in Rev. 16 must be interpreted in connection with the world-wide Armageddon slaughter of the forces of spiritual Babylon.

Daniel's last long prophecy commences with Cyrus (Dan. 10: 1)—who came from the east or the sun-rising leading lesser "*kings*" (Jer. 50: 41; 51: 11, 28), overthrowing Babylon by drying up the waters of the Euphrates, and bringing deliverance to God's people—and ends with Michael, Jesus, the Almighty Son of God—Who comes from the east or from the sun-rising to bring deliverance to His people in the hour of extremity (see Dan. 12: 1; GC. 635-637; E.W. 283-285) by drying up the persecuting waters of the Euphrates and completely destroying spiritual Babylon. God's wrath will be poured out upon the persecuting people of Babylon: and "the King of kings," with all the triumphant hosts of angels and leaders of other worlds who were here when this world was created, together with the saints who had been resurrected and translated to be "kings and priests unto God" in association with Christ in His heavenly ministry, will be seen in the radiant, eastern skies. "And the sixth angel poured out his vial upon the great river Euphrates; and the *water thereof was dried up*, that the way of the *Kings of the east* might be prepared." "Even so, come, Lord Jesus." All persecutors, and workers of evil, will be destroyed in "the *battle* of that great day *of God Almighty*." "And at that time *Thy people shall be delivered*, every one that shall be found written in the book."

CHAPTER XXVI.

THE PRINCIPLE GOVERNING THE USE OF UNFULFILLED CONDITIONAL PROPHECIES.

God wastes nothing: Jesus commands us to "gather up the *fragments* . . . that *nothing* be lost." John 6: 12. Unfulfilled predictions are not to be regarded as useless words: God would not have useless matter in His Holy Word. While these unfulfilled predictions could have been retained in the Scriptures to show the promises God had made on condition of obedience, yet, that surely would not be sufficient reason for the inclusion of whole chapters if, otherwise, they were merely unprofitable words. As each part of the Scriptures "is given by inspiration of God, and is *profitable* for doctrine, for reproof, for correction, for instruction in righteousness: that the man of God may be perfect, throughly furnished unto all good works" (2 Tim. 3: 16, 17), the inclusion, in the Bible, of these unfulfilled prophecies means that they still have a purpose in the plan of God. We are to heed "*every* word" in the Bible. Matt. 4: 4. In Matt. 21: 41-43, Jesus taught that the church—God's spiritual nation (1 Pet. 2: 9, etc.)—is heir to all the privileges and blessings which had been promised to Israel. This is the teaching of all the writers of the New Testament. God's servant has written: "Warning, admonition, promise, *all are for us*, upon whom the ends of the world are come." 6T. 410. "*We* are numbered with *Israel. All* the instruction *given to the Israelites of old* concerning the education and training of their children, *all the promises of blessing through obedience, are for us.*" Min. of Healing, p. 405.

The promises of blessings to obedient Israel, of victory over their foes, etc., described in such prophecies as Ezek. 38, 39, 40-48; Joel 3; Zech. 14, etc., are thus promises of blessings for the true Israel of God in the last days. In their last-day application in relation to spiritual Israel these promises become *pictures* which, *like parables,* are to be understood in a general sense without undue emphasis upon the local details which would have been fulfilled in a national sense had they been fulfilled to national Israel in the literal land of Israel. As stated in my "What is Armageddon?" pp. 65,

66: "Certain local matters in those *conditional* prophecies drop from view in the world-wide application of those predictions in connection with the church. In an *imagery, as in a parable,* a meaning is not to be sought for in every detail, for the main purpose is to provide a *general word-picture.* Many illustrations could be given . . . Ezek. 38, 39 pictures an assault against Israel by a vast combined army. Through the intervention of God, the evil forces seeking the destruction of Israel are themselves destroyed. To complete this description of absolute victory for Israel, the latter are pictured as gathering their dead enemies and burying them. See Ezek. 39: 11-15. This feature of the portrayal of the outcome of Armageddon is not to be taken literally—that would contradict Jer. 25: 33, where we are informed that those slain in Armageddon, 'shall *not be* lamented, neither *gathered, nor buried,* they shall be dung upon the ground.' Ezek. 38, 39 is an *imagery,* and, therefore, the local details (including the points of the compass) are not to be interpreted literally, but only as parts of a word-picture. Jer. 25. 33 is a straight-out statement *without imagery.* Hence, while the two prophets speak of the same thing and appear to contradict each other, the apparent discrepancy is due to the fact that Ezekiel's vision is in the form of an imagery."

Referring to this vision of Ezekiel, Carlyle B. Haynes, in his "Blackout of Civilization," p. 80, says: "There he saw the countless *foes of God* marshalling themselves to battle against Jehovah *like the gathering of a great tempest.*" If we interpret this prophecy in terms of an *imagery,* or a general *word-picture,* setting forth the dramatic scenes in the final conflict of the great controversy between Christ and Satan, we employ it in the way God intended. The call to the fowls of the heavens and the beasts of the earth to come and eat the flesh of the *enemies* of *Christ* and *His spiritual Israel* (Ezek. 39: 3-9, 17-23; Rev. 19: 17, 18) is to be interpreted in the same manner, namely, as an *imagery* depicting the *completeness* and the *final* nature of the victory of Israel over her foes. As all life—except the church—will be slain at Christ's coming (Zeph. 1: 1, 2, 3; Jer. 4: 25-27, etc.), no beasts or birds will be left upon the earth to eat the flesh of Israel's enemies, scattered as "dung upon the ground" (Jer. 25: 33), throughout the whole earth. These details, and others, such as Israel for "seven months" (Ezek. 39: 11-16) burying those slain in "the final conflict," and for "seven years" (Ezek. 39: 9, 10) burning up the weapons of their adversaries, are not to be applied in a *literal* sense. Following "the final conflict," when the enemies of spiritual Israel will be destroyed, the earth will be desolate, without an inhabitant. Jer. 4: 23-27; Zeph. 1: 2, 3, etc. After the second advent, Israel will not be left on the earth for a moment—certainly not for "seven months" or "seven years." According to the principle of a day for a year, seven months equals 210 years, and seven years becomes a period of 2,520 years! It is impossible to apply the prophecy of Ezek. 38, 39 in a *literal*, Palestinian sense and make it harmonize with the rest of the Scriptures concerning the Third Angel's Message.

Those things which *could have happened* in the experience of literal Israel, had they been faithful, are no longer to be *literally* fulfilled, for the prophecy now applies *spiritually* in connection with *spiritual* Israel: those things which, because of their strictly local nature, pertained to national *Israel* in connection with certain localities, do not apply in detail to spiritual and world-wide Israel, but are merely included in the general picture of the *imagery*.

The principle governing the understanding of Biblical imagery (which is a form of parable, or pen picture) is similar to that governing the interpretation of parables. Writing concerning the proper understanding of parables, the Rev. Norman L. D. Webster, B.A., says: "Speaking broadly, when Jesus told a parable it was to illustrate some *one outstanding truth*. To get the full benefit of the parable we need to grasp *that one truth*, and not to lead ourselves into a fog or a maze of bewilderment by trying to emphasise *unimportant details* and trying to get all sorts of *absurd meanings out of these details*."

The parable of the rich man and Lazarus is used, by many, to teach the conscious state of the dead and the lake of fire and eternal torment. We know that such was not the purpose for which Christ gave the parable. His main objective was to point out by means of beliefs well known to the Jews, themselves, that at death *our eternal destiny is fixed*, and that after death, no one can cross the chasm from unpreparedness to readiness for heaven. The *details* of this parable should be seen merely as contributing to a general picture, by which Jesus taught the one solemn truth that death decides our eternal destiny: after death it is too late for the alteration of character.

The details of the story of the prodigal son were not given to teach that eating the "fatted calf" is God's ideal diet; or that men should wear rings, etc.

In His illustration of the suddenness of the close of probation and the coming of the day of the Lord, Jesus said He would come like a thief in the night. Obviously, if we endeavour to apply the details of this illustration, we have the incongruity that Jesus is coming to steal like a thief. No, He is not coming to steal; but He will come *unexpectedly* like a thief, Matt. 24: 42, 43. And so we could go on, pointing out that in illustrations, parables and imageries we look for the outstanding picture, being careful not to unduly emphasise the details. This principle applies in the conditional prophecies: the details which could have been fulfilled in connection with national Israel in Palestine are not to be unnecessarily enlarged, or dwelt upon. The *spiritual* application of *conditional* prophecies lifts them into the category of *imagery and parable*, which are given to provide *general pictures* teaching *spiritual*, worldwide truths. The unfulfilled conditional prophecies now apply *spiritually in relation to the church.*

CHAPTER XXVII.

LITERAL INTERPRETATIONS LIMIT IN TIME AND PLACE IMPORTANT SCRIPTURES RELATING TO THE THIRD ANGEL'S MESSAGE: SPIRITUAL INTERPRETATIONS ARE WORLD-WIDE AND UNLIMITED IN TIME—UNTIL THE SECOND ADVENT.

Spiritual things are *world-wide* in scope, whereas *literal* things are *limited* in *time* and *place*. For example: when a prediction concerning Israel is applied in a *literal* sense to Palestine, that prophecy is *limited* to that particular *locality*, and it is also limited to a particular *time*. Take the prophecy in Joel 2: 23-27. Early and latter rains are predicted to fall upon the "land" of Israel. V. 18. Futurists apply this passage to *literal* rains which, they say, are now beginning to fall in Palestine. Such an application *limits* the prophecy in regard to both *time* and *place*. But the spiritual application is world-wide in scope and, in a limited degree, continuous in time, during this "dispensation of the Holy Spirit." While we look for the Holy Spirit to be poured out in a *special* way in the closing days of the work of the preaching of the message, yet it is true that down through all the centuries of the Christian era people have prayed for the outpouring of the Holy Spirit and God, in fulfilment of this passage of Scripture, has given them rains—"showers of blessing" (Ezek. 34: 26)—according to the seasons of the workings of the Holy Spirit upon the hearts of individuals or churches. By studying A.A. 54, 55; T.M. 399, 506-512, etc., it will be seen that the Spirit of Prophecy, in harmony with the Scripture, teaches that, while Pentecost was the "early rain" and the special manifestation of the Holy Spirit in the last days is the "latter rain" yet, throughout this dispensation, *individuals* have received their early and latter rains to quicken spiritual life and to prepare the character for heaven. Thus the prophecy of Joel 2: 23-27 has a world-wide, *spiritual* fulfilment throughout "the dispensation of the Holy Spirit." T.M. 511.

At the time of the second advent the harvest will be reaped. The Saviour declared: "the harvest is the end of the world; and the reapers are the angels." Matt. 13: 30, 39, 40. Rev. 14: 14-20 pictures the reaping of "the harvest of the *earth.*" While there will be the reaping of "the harvest of *the earth*" at the end of the world, yet from the commencement of the plan of redemption there has been a reaping of the harvest. Jesus said: "The harvest truly is plenteous, but the labourers are few; pray ye therefore the Lord of the harvest, that He will send forth labourers into his harvest." Matt. 9:37,38; Luke 10: 2. "Say ye not, There are four months, and then cometh harvest? behold, I say unto you, Lift up your eyes, and look on the fields; for they are white *already to harvest.*" John 4: 35-38.

The Papal teaching of the dignity and power of the Roman Catholic priesthood is another, of many examples, illustrating that Satan deceives by limiting to earthly persons or places truths which apply in a universal sense to the body of the church. The members of that church are educated to believe that the keys of heaven and hell are in the hands of the *priest.* By wrong interpretations of Matt. 16: 18, 19; John 20: 22, 23, the people are taught to believe that the *priest* can bind and loose, and remit sins. The New Testament teaches that *every believer is a priest* (see Rev. 1: 6; 5: 10; 20: 4; 1 Pet. 2: 5, 9, etc.) offering up "*spiritual* sacrifices, acceptable to God by Jesus Christ." "Let us *offer* the *sacrifice* of praise to God continually." Heb. 13: 15. "*Present* your bodies a living *sacrifice,* holy, acceptable unto God, which is your reasonable service." Rom. 12: 1.

To the *church as a whole*—with *each* individual sharing *alike* in privelege and power—has been committed the solemn charge of handling the keys of heaven and hell by bringing the knowledge of salvation from sin, by bringing the sinner into contact with the Saviour, and by prayer leading the sinner to lay hold on eternal life. As the church joins with the Saviour in the work of salvation, she becomes a channel of blessing to all who accept her message; but those who reject will be destroyed in the day of the Lord's wrath. Thus the power of life and death is not in the hands of a few *literal* priests, but belongs to the *whole church, every* member of which is a *spiritual* priest offering up "*spiritual* sacrifices." The error lies in the *limitation* placed upon that which God intends should be applicable to His children in *all the world.* The same error—of *limiting* to *time* and *place* truths that are world-wide —appears throughout Satan's counterfeit system of interpretation.

The Futuristic interpretation also limits to time and place the prophecies picturing "the final conflict" between Israel and her enemies. Ezek. 38, 39; Joel 3; Zech. 12, 14; Rev. 16: 12-16, etc. While having a *special* application in the last days, yet, in a certain measure, they have been applicable to individuals and the church in all places and at all times during the Christian era. Notice Joel 3: 14, which reads: "Multitudes, multitudes in the valley of decision." How often this passage has been mis-applied in connection with the erroneous Palestinian interpretation teaching a gathering of warring nations in "the valley of Jehoshaphat." "Multitudes" are pictured as being then "in the valley of decision." By that *literal* interpretation the prediction is *limited* to that *time* and *place*. When the whole setting is *spiritually* applied in connection with Christ and spiritual Israel, Joel 3 becomes a message applicable, in a general sense, throughout the Christian era. There has always been enmity between the followers of Satan and those who love the Lord; there has always been a mustering of the forces of Satan against the church; in a sense, people have always been before the throne of God for judgment; there have always been multitudes in the valley of decision; but, as the finale of the great controversy draws near, these predictions also have *special* significance in relation to the final gathering of Satan's army against the church; in relation to the final judgment day, when "multitudes" will be "in the valley of decision" for the last time.

How incongruous to teach from Joel 3 both a *literal* gathering of nations "into the valley of Jehoshaphat" for "Armageddon," and the *spiritual* application of the statement "multitudes in the valley of decision"! How incongrous, when "the *valley* of decision" *is* "the *valley* of Jehoshaphat," and the "nations" are the "multitudes"! The "multitudes," or "nations," are not gathered "into" the *literal* "valley of Jehoshaphat" (it is far too small); but they are spiritually gathered before God in the *symbolical* "valley of Jehoshaphat." How incongruous to limit the "multitudes in the valley of decision" to Palestine, during the 6th plague, and to thus apply this verse after probation has closed and all "decisions" for eternity have been made! The Spirit of Prophecy applies Joel 3: 14 to the time of the preaching of the gospel; to the "multitudes" *now* in all the world: "The destinies of souls are balancing. *Multitudes are in the valley of decision.* . . . Prompt, energetic action may save an undecided soul." 4T. 446; 6T. 406.

The Bible and the Spirit of Prophecy refer to the age-long struggle between Christ and Satan as the "war," or "battle," or "controversy." This "war," or "battle," is described by the

Revelator from its commencement in heaven (Rev. 12: 7) until its close (Rev. 12: 17; 13: 4, 7; 16: 14; 17: 14; 19: 11; 20: 8). "Armageddon," the "battle . . . ' of God Almighty," is the *finale* of this world-wide, age-long conflict between the forces of good and evil. The erroneous belief that such passages as Rev. 16: 12-16; Ezek. 38; 39; Joel 3; Zech. 14, etc., refer to a literal Palestinian conflict of nations in the last days limits to place and time that which, in principle, has been in progress in all the world throughout human history. In contrast, the spiritual interpretation of these prophecies, while teaching that they have a *special* significance in the description of the final conflict, also shows that, *in principle*, they have been applicable in a limited sense to individuals and the church throughout the conflict between good and evil. While the literal interpretation limits the usefulness of these prophecies to Palestine and to the last hours of human history, the spiritual interpretation shows that they have had a spiritual significance for hundreds of years. One of the tests of the true interpretation of these prophecies concerning Israel is the value to the individual.

The teaching of a military "Armageddon," based upon the erroneous interpretations of prophecies relating to Israel and her enemies, limits to place—to Palestine—and limits to time—to the very last hours of this world's history when the literal interpretation of these prophecies cannot be of spiritual value to the individual or church—truths which are now applicable to the church in all the world.

Satan counterfeits by limiting to Palestine in relation to the *literal* Jews that which the Third Angel's Message applies spiritually in relation to *spiritual* Israel in all the world.

The spiritual interpretation of such prophecies as Rev. 16: 12-16; Ezek. 38; 39; Joel 3, etc., shows that they have contained a message to individuals, as well as to the church, at any time and place, but that their culmination concerns the world-wide final conflict.

A study of the prophecies in the Apocalypse relating to the closing scenes reveals that events reach a *culmination* at that time. The message of the second angel, given first in 1844, will, in the final hours of probationary time, be sounded with greater power throughout the world. See G.C. 389, 390; 603. The gathering, or uniting, of the remnant church is now in progress. See Isa. 11: 11, 12; P.K. 373, 376; E.W. 74, 75; 6T. 133; 7T. 172; 9T. 51, etc.

"The agencies of evil are combining their forces, and consolidating. They are strengthening for the last great crisis." 9T. 11. See further extracts from the Spirit of Prophecy given in "What is Armageddon?" pp. 37-44. The gathering of "the kings of the earth and of the whole world," described in Rev. 16: 14-16, does not refer to a sudden military gathering of nations to Megiddo, but refers to the culmination of the work of deception carried on through the years by Satan in his preparation to "unite" the world to "join" him "in his last struggle" against God. See GC. 623, 656; T.M. 465.

In "The Great Controversy," pp. 561, 562. we read·—

"Satan has *long been preparing* for his final effort to deceive the world. . . . Little by little he has prepared the way for his master-piece of deception in the development of Spiritualism. He has not yet reached the *full* accomplishment of his designs; but it will be reached in the last remnant of time. Says the prophet: 'I saw three unclean spirits like frogs . . . they are the spirits of devils, working miracles, which go forth unto the kings of the earth and of the whole world, to gather them to the battle of that great day of God Almighty.' (Rev. 16: 13, 14).

This extract shows that "the battle of that great day of God Almighty "comes as the *culmination* of world-wide events. By the time of the 6th plague "the wicked have *fully* united [or "gathered"] with Satan in his warfare against God." G.C. 656.

CHAPTER XXVIII.

"ALL THINGS ARE YOURS" (1 Cor. 3: 21, 22): SPIRITUAL INTERPRETATIONS OF THE *LITERAL PAST* AND OF THE *LITERAL FUTURE* APPLY TO SPIRITUAL ISRAEL *NOW*

"*All* Scripture is given by . . . God, and is *profitable.*" 2 Tim. 3: 16, 17. The historical narratives of Israel's past glories, the unfulfilled prophecies that would have been fulfilled had Israel met the conditions, the prophecies which describe the glories of heaven and the new world: "ALL" Scripture, whether dealing with the past, the present, or the future, is spiritual food for the church *now*. As shown previously, the New Testament writers spiritually applied the literal things of Israel mentioned in the Old Testament, when recording truths for the people of this "dispensation of the Holy Spirit." The Scriptures are built upon this principle that "all things are" ours *now*: that the things of the past and the things promised to the faithful in the hereafter have their *spiritual* counterpart *now*.

Through the prophetic descriptions in God's Word, heavenly things are now spiritually seen by the eye of faith: the saints now behold them in spiritual vision, before *literally* beholding them in the eternal kingdom. "God *hath* revealed them unto us by His Spirit." 1 Cor. 2: 9, 10.

The church is now a temple, "Whose Builder and Maker is God." Vol. 9 Test., p. 180, refers to the latter statement (Heb. 11: 10) and applies it to the church. The church is also the spiritual New Jerusalem, in which God now dwells, as He will dwell eternally in the visible, literal New Jerusalem, the metropolis of the new world. See also Heb. 12: 22, 23; Ephes. 2: 21, 22; John 14: 23. The New Jerusalem "hath foundations" (see Heb. 11: 10; Rev. 21: 14, 19, 20)—so has the church. 1 Cor. 3: 11; Ephes. 2: 20, etc.

There is a *spiritual* temple on earth, and a *visible, literal* temple in heaven. See texts given previously; also Rev. 11: 1, 2; G.C. 266; T.M. 17; A.A. 595; P.K. 36. While the work of measuring (the judgment), referred to in Rev. 11: 1, 2, takes place in the literal temple in heaven, the judgment message is being sounded on the earth. This message calls all to measure up to the standard required by the judgment, which is convening in the literal temple above. The *literal* things of Israel have their *spiritual* application on the earth until the second advent. The *spiritual* temple—the spiritual Jerusalem—continues until it merges into the *literal* things of the eternal kingdom.

The prophetic pictures of the *literal* things of the new world apply also, in a spiritual sense, to the church. The Holy City is said to be "measured"; also the church. See Rev. 21: 15; 11: 1, 2; Ezek. 48: 16, 20; Rev. 21: 16; Ezek. 48: 31; Rev. 21: 12, 13; Ezek. 48: 30-34; and Rev. 21: 12-17. What is said of the *literal* city in heaven is also said of the church, the *spiritual* dwelling place of God.

"Behold, I make all things new" (Rev. 21: 5) is God's promise concerning the eternal kingdom. "Behold, all things are become new" (2 Cor. 5: 17), declared Paul of those "in Christ." The *spiritual* application in connection with the church comes before the *literal* application to the eternal kingdom.

The New Jerusalem is declared to be "*the bride, the Lamb's wife.*" Rev. 21: 9. In M.H., p. 356, we read: "He Himself is the Bridegroom; *the bride is the church.*" See also G.C. 381, and notice the texts of Scripture quoted therein; also Ephes. 5: 23-33; Rom. 7: 1-4, etc. Commenting on Rev. 22: 17, which reads "And the Spirit and *the bride* say, Come," the Spirit of Prophecy says: "The church is to say, Come." 9T. 43. The verses in the Revelation prior to this statement refer to the New Jerusalem as "*the bride.*" The Spirit of Prophecy teaches that *the church is the bride* of Christ: but it also teaches, just as plainly, that *the New Jerusalem is Christ's bride.* "The marriage represents the reception by Christ of His kingdom. The holy city, the New Jerusalem, which is the capital and representative of the kingdom, is called 'the bride, the Lamb's wife.' . . . *Clearly, then, the bride represents the holy city.*" G.C. 426, 427; E.W. 251. Christ is now married to His church: His "marriage" to His kingdom (the New Jerusalem is "the capital and representative of the kingdom") takes place just before He returns to the earth. Matt. 25: 1-13; Luke 12: 36. Christ's marriage to the *spiritual* bride (the church) precedes His marriage to His kingdom, with its *literal* things.

His *spiritual* glory in the church precedes the manifestation to the church of His *literal* glory. Col. 1: 26, 27; Luke 17: 20, 21;

2 Thess. 2: 14; 1 Pet. 4: 14; Isa. 40: 1-5 (see P.K., p. 689, where Isa. 40: 5 is *spiritually* applied, and p. 733, where it is *literally* applied in connection with the kingdom of glory); Hag. 2: 3, 7-9; 1 Pet. 1: 10-12; John 17: 22; 1: 14; 12: 41, 45; Ex. 33: 18-22; 34: 5, 6; Isa. 42: 8; 48: 11; Matt. 25: 31; John 17: 24, etc.

Texts describing the new earth have a present *spiritual* application in the experience of the church. See 6T. 24, 308, where Isa. 35: 1, 2 is *spiritually* applied; also 6T. 308, where Isa. 55: 13 (another new earth text) is *spiritually* applied to the church.

Spiritual birth precedes the regeneration of the *physical* world. John 3: 3-7; Titus 3: 5; Matt. 19: 28.

Spiritual salvation, or redemption, occurs before *physical* redemption. Matt. 1: 21; John 1: 12; 3: 36; 1 John 5: 11, 12; Rom. 14: 17; Acts 13: 22, 23; 5: 30, 31; Luke 2: 30-32; Rom. 8: 23; Luke 21: 28.

Spiritual robes of salvation are worn now; eternal robes are to be worn from the time of the second advent. Isa. 61: 10; Rev. 3: 4, 5, 18; 4: 4; 6: 11; 7: 9, 13, etc.

God's people now *spiritually* "follow the Lamb withersoever He goeth"; they *literally* follow Him in His eternal kingdom. Rev. 14: 4; C.O.L. 223; A.A. 591.

Spiritual fire precedes *literal* fire. D.A. 107, 108.

The *spiritual* kingdom of grace precedes the *literal* kingdom of glory. Col. 1: 12, 13; Heb. 4: 16; Matt. 25: 31, etc.

We mount up on *spiritual* wings before we mount on *literal* wings. Isa. 40: 31; E.W. 19; G.C. 677, etc.

The pure in heart see God *spiritually*—see His character revealed everywhere in the Scriptures and in nature (Isa. 40: 5; Ephes. 3: 21; Ex. 33: 18; 34: 5, 6)—before they *actually* see Him. Matt. 5: 8; Rev. 22: 4.

We stand before the throne of God *spiritually* (in the Investigative Judgment, etc.; 1 Kings 17: 1, etc.) before we *literally* stand there. 2 Cor. 5: 10; Rom. 14: 10; Rev. 20: 12; 7: 15.

God's name is *spiritually* written on our foreheads before it is literally written there. Rev. 3: 12; 7: 2-4; 14: 1; 22: 4; E.W. 15, 58.

The Bible is now the *spiritual* tree of life: the eternal, *literal* tree of life will be literally seen and partaken of by the saved after the second advent. Prov. 3: 18, 22; 15: 4; Phil. 2: 16; 1 Pet. 1: 23; M.H. 66, 122, 173, 199; A.A. 478.

We drink of the *spiritual* water of life (Rev. 22: 17) before we drink of the *literal* water of life which "proceeds out of the throne of God and of the Lamb." Rev. 22· 1, 2. See also John 4: 10, 14; 7: 38, 39; Ezek. 47: 1-12; A.A. 13-16; 7T. 24; 9T. 96. The saved literally see the "pure river of water of life" after the second advent.

The *spiritual* shaking occurs before the *literal* shaking. The *literal* shaking of the mountains of the earth at the second advent is mentioned in PP. 340; IT. 184; Joel 3: 16; Heb. 12: 26; Rev. 16: 18. Hag. 2: 6, 7, 21, 22 also mentions the physical upheavals at the second advent. Paul, in Heb. 12: 26-28, connects the *spiritual* and *literal* shakings. After quoting Hag. 2: 6 (which reads: "Yet once more I shake not the earth only, but also heaven"), he says: "And this word, yet once more, signifieth the removing of those things that may be shaken [margin], as of things that are made, that those things which cannot be shaken may remain." From *literal* shakings to take place at the second advent he refers to a *spiritual* shaking which will precede the literal. The *spiritual* shaking is mentioned by the Spirit of Prophecy in IT. 355; 9T. 15, 16, 22, 179-182; E.W. 50, 269-273; T.M. 112; 6T. 332.

The *spiritual* wall of Babylon (the false Sabbath) will fall (Jer. 51: 44; Ezek. 13: 10-16, etc.) when the beast's power collapses (Rev. 19: 20): the *literal* walls of the Babylonian cities will also fall. Rev. 16: 19; Ezek. 38: 19, 20.

Spiritual fire is to devour spiritual Babylon. Jer. 50: 32; 51: 32, 58; Rev. 17: 16; 18: 6-9, 18; 19: 3. At Christ's second advent and at the end of the millennium *literal* fire is employed in the destruction of Babylon. 2 Thess. 1: 7-9; 2: 8; Rev. 19: 20; Ps. 50: 3-5; 97: 3-5; G.C. 638, 641, etc.

Our Lord comes to us *spiritually*, arising in our *spiritual* east as "the Sun of Righteousness" with "healing in His wings" (Mal. 4: 2), before He *literally* appears in the eastern skies at His second advent. P.K. 688; G.C. 632; C.O.L. 415-421; D.A. 22, 48, 464, 468, 677, 680, 755, 801; M.H. 251; 6T. 67, 115, 479; 7T. 74, 195, etc. To the Christian there is a *spiritual* east before the *literal* east. The Scriptures liken our new experience in Christ—of coming "out of darkness into His marvellous light" (1 Pet. 2: 9)—to the dawning of a new day after the darkness of the night. He is "the Sunrising" (Luke 1: 78, margin) in our *spiritual* experience, before He comes as "the sunrising" at His second advent. Rev. 7: 2; 16: 12.

Joel 3: 14 has a *spiritual* application now. 6T. 406; 4T. 446. In the final scenes, the "multitudes" who have rejected God will then be in the valley of concision, or *destruction*.

The church is now encompassed by a *spiritual* wall, as a protection against the assault of Satan's forces: at the end of the millennium the *literal* walls of the New Jerusalem will protect her against Satan's attacking forces. Zech. 2: 5; T.M. 18; D.A. 323, 324; A.A. 600; Rev. 20: 8; Isa. 60: 18.

The description of the Messiah's seat of government, given in Isa. 54, is *spiritually* applied to the church, and is also employed to describe the *literal* New Jerusalem. P.K. 724, 725, etc.

The *spiritual* attack upon, and the surrounding of Christ's church takes place before the *literal* attack upon, and the surrounding of the New Jerusalem. Isa. 54: 15-17; Rev. 14: 20; 20: 8, 9.

We stand "with" Christ on *spiritual* Mt. Sion before we stand "with" Him on the *literal* Mt. Zion. Ephes. 1: 3; Isa. 58: 14; Rev. 14: 1.

We stand "with" Christ in the *spiritual*, world-wide conflict of the last days, when enemies *spiritually* "gather," or "unite," against Christ and His church (Rev. 17: 13, 14; Rev. 16: 13-16; 19: 11-21): we *literally*, visibly stand with Him inside the *literal* New Jerusalem when His enemies *literally* gather outside the holy city. Rev. 20: 8, 9, etc.

Thus we see that the *literal* of the *past*—of Israel's literal kingdom—and the *literal* things of the *future* kingdom of glory have their *spiritual* application in this "dispensation of the Holy Spirit." If this principle is not followed when interpreting prophecies, confusion and error will result. Most of the last-day prophetical errors originate from applying *literally during this dispensation* the *literal* things of Israel's kingdom of the past and the descriptions of the new world. The principle revealed in the New Testament and in the Spirit of Prophecy shows that *the things of Israel* are to be literally applied until the time of Christ's death—which terminated the law of types and shadows *pertaining to Israel* in Palestine—and then, with the literal things of the eternal kingdom, applied *spiritually until the second advent.*

CHAPTER XXIX.

THE TRIPLE APPLICATION OF THE PROPHECIES PERTAINING TO ISRAEL: *"RIGHTLY DIVIDING* THE WORD OF TRUTH." 2 Tim. 2: 15.

In previous chapters we have shown that the Bible is written on the principle of "multum in parvo," or much in little. It is a book written on definite principles, harmonizing logic with spiritual vision. The principles of enlargement by repetition, of the first things foreshadowing the last, the world-wide symbolized in the local things of the past, types and antitypes, past events "acted parables" of future things, "double" applications, etc., prove that nothing in the Scripture is useless or wasted: that the *past* and the *future* are profitable for the *present*.

The principle of going back to where a thing commences and returning by means of a progressive cycle on an ascending scale is clearly seen in Scripture and in nature. In the musical world, this principle is represented by the octave. The octave brings us back to begin again on the same note, but an octave higher. This note, which is eight above the same note below, has so many more vibrations. This same principle is also manifested in light and in colours. The repetitions and antitypes of prophetic imagery (with which the Revelation is replete) are always magnifications of the historical basis upon which they rest. In chapter 21 we referred to the Epanados employed in Rev. 1, which illustrates the law of repetition, whereby the last comes back to the first, but on a higher note, or greater number of vibrations—if we regard it in the terms of the octave. See my "Christ Conquers," pp. 123-139, for further consideration of the use of the number 8 in the Scriptures in relation to this principle. The world is to be restored to its Edenic state at the commencement of the eighth millennium from creation. Previously we have shown that the things in the commencement of Genesis mentioned as lost to man because of sin are restored at the close of the book of Revelation.

Throughout the natural world God illustrates the principle of the progressive cycle on an ascending scale (i.e., a "spiral"). In the study of phyllotaxis—the branch or leaf arrangement of trees and plants—we find that each tree or plant has its normal mathematical number. Commencing with a certain branch or leaf, the stem is circled once, or more, according to the mathematical number of the tree, before the next branch or leaf appears directly above the one from which we commenced to count—and so on up the trunk or branch. Thus, on the spiral system, we recommence to count with the original number—only higher up the tree or plant.

The principle of going back and commencing again by means of a progressive cycle is seen in the days of the week, the months of the year, the seasons, the revolutions of the moon around the earth, the earth around the sun, the sun around its central star, and in all the worlds revolving around the throne of God.

"The sun also ariseth, and goeth down, and hasteth to his place where he arose. The wind goeth toward the south, and turneth about unto the north; it whirleth about continually, and the wind returneth again according to his circuits. All the rivers run into the sea; yet the sea is not full; unto the place from whence the rivers come, *thither they return again*." Eccles. 1: 5-7.

"For as in Adam all die, even so in Christ shall all be made alive." 1 Cor. 15: 22. Christ restores man back to life.

"Behold, I make all things new." Rev. 21: 5. The earth will be restored to even greater glory than before.

This principle in the economy of God—of going back to the commencement on a progressive, ascending scale—must not be overlooked in the interpretation of Bible prophecies. Those things which are introduced in the early parts of the Bible are repeated and enlarged until, in the New Testament, and especially in the Revelation, they are employed in a world-wide sense. "In the Revelation all the books of the Bible meet and end." A.A. 583, 584. A true interpretation of the Scriptures enables us to see in each part that makes up the whole an indication that it is a part of a general plan: that the whole is indicated in the part—as the general shape of the tree is often indicated in the leaf. The Revelation demonstrates principles upon which the whole of the Bible is written. As things mentioned in the early chapters of the Bible are referred to in later books, so, similarly, things mentioned in the early chapters of the Revelation are later referred to in this book. Notice the following examples:—

Christ's second advent. Rev. 1: 7; 3: 3, 11, 20; 6: 14-17; 11: 17, 18; 14: 14-20; 16: 12; 19: 11-21.

The wailing and destruction of the wicked. Rev. 1: 7; 6: 14-17; 19: 11-21.

The seven stars. Rev. 1: 16, 20, 13 compare Rev. 2: 1; 3: 1.

The first and the last. Rev. 1: 8, 11, 17; 2: 8; 22: 13.

Was dead, and is alive. Rev. 1: 18; 2: 8.

A sharp, two-edged sword. Rev. 1: 14, 16; 2: 16; 19: 15.

Eyes as a flaming fire. Rev. 1: 14, 15; 2: 18; 19: 12.

The seven Spirits. Rev. 1: 4; 3: 1; 4: 5; 5: 6.

The faithful Witness. Rev. 1: 5; 3:14; 6: 10; 19: 11.

The true witness. Rev. 3: 14; 19: 11; 22: 6.

The tree of life. Rev. 2: 7; 22: 2.

Jews. Rev. 2: 9; 7: 1-8; 14: 1; 21: 12.

Saints have power over the nations. Rev. 2: 26, 27; 17: 14; 20: 4; Ps. 149: 5-9.

Coming as a thief. Rev. 3: 3; 16: 15.

White raiment. Rev. 3: 5; 6: 11; 7: 14; 19: 8.

Door of sanctuary shut. Rev. 3: 7, 8; 11: 19; 15: 5-8; 16.

The synagogue of Satan. Rev. 2: 9; 13: 6, 8, 14-18; 3: 9; etc.

Where Satan's seat is. Rev. 2: 13; 13: 3; 18: 2.

Queen Jezebel, who influenced her husband, at the head of the state, to lead Israel into sun-worship. Rev. 2: 20; 18: 7.

Hour of test. Rev. 3: 10; 13: 8-18; 14: 6-12.

Warning of the Judgment. Rev. 3: 14-21; 14: 6-12, 14-20; 15; 16.

The 24 elders. Rev. 4: 4, 10; 5: 8, 14; 11: 16; 19: 4.

The four beasts. Rev. 4: 6; 5: 8, 14; 6: 1, 3, 5, 6, 7; 19- 4.

The temple. Rev. 3: 12; 7: 15; 11: 1, 2; 14: 15, 17; 15: 5-8.

The holy city. Rev. 3: 12; 11: 1, 2; 14: 20; 21; 22.

God's name. Rev. 3: 12; 14: 1. (See 1 Kings 8: 16-20, 29, 44, 48; Deut. 12: 5, 11, 21, etc.)

God's name in the fourth Commandment. Rev. 7: 1-4; 14: 1.

The Lord's Day. Rev. 1: 10; 7: 1-4; 14: 1, etc.

The seven lamps or seven Spirits. Rev. 1: 4; 3: 1; 4: 5; 5: 6.

The prayer altar. Rev. 5: 8; 8: 3; 9: 13; 14: 18.

Kings and priests. Rev. 1: 6; 5: 10; 20: 4.

The kings of the earth. Rev. 1: 5; 6: 15; 16: 14; 17: 12 -14; 19: 19.

Thus we see illustrated in the Revelation the principle of employing again that which has been mentioned previously. The 6,000 years of struggle between the forces of good and evil are fuller developments of the words of Gen. 3: 15. Genesis is known to Bible students as "the seed plot of the Bible." Similarly, the early chapters of the Revelation contain the germ of later developments. By repetitions of the seed thought presented in the early chapters of his book (Rev. 1: 7, etc.), the Revelator works towards the great climax in the struggle between the forces of God and of Satan—the slaughter of the enemies of spiritual Israel in the antitypical Megiddo conflict. He would not depart from his theme of outlining the final clash between Christ and Satan—towards which he had been moving all through his book—in order to depict a conflict between nations. To apply "the kings of the east" of Rev. 16: 12 to Japan, China, etc.—nations which are not mentioned, or even hinted at, in the book—is entirely foreign to the theme of the Revelation. But a grand culmination of all the pictures and repetitions from Rev. 1: 7; 6: 14-17 to Rev. 19: 11-21 is seen when Rev. 16: 12 is applied to the glorious appearing of Christ (with His vast retinue of angels, etc.) in the eastern skies as He comes to deliver spiritual Israel, and to destroy spiritual Babylon.

In describing the scenes of the conflict over the keeping of the Commandments of God, the Revelator takes his imagery from previous portions of the Scriptures. He employs the experiences of ancient Israel in his pictures outlining the final conflict. The past is used to describe the present—in a spiritual, world-wide sense.

THE TRIPLE APPLICATION OF THE PROPHECIES PERTAINING TO ISRAEL.

In earlier chapters we have shown that the *literal* application belonged to the days of *literal* Israel: to the days when the *literal* glory of God was manifested, and things were upon a *literal, national* basis. In this "dispensation of the Holy Spirit," the things of Israel apply *spiritually*. Later, in the eternal kingdom, where the *literal* glory of the Lord will be revealed again, things pertaining to Israel will be literal.

The principle of the triple application enables us to "rightly divide the word of truth." This triple application of the prophecies causes all things to fall into their respective places, in—

(1) The *national* kingdom of God, in the time of the *literal* economy: centred in Jerusalem, and pertaining to the land of Israel.

(2) Christ's *spiritual* kingdom: centred in spiritual Jerusalem, the church, and embracing the world.

(3) Christ's eternal kingdom: with His seat of government *literally* centred in the New Jerusalem.

Christ is the centre of each of the three-fold applications of the prophecies of the blessings to, and the designations, etc., of Israel.

EXAMPLES OF THE TRIPLE APPLICATION.

NATIONAL ISRAEL.	SPIRITUAL ISRAEL.	NEW WORLD.
Literal Kingdom: Visible King, City, Temple, Sacrifices, Altars, etc.	Spiritual Kingdom. Luke 17: 20, 21, margin; 1 Pet. 2: 5, 9; 1 Cor. 10: 3, 4· Col. 1: 13; AA. 30, 28, 39; GC. 347, 348; DA. 506; Heb. 4: 16; Heb. 8: 1; Zech. 6: 13, etc.	Literal, Visible Kingdom. Rev. 21, 22, etc.
Holy Nation. Ex. 19: 5, 6.	Holy Nation. 1 Pet. 2: 9; Zeph. 2: 1; Matt. 21: 43.	Holy Nation. Isa. 26: 2; 51: 4, 7; 66: 22, 23.
Kingdom of Priests. Ex. 19: 5, 6.	Kingdom of Priests. 1 Pet. 2: 5, 9; Rev. 1: 6; Rev. 4: 4; 5: 10.	Kingdom of Priests. Rev. 20: 4; 3: 21.
A Peculiar Treasure. Ex. 19: 5, 6.	A Peculiar Treasure. 1 Pet. 2: 9.	A Special Treasure. Mal. 3: 17, margin.
God's People. Hos. 1: 9-10; Rom. 9: 6-8.	God's People. 1 Pet. 2: 9.	God's People. Rev. 21: 3.
A Holy People. Deut. 7: 6.	A Holy People. 1 Pet. 1: 15, 16.	A Holy People. Rev. 20: 6; 22: 11.
A People of Inheritance. Deut. 4: 20.	A People of Inheritance. Eph. 1: 18.	"Eternal Inheritance." Heb. 9: 15.
Israel's Shepherd. Jer. 31: 10.	Israel's Shepherd. John 10: 11.	Israel's Shepherd. Rev. 7: 17.
Israel's Salvation. Isa. 45: 17.	Israel's Salvation. Heb. 5: 9; 9: 15.	Israel's Salvation. Rev. 19: 1.
God's Tabernacle Among Israel. Lev. 26: 11.	God's Tabernacle Among Israel. John 1: 14.	God's Tabernacle Among Israel. Rev. 21: 3; Ezek. 37: 26-28.
Seven Lamps in the *Literal* Temple. Ex. 25: 31-37.	Seven Lamps in the *Spiritual* Temple, the Church. Rev. 1: 12, 13, 20; 2: 1.	Seven Lamps Burning in the Heavenly Temple. Rev. 4: 5.
Literal Priests Wore "Fine Linen" Called "Holy Garments." Lev 6: 10; 16: 4, 32; Ezek. 44: 17, 18.	*Spiritual* Priests Now Wear *Spiritual* "Holy Garments." Isa. 61: 10; Rev. 3: 4, 5, 18; 6: 11, etc.	In Heaven, the Saints Wear "White Robes." Rev. 4: 4; 7: 9, 13, etc.
God Walked Among Them. Lev. 26: 12.	God Walks Among His People. 2 Cor. 6: 16-18.	God Dwells With His People. Rev. 21: 3.

National Israel.	Spiritual Israel.	New World.
Christ Married to His People. Isa. 54: 5; Jer. 3: 14; Hos. 2: 19; Jer. 6: 2; 31: 32.	Christ Married to the Church. Ephes. 5: 23-33; 2 Cor. 11: 2; Jas. 4: 4; Rom. 7: 1-4; Rev. 12 (Christ's bride); MH. 356.	Christ Married to the New Jerusalem. Rev. 21: 9; 19: 7-9; Matt. 25: 10; Luke 12: 36.
Christ Reigned in Jerusalem. 1 Chron. 29: 3; Zech. 8: 3; Ps. 132: 13; 43: 2; Matt. 5: 35; Zech. 2: 5, 10, 11; Joel 3: 21; Isa. 2: 2; Micah 4: 2.	Christ reigns in the Church. Ephes. 2: 20-22; 1 Cor. 3: 16; 2 Cor. 6: 16; John 14: 16-23. Acts of Apostles, pp. 11, 12, 600.	Christ Will Reign in the New Jerusalem. Rev. 22: 1, 3.
Literal Gathering to Jerusalem—for their festivals, etc.	Spiritual Gathering to Jerusalem—the Church. Isa. 11: 11, 12; PK. 375, 376; E.W. 74, 75; 6T. 133; 7T. 172; 9T. 51; Isa. 60: 3, 4, 6, 7, 9; PK. 375; AA. 595; Rev. 18: 4.	Literal Gathering to the New Jerusalem. Rev. 21: 24-27; 22: 14; Isa. 66: 22, 23.
Literal Zion. Ps. 50: 2; 2: 6.	Spiritual Zion — the Church. Joel 2: 32; Rom. 10: 13; Isa, 28: 16; 1 Pet. 2: 6-8; Isa. 59: 20; Rom. 11: 26; Ps. 2: 6.	Eternal Zion. Rev. 14: 1; Ps. 2: 6.
Enemies *Literally* Gathered Against Israel. Isa. 8: 7, 8; 36: 1, 2, 37; 54: 15, 17; Ezek. 38, 39; Zech. 12: 3, 9; 14: 1, 2.	E n e m i e s *Spiritually* Gather Against the Church. Isa. 54: 15, 17; Rev. 14: 20; 16: 14-16; 17: 14; 19: 19; Zech. 12: 3, 9; 14: 1, 2; Ezek. 38, 39; Joel 3, etc.	Enemies *Literally* Gather Against the Saved Within the. New Jerusalem. Rev. 20: 8, 9.

Many more examples of this triple application of the Scriptures could be given, for the principle is employed throughout the Bible. This triple application, which arises out of the nature of the Trinity, simplifies the understanding of the Scriptures, as it causes all things to automatically fall into their proper places. , That which was *literal* in relation to *national* Israel centred in *literal* Jerusalem is given its "double," or *spiritual,* application in relation to Christ's *spiritual* kingdom of grace centred in *spiritual* Jerusalem, the church; and its triple application—which is *literal*—in relation to the New Jerusalem. The same pictures which are *spiritually* applied before the second advent, have their triple—their final—application, in a *literal* sense, in connection with the *literal* New Jerusalem.

The *millennium* is the dividing line between the *spiritual* application of this dispensation and the future *literal application*. This is clearly taught in the Revelation and in the Spirit of Prophecy. That which is literal *after* the millennium has a spiritual application *before* the millennium. We need to apply this principle to understand the Scriptural teaching concerning Armageddon, before, and after the millennium.

CHAPTER XXX.

SPIRITUAL LESSONS FROM THE NEW JERUSALEM: FURTHER PROVING THE BIBLE PRINCIPLE OF THE *SPIRITUAL* APPLICATION *BEFORE*, AND THE *LITERAL* APPLICATION *AFTER*, THE MILLENNIUM.

After the millennium, the literal "holy city, new Jerusalem, coming down from God out of heaven, prepared as a bride adorned for her husband" (Rev. 21: 2), will descend to the place prepared by God, in the locality which, at one time, was the *literal* land of Israel. Compare Rev. 21: 2 with Zech. 14: 4. Then, *literal* things of the eternal kingdom will be centred in the New Jerusalem as, similarly, the *literal* things of national Israel had centred in old Jerusalem. During the Christian era, the church—spiritual Jerusalem—is the centre of *spiritual* things. The millennium is the dividing line on earth between the *spiritual* things centring around *spiritual* Jerusalem—the church—and the *literal* things centring around the *literal* New Jerusalem. Just as the terminology of national Israel is employed to describe the church, so the language descriptive of the New Jerusalem is also applicable to the church: it is applicable to the church *now*, during the kingdom of grace, but *after* the millennium it is applicable to the *literal* New Jerusalem.

BEFORE THE MILLENNIUM: THE *SPIRITUAL* JERUSALEM (THE CHURCH).	AFTER THE MILLENNIUM: THE *LITERAL* NEW JERUSALEM.
Church—a city. Matt. 5: 14; Isa. 62: 12, 1, 4; 54: 1-17; 60: 11-20; 1 Cor. 6: 16; A.A. 11, 12.	"The holy city, New Jerusalem." Rev. 21: 2, 9-27; 22: 1-5, 14-17, 19; Isa. 52: 1; Gal. 4: 26; Heb. 11: 10; 12: 22; 13: 14; Rev. 3: 12.
Church—city and temple. G.C. 266; TM. 17; AA. 595; 6T. 363; AA. 599; Mt. Blessing 216; 9T. 180; PK. 36; Rev. 11: 1-2.	Temple and city inseparable. Rev. 3: 12; Ezra 1: 2-5; Dan. 9: 16-18; Ezek. 40-48; Isa. 60: 11-14; 1 Kings 8: 29, 38, 41-44; Num. 2: 2-17; Ex. 29: 45-46; 25: 8; Ezek. 43: 7-9; 37: 26-28; Rev. 21: 1-3, 5. "In the city I saw a temple." E.W. 32. (Rev. 21: 22, see GC. 676.)

The church measured: "His church is to be a temple . . . the angelic architect has brought his golden measuring rod, that every stone may be hewed and squared by the divine measurement." T.M. 17; 7T. 219. See Rev. 21: 15-17; 11: 1-2; Zech. 2: 1-2; Ezek. 40-48.

Church is born from above. John 3: 3, 7, 31; James 3: 15-17.

Church is the bride. Jer. 6: 2; 2 Cor. 11: 2; Ephes. 5: 23-32; Rom. 7: 1-4.

"The bride is the church." M.H., p. 356. 6T. 23 applies Isa. 54: 2 to the church: "The words of the Lord in the fifty-fourth of Isaiah are for us." Mt. Bless., p. 100; P.K. 374: "He heard the Lord saying of the gospel church . . . and he heard the commission." Isa. 54: 2, 3 is then quoted.

Church—bride—is to develop character so that she may live with Christ. Rev. 3: 4; 19: 7, 8; G.C., p. 428; C.O.L. 307-312. "That I may present you as a chaste virgin to Christ." 2 Cor. 11: 2; Isa. 54: 5; 61: 10; Matt. 25: 1-11; Rev. 14: 4.

"Ye are the temple [sanctuary R.V.] of the living God; as God hath said, I will dwell in them . . . and they shall be My people." 2 Cor. 6: 16; Lev. 26: 11, 12; Ezek. 43: 7; 37: 26-28; 1 Cor. 3: 16, 17; 6: 19; John 2: 19-21; P.K. 36; T.M. 17; A.A. 595-598; 8T. 246.

The church has Christ tabernacling with her. John 1: 14, R.V.; Matt. 1: 23: "God with us." Matt. 28: 18-20; John 14: 23.

"The place of My throne." Ezek. 43: 7. "The Lord is there." Ezek. 48: 35. Ezekiel's city and temple are a representation of the church and of the individual wherein God reigns. John 14: 21-23; Rom. 8: 9-11; 5: 17-21; 6: 12-16, etc.

Temple and city measured. Rev. 11: 1-2; 21: 15-17; Zech. 2: 1-2; Ezek. 40: 3-49; 41; 42; 43; 48: 31-35.

"Coming down from God out of heaven." Rev. 21: 2.

"Bride adorned for her husband." Rev. 21: 2. "The bride, the Lamb's wife." Rev. 21: 9, 10.

"The bride represents the holy city." G.C., p. 426; E.W., p. 251. Isa. 54: 5; 2 Cor. 11: 2; Isa. 61: 10; in margin of Rev. 21: 2 show translators coupled the literal, heavenly bride with the spiritual, earthly bride. Also see Rev. 19: 7, with marginal references.

"Prepared as a bride adorned for her husband." Rev. 21: 2. "His wife hath made herself ready." Rev. 19: 7. See also Isa. 54: 5; 61: 10.

"The tabernacle of God is with men, and He will dwell with them, and they shall be His people." Rev. 21: 2-5.

"The throne of God and of the Lamb shall be in it." Rev. 22: 3. See also Ezek. 48: 35; Jer. 3: 17; Joel 3: 21; Zech. 2: 10; Rev. 21: 3, etc.

316

"Blessed are they that mourn, for they shall be comforted." Matt. 5: 4. Isa. 61: 2-3: "To comfort all that mourn; to appoint unto them that mourn in Zion, to give unto them beauty for ashes, the oil of joy for mourning, the garment of praise for the spirit of heaviness." Luke 4: 18; John 16: 20; 2 Cor. 1: 3-7.

"He that hath the Son hath everlasting life." John 3: 36; Rom. 1: 17; Gal. 2: 20; 3: 11; Heb. 10: 38; 1 John 5: 10-13.

"Put off concerning the *former* conversation the old man." Eph. 4: 22; Col. 3: 9; Heb. 12: 1; Rom. 6: 1-6; 7: 24. "In Christ . . . old things are *passed away.*" 2 Cor. 5: 17.

"*All things* are become *new.*" 2 Cor. 5: 17. "If any man be in Christ, he is a *new creature* [Variorum Bible and R.V., margin "creation"]: old things are passed away; behold, all things are become new." See also Gal. 6: 15; Col. 3: 9, 10; Ephes. 4: 22-24.

"Jesus the *beginner* and *finisher* of our faith." Heb. 12: 2, margin. Phil. 1: 6, margin: "He which hath *begun* a good work in you will *finish* it." Rev. 3: 14.

"Whatsoever we ask we receive of Him, *because* we keep His commandments, and do those things that are pleasing in His sight." 1 John 3: 22. Isa. 1: 19; Ex. 19: 5; Gen. 22: 18; Heb. 5: 9. If we obey, the Holy Spirit is given. Acts 5: 32. The Spirit "brings all other blessings in its train." AA. 50; C.O.L. 327, 419.

"Obey My voice, and I will be *your* God, and ye shall be *My people.*" Jer. 7: 23; 11: 4-7; Zech. 8: 8; Heb. 8: 10. "I will be a Father unto

"And God shall wipe away all tears from their eyes, and there shall be no more death, neither sorrow, nor crying. Rev. 21: 4. See also Isa. 35: 10; 61: 3; 65: 19.

"No more death." Rev. 21: 4.

"The *former* things are *passed away.*" Rev. 21: 4.

"Behold, I make *all things new.*" Rev. 21: 5.

"I am Alpha and Omega, the *beginning* and the *end.*" Rev. 21: 6. "The *beginning* and the *ending.*" Rev. 1: 8.

"He that overcometh shall *inherit all things.*" Rev. 21: 7.

"And I will be *his* God, and he shall be *My son.*" Rev. 21: 7.

you, and ye shall be My sons and daughters, saith the Lord Almighty." 2 Cor. 6: 18.

Angels lead us to the church. Acts 8: 26. Rev. 14: 6-9: Angels have oversight of church. Dan. 9: 21-22; Angels make Bible plain to us. Heb. 1: 14: Ministering spirits to the church.

"In the visions of God brought he me into the land of Israel, and set me upon a *very high mountain,* by which was the frame of a city." Ezek. 40: 2. John's description of the New Jerusalem is partly based upon Ezekiel's vision. The Spirit of Prophecy applies Ezekiel's vision to the church. Ezekiel's temple and city will not be *literally* built in the land of Israel: the vision has a *spiritual* fulfilment in the church—its *literal* counterpart is in the New Jerusalem. Heb. 13: 14; 11: 16, 10.

"The spirit of *glory* and of God resteth upon you." 1 Pet. 4: 14. "Called you out of darkness into His marvellous light." 1 Pet. 2: 9. Acts 26: 18; Eph. 5: 8; Col. 1: 13; 1 Thess. 5: 4-5; 2 Cor. 4: 4.

"For I, saith the Lord, will be unto her a *wall* of fire round about." Zech. 2: 5. This promise to Jerusalem is applied by the Spirit of Prophecy to the church: the "Holy Spirit . . . is to be to His church as an encompassing wall of fire." T.M. 18. "What a God is our God! He rules over His kingdom with a diligence and care; and He has built a hedge—the ten commandments—about His subjects, to preserve them from the results of transgression." CT. 454.

"There were sealed a 144,000 of all the tribes of the children of Israel." Rev. 7: 3-8. *Twelve* thousand of each of the *twelve* tribes are sealed.

"And there came unto me one of the . . . *angels* . . . saying, Come hither, I will shew thee the bride, the Lamb's wife." Rev. 21: 9.

"And he carried me . . . to a *great and high mountain,* and shewed me that great City, the holy Jerusalem descending out of heaven from God." Rev. 21: 10. See also Ezek. 40: 2.

"Having the *glory* of God." Rev. 21: 11.

"And had a *wall* great and high." Rev. 21: 12. See Ezek. 48: 31-34.

"And had *twelve* gates . . . and names written thereon, which are the names of the *twelve* tribes of Israel." Rev. 21: 12. See also Ezek. 48: 31-34.

318

The *three* angels' messages show the way into the spiritual Jerusalem. Rev. 14: 6-12, etc.

"Jesus Christ, both in the Old and New Testament, is called a *foundation*. Isa. 28: 16; 1 Cor. 3: 11. Other *foundation* can no man lay, than that is laid, which is Jesus Christ. And the abovementioned passage in Isa. 28: 16 is cited by Peter, and applied to Christ, 1 Pet. 2: 6."—Cruden.

"The *foundation* of God standeth sure." 2 Tim. 2: 19; Gal. 2: 9; Rev. 3: 12; Ephes. 2: 20. 1 Cor. 3: 9-15 makes it clear that we build on Christ the foundation.

"The angelic architect has brought his *golden measuring* rod from heaven, that every stone may be hewed and squared by the divine *measurement*." T.M. 17. Ps. 48: 12-13; 122: 3. "The holy city (the true church)." GC. 266. See Rev. 11: 1. The spirit of Prophecy has given us a spiritual interpretation of the temple of Ezekiel. Hence the measuring of it, which is identical with the measuring of the holy city, shows that the New Jerusalem has a church aspect to-day. The measuring of Jerusalem mentioned in Zech. 2 refers to the church.

The church is perfectly symmetrical; Christ is the foundation, and every stone is measured and polished by God. Twelve is the kingdom number. There were 12 tribes of Israel; the church had 12 apostles; the New Jerusalem has 12 foundations; 12 gates; the tree of life bearing 12 fruits, etc. The remnant of spiritual Israel is said to number 144,000 (Rev. 7: 4; 14: 1) —the same number as the cubits in the measurement of the wall mentioned in v. 17. Rev. 21.

"On the east *three* gates; on the north *three gates;* on the south *three* gates; and on the west *three* gates." Rev. 21: 13. See also Ezek. 48: 31-34.

"And the wall of the city had twelve *foundations,* and in them the names of the twelve apostles of the Lamb." Rev. 21: 14. See also Heb. 11: 10.

"And he that talketh with me had a *golden reed* to *measure* the city, and the gates thereof, and the wall thereof." Rev. 21: 15. See also Ezek. 40: 3 and onwards, which pictures the angel measuring everything with the measuring reed. Zech. 2: 1-2: "A *measuring* line in his hand . . . to *measure Jerusalem,* to see what is the breadth thereof, and what is the length thereof." Rev. 11: 1: "And there was given me a reed like unto a rod . . . rise, *measure* the temple."

"And the city lieth four-square, and the length is as large as the breadth; and he measured the city with the reed, *twelve* thousand furlongs. The length and the breadth and the height of it are equal. And he measured the wall thereof, an *hundred and forty and four cubits,* according to the measure of a man, that is, of the angel." Rev. 21: 16-17.

"Foundation . . . Jesus Christ . . . if any man build upon this foundation, gold, silver, and precious stones." 1 Cor. 3: 11-12. Gold symbolises divine character. Rev. 3: 18. '"Gold tried in the fire"— i.e., free from dross, or sin. 2 Sam. 22: 31; Ps. 18: 30, margin; Zech. 13: 9; D.A. 280; C.O.L. 158; 4T. 88-89.

"Through the ages . . . the building of God's temple has never ceased. We may look back through the centuries, and see the living stones of which it is composed gleaming like jets of light. . . . Throughout eternity these precious jewels will shine. . . . The flashing light of these polished stones. . . . We are to bring to the foundation material that will stand the test of fire— gold, silver, and precious stones, 'polished after the similitude of a palace'." AA. 598-599. PK. 724, 725 quotes Isa. 54: 11-17—which mentions the precious foundation stones—in relation to the church.

"The kingdom of heaven is like unto a merchantman, seeking goodly pearls: who, when he had found one pearl of great price, went and sold all that he had, and bought it." Matt. 13: 45, 46. Christ is the pearl. (See C.O.L., pp. 115-121.) He is the entrance into the church. Christ provided "a new and living way." Heb. 10: 20. A pearl is made by suffering: Christ "suffered for us." 1 Pet. 2: 21; 1: 11. "We must through much tribulation enter into the kingdom of God." Acts 14: 22.

"Pure gold," clear, like glass, represents the divine purity of the path the church must tread to God's throne. Rev. 3: 18; Heb. 12: 14; Matt. 5: 8; 2 Cor. 7: 1; Ephes. 5: 5; Matt. 7: 13, 14. The sacred vessels and the furniture of the

"And the building of the wall of it was of Jasper; and the city was pure gold, like unto clear glass." Concerning the building of the wall the Var. Bible says, "i.e., work above the foundation." Rev. 21: 18.

"And the foundations of the wall of the city were garnished with all manner of precious stones." Rev. 21: 19-20. See also Isa. 54: 11-12.

"And the twelve gates were twelve pearls; every several gate was of one pearl." Rev. 21: 21.

"And the street of the city was *pure gold*, as it were transparent glass." Rev. 21: 21.

Before the Millennium:	After the Millennium:

holy places of the sanctuary and temple were made of gold.

"Called . . . into His marvellous *light.*" 1 Pet. 2: 9; Ps. 36: 9; 84: 11; Mal. 4: 2; John 9: 5; 2 Cor. 4: 4. The Bible teaches that God and Christ are the light of the church. See chapter 25 dealing with "The Kings from the Sunrising." Isa. 60: 18, which gives a description of Jerusalem, is applied in G.C. 675 and PK. 730 to the New Jerusalem; but in PK. 375 and AA. 595, Isa. 60: 10, 11 is applied to the church.

"And the city had no need of the sun, neither of the moon, to shine in it: for the *glory of God did lighten it,* and the *Lamb is the light* thereof." Rev. 21: 23. "The *Lord God giveth them light.*" Rev. 22: 5. See also Rev. 21: 24, 25; Isa. 60: 19, 20, etc.

People from all nations are now walking into the church. The Revelator (Rev. 21: 24-26) quotes from Isa. 60: 10, 12. PK. 375 and AA. 595 apply Isa. 60: 10, 12 to the church to-day. What will be *literally* true on earth in the eternal kingdom has a *spiritual* application to the church now.

"And the nations of them which are saved shall walk in the light of it; and the kings of the earth do bring their glory and honour into it. And the gates of it shall not be shut at all by day: for there shall be no night there. And they shall bring the glory and honour of the nations into it." Rev. 21: 24-26. See also Isa. 60: 10, 11.

"Thy people also shall be all righteous." Isa. 60: 21. "O Zion, put on thy beautiful garments, O Jerusalem, the holy city; for henceforth there shall no more come into thee the uncircumcised and the unclean." Isa. 52: 1. In 9T. 108, 6T. 434, this verse is applied to the church to-day. In PK. 725 the same text is applied to the New Jerusalem.

"And there shall in no wise enter into it anything that defileth." Rev. 21: 27; Isa. 60: 21; Joel 3: 17; Isa. 52: 1; 35: 8, etc.

"*Living water* . . . a well of water springing up into everlasting life." John 4: 10-14. "Out of his belly shall flow rivers *of living waters. But this He spake of the Spirit.*" John 7: 37-39. "*Living waters* shall go out from Jerusalem." Zech. 14: 8; Isa. 12: 3; 55: 1, etc. "And whosoever will, let him take the *water of life freely.*" Rev. 22: 17. To-day we partake of the *spiritual,* living waters: in the eternal kingdom we shall drink *literal* waters.

"A pure river of *water of life* . . . proceeding out of the throne of God and of the Lamb." Rev. 22: 1. "I will give unto him that is athirst of the fountain of the *water of life* freely." Rev. 21: 6. See also Ezek. 47: 1-12; Zech. 14: 8; Joel 3: 18.

"And by the river upon the bank thereof, on this side and on that side, shall grow all trees for meat . . . it shall bring forth new fruit according to his months . . . and the leaf thereof for medicine." Ezek. 47: 12. "Wonderful is the work which the Lord designs to accomplish through *His church.* . . . The *picture of this work is given in Ezekiel's vision* of the river of healing." AA., pp. 13, 14; 7T. 171, 236; 6T. 227, 288.

"Christ . . . brings us to *His Word,* and from *the tree of life* presents to us leaves for the healing of sin-sick souls." AA. 478; MH. 66, 122, 173, 199; 6T. 393.

The Bible is the tree of life—in the • midst of the church. The Living and the written Word go together.

"On either side of the river: was there the tree of life, which bare twelve manner of fruits, and yielded her fruit every month; and the leaves of the tree were for the healing of the nations." Rev. 22: 2.

"The tree of life . . . and the leaves of the tree were for the healing of the nations." Rev. 22: 2. See also Ezek. 47: 12; Gen. 2: 9.

The tree of life was in Eden: it was translated to heaven (P.P. 62) and is now "in the midst of the Paradise of God." Rev. 2: 7.

BIBLE.	JESUS.	BOTH ARE
Mark 7: 13.	Rev. 19: 13.	Word of God.
Phil. 2: 16.	1 John 1: 1.	Word of life.
2 Tim. 3: 15.	Heb. 7: 26.	Holy.
Ps. 119: 140.	1 John 3: 3.	Pure.
Heb. 4: 2.	1 Cor. 1: 24.	Powerful.
Rev. 21: 5.	Heb. 3: 1, 2.	Faithful
Ps. 33: 4.	1 John 2: 29.	Righteous.
John 17: 17.	John 14: 6.	True.
John 6: 63.	John 14: 6.	Life.
Ps. 119: 105, 130.	John 1: 8, 9.	Light.
John 6: 63.	John 3: 34.	Spiritual.
Ps. 19: 7; 18: 30.	Isa. 28: 16.	Sure.
Matt. 4: 4.	John 6: 35.	Food.
Heb. 4: 12.	Matt. 12: 25.	Discerners of thoughts and hearts.

Sabbath-keepers have the Father's name *spiritually* written in their foreheads. Rev. 3: 12; 14: 1; 7: 1-4.

"His name shall be in their foreheads." Rev. 22: 4.

"Beware of *dogs,* beware of evil workers." Phil. 3: 2. "But if ye *bite* and *devour* one another, take heed that ye be not consumed one of another." Gal. 5: 15; Isa. 56: 10, 11. The wicked will be out-

"For without are *dogs.*" Rev. 22: 15.

side the city at the end of the millennium, ready to devour · the righteous; similarly, those who now bite and devour are not really in the church.

The "bride" in Rev. 22: 17 refers to both the church and the New Jerusalem. The Spirit, through the church — the earthly, *spiritual* bride—says "Come." See 9T. 43. Also, through the descriptions of the *literal bride*, New Jerusalem, the Spirit says "Come." We *spiritually* drink of the waters of life now; we *literally* drink in the eternal kingdom.

"And the Spirit and the bride say, Come. And let him that is athirst come. And whosoever will let him take of the water of life freely." Rev. 22: 17.

The description applying both to the New Jerusalem and its *spiritual* counterpart, the church, further proves the principle that those things which apply *literally* on earth *after* the millennium are *spiritually* applied *before* the millennium.

CHAPTER XXXI.

THE TEACHING OF A LITERAL, PALESTINIAN "ARMAGEDDON" VIOLATES THE BIBLE PRINCIPLE THAT THINGS WHICH APPLY *LITERALLY AFTER* THE MILLENNIUM APPLY *SPIRITUALLY BEFORE* THE MILLENNIUM.

Previous chapters demonstrate the principle that things which apply *literally after* the millennium apply *spiritually before* the millennium. The following prophetic descriptions concerning Armageddon further illustrate the operation of this principle:—

SPIRITUAL BEFORE THE MILLENNIUM.	LITERAL AFTER THE MILLENNIUM.
The *spiritual* Jerusalem, the church. Rev. 11: 1, 2; G.C. 266; Rev. 14: 20; Joel 2: 32, etc.	The *literal* New Jerusalem. Rev. 21: 22.
Spiritual Israel is now coming out of spiritual Babylon, and is *spiritually* gathering within the *spiritual* Jerusalem. Rev. 18: 4; Ephes. 2: 20-22; Rev. 11: 1, 2; Isa. 11: 11, 12; E.W. 74, 75.	The saints will be *literally* within the *literal* New Jerusalem.
The *spiritual* enemies of *spiritual* Israel *spiritually* "gather," or "unite." .. The Greek word for "gather" in Rev. 16: 14, and "gathered" in Rev. 16: 16; 19: 19, etc., is "Sunago"—derived from "sun." Dr. Strong gives "union" as the first definition of "sun." Mrs. E. G. White very often employs the word "united" in describing the spiritual armies engaged in the coming conflict. See Vols. 5T. 449, 524; G.C. 582, 590, 604; T.M. 39, etc. In G.C. 623 we are given the Lord's interpretation of Rev. 16: 14. When quoting this verse God's servant uses the word "unite"—referring	The enemies of the saints *literally* "gather" around the *literal* New Jerusalem. Rev. 20: 8, 9.

to a spiritual gathering—instead of the word "gather," which is in the text. See also G.C. 561. 562, 656; T.M. 465, etc. For further study see my other publications.

Before the millennium, Satan *deceives* the people of *spiritual* Babylon concerning the *spiritual* "mark"— the false Sabbath, the mark of *spiritual* Babylon's power. See Rev. 12: 9; 13: 13, 14. "He *deceived* them that had received the *mark* of the beast." Rev. 19: 20.

To further his deception concerning the *spiritual* mark Satan works *"miracles."* The *"miracles"* which "the spirits of devils" perform in conjunction with the dragon, beast, and false prophet (Rev. 16: 14) are not connected with military matters. These *miracles, signs,* or *wonders,* referred to in Scripture, demonstrate the *spiritual* power possessed by the persons who perform them—whether on God's side, or on Satan's. The original word is employed in the Scripture at least 77 times, but *not once* is it used in a national or international sense. See Luke 23: 8; John 2: 11, 23; 3: 2; 4: 54; 6: 2, 14, 26; 7: 31; 9: 16; 10: 41; 11: 47; 12: 18, 37; Acts 4: 16, 22; 6: 8; 8: 6; 15: 12; Rev. 13: 13, 14; 16: 14; 19: 20, etc. In the final conflict, in order to obtain from worldly rulers and people support for the enforcement of Sunday laws, the dragon, the beast, and the false prophet will work "miracles." Through the deceptive powers of spiritualism the world will be led to "war" against God's law. For further study see my other publications.

Before the millennium, Satan wages a *spiritual* "war" against spiritual Israel. Rev. 12: 17. He does this through the enforcement of Sun-

After the millennium, Satan *deceives* the wicked to believe that they have been resurrected by his power, and that by his power they will take the holy city. "Satan shall . . . go out to *deceive* the nations." Rev. 20: 8, 9. After the millennium, Satan's deception concerns *literal* things.

To further his deception concerning the taking of the literal Jerusalem, "Satan works *wonders* to support his claim." G.C. 663.

After the millennium, Satan will wage a *literal* "war," or "battle," against the literal New Jerusalem. "Satan shall . . . gather them together to

day laws. G.C. 592, etc. The word "battle" mentioned in Rev. 16: 14; 20: 8, and the word "war" of Rev. 12: 7, 17; 13: 7; 19: 19 come from the same Greek word, "polemos." The same conflict is referred to—the controversy between Christ and Satan. "The battle [Greek, "polemos"] of that great day of God Almighty" refers to the slaughter of those who have made spiritual "war" upon spiritual Israel.

When describing the destruction of the enemies of spiritual Israel at the second advent, the Revelator quotes from Ezekiel's prophecy (compare Rev. 19: 17-20 with Ezek. 39: 17-20), which pictures Gog's army attacking Israel and being utterly destroyed by God.

When describing the destruction of the enemies of spiritual Israel at the second advent, the Revelator says that Christ "treadeth the winepress of the fierceness and wrath of God." Rev. 19: 15. This statement refers back to the prophecy concerning the destruction of Edom and Bozrah. See Isa. 34: 1-10; 63: 1-6. The Edomites were the enemies of ancient Israel. As shown in a previous chapter, the meanings of the names "Edom" and "Bozrah" are of special significance in relation to the treading of the winepress of God's wrath in the battle of Armageddon.

When describing the destruction of those who reject the Third Angel's Message delivered by spiritual Israel, the Revelator quotes from the prophecy of Isa. 34: 6-10, which concerns the burning of the land of Idumea. See Rev. 14: 9-11; 18: 9, 18; 19: 3, and notice the same words employed as in Isa. 34: 9, 10.

battle." "All immediately begin to prepare for battle. Skilful artisans construct implements of war. Military leaders, famed for their success, marshal the throngs of warlike men into companies and divisions. . . . With military precision, the serried ranks advance . . . to the city of God." G.C. 664.

When describing the destruction of the enemies of the saints at the end of the millennium, the Revelator quotes from Ezekiel's prophecy (compare Rev. 20: 8, 9 with Ezek. 38; 39), which pictures Gog's army attacking Israel and being utterly destroyed by God.

When describing the destruction of the enemies of the saints inside the New Jerusalem at the end of the millennium, the Revelator says "And the winepress was trodden without the city." Rev. 14: 20.

When describing the destruction of the enemies of the saints in the New Jerusalem at the end of the millennium, the Revelator quotes from the same prophecy relating to the burning of the land of Idumea, and employs the same words. Rev. 20: 10; 21: 8.

Thus, the same principle that things applying *literally after* the millennium have a *spiritual* application *before* the millennium is seen to operate in the prophetic descriptions concerning Armageddon. As *nothing* in the Revelator's *post*-millennial descriptions pertaining to Jerusalem, Israel and her enemies has a *literal* application *before* the millennium, the teaching of a *pre*-millennial *literal* gathering of nations to Palestine is out of harmony with the teaching of the Scriptures.

The belief of a literal, military gathering to Palestine for a literal "war" before the millennium violates the principle of interpretation which shows that the "war," or "battle," against the literal city of God *after* the millennium has its *spiritual* counterpart *before* the millennium in the gathering of spiritual forces against God's spiritual city, the church. The Revelator's descriptions link together the events concerning *spiritual* Israel (the spiritual Jerusalem) *before* the millennium and those concerning the saints in the New Jerusalem *after* the millennium. The 1,000 years between the events associated with the *spiritual* Jerusalem at the time of the second advent and those associated with the *literal* Jerusalem at the third advent are *not symbolic* years—not 360,000 years, reckoned by the day for a year principle employed in prophetic *symbolism*—because the spiritual dispensation ends at the second advent.

Notice other examples showing that the spiritual application precedes the literal—with the millennium dividing the two:—

At Christ's second advent, all nations then living are spiritually gathered before His judgment throne. Matt. 25: 31, 32.

After the millennium, all the unrighteous of all ages literally gather before Christ's throne of judgment. Rev. 20: 11-15; G.C. 664-671.

Before the millennium, there is a spiritual gathering of the tares. Matt. 13: 30, 40; 7T. 84; 5T. 384, etc.

After the millennium, the tares literally gather around the holy city, and are then literally burned. Rev. 20: 8-15.

Before the millennium, the spiritual enemies of spiritual Israel are to have a *spiritual* resurrection. See Rev. 17: 8, 11. The significance of the number eight, referred to in Rev. 17: 11, is shown in my "Christ Conquers," pp. 123-139. The number eight is used in the Bible as a symbol for resurrection to life and power. When restored to life and power, the enemies of spiritual Israel make spiritual "war" upon her. The seventh head of the

After the millennium, the enemies of the saints inside the New Jerusalem will be *literally* resurrected. When restored to life and power, the enemies of the saints will make literal "war" upon the New Jerusalem. In its larger fulfilment after the millennium, the 7th head, which is "the eighth" (Rev. 17: 11), is a combination of *all* the resurrected enemies of the saints who have lived throughout human history.

beast of Rev. 17 represents a combination of all the enemies of spiritual Israel.

Spiritual Babylon is to be spiritually burned with fire before the millennium. See Rev. 17: 16; Rev. 18: 8, 9, 18; 19: 3. Literal Babylon was burned with literal fire. Jer. 50: 32; 51: 25, 58.	After the millennium, the enemies of the saints will be literally burned with fire. Rev. 20: 9-15.

Confusion prevailing throughout the religious world to-day concerning last-day prophecies is caused by a failure to understand the prophecies pertaining to "Israel." The Third Angel's Message gives the *spiritual* meaning of "Israel" and those things pertaining to her, thus showing the *spiritual* application *before* the millennium and the *literal* application *after* the millennium. What the "Babylonian" theologians expect to *literally* transpire on earth *during the millennium is now being spiritually fulfilled:* the *literal* fulfilment *on earth* of the prophecies pertaining to Israel takes place *after* the millennium.

CHAPTER XXXII.

AFTER THE MILLENNIUM—THE CONSUMMATION OF BIBLE PROPHECIES.

God's promises to man could not have been fulfilled without the first advent of our Lord; they could not all be fulfilled without the second coming of Christ at the commencement of the 1,000 years; they will not be completely fulfilled without the third coming of Christ at the end of the millennium. Throughout Scripture and human history all things move towards the consummation of the plan of redemption, which occurs after the millennium. Important though the second coming of Christ undoubtedly is, the prophecies also point beyond the glories and wonders of the second advent to His third coming after the millennium: they point to the finale of the controversy between Christ and Satan; the destruction of all sinners and the results of sin; the completion of the plan of redemption, and the commencement of the eternal kingdom. Note the following examples which demonstrate that the consummation of the prophecies occurs after the millennium:—

THE SECOND ADVENT: BEFORE THE 1,000 YEARS.	THE THIRD ADVENT: AFTER THE 1,000 YEARS.
Jude 14, 15. Jesus comes with His holy ones "to execute judgment upon" all who are alive at the second advent. 6T., p. 392; G.C., pp. 299, 426 quote Jude 14, 15 in connection with the second advent.	Jesus comes with His holy ones "to execute judgment upon all" the unsaved from the commencement of sin—evil angels and men. G.C. 549 quotes Jude 14, 15 in connection with events after the millennium.
Job 19: 25, 26. "He shall stand at the latter day upon the earth." Jesus stood "upon the earth" at His first advent: He will resurrect the dead at His second advent, but will not "stand upon the earth" (1 Thess. 4: 16-18); He will again literally stand "upon the earth" after the millennium.	After the millennium. "His feet shall stand in that day upon the Mount of Olives." Zech. 14: 4.

The Second Advent:

John 5: 25-29. The resurrection of the righteous occurs at the second coming of Christ.

2 Thess. 1: 7-9. Jesus comes "in flaming fire, taking vengeance"—punishing and destroying.

Gen. 3: 15. At the second advent, Christ bruises Satan. Rom. 16: 20; Rev. 20: 1-3. (At the first advent Satan bruised Christ. Gen. 3: 15 has a triple application.)

The prophecy of Dan. 2. At the second advent, the stone destroys the ten kingdoms represented by the ten toes.

The prophecy of Dan. 7. At His second advent, Christ is given "dominion, and glory, and a kingdom, that all people, nations, and languages should serve Him." Dan. 7: 14.

The prophecy of Dan. 10 to 12. Daniel stands in his "lot" in the Investigative Judgment.

The prophecy of the seven trumpets. Rev. 8 to 11. "The kingdoms of this world become the kingdoms of our Lord" at the second advent. Rev. 11: 15.

At His second advent, Jesus "destroys them that destroy the earth." Rev. 11: 18. At His second advent, Jesus "gives reward unto" His servants. Rev. 11: 18; 22: 11, 12.

The Third Advent: .

The resurrection of the wicked takes place after the millennium. See Rev. 20: 3-6.

All the wicked are finally punished and destroyed after the millennium. Those who are alive at the second advent are destroyed; but the second death, from which there is no resurrection, takes place after the millennium. See Rev. 20: 6; 21: 8.

After the millennium, Satan is destroyed. Rev. 20.

The complete and final destruction of all the people of the kingdoms represented by the various metals, and the establishment of the eternal kingdom of Christ ("the stone that smote the image . . . filled the whole earth") occurs after the millennium.

The eternal kingdom is not established on this earth until after the millennium. V. 27.

Daniel stands in his "lot" in the eternal Canaan. Dan. 12: 13.

Jesus "shall reign for ever and ever" (Rev. 11: 15) on this earth after the millennium.

After the millennium, Jesus destroys all the wicked who have destroyed the earth. After the millennium, Jesus gives rewards unto His servants—they inherit the earth, and share His throne. Matt. 5: 5; Rev. 3: 21.

The Second Advent:

Dan. 7: 11. The Roman beast exists until it is slain at the second coming of Christ.

2 Thess. 2: 3-8. "The man of sin . . . the son of *perdition*" is destroyed "with the brightness of" Christ's second advent.

Rev. 19: 20. "The beast . . . and the false prophet are cast into a lake of fire" at the second advent. Christ's glory is so brilliant—"the fiery stream" which issues before Him" (Dan. 7: 10)—and so envelopes the earth (Ps. 18: 12-15; 50: 3-5; 97: 3-5), that to John in vision the lake of fire which destroys the wicked at the end of the 1,000 years appeared to commence at the time of the second advent. "Fierce lightnings leap from the heavens, enveloping the earth." G.C. 637. "Like consuming fire . . . wrapped in flaming fire." p. 641.

The Third Advent:

After the millennium, it is "given to the burning flame."

After the millennium, "ungodly men" go into *"perdition."* 2 Pet. 3: 7. Then, "the son of *perdition*" (2 (Thess. 2: 3) "goeth into *perdition.*" Rev. 17: 11.

After the millennium all the wicked are "cast into the lake of fire . . . where the beast and the false prophet are [or, "were"]." Rev. 20: 10.

The prophecies which have a fulfilment at the second advent have their *complete* fulfilment at the end of the 1,000 years. Though the prophecies concerning Armageddon have a *spiritual* fulfilment at the second advent, they have their *complete* fulfilment *after* the millennium.

CHAPTER XXXIII.

ARMAGEDDON—BEFORE, AND AFTER THE MILLENNIUM: THE SPIRITUAL APPLICATION BEFORE, THE LITERAL APPLICATION AFTER THE MILLENNIUM.

Under the word "Armageddon," in "The Index to the Writings of Mrs. E. G. White," p. 115, we are directed to G.C., pp. 663, 664, 671, 672. The "General Index" of "The Great Controversy" also directs to pages 663, 664 for reference to "the last great battle" and "those engaged in it." These pages in "The Great Controversy" describe the massing of Satan's mighty army to attack the New Jerusalem after the millennium. To apply "Armageddon" also to the attack on the holy city after the millennium, as indicated in "The Index to the Writings of Mrs. E. G. White" and the "General Index" of "The Great Controversy," is in harmony with the Word of God. As shown in my "What is Armageddon?" and "Armageddon—the Time of Spiritual Israel's Deliverance," the Spirit of Prophecy teaches that "Armageddon" is the finale of the great controversy between Christ and Satan, before, and after the millennium. The Spirit of Prophecy makes not the slightest reference to a Palestinian "Armageddon," for such teaching, as we have shown, is opposed to the truth of the Third Angel's Message. By the teaching of a Palestinian "Armageddon" Satan seeks to blind many to God's last-day message.

As shown in my "What is Armageddon?" pp. 37-44, etc., the Spirit of Prophecy employs the words "battle," "controversy," "conflict" and "struggle" as synonyms for "war." The words "war" or "battle" mentioned in Rev. 12: 7, 17; 13: 4, 7; 16: 14; 17: 14; 19: 11; 20: 8 are from the same Greek word, and some translators keep to the one designation from the time this "war" is mentioned in Rev. 12: 7. The "war," or "battle," mentioned from Rev. 12: 7 to Rev. 20: 8, refers to the same great "controversy," "conflict," or "struggle" between Christ and Satan. "The last great *conflict* between truth and error is but the final *struggle* of the long-standing *controversy* concerning the law of God. Upon this *battle* we are now entering—a *battle* between the laws of men and the precepts of Jehovah. . . . The agencies which will unite [or gather] against truth and righteousness in this *contest* are now actively at work." G.C. 582. "There was *war* in heaven. Angels engaged in the *battle;* Satan wished to conquer the Son of God." E.W. 146. Notice in the next extract that *"conflict"* is employed instead of *"war."* "The great *conflict* that Satan created in the heavenly courts is soon, very soon, to be forever decided. Soon the inhabitants of the earth will have taken *sides,* either *for* or *against* the government of heaven." 7T. 141. "We are to . . . understand the progress of events in the *marshalling of the nations* for the *final conflict of the great controversy."* 8T. 307. "Already the *inhabitants* of the earth are *marshalling* under the leading of the prince of darkness, and this is but the beginning of the end." 8T. 49. *"The Sabbath question* is to be the issue in the *great final conflict* ["war," or "battle"] in which *all the world will act a part."* 6T. 352. See "What is Armageddon?" for further extracts from the Spirit of Prophecy concerning "the *marshalling* of the nations for the final *conflict* of the *great controversy"*—the spiritual *"war,"* or *"battle,* between the forces of good and evil. The "war," or "battle," which the Revelator describes from its commencement in heaven (Rev. 12: 7) until its close (Rev. 20: 8), is "the war" between Christ and Satan depicted in "The Conflict of the Ages" series of the Spirit of Prophecy. The Bible and the Spirit of Prophecy teach that the "battle" (Rev. 20: 8) *after* the millennium is the *same* "battle," or "war" (Rev. 12: 17; 16: 14; 17: 14; 19: 11-21) as *before* the millennium. Before the millennium, Satan attacks Christ in His church, the *spiritual* Jerusalem; after the millennium, Satan attacks Christ and His church within the *literal* Jerusalem: *before* the millennium, the *"war"* is a *spiritual* uniting to attack the *spiritual* centre; *after* the millennium, it will be a *literal* gathering and a *literal* attack upon the *literal* centre—the holy city. Before, and after the millennium, it is the same "war," "battle," or "controversy" between Christ and Satan.

JERUSALEM, THE STORM CENTRE OF THE GREAT CONTROVERSY.

In the book of Revelation, the storm centre of the ages is the city of Jerusalem, the name of which means "foundations of *peace";* Jerusalem, the city of "the Prince of *Peace."* To correctly understand the Revelation, Jerusalem must be interpreted as the centre of the battle beween good and evil. In the Old Testament, Jerusalem was the literal centre of national Israel, and many of Israel's national enemies came against Jerusalem—the city of "peace." Though foes were without, peace reigned within the city when Israel was faithful. In this we see typified the church as a whole, and also each individual. Through their allegiance to the God of Israel, the church and individual Christians become the centre of attack by foes who are stirred to "war" against the Holy Son of God within. But, while spiritual enemies gather outside the walls of "the holy city" (Rev. 11: 2, etc.), the heart is at peace with God. At the end of the millennium, when the law of the spiritual interpretation of the things of Israel does not operate, the things pertaining to Christ and His people will apply literally. Then, Jerusalem will still be the centre within which "the Prince of Peace' reigns, but enemies, bent on "war," will literally gather outside.

Enemies of the people of God who literally gathered around and attacked ancient Israel's literal city of "peace" are brought into the spiritual imagery of the Revelation as types of the enemies who spiritually gather around to attack the spiritual city of spiritual Israel. The Revelation carries this representation through until the end of the millennium then, *all* the literal enemies of ancient Israel and *all* the enemies of the church will literally gather around the literal city in which reigns the visible Son of God, the Prince of Peace, the Destroyer of the evil which makes "war" on Him, and on His people.

In the prophecy of Joel, as in other prophecies of the Bible, Jerusalem is the centre—literal Jerusalem in the days of literal Israel; spiritual Jerusalem in the days of spiritual Israel; and the literal New Jerusalem at the end of the millennium. In Joel 2: 32, deliverance from the foes without the city is vouchsafed to "the remnant" within Jerusalem. This was literally true in the history of national Israel (see 2 Kings 18: 17-37; 19: 1-37; Isa. 37: 32-36, etc.) when they were faithful to God; it is spiritually fulfilled now, in the days of spiritual Israel; and will again be literally true at the end of the millennium. The triple application of these prophetic descriptions concerning Israel becomes very clear to the searcher for truth.

BEFORE AND AFTER THE MILLENNIUM.

All the proper names, places and designations of the Revelation are employed in a symbolical sense until the Revelator's description of the holy city—New Jerusalem—*at the end of the millennium.* Thus the Lord shows the principle to be employed in "rightly dividing" *the Apocalypse* and *other parts of the Holy Scriptures.* The millennium is the dividing line between the application of the *spiritual* and the application of the *literal,* just as the cross terminated the literal, national, *typical* system and introduced the period of the *antitypical, spiritual* church application. The Revelation clearly reveals this triple application of the things of Israel, which comprehends:—(1) The literal, national dispensation of ancient Israel; (2) The spiritual, or "church," dispensation of spiritual Israel, during which the terminology of national Israel is spiritually employed; (3) The literal and visible things of the eternal kingdom. This principle of "rightly dividing" is clearly seen even on the surface of the structure of the Revelation.

The Apocalypse, which is "The Revelation of Jesus Christ" in His work, past, present and future, is *a revelation of the whole Bible, and shows the true interpretation of all that pertains to Israel —past, present and future.* The prophecies of Ezekiel, Daniel, Zechariah, Joel, etc., should be interpreted in harmony with the principle of the triple application of the things of Israel so clearly revealed in the Revelation.

The Spirit of Prophecy declares that the *"symbols* and *figures"* of the Revelation "mean so much to *us"*—spiritual Israel, the church. The Spirit of Prophecy also declares that an understanding of the Revelation requires "close, prayerful study." A prayerful study of the description of the final conflict in Rev. 16: 12-16 reveals that it concerns spiritual Israel and her enemies.

A thorough study shows the connection between Rev. 16: 12-16; 19: 11-21; Isa. 34; 63: 1-6; Ezek. 38; 39; Zech. 12; 14; Joel 3, etc. In his commentary on Revelation, Scott says: "The coincidence between this prophecy (Rev. 16: 12-16), and those above referred to [Ezek. 38, 39; Joel 3; Zech. 14; Isa. 34, etc.] as unfulfilled prophecies in the Old Testament, is worthy of special notice by all who would *patiently* investigate the *true* meaning of them, and not run away with *hasty* and *crude* and *partial,* though *plausible,* interpretations, *grounded on incidental resemblances.*"

The same principle must be followed when interpreting each of the above passages of Scripture, for the Word of God is a united, harmonious whole. *If* Ezek. 38, 39 picture a *literal* gathering of nations from the "four *quarters"* (compare Rev. 20: 8 and Ezek. 38: 6, and notice the word "quarters") to attack *literal Israel* in Palestine, then a literal gathering of nations would be pictured in

Rev. 16: 12-16. But this interpretation would violate the law followed throughout the Apocalype, which reveals that the places and designations mentioned in the Revelation are *symbolically employed until after the millennium.* If Ezek. 38, 39 and Rev. 16: 12-16 predicted a literal gathering of nations around literal Jerusalem, then Zech. 14 must also refer to such. But that interpretation would be out of harmony with the Spirit of Prophecy, which applies these verses in Zech. 14 in relation to the spiritual gathering of the enemies of spiritual Israel in "the final conflict" over the enforcement of Sunday laws. Joel 2: 32 predicts the "deliverance" which will come to "the remnant" *"in Mount Zion and in Jerusalem."* This prophecy is applied by the Spirit of Prophecy in connection with spiritual Israel in spiritual Jerusalem. Joel 3 is the *continuation of the same prophecy:* the gathering of the nations around Jerusalem and the "deliverance" of Israel "in Jerusalem" can refer only to a *spiritual* gathering *before* the millennium, and to a *literal* gathering of the enemies of Israel around the *literal* New Jerusalem *after* the millennium. This is precisely the way Joel 3 is interpreted in the Spirit of Prophecy. To ensure perfect harmony in our interpretation of the Word of God, all these prophecies concerning Israel, who, in the New Testament, is clearly declared to be the church, must be interpreted *spiritually* before the millennium, and *literally* after the millennium. "Christ the Revelator" (see G.C. 342) has revealed the *principle* by which *all other parts of the Scriptures relating to Israel* are to be interpreted.

In G.C., p. 266, we are given the interpretation of "the holy city" mentioned in Rev. 11: 2: "The holy city *(the true church)* shall they tread under foot forty and two months. . . . The periods here mentioned—'forty and two months,' and 'a thousand and two hundred and three-score days' — are the same, alike representing the time in which *the church of Christ* was to suffer oppression from Rome." In other places, also, the Spirit of Prophecy interprets "the holy city," *Jerusalem,* as the symbol of "the *true church,*" "the *church of Christ.*" Therefore, as the Spirit of Prophecy applies *literally* (see G.C. 676, etc., etc.) the Revelator's description of "the holy city" in Rev. 21: 22 (which comes into the description of events to occur *after* the millennium), it is further evident that the Spirit of Prophecy teaches the triple application of the things of Israel: *literal* in the days of ancient Israel. *spiritual* in this "dispensation of the Holy Spirit," and *literal* again *after* the millennium.

Following this divinely-given principle of interpretation, we know that the words in Rev. 14: 20, "And the winepress was trodden *without the city,"* depict the slaughter of the wicked outside the *spiritual* city, the church, *before* the millennium, and the slaughter of the wicked outside the *literal* New Jerusalem *after* the millennium. Rev. 20: 8, 9. In harmony with this Biblical principle of interpretation, the Spirit of Prophecy applies such prophecies as Zech. 14, Joel 3, etc., *spiritually before* the millennium, and *literally after* the millennium. Zech. 14 depicts a gathering of *"all nations* against *Jerusalem* to battle [historically, and partially fulfilled in the experience of rejected, *literal* Israel, in A.D. 70, when the Roman armies, made up of many nationalities, destroyed the nation and city of *literal* Israel]. . . . Then shall the Lord go forth against those *nations,* as when He fought in the day of battle [because of their sins, God could not protect *national* Israel, but deliverance is assured obedient, *spiritual* Israel] . . . and this shall be the *plague* wherewith the Lord will smite all the people that have *fought against Jerusalem."* G.C., pp. 656, 657, applies these verses to the destruction of those who seek to destroy the remnant church, which is promised "deliverance" *"in Mount Zion* and *in Jerusalem."* Joel 2: 32. The Spirit of Prophecy interprets "all the people" (v. 12), "all *nations"* (v. 2) who fight against *Jerusalem* to be the leaders of *religion* (see G.C. 654, 655, 656) assisted by the multitudes who endeavour to destroy the church. Notice the following extract from Early Writings, p. 289: "The wrath of God in the seven last plagues had been visited upon the inhabitants of the earth, causing them to gnaw their *tongues* [see Rev. 16: 10, 11, and observe the reference to Zech. 14: 12: 'the *plague* wherewith the Lord will smite all the people that have fought against Jerusalem . . . their *tongue* shall consume away in their mouth'] for pain, and to curse God. The *false shepherds* had been the objects of Jehovah's wrath. Their eyes had consumed away in their holes, and their *tongues* in their mouths, while they stood upon their feet [referring to Zech. 14: 12] . . . the wicked multitude turn their rage upon one another [this refers to Zech. 14: 13]. The earth seemed to be deluged with blood [see Rev. 14: 20], and dead bodies were from one end of it to the other."

These references from the Spirit of Prophecy show that prophecies of the *gathering* of "all *nations"* to fight against Israel and *Jerusalem* refer to a uniting of the forces of evil to attack spiritual Israel, the church, in the last days. See my "What is Armageddon?" pp. 37-44, for proof that the Revelator's statement that the nations "gather" means they spiritually "unite." In the interpretation of Zech. 14 given above, the Spirit of Prophecy declares that those who fight "against *Jerusalem*" are *"false shepherds"*— not military leaders. The place of contest is not around *literal* Jerusalem, but around *spiritual* Jerusalem, the church; and the "place" where they are *"plagued"* and destroyed is not Palestine, but *"the earth."* The great hosts destroyed are *not military armies,* but *"the wicked multitude."* Thus the Spirit of Prophecy shows the true interpretation of those prophecies depicting the *gathering* of *"nations"* to Palestine, Jerusalem, and Mount Zion. Upon this principle of the *spiritual* application *before* the millennium, and the *literal* application *after* the millennium, God's servant bases her interpretations of Holy Writ, thus proving to be in harmony with all the inspired prophets of God.

ZECHARIAH 14 AND JOEL 3: THE SPIRITUAL FULFILMENT BEFORE, AND THE LITERAL FULFILMENT AFTER THE MILLENNIUM.

Commenting on Zech. 14: 1, 2, Dr. Clarke says:—

"From this great Jewish tragedy [the destruction of Jerusalem in A.D. 70] the prophet immediately passes to the *utter destruction of the enemies of Christianity in the latter days."*

Place "church" or "the remnant" instead of "Christianity" and this extract would be in harmony with the true interpretation of this prophecy in relation to the *spiritual* conflict of the last days.

The Spirit of Prophecy applies Zech. 14 and Joel 3 to the final conflict, showing that they have a *spiritual* application *before* the millennium, and a *literal* application *after* the millennium.

ZECH. 14.	SPIRITUAL: *BEFORE* THE MILLENNIUM.	LITERAL: *AFTER* THE MILLENNIUM.
V. 2. "I will gather all nations against Jerusalem to battle." (Literally fulfilled in the siege of Jerusalem, A.D. 70.)	Rev. 14: 20; 16: 14-16; 17: 14; Isa. 54: 15, etc. Nations spiritually "gather," or "unite," to destroy the church — *spiritual* Jerusalem.	Rev. 20: 8 9. Nations *literally* gather to attack Israel in the *literal* New Jerusalem.
V. 3. "Then shall the Lord go forth, and fight against those nations." (Because of their sins, God did not fight for the literal Jews in A.D. 70.)	Rev. 16: 12-16; 17: 14; 19: 11-21, etc. The Lord will fight against the people who attack His spiritual Jerusalem. They will be slain in the slaughter of *"Armageddon."*	Rev. 20: 8, 9. God will send down fire from heaven to *destroy the armies* which literally gather around the New Jerusalem.

338

Zech. 14.	Spiritual:	Literal:
V. 4. "And His feet shall stand in that day upon the Mount of Olives, which is before Jerusalem . . . and the Mount of Olives shall cleave in the midst thereof . . . and there shall be a very great valley."		E.W. 17, 51, 53, 281; 1T. 67, 68; G.C. 662, 663. *Literally fulfilled at the end of the millennium.*
V. 5. "And ye shall flee to the valley or the mountains."	Rev. 6: 15-17; Isa. 2: 19-21. Spiritual Babylonians flee to the mountains.	E.W. 53. "Those who flee at that time are the wicked, who have just been raised." Thus the Spirit of Prophecy gives this verse its *literal* fulfilment at the *end of the 1,000 years*
V. 5. "And the Lord my God shall come, and all the saints with thee.'	Jude 14, 15. Christ comes with His angels to deliver spiritual Israel and to destroy their enemies.	E.W. 53, 17, 51, 291. *Literally* fulfilled at the *end of the 1,000 years:* the saints descend with the New Jerusalem to the place where the *literal* land of Israel had been located.
V. 6, 7. Light to shine in all the world.	Rev. 18: 1. The light of the Third Angel's Message is to shine spiritually in all the world. P.P. 237.	Rev. 21: 23, 24; 22: 5. *Literal* light for the saints *after the millennium.*
V. 8. "And it shall come to pass in that day, that living waters shall go out from Jerusalem."	John 4: 10-14; 7: 37-39; Ezek. 47: 1-12; A.A. 13; 6T. 227, 228, 230; C.H. 210; 7T. 171, 172. *Spiritually* applied to the church now.	Rev. 22: 1, 2, 17; Joel 3: 18. *Literally fulfilled* in the experience of the saints after the millennium.
V. 9. "And the Lord shall be King over all the earth."	John 1: 49; 1 Tim. 1: 17, etc. Jesus, *spiritually,* reigns in His church. Rom. 6: 12, etc.	Luke 1: 32, 33; Rev. 11: 15-17, etc. *Literally* true *after the millennium.* PP. 342, etc.
V. 11. "Jerusalem shall be safely inhabited."	Zech. 2: 4, 5. *Spiritually* applied *now.* T.M. 18; Isa. 37: 35, etc.	Rev. 20: 8, 9; 21; 22. *Literally* applied after the 1,000 years.

Zech. 14.	Spiritual:	Literal:
V. 12. Those who fight "against *Jerusalem*" are *plagued* by God; "their *tongues* consume away."	E.W. 289, 290; G.C. 657; Rev. 16: 10, 11. *Spiritual* enemies fight against *spiritual* Jerusalem; *enemies of church plagued.*	Rev. 20: 8, 9; E.W. 51, 53; G.C. 662-664. Enemies *literally* fight against the *literal* New Jerusalem.
V. 13. God confuses t h o s e who fight "against *Jerusalem*." They turn and slay each other.	G.C. 656; E.W. 290; Ezek. 38: 21; 2 Chron. 20: 23; Judg. 7: 22. *Applied to those who fight against the church* — the *spiritual* Jerusalem.	G.C. 672. Applied to those who *literally* gather against *literal* Jerusalem after the 1,000 years.

THE PROPHECY OF JOEL 3.

JOEL 3.	SPIRITUAL: *BEFORE* THE MILLENNIUM.	LITERAL: *AFTER* THE MILLENNIUM.
V. 11. "Assemble yourselves, and come all ye *heathen*, and *gather yourselves together round about.*"	E.W. 282-284; G.C. 618, 635. "Saints . . . seemed *surrounded* by the wicked inhabitants of the earth . . . the *heathen*." A *spiritual* gathering against *spiritual* Jerusalem, the church.	Rev. 20: 8, 9. Wicked assemble around the holy city. A *literal* gathering against the *literal* New Jerusalem.
V. 12. "Let the *heathen* be awakened, and come up to the valley of Jehoshaphat: for there will I judge the *heathen* round about." ("Jehoshaphat" means "God's Judgment.")	Matt. 25: 31-34. "Nations" — "heathen"— surrounding G o d ' s people are judged at the second advent. "The valley of Jehoshaphat" is no more literal in this dispensation than "My mountain" (Joel 2: 1), "Zion" (2: 1, 15, 32), "Mount Zion" and "Jerusalem" (2: 32), "the priests . . . the porch and the altar." 2: 17. In the New Testament all of these are *spiritually* applied in *relation to the church.* The literal valley of Jehoshaphat was located outside Jerusalem (see G.C.	Rev. 20: 11, 12. All the unsaved literally stand before God's judgment throne at the end of the 1,000 years.

Joel 3.	Spiritual:	Literal:
	33, 37); the *symbolic* "valley of Jehoshaphat," where *spiritual* Israel's enemies are judged, is outside the *spiritual* Jerusalem.	
V. 9. "Proclaim ye this among the *Gentiles*"— the enemies of Israel. See "What is Armageddon?" pp. 7-10.	Ephes. 2: 11-19. *Gentiles* are those who are not Israelites. Rev. 11: 2. The Papal church stated to be "Gen-	Rev. 20: 8, 9, etc. All Israel inside the holy city—Gentiles outside. Rev. 22: 15.
V. 9. "Proclaim *war* . . . let all the men of war draw near."	Rev. 12: 17. "War" against the remnant church. "In every quarter companies of *armed* men . . . are preparing for the work of death." G.C. 635. Men are *arming to attack spiritual Jerusalem,* the church.	"As the New Jerusalem . . . comes down out of heaven. . . . Now Satan *prepares* . . . He will *marshal* all the armies of the lost under his banner . . . Skilful artisans construct *implements of war. Military* leaders . . . *marshal* the throngs of *warlike* men . . . with *military* precision, the serried ranks advance . . . to the *city of God* . . . the *armies* of Satan *surround* the city, and make ready for the onset." G.C. 663, 664.
V. 10. "Let the *weak* say, I am strong."	Rev. 17: 13. "These . . . give their power and strength unto the beast." Rev. 13: 16. The weak and the strong receive the mark of the beast. "Mighty men, and every bondman." Rev. 6: 15.	"Satan works wonders to support his claims [concerning the New Jerusalem which has come from heaven]. He makes the *weak* strong, and inspires all with his own spirit and energy." G.C. 663.

The prophecies depicting nations gathering to Palestine to attack Israel and Jerusalem are shown by the Spirit of Prophecy to apply *spiritually before* and *literally after* the millennium. This principle is adhered to throughout the Spirit of Prophecy, and is in

341

harmony with the principle clearly shown in the book of Revelation.

ZECHARIAH 12 AND ARMAGEDDON.

Rev. 19: 11-21 describes the coming of Christ, with "the *armies* of heaven," to "make *war*" on "the beast, and the kings of the earth, and their *armies gathered together* to make *war* on Him that sat on the horse, and against His *army*." 6T. p. 406 applies these verses in connection with "the battle of Armageddon." Rev. 19: 11-21 contains direct references from Joel 3 and Ezek. 38; 39, and these in turn are linked with Zech. 14; 12: 2-4, 8, 9, 11; Isa. 34; 63: 1-6. Rev. 14: 19-20, which is definitely connected with Rev. 19: 15, states that "the winepress" will be "trodden *without the city,* and blood "will come out of the winepress, even unto the *horse bridles.*" "Armageddon," "the mountain of slaughter," will occur *"without the city."* Zech. 12 says that "all the people *round about*" will lay siege "both against Judah and *against Jerusalem,"* and that God "will smite every *horse* with astonishment, and his rider with madness." Vs. 2-4. "I will seek to destroy all the *nations* that shall *come against Jerusalem."* V. 9. "In that day shall there be a great *mourning* in Jerusalem, as *the mourning* of Hadadrimmon in the valley of *Megiddon."* V. 11.

Dr. Adam Clarke's comment on Zech. 12 is worthy of notice. At the head of the chapter he says:—

"The first part of this chapter, with several in chapter XIV, relates to an invasion that shall be made on the inhabitants of Judea and Jerusalem in *the latter ages of the world. . . .* It also describes, in very magnificent terms, the signal interposition of God in their favour."

Concerning v. 2 he says:—"The *Babylonians,* who captivated and ruined the Jews, shall in their turn be ruined."

"I incline to think that what is spoken in this chapter about the Jews and Jerusalem belongs to the glory of the latter times.' *Shall be in the siege.* This may refer to some war against the church of Christ, *such as that mentioned in Rev. 20: 9."*

Verse 8 of Zech. 12 reads: "In that day shall the Lord defend the inhabitants of Jerusalem; and he that is feeble among them at that day, shall be as David; and the house of David shall be as God, as the angel of the Lord before them." Dr. Clarke comments:—

"So clear, full, and efficient shall be the salvation of believers under the *gospel,* that the *feeblest* among them shall be as strong, as full of courage, and as successful as David when he went against Goliath. . . . The *family,* the *church* of the *true David,* the Lord *Jesus,* shall be as the angel of the Lord; shall *stand in the divine presence* like *Gabriel. . . .* Thus the house of David, the *true Christians,* shall here walk *with, after,* and *before God."*

The time of severe test to the church (Rev. 3: 10) is forecast in Zech. 12 and 14: but the believers of the Third Angel's Message will be strengthened by the outpouring of the Holy Spirit, and thus prepared for the final struggle when the whole world is against them. The servant of the Lord writes:—

"The power of God had rested upon His people; they had accomplished their work, and *were prepared for the trying hour* before them. They had received the latter rain, or refreshing from the presence of the Lord." E.W., p. 279.

"And the people of God are *thus prepared to stand in the hour of temptation,* which they are soon to meet." E.W. 277.

Zech. 12: 9 reads:—

"And it shall come to pass in that day, that *I will seek to destroy all the nations that come against Jerusalem.*"

Dr. Clarke comments:—

"When this time shall arrive. all nations that will not receive the faith of our Lord Jesus [the Third Angel's Message] shall be destroyed, when the long-suffering of God shall no longer wait upon them."

Dr. Clarke's interpretation of this chapter—the spiritual application which he makes in relation to the church, the reference to the close of probation, and to the surrounding of the New Jerusalem at the end of the 1,000 years (Rev. 20: 8, 9)—illustrates the interpretation given by many godly men concerning these predictions of Jerusalem being attacked by the nations.

In this same chapter (Zech. 12) we read concerning "the mourning of Hadadrimmon in the valley of *Megiddon,*" which "becomes the poetic expression for the deepest and most despairing grief; as in the Apocalypse (Rev. 16: 16) Armageddon, in continuance of the same *imagery,* is represented as the scene of terrible and final conflict." Smith's Bible Dictionary. Thus a study of Zech. 12 shows that this chapter is connected with the final conflict which *rages around the remnant church—the spiritual Jerusalem* —and culminates in the slaughter of Armageddon. God destroys the nations which are gathered around His spiritual city—the church. Dr. Clarke's coupling of Zech. 12 with Rev. 20: 9 is correct, for an attack is made against the *spiritual* Jerusalem before the millennium, and an attack upon the *literal* New Jerusalem at the end of the millennium. The slaughter of the wicked, in both instances, is "without the city." "Jerusalem," in Zechariah's prediction, refers to the church *before* the millennium, and to the New Jerusalem *after the millennium.* The battle of Armageddon will be fought "without the city" both before and after the 1,000 years. "The siege both against Judah and Jerusalem" (Zech. 12: 2), the gathering of the nations around Jerusalem (Zech. 12: 2, 4, 9; Joel

3, etc.), the slaughter in "the valley of Megiddon" (Zech. 12: 11) when "the Lord [shall] go forth, and fight against those nations" (Zech. 14: 3) and shall destroy "all *nations*" which "*gather* . . . against *Jerusalem* to battle" (Zech. 14: 2; 12: 2; Joel 3, etc.) refer to the final conflict and the destruction of the enemies of the *church*.

THE FINAL DESTRUCTION OF ISRAEL'S ENEMIES.

Terrible as the slaughter of the wicked will be in the first phase of Armageddon *before* the millennium, it will be vastly more terrible *after* the millennium, for then it will involve *all* the resurrected wicked from the days of Cain to the second advent. All the persecutors of the people of God will be there with hatred still in their hearts for God and His saints. Haughty Pharaoh will be there seeking to "pursue" spiritual Israel to death; the Edomites with their "perpetual" hatred of Israel will be there; the kings of Canaan who were destroyed at Megiddo will be there to again take part in a devil-controlled conflict; the proud Assyrians and the Babylonians from the region of the Euphrates will once more march towards the land of Israel; the Scythian kings (who anciently went by the name of Gog—see Pocket Commentary on Rev. 20: 8), the unsaved Armenians (house of Togarmah), Gomer and all his bands, the Persians, Ethiopians, Libyans, the unregenerate of Sheba, Dedan, and "the merchants of Tarshish with the young lions thereof" will be there; "the beast," and "the false prophet" and all who have persecuted spiritual Israel will be there. But Immanuel —"God is with us"—will be there—personally, visibly—to deliver His people and to destroy their enemies. The same fratricidal bloodshed which occurred among the enemies of Israel gathered against spiritual Jerusalem, the church, before the millennium (see Zech. 14: 13; Ezek. 38: 21; Judg. 7: 22; 1 Sam. 14: 20; 2 Chron. 20: 23; G.C. 657) will be repeated on a vaster scale around the literal New Jerusalem at the end of the millennium. The lost, realising that they have been "*deceived*" (Rev. 20: 3, 8, 10; G.C. 663), turn upon those who have led them to their eternal doom, and there is colossal slaughter.

"Those who have united with him [Satan] see the total failure of his cause. . . . He rushes into the midst of his subjects, and endeavours to inspire them with his own fury, and arouse them to instant battle. But of the *countless millions* whom he has allured into rebellion, there are none now to acknowledge his supremacy. His power is at an end. The wicked are filled with the same hatred of God that inspires Satan; but they see that their case is hopeless, that they cannot prevail against Jehovah. Their *rage is kindled against* Satan and those who have been his agents in deception, and with the fury of demons they turn upon them. . . . 'Every battle of the warrior is with confused noise, and garments

rolled in blood; but this shall be with burning and fuel of fire' (Isa. 9: 5)."
G.C. 672.

Sin is selfishness and ends in mutual slaughter. A world in rebellion against God ends in man hating man; in neighbour slaying neighbour.

The fires of God fall upon the wicked as they are engaged in slaughtering each other. "And fire came down from God out of heaven, and devoured them. And the devil that deceived them was cast into the lake of fire and brimstone." Rev. 20: 9, 10. "The day that cometh shall burn them up, saith the Lord of hosts, that it shall leave them neither root nor branch." Mal. 4: 1. "And never shalt . . . be any more." Ezek. 28: 19. "The great controversy is ended. Sin and sinners are no more. The entire universe is clean." G.C. 678.

THE THIRD ANGEL'S MESSAGE PREPARES FOR THE ETERNAL KINGDOM.

The prophets saw beyond the destruction of the unrighteous and the cleansing of the world at the end of the millennium to the establishment of the eternal kingdom. Only a kingdom built upon love can endure throughout the endless ages. To-day, the Third Angel's Message is calling ·out of spiritual Babylon a people who will obey God's commandment "thou shalt love the Lord thy God with all thy heart, and with all thy soul, and with all thy mind, and with all thy strength . . . and . . . thou shalt love thy neighbour as thyself" (Mark 12: 30, 31): a people who will share in the glories of the new world.

The Third Angel's Message calls for purity of heart and purity of doctrine. Only "the pure in heart . . . shall see God." Matt. 5: 8; Heb. 12:14. Purity of heart seeks purity of doctrine; purity of doctrine upholds and develops purity of heart. "Ye have purified your souls in obeying the truth." 1 Pet. 1: 22. God has ordained that by prayer and the study of His Word we shall be "changed . . . from glory to glory, even as by the Spirit of the Lord." 2 Cor. 3: 18. "That perfection of character He [God] requires can be obtained only by becoming familiar with His Word." Counsels to Teachers," p. 454.

The Third Angel's Message is calling a people to come out of Babylon to "the faith of Jesus." "These are they which were not defiled with women" (Rev. 14: 4)—*not defiled with the teachings of apostate churches.* The teachings of the Third Angel's Message are based upon definite principles which the Lord has clearly revealed in the Scriptures to instruct His children and to safeguard them from error. "None but those who have fortified their minds with the truths of the Bible will stand through the last great conflict." G.C. 593.

Light upon the Scriptures is to increase until the end (see Dan. 12: 4; 8T. 322; A.A. 283; G.C. 312, 677, 678; 5T. 704, 706; Isa. 9: 6, etc.); but truth will always be in harmony with the united testimony of the Scriptures—"the testimony of Jesus"—against which Satanic deceptions cannot prevail.

The Third Angel's Message calls spiritual Israel to "follow the Lamb *whithersoever He goeth"* (Rev. 14: 4). Those who *spiritually* follow Him now will *literally* "follow the Lamb whithersoever He goeth" (C.O.L. 223; A.A. 591) throughout eternity.

"Israel shall be saved in the Lord with an everlasting salvation . . . world without end." Isa. 45: 17. "Unto Him be glory in the *church* by Christ Jesus throughout all ages, world without end, Amen." Ephes. 3: 21.

For other titles by Louis F. Were, or for a free catalog of books, videos, audio tapes and more at discount prices, contact:

Laymen Ministries

LMN Publishing International, Inc.
HC 4, Box 94C
St. Maries, ID 83861

Phone: (208) 245-5388
Fax: (208) 245-3280
Toll free order line: 1-800-245-1844
email: lmnpubint@nidlink.com
Visit our website at www.lmn.org

Laymen Ministries is a self-supporting, privately funded 501 (c)3 nonprofit corporation. We exist to encourage lay people in all parts of the world that they are an essential element in seeing the three angels' messages triumph in our generation. It is our goal to help establish lay ministries—to educate in practical religion, promote the publishing and distribution of literature, and promote family-oriented ministry. More information on our current international projects is available by contacting our office.

An Adventist Apocalypse

By Ellen G. White

A compilation of hundreds of quotations from unpublished letters and manuscripts covering a wide range of issues and events that will confront the people of God in the last days. Much of this material is previously unreleased, nowhere else to be found.

This is a paperback version with easy to read type. Learn what God's messenger had to say about preparing for the coming conflict, the working of the enemy, the Latter Rain, events preceding the Second Coming, the Loud Cry, what will happen within the church, how God will sustain His children, the Judgment... and too many more topics to list. 160 pages.

Retail Price: $9.95. **Discount Price: $8.25** + S&H

The Sanctuary Series

Five *Sanctuary* volumes under one cover

By Arla Van Etten

Each detail of Type (earthly sanctuary) and Antitype Counterpart (heavenly sanctuary) is presented side by side in an easily understood format, with texts and references for study. Designed for youth, but with ample content to provide adults with a fascinating, in-depth study, as well.

240 pages, paperback. This edition contains:

The Young People's Sanctuary Series

Volume 1:   *The Camp Around*
Volume 2:   *The Courtyard*
Volume 3:   *The Offerings*
Volume 4:   *The Tent Tabernacle*
Volume 5:   *The Holy Days and Feast Days*

Retail Price: $17.95 **Discount Price: $16.50** + S&H

Bible Students' Library

The *Bible Students' Library* series was originally published between 1889 and 1905 and was written by the Adventist pioneers. These booklets clearly present the principles of our faith. Excellent for your own study or for a witnessing tool. Most are under 30 pages and priced under $1.00, and all are small enough to fit in a pocket or purse. Additional savings when bought in lots of 100 or more.

Includes such titles as:
Baptism, Its Significance
Can We Keep the Sabbath?
Christ Tempted As We Are
The Immortality of the Soul
Justified by Faith
Living by Faith
Privilege of Prayer
The Sufferings of Christ
Sunday: The Origin of Its Observance in the Christian Church
....and more....

Apples of Gold Library

Also written by the Adventist pioneers and published between 1893 and 1905 as tracts especially designed to fit in an envelope for mailing to friends and family. These little gems are excellent for your own study and for distribution in literature racks, evangelism, and personal witnessing.
Priced at only **$.25 each, or $.10 each for 100 or more.**

Includes such titles as:
The Christian's Privilege
God's Word the Parent's Guide
Hope in Trials
The Power of Forgiveness
The Power of the Word
Three Sabbaths
What Must I Do to Be Saved?
....and more....

Who is Laymen Ministries?

Laymen Ministries is a missionary organization which originally began with a work of republishing some of the out-of-print works of early Christian pioneers. Today, in addition to our publishing work, we also train and equip laymen in many parts of the world to do translation, layout, and publishing of materials that will help spread the news of God's great love and Jesus' soon return. We have a video production facility from which we provide various programs for video, satellite TV broadcast, and culturally adapted materials in their native languages for use in 3rd world countries. We also support evangelism and training of laymen as pastors, Bible workers, and literature evangelists, as well as providing medical outreach and life-style training to help people live happier, healthier lives.

If you would like to learn more about the work we do, and about some of the fascinating projects we are involved in, please contact our office to receive your FREE subscription to our magazine, which contains exciting mission updates, as well as timely articles to strengthen and encourage laymen in all walks of life.

(208)245-5388
(800)245-1844
Fax: (208) 245-3280
email: lmnpubint@nidlink.com
Visit our website at www.lmn.org